W9-APT-939

Robert V. Prescott, Ph.D

Introduction
to Forensic
Psychology

Introduction to Forensic Psychology

Issues and Controversies in Crime and Justice

Bruce A. Arrigo

Institute of Psychology, Law and Public Policy
California School of Professional Psychology
Fresno, California

ACADEMIC PRESS

A Harcourt Science and Technology Company

San Diego   San Francisco   New York   Boston   London   Sydney   Tokyo

Academic Press
A Harcourt Science and Technology Company
525 B Street, Suite 1900, San Diego, California 92101-4495, USA
http://www.academicpress.com

Academic Press
Harcourt Place, 32 Jamestown Road, London NW1 7BY, UK

Library of Congress Catalog Card Number: 99-63961

International Standard Book Number: 0-12-064350-2

PRINTED IN THE UNITED STATES OF AMERICA
00   01   02   03   04   SB   9   8   7   6   5   4   3   2

For Marc: Sometimes close, often deep, always my brother.

Contents

PART I

Police and Law Enforcement

1   Adult Forensics

2   Juvenile Forensics

PART II

Court and the Legal System

6 *Juvenile Forensics*

7 *Civil Forensics*

8 *Family Forensics*

PART III

Corrections and Prison Practices

9 *Adult Forensics*

About the Author

BRUCE A. ARRIGO is Professor of Criminology and Forensic Psychology and Director of the Institute of Psychology, Law, and Public Policy at the California School of Professional Psychology–Fresno. Prior to his career in academe, he was a community organizer and social activist for the homeless, the mentally ill, the working poor, the frail elderly, and the chemically addicted. He is the author of more than 60 journal articles, academic book chapters, and scholarly essays exploring theoretical and applied topics in critical criminology, criminal justice and mental health, and the sociology of law. His recent scholarship has appeared in such periodicals as *Criminal Justice and Behavior; Crime, Law, and Social Change; Justice Quarterly; International Journal of Law and Psychiatry; Critical Criminology; Journal of Offender Rehabilitation; Social Justice; Law and Psychology Review;* and the *International Journal for the Semiotics of Law.* He is the author, coauthor, or editor of 4 books. His most recent book-length projects include *Madness, Language, and the Law* (1994); *The Contours of Psychiatric Justice* (1996); *Social Justice/Criminal Justice: The Maturation of Critical Theory in Law, Crime, and Deviance* (1998); and, with T. R. Young, *The Dictionary of Critical Social Science* (1999). Professor Arrigo is also the editor of the peer-reviewed quarterly *Humanity and Society* and the founding editor of the periodical *Journal of Forensic Psychology Practice.*

Acknowledgments

This textbook could not have been written without the thoughtful, diligent, and insightful assistance of many students. One of the pleasures of higher education is that *faculty* get to learn *from* those who we teach. From the inception of this project in 1996 to its present-day from, I have gained considerably from countless students. The individuals with whom I have worked contributed substantially to the research, drafting, and editing of this book. In many ways, *Introduction to Forensic Psychology: Issues and Controversies in Crime and Justice* is a collaboration. I am eternally grateful to my (student) colleagues. Participants in this project include those listed below.

Senior Researchers

David Mitroff	Stacey Shipley
Janna Oddie	Alexa Wasserman
Jennifer Santman	Christopher Williams

Assistant Researchers

Carol Fowler	Catherine Purcell
Debbie Margulies	Jeffrey Tasca

Senior Writers

Janna Oddie	Christopher Williams
Jennifer Santman	Edward Zawadski
Stacey Shipley	

Assistant Writers

Toni Backman	Clint Soares
Debbie Margulies	Jeffrey Tasca
David Mitroff	Alexa Wasserman
Catherine Purcell	Laura White

Senior Copyeditors

Toni Backman	Carol Fowler

Preface

What *Is* Forensic Psychology?

Forensic psychology is a growing and popular field of inquiry. Its allure, in part fueled by sensationalized and glamorized media images, features psychologists tracking down serial killers, treating sexual psychopaths, and studying the criminal mind. Indeed, as a teacher, I see many of my students expressing considerable enthusiasm for careers as "profilers" engaged in the behavioral science pursuit of crime scene analyses. While there is certainly a need for trained specialists in this domain of forensics, the field itself is considerably more vast.

The expanse of the field is rooted in its sundry models of instruction and practice. Clinical practitioners emphasize the assessment, diagnosis, and treatment of different civil and criminal forensic populations. Law/psychology practitioners emphasize the development of the legally trained specialist whose overlapping skills in courtroom processes and human behavior make for a formidable expert in the treatment and policy arenas. Law–psychology–justice practitioners emphasize the development of a cross-trained specialist whose integrative knowledge base in psychology, criminology, organizational analysis, policy studies, and law readies the person for the increasing demands of a multifaceted profession. If appropriately prepared, this specialist moves skillfully among those in the psychotherapeutic, management, and advocacy communities.

Clearly, each of these models includes a unique set of strengths and limitations. What each of these approaches shares, however, is that its collective vision of forensic psychology is not so narrowly defined or so unidimensionally depicted as is the impression created for us by the popular media. Much of what forensic experts do is not stylish or seductive. Indeed, if anything, much of the work is often tedious and technical. This is not the same as suggesting that the contributions of forensic psychologists are insignificant or trivial to society. Nothing could be further from the truth.

Forensic psychologists are invested in crime and justice. They examine issues, controversies, social problems, psychological states, and other complex phenomena within the adult, juvenile, civil, and family domains of professional practice. They may not define the parameters of their work as such; however, they are unquestionably committed to this enterprise. What links various forensic specialists together, regardless of their particular academic orientation, is the problem of violence (e.g., physical, sexual, psychological, and symbolic) and its impact on different individuals or groups (e.g., offenders, victims, police officers, correctional guards), so that the experiences of intrapsychic pain, interpersonal conflict, and social unrest are identified, reduced, and, perhaps, altogether eliminated. Thus, it is not surprising that many people view the forensic arena as the study of psychology and law within the mental health and criminal/civil justice systems. In addition, though, forensic psychology is the study of both these disciplines and systems precisely where they intersect. Without question, at the crossroads of the field are a host of pressing general public concerns that warrant careful examination and close scrutiny by competently trained specialists.

Why Study Forensic Psychology?

The thoughtful study and effective practice of forensic psychology are compelling responses to the problems posed by crime, victimization, trauma, and other forms of violence. They are also laudable solutions to the demands placed upon us for restoring justice to society. These overlapping and interdependent aims are significant, and those interested in the field would do well to consider how these observations are integral to the successful administration of this specialty area.

Forensic psychology is not simply about reacting to crime. Yes, the discipline does address such disturbing and perplexing questions as: What do we do with kids who kill? What are the causes of prison riots? Are the mentally ill dangerous? Why do the police use (deadly) force? These matters, however, address only the violence variable. In addition, the field considers a number of related concerns that are equally critical and enduring: How do officers mediate conflict? Is the "least restrictive alternative" made available to the psychiatrically disordered? How do the legal and psychological communities promote the best interests of the child in forensic decision making? What treatment and care are available to mothers in prison? These subjects evaluate the justice variable. Forensic psychology, then, is as much about responding to crime and victimization as it is about preventing it or, better still, promoting peace and well-being whenever possible.

Organization of the Book

A textbook about the field of forensic psychology as defined above is therefore potentially quite useful, illuminating, and appealing. The organization of *Introduction to Forensic Psychology: Issues and Controversies in Crime and Justice* is distinct from that of other similar books on the market. This text is distinguishable from its competitors in four ways.

First, readers will note that the book is divided into three broad sections: (1) Police and Law Enforcement, (2) Court and the Legal System, and (3) Corrections and Prison Practices. For those more familiar with conventional psychology texts, this approach will be different and becoming acquainted with it may take some time. This strategy, however, is worthwhile. The three overarching components of the criminal justice system encompass the dimensions previously identified. Thus, as a starting point, working from within the police, court, and correctional orientations to forensic psychology makes perfect sense.

Second, each of the three broad sections to the text includes four subsections, creating a total of 12 chapters. These subsections include: (1) Adult Forensics, (2) Juvenile Forensics, (3) Civil Forensics, and (4) Family Forensics. For those comfortable with standard criminal justice textbooks, this approach will be unusual and familiarizing oneself with it may be awkward at first. Again, though, there is a justification for this strategy. The broad domains of (forensic) psychological practice emphasize these intervention areas. Thus, delineating the chapters accordingly is an appropriate and necessary way in which to define the contours of the police, court, and corrections sections.

Third, within each subsection of a given chapter, a number of selected issues or controversies are presented. Collectively, these topics do not exhaustively canvass the depth of a particular chapter's thematic possibilities. Rather, the carefully chosen entries reveal the diversity contained within the subspecialty area of forensic psychology under investigation. For example, Chapter 5 addresses several adult forensic topics in the court and legal system. The reader is introduced to where and how forensic professionals are called upon during the plea bargaining phase of a case, during the trial's unfolding, and following conviction. Traditional psychology and criminal justice textbooks tend not to adopt an issues/controversies perspective. I suggest that given the nature of the field, this approach is as logical to the introductory analysis of the forensic discipline as it is essential.

Relatedly, the core organizing theme for the selection of entries deliberately focused on capturing the breadth and variety of topics within a subspecialty domain of forensic psychology. This meant that some otherwise noteworthy issues had to be dismissed because they did not advance this goal. Moreover, the process of choosing topics was based on the promotion of introductory (rather than intermediate or advanced) knowledge and practical (rather than conceptual or technical) utility. Again, several worthwhile entries had to be omitted because they did not support this end.

Fourth, over 60 individual entries (i.e., topics) are found in *Introduction to Forensic Psychology: Issues and Controversies in Crime and Justice*. Most chapters examine between four and six topics. It is easy to imagine adding more entries within each chapter. Indeed, each chapter, if appropriately developed as such, could become the basis for its own, freestanding textbook. Standard introductory textbooks in psychology or criminal justice present students with a much more limited number of topics to investigate, but considerable depth is given to those matters that are reviewed. In *Introduction to Forensic Psychology*, greater care is given to the expanse of the field. Certainly, this sacrifices depth of critical analysis. But the aim of the book is to demonstrate something about the volume of compelling or "cutting edge" controversies influencing the development of the field. This is important to readers, particularly those who are cultivating interests in the field for future career possibilities.

Each section or entry of the textbook follows a structured format. The format includes a brief introduction, a case illustration, a review of the literature, an assessment of policy implications, and suggestions for future research. Most entries are between 4 and 6 pages long. Readers expecting to learn about the details of any one issue or controversy in a given chapter may be disappointed. Again, however, the book is designed to canvass an emerging field of inquiry that continues to grow considerably.

Additionally, because the organization of the project does not permit any more systematic assessment than what a provisional analysis would yield, the sections move very quickly and easily from one to the next. Readers could just as simply start in the middle of one chapter, explore a particular section, and then start at the beginning of the chapter and read to its completion. Either approach will not detract from the learning. To explain the broader context in which each individual chapter is organized, overviews introduce the material. The case illustrations (some factual and some fictitious) demonstrate the real-word impact or application of the issue investigated. The policy implications and future research sections are indicators of what needs to be done in a given subspecialty area. Policy implications address the current impact on the field given the state of knowledge regarding the individual entry. Future research considers where and how additional investigations could improve our understanding of the examined issue in relation to other facets of society. These include programmatic, scientific, political, economic, legal, and other notable remedies.

In many ways, *Introduction to Forensic Psychology: Issues and Controversies in Crime and Justice* is a primer to the field. There are competitors; however, I believe that none attempts to so dramatically and comprehensively capture the breadth of the discipline. This project, then, arguably fills this gap in the literature. Mindful always that forensic practitioners operate within the justice and mental health systems, this book endeavors to reveal something about the complexities of where and how the forensic process succeeds and fails for those individuals and collectives who are most directly impacted by it. Clearly, a book of this sort can reveal but a tiny fraction of all that occurs in the functioning of a discipline. But it can offer us information that is useful, worthwhile, and insightful. I invite the readers, whether students or practitioners, to discover the possibilities contained in this book and to consider where and how such observations may serve them in their own educational pursuits or professional development.

Bruce A. Arrigo
Fresno, California
Spring 1999

PART I

Police and Law Enforcement

CHAPTER 1

Adult Forensics

OVERVIEW

Traditionally, the fields of law enforcement and psychology have made for strained if not strange bedfellows. Policing by its very nature requires that officers necessarily and responsibly exercise restraint and caution, be alert and suspicious, and exert power and force where appropriate. Psychology, by contrast, encourages considerable openness, reflection, and introspection. In short, the "protect and serve" function of policing does not seem easily assimilable with the "touchy-feely" sentiment of psychology. This notwithstanding, there are certainly a number of instances where the tools of psychology help officers interface with the public (for example, see the sections on police and the mentally ill, policing and minority populations, and police as mediators in domestic disputes).

Perhaps nowhere else is the tension between law enforcement and psychology more evident then in the adult forensic arena. In this chapter, five issues and/or controversies are examined, exploring different facets of this relationship. These issues/controversies include (1) power, authority, and discretionary decision making; (2) the use of force; (3) evidence tampering; (4) adult criminal profiling; and (5) coerced confessions. Clearly, there are a number of other domains where the psychological sciences impact the practice of policing; however, the selected topics were carefully chosen because they collectively suggest considerable breadth in forensic application. In other words, the adult forensic section of policing canvasses a wide array of law enforcement psychology topics, reflecting the expanse of the field.

Police officers exercise power, authority, and discretion in decision making. Not only is it important to know where and how this behavior manifests itself, it is equally significant to assess the thought and perceptual processes (e.g., demeanor of the suspect) that give rise to police action or inaction. Police officers also, on occasion, use force. What are the psychological variables that impact the use of it, and what "dangerous" circumstances inform an officer's decision to use excessive and even deadly force?

Law enforcement personnel confront difficult cases where evidence, necessary for clear and certain conviction, is not always as fully developed as it could be. What motivates an officer to tamper with evidence? What ethical and/or moral factors contribute to an officer's understanding of this behavior?

State and federal law enforcement personnel investigate crimes that are committed by very troubled individuals. This has lead to the criminal profiling of offenders. What are the personality and behavioral characteristics that officers consider when evaluating the profile for a serial homicide killer, a mass murderer, a sex offender, or other seriously disturbed persons? How do these processes contribute to the apprehension of offenders?

Police officers are responsible for eliciting information from suspects that may result in a confession. What psychological and sociological techniques, manipulative or otherwise, do law enforcement personnel employ to arrive at (in-)voluntary confessions? How, if at all, do officers balance the suspect's right against self-incrimination with the precinct's and/or the public's demand for apprehension of (factually) guilty criminals during the interviewing phase?

These and other questions are examined in the various sections of Chapter 1. This chapter, therefore, demonstrates that psychology is very much a part of what happens in ongoing police practices. Interestingly, however, we know very little about the extent of its role in routine law enforcement. What we do know suggests that the implications for officers, for police departments, for suspects/offenders, for the public at large, and for communities in general are considerable. More research on the identified controversies is needed. Better evaluations of how the adult forensic arena of policing and psychology interface is essential. These conditions are necessary if we are to address the problem of crime and the search for justice at the crossroads of psychology and law enforcement.

POWER, AUTHORITY, AND DISCRETIONARY DECISION MAKING

Introduction

Effective law enforcement must take into account, and encompass, a wide variety of processes and decision-making steps. Officers must decide whether to arrest an individual, give a citation, or simply release a citizen with a warning. These decisions, however, are never cut-and-dried, and often they fail to be consistent. An officer's decision in handling a situation depends on the offense, the background and personality of the responding officer(s), and the demographic background of the offender. This section discusses the discretionary decisionmaking process within law enforcement, drawing on the officer's perceived or given power and authority to make law-enforcing decisions. The following scenario is commonplace, deals with alternating forms of police discretion, and is a typical complaint of citizens.

> While driving down an interstate, you are pulled over by a police officer. The officer, upon reaching your car, begins to discuss with you in a somewhat stern voice, the rules and/or regulations of the road and every way in which you have violated them. To your dismay, you are informed that you are receiving a ticket, to which you may plead "guilty" or "not guilty," and will be required to pay a hefty fine.
>
> The following week, you are told by a friend of yours that they too, were pulled over just yesterday on the same interstate. However, you are surprised to discover that this friend did not receive a ticket, and in fact was released without even a warning. Upon further discussion, you also discover that you were clocked at the same speed and were pulled over in the same area of interstate.
>
> You can't help but wonder why you recived a citation and your friend did not. Was it because you are significantly younger than your friend, or was it because you are of a different race or sex? Aggravated, you complain to all who will listen about the lack of fairness and consistency in traffic ticket citations.

Scenarios such as these have been the subject of controversy for some time. Some researchers have even attempted to quantify the nature of traffic stop citations in addition to contributing and noncontributing factors in receiving a traffic citation (Corbett & Simon, 1991; Koehler & Willis, 1994). The process behind police decision making is discussed within this section as are the contributing factors that enable police to discern between decisions in various circumstances.

Literature Review

A survey examining the responses of over 1000 people, including police officers, probation officers, prosecuting attorneys, defense attorneys, judges, community leaders, and ordinary citizens, found striking differences in police practices and decision making. Compared to all other groups, police officers were found to be more harsh in their treatment of curfew violators and those involved with drugs and alcohol, prostitution, and vandalism. Further, it was discovered that decision-making practices of police officers were found to be related to the experience of the officer, in addition to their educational level. More specifically, the higher the officer's education, the less harshly police officers treated offenders. Also, officers were found to act more harshly during the early years of police service, become more tolerant during their mid-level years, and become again more harsh toward the end of their careers (Icove, 1994).

Discretionary decision making by law enforcement officers is closely tied to the concept of police ethics and morality. To demonstrate this, H. S. Cohen and Feldberg (1991) discussed the necessary empowerment of police and their ability to exercise power. The authors stated that "[p]olice have considerably more authority over others than most people in society and, consequently, have more opportunities to use that authority in impermissible ways" (p. 7). Therefore, decision making by police is, at times, a result of personal judgments and natural biases. The authors concluded by stating that police must retain all the discretionary power that they currently possess. However, this power must be exercised cautiously, since the effects of police officer decisions affect the community in a multifaceted manner and have potential ramifications that may be unseen.

From a psychological standpoint, decision making encompasses a wide variety of cognitive processes. The ability to organize data, to synthesize that data, and to translate the results into an appropriate behavioral outcome is clearly a complicated process. It is no surprise, then, that police make some decisions based on suspect behavior and their interpretation of that behavior. Suspects' behavior may help the officer to gather particular data regarding a situation, to assess the potential danger of the situation, and to form effective strategies to deal with the predicament.

The above paradox has been debated by numerous criminologists, psychologists, and other scientists (Fyfe, 1996; Klinger, 1996; R. J. Lundman, 1996a; R. E. Worden, Shepard, & Mastrofski, 1996). For example, Klinger (1994) discovered that the demeanor of citizens had an impact on police decisions to arrest. More specifically, Klinger detailed a two-phase process by which officers interact with citizens: there is (1) a "pre-intervention" phase that incorporates the circumstances that bring a police officer to the intervention with citizens and (2) an "interaction" phase that begins when the officer actually deals with the citizen and ends when these two parties separate from each other. During these encounters, the citizen's demeanor comes into play and influences how an officer may deal with an arrest decision. However, demeanor was found to have an effect on an officer's decision to arrest only when demeanor included illegal conduct (Klinger, 1994).

As an opposing viewpoint, R. J. Lundman (1996b) stated that demeanor has a larger effect on police decisions to arrest and is not confounded by research flaws to the degree that Klinger purports. Previously unpublished results of drunk-driving encounters were used in order to determine whether demeanor and other extralegal variables had an effect on an officer's decision to arrest when the effects of the crimes themselves were statistically controlled. It was found that the effects of demeanor vary with how the citizen's demeanor was presented to the officer. More specifically, race and social class had effects on decisions to arrest. Members of minority classes were arrested more often, while members of the economic upper-class were also cited more often, due to the officers' beliefs that they can better afford the monetary fines.

Police face a wide variety of law enforcement situations every day. These range from minor traffic stops to interventions dealing with robbery and other serious offenses. The decision to either arrest or not arrest varies as a function of a police officer's experience and outside influences. The "leniency thesis," for example, states that police treat males who abuse their female spouses less punitively than other violent offenders. In fact, research has demonstrated that 13% of male-on-female assaults result in arrest, while 28% of other assaults result in arrest (Fyfe, Klinger, & Flavin, 1997). These results indicate that police do make decisions based on certain aspects of situations, some of which may be individual personal biases.

Social psychology and industrial/organizational psychology have also made attempts to clarify the nature of police decision making. The psychological forces behind drinking-under-the-influence (DUI) enforcement has been the focus of at least one particular study (Mastrofski, Ritti, & Snipes, 1994). This research has offered an "expectancy theory" of discretionary decision making. This theory is a model of motivation and performance based on worker perception and, to a degree, their expected outcomes.

It is clear then, that police do make discretionary decisions based on a variety of factors. These decisions are based on a variety of internal and external influences. These influences allow the law enforcement officer to weigh these factors and make decisions based on their perceived levels of authority.

Forensic Psychology and Policy Implications

In theory, all police decisions are made on the basis of law enforcement policy. Each police department has its own set of individual codes and policies, although many of these policies share similarities between departments. However, law enforcement must remain, to the largest degree possible, consistent. Therefore, the development of policies ensuring that police discretion and decision making remain consistent is warranted.

At its most basic level, police must ensure that courtesy be extended to citizens at all times in order to perpetuate the notion that police are, in fact, public servants who have the safety of the general public as their primary interest. Overt use of force by a police department demonstrates to the public a sign of inherent weakness in that police department's ability to effectively and fairly handle situations (Wadman & Ziman, 1993). Unfortunately, departments often see the use of force as too necessary and exercise it in a loose manner. A police force which uses more courtesy demands a certain level of respect and mutual value between the citizenship and the law enforcement agency.

The methods in which police handle serious and nonserious crimes has also been investigated with the purpose of understanding more fully the decision-making process of officers. The goal of this research is policy reform in establishing consistent policing. Crank (1992), for example, found that factors such as the presence of minorities, location of the actual police department, number of police on the force, the supervisory ratio of departments, and other variables correlate significantly with the amount of arrests made. Research which spells out specific influences on police decision making could be used to form policies which are found to best suit the public in terms of appropriate numbers of arrests and other law enforcement decisions.

Suggestions for Future Research

Research examining the psychological processes underlying police discretionary decision making is of current interest in both the psychological and criminological literature. While the topic of demeanor and police decisions to arrest have been examined scientifically, specific modalities involving police decisions to arrest and methods of police intervention are still areas of research worthy of investigation.

Police expectancy theory, for example, is an area of research that is needed. Mastrofski et al. (1994) state that broader and more diverse samples of department examination will help in the development of theories attempting to explain cognitive models of police decision making. These authors further state that the effects of expectancy theory could be tested by focusing to a larger degree on actual police arrest decisions rather than examining police arrest totals post hoc.

More systematic analyses of citizen behavior, which are likely to result in arrest decisions, should be explored more fully. The majority of studies indicate that illegal behavior will result in police decisions to arrest. However, it may also follow that other citizen behaviors besides those that are blatantly illegal will result in either arrest or citation. Research examining these processes is needed and certainly warranted.

There is also a lack of psychological research examining a police officer's personality and its relation to arrest likelihood. Although some studies exist which have attempted to quantify the typical police personality, virtually no research exists which attempts to correlate police personality characteristics, such as overcontrolled hostility and passivity, with an officer's likeliness to arrest.

USE OF FORCE

Introduction

The question of force used by police first came to attention in 1974, in Memphis, Tennessee, when a 15-year-old boy named Edward Garner broke into a home and stole 10 dollars and a purse. At the arrival of the police, Garner, who was unarmed, fled from the home and ran across the backyard. As the police began pursuit of the suspect, Garner reached a six-foot fence surrounding the yard. In an attempt to avoid police custody, he continued to flee and began to climb over the fence. The police officer, fearing that the suspect would get away if he made it over the fence, fired at the back of Garner's head and killed him.

The decision to use force in the apprehension of a citizen, whether it be excessive or deadly, ultimately lies in the hands of the police officer at the moment of conflict. Although the goal of the officer is always to resolve a conflict in the most peaceful manner, it is understood that there are situations in which a peaceful resolution is not possible. Guidelines are established to assist the officer, who at times must make a "split-second" decision as to the type of force necessary. In order to set these guidelines behind the use of force, it is first necessary to understand how dangerous situations in need of force unfold and the decisions that follow.

Literature Review

The history behind the police officer's right to use force dates back to common law under English rule. Known as the "fleeing felon" law, common law states that a police officer could use deadly force in situations that must protect the life of the officer or an innocent third party, to overcome resistance to arrest, or to prevent the escape of any felony suspect (Inciardi, 1993; Pursley, 1994). The loose generalization of the "fleeing felon" law leaves a series of questionable circumstances and issues that remain unaddressed due to the changing criminal activities of our present day. Our current legal system now classifies more crimes as felonies, which in turn allows for more felony-related crimes that are not necessarily dangerous nor life- threatening. Furthermore, technology provides more effective means of communication and organization within police forces that can aid in the apprehension of criminals (Pursley, 1994).

Such unspecified circumstances established by the "fleeing felon" law were left to the discretion of the police jurisdiction. Many jurisdictions continued to use the common law guidelines until the landmark decision in *Tennessee v. Garner* (1985) that sought to outline the qualifications of the use of force in a constitutional frame. It was argued that the level of force the officer used against Edward Garner was extreme and unnecessary given the circumstances of the crime. Following *Tennessee v. Garner*, the use of force was restricted to circumstances where it is necessary to prevent the escape of a suspect who is believed to be a significant threat to the officer or others (Inciardi, 1993).

Within the creation of more defined standards of the use of force lies the exploration of the motives, behavior, and decision-making process that underlie such an action. Many social scientists have researched these aspects and have offered some insights that can serve as an aid in organizing such standards of force. In the past, the problems associated with the use of force were seen as the result of "a few bad apples" within the police community. Such an explanation is weighted in the view that many police officers possess a stereotypical aggressive and authoritative nature. This concept has received a great deal of attention within the public due to the highly controversial Rodney King incident (see the following case illustration). Although the officers involved maintained they acted according to police standards and that such force was necessary in the apprehension of King, the beating of Rodney King has been cited as a clear representation of the use of excessive force and stands to support the idea of the authoritative and aggressive police officer.

> In the early morning hours of March 3, 1991, in a suburb of Los Angeles, police began a high-speed chase in pursuit of a suspect who was driving recklessly and believed to be dangerously intoxicated. The driver, Rodney King, led police on a chase that reached approximately 100 m.p.h. and ended when he reached an entrance to a park which had been closed off with a cable. After King, who was unarmed, stepped out of his car, police attempted to restrain him by striking him with a TASER gun and then followed by beating him repeatedly with their batons. King suffered multiple fractures, broken bones, and internal injuries. As this was occurring, a citizen who lived across from the park grabbed his video camera and proceeded to record the event. The tape was then sold to television stations which broadcasted the tape nationwide. Initially the officers were acquitted in court, although upon appeal two of the four officers were convicted of excessive use of force. The King incident produced widespread public outrage that spawned numerous questions and concerns about police power and brutality.

Following the Rodney King incident, many police departments looked to establish a clearly defined set of guidelines for the use of excessive and deadly force. However, more recent explanations of force suggest it is impossible for such specified standards to be established and maintained because the act of force is based on a "split-second" decision that involves an immediate analysis of the situation by the police officer (Fyfe, 1985). Such an analysis is accompanied by intense stress and the possibility of a life-threatening situation. Some experts believe that to expect an officer to make an appropriate decision under these circumstances is unrealistic.

In contrast, there have been several studies that attempt to understand the process by which an officer makes his or her decision and the circumstances behind these decisions. Binder and Scharf (1980) researched the circumstances that evolved during a conflict and developed a four-phase model that describes the steps involved at the final decision to use deadly force. This model submits that "the violent police–citizen encounter is considered a developmental process in which successive decisions and behaviors by either police officer or citizen, or both, make the violent outcome more or less likely" (Binder & Scharf, 1980, p. 111). The model consists of the Anticipation Phase, Entry and Initial Contact Phase, Information Exchange, and Final Phase. Each phase describes the emotional as well as the environmental details as they unravel in a potentially violent situation. The Anticipation Phase is composed of the immediate involvement of the officer when he or she is first called to intervene and the information that is relayed as a result. Entry and Initial Contact include what the officer is confronted with when arriving at the scene and the development of the crisis. The Information Exchange Phase consists of any verbal or nonverbal exchange of information between the suspect and the officer which also contributes to the officer's assessment of the dangerousness of the situation. In the

Final Phase, the officer makes the decision of whether to use force by incorporating the information received in the previous phases as well as any final action by the suspect or immediate threat.

As described, this model reflects the application of a series of decisions actively made by the police officer. Appropriate decisions are made when the police officer consciously evaluates the situation based on the development of the event. Many police departments have used a similar philosophy in developing a series of guidelines which establish a more definitive circumstance for the use of force. Such policies can aid the officer in making a rational decision in a time of great pressure.

Forensic Psychology and Policy Implications

One way to combat the chances of using force unnecessarily is by incorporating effective training programs that will prepare an officer in the event that such a quick decision must be made (Ross & Jones, 1996). Developing extensive policies that outline the criteria which may necessitate the use of force can act as means of training police officers to recognize the key elements involved. These key elements include specific response levels on the part of the officer that must be evaluated during the course of the confrontation. Providing officers with applicable response levels such as appropriate dialogue and verbal direction with the citizen, appropriate means of restraint, and the use of weapons and incapacitation can alleviate some of the intense pressure in that "split-second" decision. In addition, such policies can address the various subject factors such as age, size, seriousness of crime, and weapons usage as compared to the officer's factors of size, number of officers present, an officer's defensive tactics, and legal requirements. As explored in the Edward Garner case, his youth and the fact that he was unarmed and had not committed a dangerous crime would indicate under such a policy that deadly force was not appropriate in the context of the situation. Similarly, in the Rodney King case, an implication of policy could prevent questions as to the amount of force that is necessary to subdue a suspect. Such guidelines have been proven to be highly effective in the fast-paced discretionary decision making that is necessary in such an event.

Another effective means of preventing unnecessary use of force would be in the screening and counseling of those officers who reveal a greater propensity toward violence (Scrivner, 1994). These provisions would allow the police departments to gain more responsibility over the likelihood of an incident to occur rather than to rely solely on the circumstances of the crime or on the suspect.

In addition, monitoring officers' behavior can also serve as a defense against unnecessary use of force (Scrivner, 1994). By alerting supervisors to those officers who demonstrate behavior that suggests a risk for violence, intervention techniques can be performed early. In addition, monitoring officers in the field can provide a role model to other officers as well as aid in the enforcement of the policies established within the department.

Suggestions for Future Research

There is a great need for further research in the evaluation of the environmental aspects that lead to the need for force. As discussed, the environment in which the situation arises can determine the need for force and the potential outcome of such force. With a more complete understanding of how the environment develops, what role the environment plays, and how the environment can be manipulated for safety, we can hope to use force as a means to uphold justice with minimal conflict. Furthermore, there is a need to understand the psychological as well as the sociological aspects of the use of force. It is necessary to understand the emotional and cognitive functions of both the suspect and the police officer involved in such a crisis. It is essential to research areas such as if and how gender and ethnicity relate to the use force by officers. These environmental, sociological, and psychological applications can be beneficial in training police officers to recognize the scenarios that develop and can facilitate that final decision of whether to use force.

EVIDENCE TAMPERING

Introduction

The O. J. Simpson trial brought into the limelight an increasingly notorious portion of criminal investigation—the tampering of evidence. Much attention was given to the notion that Simpson may have been framed by the Los Angeles Police Department, who was accused of planting blood evidence in his Bronco and bloody clothing in his house. Relatively little attention, however, is given to other aspects of evidence tampering. In what ways could an officer tamper with evidence? What motivates a police officer to tamper with evidence? Are there any steps that can be taken to prevent such occurrences? These questions are examined in this section, as are other issues related to evidence tampering.

The following fictional vignette provides an illustration of evidence tampering (Klockars, 1984).

> Mike, an experienced and talented detective, was the chief investigating officer on a case that involved a series of rapes, kidnappings, and robberies that were all committed by the same person. In each of the cases the rapist knocked on the front door of the home, talked or forced his way in, and, finding that the woman was alone or only small children were present, took her to a bedroom and raped her. In all, the rapist victimized five women in this way.
>
> The third rape was, however, different from the others in that as he was raping his victim someone came to the front door and rang the bell. This frightened the rapist and he fled through a rear window, leaving a shoe behind. Normally the shoe would have been placed with other physical evidence from the scene in a police evidence room, but Mike took possession of the shoe himself so that it might be used to give the rapist's scent to some specially trained tracking dogs who would follow it from the victim's home. The

dogs followed the scent through city streets for roughly two miles before they lost it at the door of a popular after-hours club.

   Instead of returning the shoe to the evidence room, Mike placed it in the back of one of the bottom drawers in his desk, a desk which is never locked. It sat in the desk drawer for weeks until Mike brought it out to compare it with a shoe that was recovered in a search of the rapist's lodgings. It was a perfect mate to the shoe from Mike's desk. What Mike realized after he had made the match was that by keeping it in his unlocked desk drawer he had compromised, if not destroyed, the chain of continuity that would have to be established to introduce the shoe from the victim's home into evidence in court. What he did was forge an evidence receipt with the cooperation of the officer in charge of the evidence room to establish that the shoe had been there all the time. (pp. 539–540)

Cases such as this cause various emotions within different people. Some feel that Mike may be justified in his evidence tampering since he knew the perpetrator was guilty and should receive jail time for his acts. Others, however, feel that the procedures of bringing an alleged criminal to justice must be followed without compromise in order to ensure that no false imprisonments are made. With today's increasing technological advancements within forensics, such as DNA testing and chemical analysis of skin and hair particles, increased opportunity for error and deliberate falsifying of evidence data is bound to occur.

   There is a surprising paucity of information addressing the topic of evidence tampering. What is available within the literature is limited in scope, and virtually no study exists on the psychological ramifications surrounding this topic. Therefore, reviewing the literature dealing with evidence tampering brings to light a broader scope encompassing such topics as types of tampering, police morality, and others.

Literature Review

The general public's perception of law enforcement is one that has always vacillated between praise and criticism. As mentioned, the O. J. Simpson trial brought much attention to the topic of "police framing," or officers that manipulate evidence in order to make a more convincing case to the jury. Why does a police officer choose to manipulate criminal evidence rather than abide by the strict standards of police detective processes? Very often, it is actually the police officers themselves who feel the jury system frequently falters, leaving too many criminals unpunished due to "technicalities."

   Evidence tampering can take a number of different forms. While evidence tampering is most often thought of as the planting of a condemning object, such as a piece of clothing, it can by some definitions incorporate many more subtleties. For example, manipulation of DNA evidence is something that cannot be detected with the naked eye. Rather, sensitive lab procedures are necessary in order to place a person at a particular location or time using genetic information. Also, perjury can be considered tampering of evidence, since verbal testimony is, by certain standards, considered a form of evidence. Theoretically, altering your verbal testimony in order to have it coincide with the case is tampering with that evidence.

Klockars (1984) describes a theory which states that police officers use a hierarchy of lying to establish domination and control, including authority, power, persuasion, and force. It is through these means, the author states, that officers obtain such necessary characteristics as governance, rule, and sovereignty. Klockars goes on to describe a concept called "blue lies," which refers to the specialty of police lying and the court's reluctance to deal with it. A hypothetical case is described in which two mentally ill brothers made accusations to the local police department that invisible aliens were pursuing them. The chief of the police department told the brothers that he called Washington and informed them of the invasion. Of course, the chief did not really notify Washington of the make-believe alien invasion. The lie served a number of purposes, however, not the least of which was bringing a sense of comfort to the brothers, who could then rest easy because the situation was dealt with (Klockars, 1984).

It is important to remember that while this "blue lie" seems and probably is a harmless means of dealing with a nonsense situation, it can be viewed as a window into the police officer's mind in examining the process of justifying lying to the citizens. Police departments are not the only ones susceptible to such occurrences. Psychiatric institutions are especially vulnerable to this type of distortion for the patient's benefit. Psychotic delusions exhibited by patients often cannot be effectively dealt with until the patient experiences a period of remitting psychosis. In the meantime, those employed within the institution will simply pacify the patient.

According to Klockars (1984), police use a number of different mechanisms to prevent addressing the potential severe feelings of moral discomfort in lying. The first is to simply refuse to admit that there is in fact a moral dilemma. A second strategy is exemption—rationalizing that a moral dilemma is really not a dilemma at all since the officer actually knows the reality of the case or situation at hand. This enables an officer to bar the case from becoming one associated with feelings of moral guilt. A good example of exemption is the case illustration presented with Mike, the police officer who manipulated a piece of evidence in order to make it admissible. Another way officers deal with potential moral dilemmas is to use what is termed "prioritization." This incorporates using a wrongdoing (e.g., lying) in order to create a more favorable outcome overall.

A particularly tangible example of evidence tampering was apparent in what is perhaps the largest evidence-tampering scandal in law enforcement history. Hansen (1994a) describes a case in which three troopers were sent to prison, three others were awaiting trial, and 40 cases came under review by the state police to examine the role of evidence tampering over an 8-year period. The article revealed that police tend to tamper, alter, and even manufacture evidence in order to make their cases more appealing and "solid." For example, troopers followed a particular pattern in altering evidence, most often fingerprints, after a suspect was identified. This scandal resulted in a reversal of one man's conviction for a 1986 robbery and double murder and the release of a woman convicted of one count each of burglary and arson. This woman had already spent over 2 years in prison for these convictions. According to one officer, "There were a lot of fingerprints found in places where they never should have been found . . . The feeling was, if you had a good suspect, it wouldn't hurt to have a few more things against him" (p. 22).

Forensic Psychology and Policy Implications

Policy implications dealing with evidence, its handling, and tampering have taken a number of different roads. Virtually every police department has a specialized procedure for handling evidence. In addition, the procedure for each type of case varies by the nature of the criminal infraction.

Arson, for example (a traditionally difficult case to prove), is subjected to a large array of evidence-handling procedures due to the temptation of evidence planting. The nature of the crime often leads to total destruction of the crime scene, often resulting in destruction of all available evidence associated with it. It is all too easy to drop a gasoline can or cigarette butt at the crime scene of an arson case in order to establish a "clean" path of criminal intent or nonintent. As a result, the Forensic Science Committee Performance Test Center has prepared minimum requirements associated with the handling and preservation of arson evidence. These include such policies as proper collection and storage equipment, identification, establishment of chain of custody, preservation, receipt, storage, and eventual disposition (Anonymous, 1984). A break in any of these links of the arson evidence chain leaves room for possible manipulation and tampering of evidence.

Police departments have joined the computer revolution in its establishment of smoother functioning, more efficient, and more powerful methods of storage and handling of forensic evidence. Genova (1989) described a new means by which a property and evidence bureau (P & E) merged with a Laboratory Information Management System (LIMS). Increasing complications associated with ever-growing piles of evidence, along with links of evidence to victim and defendant mixing, the problem of several items related to several defendants, and other problems necessitated the establishment of a modern, more efficient method of tracking evidence.

The LIMS system incorporates a series of mainframe computers used to track a piece of evidence throughout its lifespan within the police department using such features as bar-coded evidence, automatic case number assignment, and a comprehensive database of logistical data regarding the evidence. The use of an electronic wand, much like the ones used in department stores for pricing items, is used to track the physical movement of a piece of evidence from one department or locality to another within the evidence storage area. This implementation makes it

TABLE I   Alaska Statute Title 11, Chapter 56, Article 4, Section 610-AS 11.56.610 (1997)—Tampering with Physical Evidence

(a) A person commits the crime of tampering with physical evidence if the person

   (1) Destroys, mutilates, alters, suppresses, conceals, or removes physical evidence with intent to impair its verity or availability in an official proceeding or a criminal investigation
   (2) Makes, presents, or uses physical evidence, knowing it to be false, with intent to mislead a juror who is engaged in an official proceeding or a public servant who is engaged in an official proceeding of a criminal investigation
   (3) Prevents the production of physical evidence in an official proceeding or a criminal investigation by the use of force, threat, or deception against anyone
   (4) Does any act described by (1), (2), or (3) of this subsection with intent to prevent the institution of an official proceeding.

(b) Tampering with physical evidence is a class C felony.

much more difficult to remove evidence already in storage and replicate it or move it at a later time to the crime scene.

Some states regulate tampering as a crime in itself rather than as a substatute of another law such as perjury. Alaska, for example, has outlined specific guidelines used to determine whether a law enforcement agent has manipulated or otherwise distorted evidence (see Table I).

The statute described in Table I gives a sobering example of exactly how serious evidence tampering can be. Were it not deemed an extremely important portion of policing, felony charges would certainly not result from its use.

Suggestions for Future Research

While many different aspects of evidence tampering have been discussed within this section, the amount of dedicated research on this topic is indeed scanty. Some police departments have implemented antitampering policies with the intent of reducing both the temptation and actuality of evidence tampering. These policies, however, are simple and in need of research in order to determine their efficacy. Some departments now require at least two investigators to examine a given crime scene and photographs to be taken of fingerprints prior to their collection (Hansen, 1994a). Research examining the increase, decrease, or equal rates of tampering associated with these policies needs to be studied.

Psychologically oriented research is also needed in order to determine the possible causes of an officer's decision to tamper with evidence and what steps can be taken to reduce such mental states. Perhaps tampering is related solely to an officer's mistrust or distrust of the "system," feeling that additional "help" is necessary in order to bring criminals to the justice they deserve. This same feeling may be related instead to occurrences of police stress or cynicism. In either case, research examining the role of psychology in the officer's decision to tamper with evidence is lacking.

What impact does an officer caught tampering with evidence have on the courts? The police department? The general public? The Rodney King and O. J. Simpson cases bring feelings of distrust to the American judicial system. Evidence tampering has never been examined as a function of the public's trust in policing.

Many other possibilities for research exist in the topic of evidence tampering. The future will no doubt bring additional cases of police fraud associated with the manipulation of criminal evidence and will place this understudied topic into the limelight once again.

ADULT CRIMINAL PROFILING

Introduction

The area of forensic psychology dealing with criminal profiling is an increasingly popular one. A greater number of movies and prime-time television shows attempt to portray the glamorous and interesting process of profiling criminals (most often serial murderers). Although much profiling is accomplished through intuitive processes possessed by law enforcement agents or their consultants, a scientific grounding does exist for profiling and is discussed in this chapter. The following vignette provides an example of a "typical" serial murder scenario and gives a hypothesis or "profile" used to apprehend the murderer (Turco, 1990).

> The homicide scene revealed a 21-year-old woman shot on each side of the head with a small-caliber weapon. She was found nude, lying face up on the stairway of her home and had been found sexually molested. Crime scene evidence led this author to the belief that she had been murdered while walking down the stairs. The investigation led to the comparisons of similar homicides in the area and "a profile" of the perpetrator was developed. We believed he was a young, athletic male with a casual acquaintance with his victims. We believed he was nonpsychotic and "organized" in his behavior. The detective team hypothesized that he was a "smooth-talker" and capable of easily winning a woman's confidence. This led to the "hunch" that he likely had good relationships with women, at least on a superficial basis. The possibility of "splitting" was entertained as a hypothesis in which we believed the perpetrator "divided" women into good (his friends) and bad (his victims). Investigators looked for physical patterns consistent with this hypothesis. This led to an examination of telephone records of public and private phones in the geographic vicinity of sequential homicides. This revealed a pattern of telephone calls to the same phone in another city. Interviews with the suspect and his girlfriend were arranged at the time of his arrest. Police learned that following each murder he telephoned his live-in girlfriend "just to talk." Examination of his telephone bills revealed collect calls made from the vicinity of previous homicides. He was an intelligent, good-looking psychopath who was later convicted of murder. (p. 152)

Literature Review

The case illustration given above demonstrates how a series of facts regarding a particular case can be used to develop a profile of a criminal based on their behaviors. According to the Federal Bureau of Investigation (FBI), profiling is defined as a technique which serves to identify the major personality and behavioral characteristics of an offender based on an analysis of the crime the offender committed. This process generally involves seven steps: (1) evaluation of the criminal act itself, (2) comprehensive evaluation of the specifics of the crime scene(s), (3) comprehensive analysis of the victim, (4) evaluation of preliminary reports, (5) evaluation of the medical examiner's autopsy protocol, (6) development of profile with critical offender characteristics, and (7) investigative suggestions predicated upon construction of the profile (Douglas & Burgess, 1986). The authors in the same article equate the profiling process with that of making a psychiatric diagnosis. In this respect, data is obtained through assessment; situations are reconstructed; hypotheses are developed, formulated, and tested; and these results are reported back to the interested party.

The goal of any law enforcement agency is not only to enforce laws, but to apprehend those who have broken the law. However, the latter part of this process is often difficult. Investigators must struggle with a multitude of evidence, reports, and inferences regarding a particular crime. Criminals are not often immediately apprehended, leaving the law enforcement agency to deal with a criminal at large. When the crime is serious enough, as in arson, rape, or murder, a psychological or criminological profile of the subject is obtained in order to facilitate apprehension.

Criminal profiling has conceivably existed since the inception of crime itself. Documented attempts of profiling such heinous killers as Jack the Ripper date back to the 1800s. The majority of modern literature focusing on profiling examines crimes such as murder, sexual offences, and rape. These typologies are further broken down into subcategories. For example, murder is often subdivided into categories such as serial murder, sexual murder, and mass murder. Both professionals and nonprofessionals have made attempts at establishing profiles of those who have broken the law—each utilizing their own preferred school of thought. For example, West (1988) describes the extensive use of the Minnesota Multiphasic Personality Inventory (MMPI) to predict future offenders based on a series of commonly found personality characteristics. The author also discusses the use of such devices as projective measures (Rorschach, Thematic Apperception Test, etc.) and the effects of neurological insult on future aberrant behaviors.

The author also states that biological theories underlying criminal or even homicidal tendencies are becoming increasingly popular. West claims that research on genes and their correlation to aggressive criminal behaviors exists and should be further examined. The XYY sex chromosome irregularity was implicated in some studies in criminal behavioral effects through aggressive and disinhibition syndromes. Also, electroencephalograph studies examining electrical activity of brain regions also implicated biological anomalies as a possible cause of criminal behavior. The reader must be cautioned, however, that attributing an offender's behavior to a biological or brain disturbance may lead to a belief that such behavior cannot be helped due to its uncontrollable biological nature. In addition, sentencing implications may be present due to a diagnosed brain abnormality.

Turco (1990) emphasizes a psychoanalytic orientation in the production of psychological/criminological profiles of offenders. He states that a crime scene is like a projective device such as a Rorschach ink blot. There are a number of personality characteristics derived from evidence and manipulation of the crime scene which can be interpreted much like a subject's response to an ink blot. Turco's psychoanalytic background stresses the importance of early childhood experiences, relationships, and unresolved conflicts and their relation to current behavior. Further, this information can be used to predict future behaviors based on these same variables.

The FBI has done a great amount of research in the area of criminal profiling. Special agents in the FBI have developed, through archival and current case information, typical characteristics likely to be found in a particular type of offender. Hazelwood (1983) describes how a profile of a rapist can be obtained primarily through competent and informed interviewing of rape victims. He states that in profiling the rapist, three basic steps are critical: (1) careful interview of the victim regarding the rapist's behavior, (2) analysis of that behavior in an attempt to ascertain the motivation underlying the assault, and (3) a profile compilation of the individual likely to have committed the crime in the manner reported with the assumed motivation.

In establishing a profile of a rapist, Hazelwood describes how the rapist behaves within his environment relative to his personality structure. Behaviors are broken down into a number of categories and the victim is asked detailed information regarding behavior in an attempt to classify the rapist. Three basic forms of behavior are exhibited by the rapist: physical (force), verbal, and sexual. For example, the rapist who dominates his victim primarily through the use of verbal degradation and threats may be portraying a personality characteristic consistent with an intense desire to emotionally harm his victim. This may be indicative of a recent break-up between the rapist and his girlfriend. The rape therefore serves as revenge on the girlfriend through the victim in order to satisfy a psychological need. Based on this information, profilers can then begin to formulate the type of personality profile which may use rape as a means of rectification and revenge.

Other, more common techniques of profiling offenders come from gaining detailed information from a criminal population convicted of committing the same or similar crimes. These data are used to establish patterns or norms based on that particular type of offender. According to the FBI (1985b), individual development of offenders is based on two primary factors: the dominance of a fantasy life and a history of personal abuse. These factors are used to develop a working profile of a murderer. In-depth interviews of 36 sexual murderers revealed a number

TABLE II   General Characteristics, Resultant Attitudes and Beliefs, and
Deviant Behaviors of 36 Sexual Murderers[a]

Background characteristics		
Family background	Individual development	Performance
Detachment	Dominance of fantasy	School failure
Criminality	History of personal abuse	Sporadic work record
Substance abuse		Unskilled
Psychiatric problems		Poor military record
Sexual problems		Solo sex
Inconsistent discipline		
Resultant attitudes and beliefs		Deviant behaviors
Devaluation of victim and society		Rape
World viewed as unjust		Mutilation
Authority/life viewed as inconsistent		Torture
Autoerotic preference		
Obsession with dominance through aggression		
Fantasy as reality		

[a] FBI (1985a, p. 6).

of characteristics typical of this type of offender. For example, the sexual murderer
tends to be intelligent, good-looking, of average socioeconomic status, and an oldest
son or first/second born. However, they also tend to have an attitude of devaluation
toward people (having failed to form significant attachments), view the world as unjust, have an unstable or inconsistent view of authority and justice, and tend to have
an obsession with dominance through aggression. These sexual murderers also tend
to have few attachments outside their immediate families, tend to live in a created
fantasy world in which they feel comfortable, and have a history of deviant behaviors. Based on these sets of characteristics, a profile can be developed (see Table II).

Some researchers (Reming, 1988) state that the habitual criminal shares many
personality characteristics with the supercop (a police officer who consistently per-
forms within the top 90th percentile). Supercops score essentially the same on a test
measuring perceived descriptive characteristics of habitual criminals. Further, there
were similarities found between habitual criminals and supercops on such dimensions as control, aggressiveness, vigilance, rebelliousness, energy level, frankness in
expression, intensity of personal relationships, self-esteem, feelings of uniqueness,

extroversion, sociability, jealousy, possessiveness of sexual partner, tendency not to change opinions easily, philandering, and a tendency to avoid blame. These same researchers state that many of the positive traits of good police officers are also beneficial in examining the characteristics of the habitual criminal. Thus a complete understanding of officers' strengths and weaknesses may help in profiling criminals.

As previously stated, certain criminals tend to receive the spotlight in regard to psychological/criminological profiling. Not surprisingly, these crimes are often the most serious, such as homicide. It is therefore not surprising that the majority of research focuses on these criminals, since conceivably they are the most dangerous. Profiling sexual murderers seems to dominate the literature due to the nature of the crime itself. The sexual murderer often appears to be unmotivated and engages in a series of bizarre behaviors inconsistent with any other type of criminal typology.

In examining a sample of sexual murderers, the FBI (1985b) has developed a series of profile characteristics based on both demographic and crime scene traits. These traits have broken down homicide into an organized and disorganized type. Each typology allows the law enforcement agent to create a profile of the murderer, thus expediting the arrest of the suspect (Tables III and IV).

Dividing sexual murderers into organized and disorganized types allows for more accurate profiling based on information obtained through arrests. The crime scene

TABLE III   Profile Characteristics of Organized and Disorganized Murderers[a]

Organized	Disorganized
Average to above-average intelligence	Below-average intelligence
Socially competent	Socially inadequate
Skilled work preferred	Unskilled work
Sexually competent	Sexually incompetent
High birth order status	Low birth order status
Father's work stable	Father's work unstable
Inconsistent childhood discipline	Harsh discipline as child
Controlled mood during crime	Anxious mood during crime
Use of alcohol with crime	Minimal use of alcohol
Precipitating situational stress	Minimal situational stress
Living with partner	Living alone
Mobility with car in good condition	Lives/works near crime scene
Follows crime in news media	Minimal interest in news media
May change jobs or leave town	Significant behavior change (drug/ alcohol abuse, religiosity, etc.)

[a] FBI (1985b, p. 19).

TABLE IV   Crime Scene Differences between Organized and Disorganized Murderers[a]

Organized	Disorganized
Planned offense	Spontaneous offense
Victim a targeted stranger	Victim/location known
Personalized victim	Depersonalizes victim
Controlled conversation	Minimal conversation
Crime scene reflects overall control	Crime scene random and sloppy
Demands submissive victim	Sudden violence to victim
Restraints used	Minimal use of restraints
Aggressive acts prior to death	Sexual acts after death
Body hidden	Body left in view
Weapon/evidence absent	Evidence/weapon often present
Transports victim or body	Body left at death scene

[a] FBI (1985b, p. 19).

characteristics described in Table IV enable the investigator to develop a profile based solely on behaviors exhibited at the scene of the homicide, thus allowing for a psychological profile and description based on this data.

Forensic Psychology and Policy Implications

A number of U.S. Supreme court cases have dealt with the use of psychologists' and other mental health professionals' opinions regarding the goodness-of-fit of a criminal into a particular profile based on their assessment of the criminal. Much of this research stems from results obtained from the MMPI and mental status exams.

Peters and Murphy (1992) describe a variety of issues related to the admissibility and inadmissibility of mental health professionals' expert opinions of profile fitting. According to their research, every appellate court in the United States, with the exception of California, has ruled on the admissibility of expert testimony regarding the psychological profiles of child molesters. These appellate courts have consistently rejected the psychological profile concept as evidence either defending or attempting to help convict the child molester.

The psychological profile as court testimony has been used in child sexual abuse cases for three primary reasons: (1) to prove the defendant committed the crime, (2) to prove the defendant did not commit the crime, and (3) to solidify the credibility of the defendant. However, the primary reason the courts refuse to allow such evidence is because no matter how well a suspect may fit into the child molester profile, it can never prove whether the actual event took place (Peters & Murphy, 1992).

Future considerations involving the use of psychological/psychiatric testimony in relation to criminal profiles must involve continued research examining its efficacy in the court system. Policy implications will therefore depend on results obtained from developing future research in this field.

Suggestions for Future Research

One could say that the future of criminological profiling has already arrived. In years past, investigators relied only on personal knowledge bases involving experience and wisdom. Inferences were drawn based on corroboration with peers and personal hunches. In the modern computer era, comprehensive and extensive computerized databases exist which allow thousands of variables to be cross-examined between criminals, crime scenes, and case details. Computerized searches look for specific patterns, consistencies, and inconsistencies in order to determine the most likely course of action for law enforcement agents to act upon.

At the FBI's National Center for the Analysis of Violent Crime (NCAVC), experts in criminal personality profiling developed a computerized system of crime pattern analysis. This computerized system, termed VICAP (Violent Criminal Apprehension Program) uses a collection of crime pattern recognition programs to detect and predict the behavior of violent criminals. Future research is needed to examine the accuracy and reliability of such computer programs and to develop a method in which all law enforcement agencies could utilize a system on a cost-efficient, practical level. Further, the development of a national database may bring large statistical power to such evaluations. Research examining these possibilities is certainly required.

Research is also needed in order to determine the possible detrimental effects of criminal profiling. As mentioned, many courts do not allow for the inclusion of psychological profiles as evidence in courts. Will profiling a subject negatively persuade a jury to convict a potential felon if the profile is too broad or encompasses too many personality characteristics? Research is needed to determine, scientifically, if profiling is indeed efficacious.

COERCED CONFESSIONS

Introduction

No other piece of evidence is more damaging to a criminal than a stated confession. Throughout history, confessions have been obtained in a variety of ways. Due process specifically states that interrogators may use certain tactics to obtain confessions from an accused, provided that the confession is voluntary and a product of an essentially free and unhindered person. However, many tactics employed by an interrogator do not fall within these guidelines and are therefore considered "coerced." This section outlines and discusses the legal definition of a coerced confession, its psychological and sociological bases and implications, and discusses some of the specific tactics used by investigators and interrogators in obtaining confessions. The following fictional vignette provides an example in which a variety of interrogation issues, legal or otherwise, are brought into play.

> Ned and Jake, desperate for cash and needing to obtain drugs to support their addictions, decide that robbing a downtown convenience store would be a quick and convenient way to obtain money. The two arrive in Ned's car, and it is decided that Jake will run into the store, hold up the convenience clerk, and make a quick escape. Upon entering the store, Jake becomes worried and apprehensive when he realizes that the store has approximately five other people inside. Nervously, Jake approaches the clerk, pulls a gun, and demands all the money in the cash register. The clerk, unwilling to be a victim of this type of crime any longer, pulls his own firearm out from under the counter and points it at Jake. In a panic, Jake fires, killing the store clerk. Hearing a shot fired, Ned also panics and quickly drives away, leaving Jake behind. Jake, seen by numerous eyewitnesses, flees into the night on foot, only to be apprehended later by the police who take him into questioning.
>
> In the interrogation room, two officers enter and introduce themselves to Jake, who has been waiting for the officers for approximately 45 minutes in the isolated room. The officers, after offering Jake some water or use of the bathroom, quickly review Jake's Miranda rights. Jake listens and does not respond in any notable fashion. The officers then begin questioning Jake about the attempted robbery that took place earlier that evening. Jake, unwilling to give any information, states that he is innocent and wishes to speak with a lawyer. The officers tell Jake that the process can take place in one of two ways: cooperate and answer all questions immediately or cease questioning now and wait for legal counsel, thereby not cooperating with investigative procedures. Feeling somewhat intimidated, Jake concedes to answering more questions. Later, the officers come to another roadblock in Jake's testimony. He refuses to answer a question dealing with his accomplice. The officers state that if he implicates his friend in the murder of the clerk, the courts may reward his cooperation with leniency. Afraid and hopeful of a more lenient sentence, Jake admits full guilt and gives the name and description of his accomplice.

Would you consider the above confession to be coerced? If so, what specific techniques did you feel were inappropriate? The discussion to follow examines specific issues related to appropriate and inappropriate interrogation techniques. It also addresses the reason for these techniques' psychological power over many arrested subjects as well as other topics related to coerced confessions.

Literature Review

According to police procedure and the Fifth Amendment, prosecutors cannot use statements obtained by a subject as evidence in court unless the arresting party has ensured that the subject's Miranda rights have been offered and explained. The courts believe that subjects pulled from their familiar environment and surrounded by potentially intimidating authority figures may reveal information they otherwise would not give without the right to remain silent until counsel is available to them (*Davis v. United States*, 1994).

As with many laws, ambiguity exists as to exactly when a subject requests counsel. For example, during an interrogation the subject states, "Maybe I should talk to a lawyer." Does the officer interpret this as a clear request to receive counsel? If so, the interrogator must immediately stop questioning and hold the subject until a lawyer is available. If not, has the officer breached the subject's Miranda rights, creating the possibility of coercing a confession?

Three basic rules exist to aid law enforcement agents in understanding whether a subject is requesting counsel. The first is termed The Threshold of Clarity Rule and states that the subject's request for counsel meet a "threshold of clarity." Under this rule, a subject must clearly demonstrate a request for counsel. As one may guess, this rule is itself somewhat vague and offers no specific guidelines stating what is "clear."

The second rule related to the right not to self-incriminate is termed the Per Se Rule. According to this rule, any reference to counsel during an interrogation session must result in the immediate cessation of questioning and the appointment of counsel to the subject. This rule has more clarity and leaves little question as to whether the subject is indeed requesting counsel.

Last, The Clarification Rule states that if a subject makes an ambiguous request for counsel, the officers may ask for further clarification. However, if the officers, in their request for clarification, continue to discuss the arrest, the law may be breached (*Davis v. United States*, 1994).

Once a subject's Miranda rights are read and the subject waives those rights or agrees to continue questioning until counsel arrives, the interrogator may then begin questioning the subject on matters related to the crime. Officers utilize a variety of techniques in interrogation to provide them with the most important, relevant information related to the crime. As discussed in other portions of this book, the significant amount of stress felt by police often leads to an attitude of indifference or frustration. This results in tactics that ensure quick, albeit often inappropriate, justice. Given the variety of stressors and their severity, it is understandable why an officer may use underhanded tactics to obtain a confession.

For example, in the case study provided earlier, the suspect was clearly guilty of homicide and was identified by a variety of witnesses. The arresting officer, convinced that the subject is guilty, tries to expedite justice by bringing this criminal the punishment he deserves. Other cases may be encumbered with confusion and inconsistencies, and officers may then feel the need to use tactics to coerce a confession.

According to Dripps (1988), there is a conflict in every criminal case between personal autonomy and the need for evidence. Dripps states that the majority of confessions do not take place freely and with rational intellect. Rather, confessions are procured only through manipulation, irrationality of the subject, and mistakes made by the subject during interrogation. Obviously, the courts need clear evidence of guilt if a subject is to be convicted of a crime. As stated previously, the most impressive and conclusive evidence one can obtain is a confession by the accused. This evidence must not come at the expense of the subject's personal autonomy; if personal autonomy were to be sacrificed, then unlawful tactics may as well be utilized to obtain the same end.

While one may be tempted to believe that police interrogations take place in prime-time television fashion, complete with 200-watt light bulbs, 8-hour grueling question-and-answer sessions, yelling in the face of the accused, and fist pounding, the reality is that the majority of interrogations normally do not take place in such a style. Leo (1996) describes, using observations from 122 interrogations involving 45 different detectives, the processes and tactics utilized during a variety of interrogation sessions incorporating everything from homicide to property crimes. His results indicate that overall, coerced confessions occur less often than one may believe. However, he did state that he "... occasionally observed behavior inside the interrogation room—such as yelling, table pounding, or highly aggressive questioning—that straddled the margins of legality" (p. 270).

When Leo's results are broken down, we find that about 78% of the interrogated subjects ultimately waived their Miranda rights. In seven (4%) of the cases observed, the detective continued questioning the subject even after invoking their Miranda rights. The types of tactics used were: appealing to the suspect's self-interest (88%), confronting suspect with existing evidence of guilt (85%), undermining suspect's confidence in denial of guilt (43%), identifying contradictions in suspect's story (42%), behavioral analysis interview questions (40%), appealing to the importance of cooperation (37%), moral justifications/psychological excuses (34%), confronting suspect with false evidence of guilt (30%), using praise or flattery (30%), appealing to detective's expertise/authority (29%), appealing to the suspect's conscience (23%), and minimizing the moral seriousness of the offense (22%).

Less frequently used tactics were also implemented, possibly suggesting coercion: invoking metaphors of guilt (10%), exaggerating the facts/nature of the offense (4%), yelling at suspect (3%); accusing suspect of other crimes (1%), and attempting to confuse the subject (1%). In all, detectives used an average of 5.62 interrogation tactics.

Leo (1996), analyzing this data, states that according to his necessary conditions for coercion, police questioning involving coercive methods took place in only four (2%) of the cases. Further analysis of these four cases reveals that only psychologically coercive methods were used as opposed to physically coercive methods. In one case, detectives intentionally questioned a heroin addict suffering from acute withdrawal symptoms during the second day of his incarceration, knowing his symptoms were at their worst. In another case, the "good cop–bad cop" routine was utilized on a young gang member. One detective promised the youth's release if he cooperated, while the other stated that he would provide the prosecutor with incriminating information. The suspect provided the desired information and was subsequently released. All officers using coercive methods stated that they felt nothing could be lost by using coercive methods with these subjects, since they were treated essentially as informants or witnesses.

DiPietro (1993) describes a number of factors related to interrogation of subjects. He states that officers should assess the suspect's background and personal characteristics such as age, race, intelligence, and educational level before beginning interrogation. Certain subjects may be more conducive to coercive techniques, thus rendering a subsequent confession inadmissible if such techniques are used. Further, DiPietro states that some types of deceptive techniques are appropriate, given that they are not openly coercive, but that officers must not trick a subject into waiving their Miranda rights. He then gives a two-part definition of deception: (1) lies that relate to a suspect's connection to the crime and (2) trickery that introduces extrinsic considerations.

The same article describes a number of interrogation techniques which may, by some definitions, be considered coercive. The first of these are lies that connect the suspect to the crime. These include telling the subject that fingerprints were found at the crime scene when in fact they were not. Also, trickery that falsely introduces extrinsic evidence may also be considered coercive. This may include telling a subject that they will lose their welfare benefits if they are found guilty, but that leniency will be granted for cooperation. Another potentially coercive method is the effect of promises on voluntariness. This is a technique used in which an officer promises some sort of benefit to the subject in return for cooperation. Promises of leniency are also used in the facilitation of confessions, as are promises to tell higher authorities (such as the courts) that cooperation was given. Conceivably, a cooperative subject may be told that he or she will be regarded less harshly if cooperation is given.

Promises of collateral benefits such as the release of a family member or treatment for the subject's substance abuse problem are also given. More specifically, the courts have found that promises to protect the accused, promises to protect the accused's family, and promises not to arrest the defendant are considered to be coercive. Finally, threats may be viewed as inherently coercive and are therefore not allowed in the interrogation process.

While the discussion thus far has focused mainly on coercive interviewing techniques, good interviewing techniques do exist and are encouraged in virtually all interrogation situations. Hess and Gladis (1987) describe a variety of good interrogation techniques which they liken to successful advertising in marketing. These techniques include such principles as the establishment of credibility, a feeling of reciprocity, giving of compliments, conveying a sense of urgency, and casting doubts on current beliefs. These techniques, according to the authors, help the interrogator to establish a quick rapport with the subject and obtain information in a quick and easy fashion rather than resorting to coercive methods. It is hoped that discussing these principles will "demystify" the interrogation process and result in more efficient interrogations.

Forensic Psychology and Policy Implications

A variety of policy implications exist for ensuring that confessions are not obtained through primarily coercive methods. Recently, more and more police departments have utilized video recorders in the interrogation room to provide the courts with real evidence of the interrogation process, should it be sought. A survey conducted in 1990 revealed that approximately one-third of law enforcement agencies were using videotaping during the interrogation process (Geller, 1994). That number is expected to rise, giving more concrete evidence of the value of such a technique. The future will no doubt see the implications of video recording debated and discussed in the court system.

Dripps (1988) discusses the constitutional right guaranteeing the privilege against self-incrimination. He states that interpreting the constitution as an inflexible set of mores or rules results in faulty thinking and interpretation of what it may be trying to protect. For example, the privilege against self-incrimination stated in the constitution is argued by some to be tying the hands of the courts by denying the most impressive and appropriate evidence regarding a defendant's admission of guilt or innocence. Policies dealing with the privilege to not incriminate oneself in a court of law have surprisingly been absent. Clarification of this privilege, coupled with its possible ramifications, may help elucidate convictions when necessary.

Other explorable policies may include a restructuring of the Fifth Amendment, making the currently ambiguous wording more clear. Clarification of this amendment would conceivably make coercion illegal and reduce appeals dealing with the interpretation of a detective's interrogation techniques.

Suggestions for Future Research

Research studying the dynamics surrounding coerced confessions is deficient. Virtually every aspect of coercive practices involved in obtaining confessions are unstudied and in need of exploration. The videotaping procedure, previously described, lacks supporting studies that examine this procedure's psychological effects on the subject as well as on detectives' possible inhibition regarding being recorded.

Personality characteristics associated with interrogators who routinely use coercive methods have also failed to be explored. What types of personality traits make up a detective who uses coercive methods? Is it one who is "burned out" or grown overly cynical of the criminal justice system? Perhaps research investigating the level of experience required to become a routine interrogator should be examined.

What makes a particularly good interrogator? While the techniques used by certain detectives have been explored and examined, the actual characteristics associated with personality types have not. It may be that certain personality types will never, under normal conditions, develop good, efficient interviewing techniques.

What are the psychological aftereffects of the subject who has been coerced into giving a confession? Are there long-lasting psychological consequences of being deceived or tricked? What is the public's perception of coerced confessions? The public may feel that any means necessary to obtain justice are within reasonable limits. Others may feel that only the strictest of procedures should be followed, leaving little room for deviation. These topics and many more are available avenues for the continued study of coerced confessions. Interrogation must always take place; therefore the problem of coerced confession will never end.

CHAPTER 2

Juvenile Forensics

OVERVIEW

Police involvement in the lives of juveniles has varied considerably throughout the history of the United States. What is unmistakable, however, is that wayward youths can and do find themselves subject to law enforcement intervention. At the core of these interventions is a struggle over how to address the "best interests" of the child while, at the same time, maintain the public's concern for safety, order, security, and control. It is at this juncture that psychology assumes a pivotal role in the (successful) outcome of law enforcement interventions with juveniles.

This chapter examines a number of critical areas where the intersection of policing and adolescent behavior generates forensic psychological controversies. Topics explored in this chapter include (1) dealing with troubled youths, (2) policing juvenile gangs, (3) juvenile attitudes toward the police, and (4) adolescent female prostitution. The issues investigated in this chapter barely scratch the surface of where and how the interface of policing, psychology, and juvenile justice affect the lives of officers, youthful offenders, and the public at large. As with all chapters throughout this textbook, the intent here is to describe a number of the more compelling crime and justice controversies identified in the field.

Police officers confront all sorts of troubled youths. For example, some adolescents engage in underage drinking, join gangs, are truant, or become suicidal. How do police officers in their crime control interventions promote the rehabilitation of the adolescent? How do officers promote the aims of punishment?

Law enforcement personnel deal directly with youth gang members. What kind of antigang police tactics are used to inhibit membership? What sort of antigang control strategies are adopted to curb juvenile violence? What perceptions do non-gang-affiliated adolescents have about these police interventions?

Juveniles in general also harbor attitudes and beliefs about law enforcement and social control practices. Where do these adolescent perceptions come from? Can these beliefs and attitudes be changed in any meaningful way?

Police officers also find themselves responding to youths who engage in some very physically and emotionally debilitating behavior. Addressing child sexual exploitation (e.g., adolescent female prostitution) is perhaps one of the most difficult forms of police intervention imaginable. How do officers cope with the sexual victimization of children? How do the principles of rehabilitation or retribution operate with this forensic problem? Are these youths hard-core criminals or unsuspecting victims?

The field of policing deviant, risky, and/or illicit juvenile conduct is by far more complex than is described in the pages that follow. In addition, the perceptions adolescents engender regarding law enforcement behavior and practices are also more intricate and subtle than the space limits of this chapter allow. However, what is clear is the important role of psychology and the psychological sciences at the crossroads of policing and juvenile justice. As the individual sections of Chapter 2 repeatedly point out, improving relations between officers and (wayward) youths is certainly needed. The impact of such efforts potentially could improve juvenile recidivism rates and foster better, more meaningful police–community ties. One facet to this more civic-minded agenda entails additional research. The manner in which troubled youths, adolescent gangs, juvenile attitudes and beliefs, and child sexual exploitation relate to policing is not well developed in the overlapping criminological and psychological literature. Thus, as the material developed in this chapter recommends, the future success of juvenile justice and law enforcement necessitates more cross-disciplinary efforts along these and similar lines of scholarly inquiry.

DEALING WITH TROUBLED YOUTHS

Introduction

The youth of today are faced with a variety of problems that put them at risk. These problems include underage drinking and driving, drug abuse, pregnancy, suicide, truancy, gang activity, and prostitution. It is not uncommon to pick up a newspaper on any given day and find an article describing such behaviors. What follows is an illustration of how serious these problems can be.

> Jill is a 14-year-old high school student who is currently facing criminal charges for being an accomplice to murder. Jill has a history of running with the wrong crowd. Many of the crowd's activities include drinking, doing drugs, and skipping school. She has a long history of truant behavior.
>
> During the time Jill was away from school, she was burglarizing local neighborhood homes to support her drug habit. On one particular occasion, she was with her boyfriend, Mike, burglarizing a nearby residence. They were in the midst of robbing the house when the resident surprised them. Startled and scared, Mike pulled out his gun and shot the victim to death. Jill exemplifies how a life of drugs, truancy, and crime can lead to a tragic ending.

Historically, the tradition has been that the police assume ultimate responsibility for fighting crime and maintaining order. When dealing with wayward youths, the aim has been to rehabilitate the youngster, rather than to punish them. Crime statistics indicate that juvenile crime is on the rise (R. Lundman, 1993). The perspective regarding rehabilitation versus retribution for these offenders is sometimes challenged by those who feel that the criminal justice system needs to resort to punishing offenders for their crimes. Police organizations nationwide are currently questioning the effectiveness of the early strategies of crime control, which date back to the turn of the century. At present these agencies are exploring ways to combat the problem of dealing with troubled youths, either through retributive or rehabilitative measures. Police strategies to address this issue vary with each jurisdiction. Some agencies are implementing programs that target specific at-risk behaviors such as drinking and driving and drug abuse. In this section, the focus is on truant youths and juvenile delinquency. Several examples explaining how various law enforcement agencies nationwide confront these issues are presented.

Literature Review

As early as the 1800s, social reformers recognized the link between truancy and delinquency (Gavin, 1997). Truant behavior has been correlated with crimes such as burglary, vandalism, motor vehicle theft, and robbery. As a result of this relationship, law enforcement officials, community agencies, and school administrators have worked on developing various programs to address truant behavior as well as the resulting delinquent acts. The majority of these programs attempt to keep youngsters in school and to control daytime crimes. With a focus on rehabilitation, many of these programs strive to offer alternative choices for youths. The aim is to keep them out of the juvenile justice system. Depending on the policies and procedures of law enforcement and school agencies, combating truant behavior varies. The truant youths are returned to school, taken home, or taken to local police departments where the parent or guardian is contacted.

When addressing the problems of truancy and delinquency, the responsibility lies with parents; school officials; law enforcement personnel; and local, state, and federal organizations. This makes truancy and adolescent crime a multifaceted problem. Thus, it is essential to have the cooperation and support from all participants in order to successfully combat the problem.

In 1983, the Phoenix Arizona Police Department created a School Resource Officer (SRO) program in an attempt to reduce the number of truant children and juvenile delinquents. The program was funded through a 3-year federal grant. By the end of the grant period, the truancy rate at two pilot schools decreased by 73% and crimes committed on campus and in surrounding neighborhoods significantly decreased (Soto & Miller, 1992). As a result of the success, the school district agreed to continue to fund the project by paying 75% of each School Resource Officer's salary. At present, the SRO program has been expanded to include the servicing of 36 schools throughout the Phoenix area.

The officers' involved with the SRO program volunteer their time. Before being able to participate in the program, they must complete an extensive application process and pass a review procedure. Upon their acceptance, they receive intense training and education regarding juvenile issues. The SRO officers deal with problems both on and off school grounds. Their responsibilities include educating faculty and students on safety strategies to reduce crime and to recognize signs of child abuse and neglect. The officers spend a great deal of time and energy attempting to establish a good working relationship with parents living in housing projects in nearby areas. This is done in an effort to educate the parents on the importance of monitoring their child's school habits and to encourage their children to stay in school. The SRO unit is also responsible for detecting, reporting, and investigating suspected cases of child abuse and neglect.

The SRO team initiated 23,015 contacts with students, parents, school administrators, and faculty members during the 1990–1991 academic year. Officers made 476 arrests on school grounds, referred 596 cases to other social service agencies, recovered $ 14,000 in stolen property, and filed 578 truancy reports for students in kindergarten through 8th grade (Soto & Miller, 1992).

The goal and objective of the SRO program is to enforce truancy laws, educate school officials, and to build a trusting, working relationship with parents and children. These objectives are intended to serve as an effective crime prevention strategy in the hopes of combating criminal activity before it begins.

Researchers have concluded that for the purpose of predicting future criminality, the most likely juvenile recidivists are those whose first referral involves truancy, burglary, motor vehicle theft, or robbery (Snider, as cited in Gavin, 1997). Various law enforcement agencies across the country have developed truancy interdiction programs to counter both short-term and long-term effects of truancy. Nationwide, the vast majority of truancy interdiction efforts produce significant reduction in crimes traditionally associated with juvenile offenders (Gavin, 1997). The St. Petersburg Police Department in Florida decided to implement a truancy interdiction program in hopes of minimizing the relationship that exists between truancy and delinquency. The ultimate goal of this initiative was to reduce the opportunities for youths to get into trouble by informing parents to encourage their children to stay in school.

A large number of truancy interdiction programs implemented by most law enforcement agencies involve picking up truant youths and returning them to school through the involvement of their parent or guardian. Participating police departments are usually concerned with who is ultimately responsible for the interdiction and what to do with the students once they are picked up. Uniformed patrol officers are most often responsible for the interdiction. This is primarily because each uniformed patrol officer is in charge of a specific geographic area where they are cognizant of what is going on in that region. Other interdiction personnel involved with investigating truant youths include juvenile officers, school resource officers, and detectives.

One of the first obstacles the St. Petersburg Police Department faced was what to do with the truant youths once officers apprehended them. Because St. Petersburg was a large jurisdiction, the time it took officers to personally return the child to their school consumed too much of their time and took away from other duties needing attention. The St. Petersburg police officials recognized the potential problem this would pose and realized that having officers return the truant youths directly to school would not actively involve the parents in the problem. They decided to establish a centralized truancy center where the truant youths waited for their parents to pick them up, ensuring that the parents took an active role in the situation.

Once the truant youths arrive at the center via the patrol officer, a receiving officer or a juvenile detective contacts both the school and the parents and proceeds to tend to the youngster until the parents or guardians arrive. If the youngster is on probation, the juvenile officer notifies the youth's case worker immediately. The initial process was intended by program developers to be very brief in nature so that the patrol officers could get back to patrolling.

It is the responsibility of the parent or guardian to return their child to school. When they arrive at the center to pick up their child, the juvenile detective presents the parent or guardian with an accurate record of their child's attendance in an effort to make them realize the seriousness of the truant behavior. The parents are also presented with a letter signed by the chief of police and the school superintendent stressing the importance of ensuring that children go to school as well as a copy of the state statute mandating school attendance. The parents are advised that the law requires them to have their child in school and that failure to do so is a criminal act (Gavin, 1997). Before the child can be readmitted to school, their parent or guardian must bring a referral slip with the child to school. This, then, notifies school officials that the child was in custody. Many times, guidance counselors and school officials use this as an opportunity to meet with the child and parent or guardian.

Another element of the interdiction program is geared toward counseling truant youths. The juvenile detective interviews the children and asks them about their truant behavior, their home life, and other variables that may be influencing their truant behavior. They also stress to the child the importance of staying in school and getting a good education. Many times, the juvenile officers have recognized financial problems or other issues and have referred the family to the appropriate social service agency. When these situations arise, the officers give the parents lists and names of various community agencies that specialize in assisting with family problems.

When evaluating successful truancy interdiction programs, the Inglewood, California Police Department serves as an outstanding and effective model. The current literature on effective interdiction programs mentions the results as well as the ways in which the program was designed and implemented.

The City of Inglewood's program was initiated to prevent and reduce the relationship between juvenile delinquency and truancy. The project is called HOPE, "Helping Others Pursue Education." The city of Inglewood, California, worked in conjunction with five public agencies to plan the program. The five agencies involved with the project included the school district, the Los Angeles County Probation Department, the Los Angeles County Department of Social Services, the Inglewood Superior Court, juvenile judges, and the Inglewood Police Department (Rouzan & Knowles, 1985).

Police officers, assisted by school security personnel, were responsible for picking up and transporting truants to the project HOPE center. The project center is staffed full-time by a director, counselor, teacher, secretary, security guard, and a county probation officer. The atmosphere of the project center resembles that of an academic setting. The juveniles are forced to adhere to rules and are disciplined and remanded when noncompliant. Once the juveniles are apprehended by officers and taken to the center, the staff interview and counsel the youths. They are also forced to participate in a rigorous academic schedule intended to get them "back on track" with other children their age. Similar to the earlier programs mentioned, the counselors of the HOPE program emphasize parental interaction and aspire to assist the family if an emergency arises. This is usually accomplished through providing the parents with updated lists of various community service contacts. The main intent of the HOPE program is to rehabilitate the youngster and assist the family by understanding the underlying behaviors which influence the truancy. If these efforts fail, the staff probation officers direct the youth to a hearing in juvenile court.

The results of the HOPE program were extremely successful. Comparison of the school year without Project Hope (1982–1983) to the year with Project Hope (1983–1984) for the entire city of Inglewood revealed that daytime residential burglaries decreased by 32%. Auto burglaries were decreased 64%, strong-arm robberies decreased 45%, and grand theft auto dropped 36% (Rouzan & Knowles, 1985).

In order for truancy interdiction programs to effectively address the issues of truancy and delinquency, it is imperative to have parental, community, school, and police support. Studies and analyses of crime and truancy rates in communities around the country confirm that today's truants commit a significant proportion of daytime crime (Gavin, 1997). Successful truancy interdiction programs serve both long-term and short-term objectives, keeping kids in school and preventing future criminal activity. By keeping youths off the streets, the police can reduce crime today, and by encouraging youths to say in school, the police can help reduce dropout rates and prevent more serious criminal activity tomorrow (Gavin, 1997).

Forensic Psychology and Policy Implications

Police interactions with delinquent juveniles can be very challenging. With the rise of juvenile crime, it is inevitable that police are going to have a relationship with these juveniles, which often becomes quite critical in nature. The encounters they have with one another can have a profound effect on the juvenile's future. Police are often challenged by the role they play within the juvenile justice system. They vacillate between the need to help steer the youths away from a life of crime versus traditional police duties entailing crime prevention and maintaining order. When addressing issues of truancy and delinquency as well as the relationship that exists between the two, many police departments have focused on rehabilitative efforts to curtail the problem. In collaboration with other agencies, many of these programs have been effective.

When looking at juvenile delinquency from a psychological perspective, the notion of predelinquent intervention has been explored. The idea is to identify and treat youths who are inclined to have interaction with the law. Experts in the fields of psychology, sociology, and criminology who support this approach feel that youth crime is an individual problem requiring an individually oriented solution (R. Lundman, 1993).

This approach to delinquency focuses on personality problems that these youths have. Various biological, psychological, and social conditions can work together to influence the thought and behavior patterns of these individuals. According to this perspective, one's personality may predispose these juveniles to engage in delinquent activities. When looking at the example of Jill and the delinquent activities she participated in, early intervention efforts through her school should have addressed her truant behavior once it started. Treatment efforts to work with her on an individual basis, or on a family system level, should have also been attempted to identify the underlying problems.

To support predelinquent intervention, it is essential to be able to identify youths who are inclined toward a life of delinquency and then to intervene. This can be accomplished by intervening early in the youth's development. Prevention efforts should focus on the environment of the child and the relationship they have with their parents. Studies indicate that the child's home life is a key factor in delinquent behavior (Siegel & Senna, 1994). Without proper discipline and a nurturing and structured environment, the child's chances for healthy development are hindered, therefore making them more predisposed to engage in delinquent activities.

When efforts to reach the child early in development fail, it is imperative to implement treatment efforts in an attempt to reach the child before they engage in more serious offender behaviors. Mental health agencies and child welfare agencies as well as the juvenile justice system can either mandate treatment for the entire family or specifically work to assess the youth's behavioral problems.

Treatment options to address the needs of the family and the individual include alcohol and drug programs, child abuse and sexual abuse programs, or community-based programs where the focus is on a community-oriented approach. The community-oriented approach to the prevention of juvenile delinquency believes that youth crime is a community problem (R. Lundman, 1993). Whether the programs developed are targeted for the family or the individual, it is essential to have the help of local, community, state, and federal entities as well as experts in the field working together to identify and address juvenile intervention and crime prevention.

In the efforts to address the issue of juvenile delinquency and early crime prevention, the literature has identified the issue of restrictive state statutes as being a hindrance in the process. Frequently, those in charge of such programs have a difficult time trying to implement programs due to restrictive or narrowly defined state legislative guidelines. In these instances, law enforcement agencies, psychologists, and social scientists should work with state legislatures to amend those statutes which are considered too restrictive. The wording of some individual state statutes regarding compulsory school attendance does have significant impact on attempts to interdict truants (Gavin, 1997). To adapt to restrictive or unhelpful statutes, there are a number of steps program developers can take. Police administrators can work with local legislative delegations to address the issues at hand. Once the issues are discussed, the parties involved can negotiate and devise a mutual compromise that will ultimately help the youths. Statutes regarding compulsory school attendance will have a significant impact on attempts to interdict truants (Gavin, 1997). It is important to have a good working relationship with state legislatures so that they will help support and validate various truancy interdiction programs in the future.

Suggestions for Future Research

When addressing the issue of truant and delinquent youth, it is obvious that the problem is multifaceted. These issues have been a concern since the 1800s, yet with the rise of juvenile crime and the seriousness of the offenses, new efforts are being examined to combat juvenile crime.

A major area of interest for future research could address how various agencies throughout the United States are dealing with the issues of truancy and delinquency. One must keep in mind, however, that research addressing truancy in large cities incorporates more variables when compared to smaller communities.

One of the most important areas for future development is to accurately assess the repercussions these programs have on the community, the citizens, and the offenders. It cannot be emphasized enough how important it is to seek the help and support from many agencies in order to successfully combat the problems that face the youths of today. Programs and relationships need to be developed with social service organizations in order to provide effective services to juveniles.

The police have the ultimate responsibility of enforcing the laws that govern juvenile offenders. With the help of social service organizations, such as youth service bureaus, the school system, recreational facilities, and welfare agencies, coupled with parental involvement, truancy interdiction programs can help keep kids in school as well as prevent future serious crimes. Jill's case presents a very tragic and real example of how truant behavior and juvenile delinquency led one person to confront the criminal justice system.

POLICING JUVENILE GANGS

Introduction

As juvenile gangs grow in size and become increasingly violent, the community and media pressure for law enforcement officers to suppress gang activity and membership has become intense. The threat of gangs is no longer just an inner-city problem. Juvenile gangs have permeated every size of community, even branching out into rural areas (Owens & Wells, 1993). Communities are demanding action from law enforcement, and the police have had to take a more aggressive stance in their fight against gang activity. Antigang policing tactics such as gang-tracking databases and civil gang injunctions are being created and employed around the country in an attempt to suppress gang activity. If granted by the court, a civil gang injunction is a lawsuit that limits conduct by members of a gang that would otherwise be considered lawful. However, enforcement strategies alone fail to address the root causes of the juvenile gang epidemic. According to Brantley and DiRosa (1994), understanding the factors that drive youths to join gangs is the first step in confronting the problem.

Supporters of such strategies maintain that they are effective forms of gang control while opponents hold that these tactics infringe upon youths' civil liberties, particularly ethnic minorities (Siegal, 1997). It is argued that aggressive tactics broadly applied to law-abiding youths encourage negative attitudes toward officers to flourish in areas where a fragile police–community relationship already exists. Police officers have the challenge of implementing these strategies without targeting juveniles who are not affiliated with gangs. Consider the following case illustration.

Sixteen-year-old Claudio Ceja of Anaheim, California is an 11th-grader at Loara High School. From 8:00 A.M. until 2:35 P.M. he attends class. From 4 P.M. to 6 P.M. he hands out fliers for a local business. From 6 P.M. to 9:30 P.M. he completes his homework before he goes to his second job at an Anaheim convention center. But the Anaheim police do not see Ceja as a hard-working young student. In the past few years, they have stopped, detained, and photographed Ceja five times and put his photograph in the city's gang-tracking computer database. Each time, Ceja told them he was not involved with a gang. But each time they ignored his claims, he says. Despite the police attention, Ceja has never been arrested or charged with any crime. "They seem to be doing it for the fun of it," says Ceja. "They take my picture, and they put it in a gang file. But I'm not a gangster. I don't want to be identified as one." (Siegal, 1997, p. 28)

Literature Review

Aggressive policing tactics and legal interventions into the lives of gang members, particularly those that criminalize activities that are typically lawful, are becoming more widespread. However, many argue that such tactics often lead to the harassment of law-abiding youths who may fit stereotypes of a gang member as in Claudio Ceja's case, creating a negative impact on community–police relations (Hoffman & Silverstein, 1995). Cases such as Ceja's illustrate the fine line between cracking down on gang members and further alienating at-risk youths.

As the literature demonstrates, antigang policing tactics serve as an imperfect attempt to treat the symptoms and not the causes of our juvenile gang epidemic. Two of the most common antigang policing tactics are gang-tracking databases and civil gang injunctions. These policing tactics attempt gang suppression or deterrence by their speed of enforcement, certainty of punishment, and severity of sanctions, while the targeting of these sanctions is extended through an increase in gang intelligence tracking (Klein, 1995).

Gang-tracking databases are being employed as an intelligence-gathering strategy as gangs become increasingly mobile and organized. Territorial graffiti, tattoos, symbols, and specialized clothing (for example, those indicating gang colors) are all visual symbols that can indicate gang affiliation and are frequently combined with a database to provide patrol officers with identification information (Owens & Wells, 1993). Gang intelligence information gathered or received by law enforcement or juvenile-related personnel are included in the database. Police departments that utilize these gang-tracking databases detain and photograph youths who are charged with gang activity as well as those who are only suspected of it, as in Ceja's case. Youths often deny gang membership, leaving officers to distinguish between delinquent behaviors and gang behavior.

Critics of these gang databases claim that minorities are disproportionately represented. Ed Chen, staff attorney with the American Civil Liberties Union (ACLU) of Northern California stated:

> There's a racially discriminating aspect to all these programs. In every case that we've seen, the targets are Latino or African American youth. They can concentrate on young black, brown, and sometimes yellow men. It's rarely used against non-minorities. (Siegal, 1997, p. 31)

Despite claims of harassment by youths who are not affiliated with gangs, Torok and Trump (1994) state that crimes are often solved quickly or prevented altogether by stripping gang members of their anonymity. The U.S. Treasury Department's Bureau of Alcohol, Tobacco and Firearms (ATF) contends that not only do gang-tracking databases give accurate pictures of gang activities and membership but that a national intelligence network is necessary if law enforcement is to effectively confront violent gangs (Higgins, 1993).

Civil gang injunctions are also being used as a preemptive strike against gang-related crime. Using civil gang injunctions, prosecutors can prohibit members of a particular street gang from participating in criminal activities such as graffiti or possessing weapons as well as engaging in conduct which facilitates criminal activity that is typically not illegal. According to the Los Angeles City Attorney Gang Prosecution Section (1995), ". . . aggressive enforcement of an injunction enables law enforcement to effectively prevent imminent criminal activity by arresting persons for prohibited patterns of conduct which are known to precede and facilitate these crimes" (p. 325). For example, those members of the gang named in the injunction could be enjoined (prohibited) by a court from activities like wearing pagers, dressing in gang attire, flashing "handsigns," approaching and soliciting business from pedestrians and passing vehicles, or gathering at specified locations such as a city park. This is a proactive technique that is designed to enable uniformed officers to arrest gang members before a drug deal is consummated or any other gang-related crime is committed.

Critics raise the question if the desire for safe streets overrides constitutionally protected rights such as the right to free assembly and the concern of where gang members will congregate as a result of being pushed from one park or neighborhood (Pyle, 1995). Research suggests that the underlying causes for juvenile gang participation or prevention are largely ignored by enforcement strategies alone.

Forensic Psychology and Policy Implications

The current trend in gang policy involves gang suppression and deterrence, while some argue that prevention and rehabilitation possibilities are neglected. According to the Los Angeles City Attorney Gang Prosecution Section (1995), little effort is being made to change the social conditions that make juvenile gangs a viable option for a growing number of youths. Civil gang injunctions and gang-tracking databases are representative of this thrust in gang policy. Opponents question their effectiveness and maintain that the civil rights of gang members are being infringed upon.

According to Klein (1995), the gang subculture discourages the acceptance or assignment of legitimacy to police, prosecution, and court definitions of acceptable behaviors. Additionally, he states that deterrence strategies may not only inhibit the expression of fear of sanctions, but encourage the bravado that accompanies antisocial or criminal activities while increasing group cohesiveness. Recognizing the limitations of enforcement strategies alone, gang policies need to encompass more comprehensive programs addressing the root causes of juvenile gangs.

Research indicates that aggressive policing strategies might curb the incidence of gang activity in a particular area for a period of time; however, factors influencing juveniles to join gangs have tremendous psychological and sociological origins. Various factors such as a sense of belonging; the need for recognition and power; a sense of self-worth and status; the desire for a place of acceptance; a search for love, structure, and discipline; the need for physical safety and protection; and, in some instances, a family tradition motivate juveniles to join gangs (M. Walker, Schmidt, & Lunghofer, 1993). Juveniles who are drawn to gangs generally live in a subculture where attachments to families, friends, and teachers are lacking and involvement in prosocial activities are minimal or nonexistent. As a result, the stringent enforcement of gang laws or policing tactics may only decrease gang activity in one neighborhood while displacing it into another.

Forensic psychologists have a critical role in a more comprehensive strategy of gang suppression. With specialized training in the psychological aspects of a gang as well as the criminological theories and sociocultural factors that influence gang membership and activity, forensic psychologists can work in conjunction with various law enforcement agencies and school districts to identify and counsel those youths who are at risk or who are actively involved in a gang. Conflict resolution and conflict mediation strategies are being utilized by forensic psychologists working with juvenile gang members. These strategies are being used to provide these youths with the skills and insight to nonaggressively manage conflict. A structured network of aggressive policing and prosecuting illegal gang activity serves as a deterrent to active gang members. Providing educational programs, conflict resolution strategies, and professional psychological services to both juvenile gang members and those juveniles at risk of joining a gang could more effectively address the problem of juvenile gangs.

As juvenile membership continues to grow, the examination of the issues that make gangs so attractive to our youths could make a more lasting and significant impact on the gang epidemic. Research demonstrates that gangs satisfy important needs for many youths who are denied access to power, privileges, and resources. These same youths find it difficult to meet many psychological and physical needs and feel alienated and neglected at home (Glick, 1992). In the face of such strong motivating influences, being arrested or incarcerated is infrequently a deterrent.

Aggressive enforcement of antigang tactics is only one component of an overall comprehensive gang strategy that includes intelligence gathering, school intervention, graffiti abatement, vertical prosecution, community support, conflict resolution strategies, and professional psychological services. Juvenile gangs are a complex problem requiring a complex solution. According to Brantley and DiRosa (1994), the need for a coordinated response is imperative after first understanding the reasons that compel youths to join gangs.

Suggestions for Future Research

Very little research exists regarding the role of forensic psychologists working with at-risk youths or juvenile gang members. As more comprehensive programs are implemented, including prevention and rehabilitation components, comparative studies need to be undertaken to test their effectiveness. For example, which conflict resolution or mediation strategies best enable these youths to nonaggressively manage conflict? What types and durations of psychological services are the most effective? Research examining the effects of various psychoeducational and recreational programs are needed. In addition, the effects of involving families and siblings in the psychological interventions of at-risk youths should be investigated. Once programs are in place, arrest records, school dropout rates, and other forms of acting out can be monitored to determine the effectiveness of the various services being offered to the youths.

Research regarding the attitudes and perceptions that the police hold about juvenile gangs is almost nonexistent. As gangs become greater in number and increasingly violent, the effect that working with this volatile population has on police officers is a vital concern. Their perceived threat of danger and the demeanor of gang members can greatly impact officers' interactions with these youths as well as the direction of antigang tactics. Additionally, the levels of stress and its effects on officers who work in gang units is an area in need of examination. Finally, as Claudio Ceja's case demonstrates, more effective means to identify juvenile gang members should be continually explored.

JUVENILES' ATTITUDES TOWARD THE POLICE

Introduction

Juveniles' attitudes toward the police develop as a result of numerous influences in their lives. Although police officers are frequently the primary contact that adolescents have with the legal system, these experiences are only a small part of what forms their views of police officers. They learn about law enforcement from their parents, their peers, their community, the educational system, the media, and from personal contacts with the police. These attitudes are likely to have a large impact on the choices they make throughout their lives, especially as young people.

Devon is a 15-year-old African-American male who is currently living in permanent foster care, awaiting the arrival of his 18th birthday so that he may have the freedom to live on his own and make his own decisions. He states that the police are "out to get him" and that all they want to do is "ruin people's lives." Devon cannot remember a positive interaction with the police and reports that his first memory of police involvement was before the age of 3. He remembers being frightened and hiding under his bed while his parents screamed and broke things in the house. After what seemed like hours of loud noises, pushing, and hitting, he recalls two police officers dragging his father from his home, leaving his mother in a state of panic. Devon remembers watching his mother's pain and hating the men who took away the man they loved. They had stripped her of a husband and Devon of a father.

Two years later Devon learned of the police's desire to take anything that he valued from him by placing him in foster care. He will never forget the afternoon he was taken from his own home and forced to live with strangers in a house filled with other children he did not know. Devon was told that he had to live with these people because his mother did drugs and was not taking good care of him. Devon knew that things were crazy at home, but that was where his family lived. What would he do without his brothers? Where were they? He hated this new place and the new people. They would not let him see his family, the only people he knew. He blamed the police for ruining his life by taking his family from him. Now he understood why his mother always spoke so negatively of these people who were supposed to make things better.

Literature Review

Although attitudes toward law enforcement and social control have been studied quite extensively over the past few decades, researchers have focused primarily on the perceptions of adults. The fact that juveniles might have an entirely different set of attitudes and opinions, which also may have their own etiology, has been only minimally examined. However, the interaction between juveniles and the police is certainly not a recent phenomenon and does not seem to be disappearing. In fact, young people's perceptions of the police have become so important that interventions such as Police–Schools Liasons, where a police officer becomes an integral part of the children's lives in a particular school, are being introduced to change children's attitudes toward law enforcement. Interventions such as these indicate that young people tend to have a negative view of police, and in order to effectively alter their perception the etiology of these attitudes must be understood.

Unfortunately, many studies of juveniles' attitudes toward the police conducted in years past have been limited by the assumption that these attitudes are primarily a result of personal interaction with the police (Leiber, Nalla, & Farnworth, 1998). However, as investigators have become more interested in examining numerous possible influences, it becomes apparent that there are many factors which contribute to these beliefs. For example, Leiber et al. (1998) conducted a study which proposed that attitudes toward the police develop as a result of the sociocultural context of which children are a part. They specifically hypothesized that young people's attitudes "develop as a function of socialization in their communities' social environment, of their deviant subcultural 'preferences,' and of the prior effect of these sociocultural factors on juveniles' contacts with the police" (p. 151).

Leiber et al. found that juveniles' attitudes toward the police are not a direct result of police–juvenile contacts. In fact, many sociocultural factors are directly related to young people's perceptions of the police. Commitment to delinquent norms was found to be a significant predictor of negative attitudes toward the police. Race and ethnicity predicted most strongly juveniles' perceptions of police discrimination and police fairness, and minority youths tended to have more negative perceptions of the police than Caucasians. These results indicate that young people's image of the police are a direct result of their sociocultural upbringing and that in many communities the negative view of law enforcement is so much a way of life that youths may develop resistance toward the police without ever having had contact with them. This finding is also supported by a 1995 study conducted in Britain, which found that a relationship existed between the attitudes of children and adults living in the same household toward the police (Maung, 1995). This suggests the difficulty inherent in attempting to change negative views of police, social control, and the law. Many youths are taught to have disrespect for the law itself, and police are the most visible representatives of the legal system.

In a 1993 study on the attitudes of Aboriginal school children in Australia toward institutional authorities, researchers Ken Rigby and Dasia Black sought to investigate a previously found notion in non-Aboriginal children of their attitudes toward authority. Other researchers have found that Australian children have a generalized attitude toward institutional authorities that extends to a number of different individuals including both parents and the police (Rigby & Densley, 1986; Rigby, Mak, & Slee, 1989; Rigby, Schofield, & Slee, 1987; Rigby & Slee, 1987, all as cited in Rigby & Black, 1993). These studies further report that juveniles tend to have generally positive attitudes toward institutional authorities, although these studies did not include any Aboriginal youth. In Rigby and Black's 1993 study, they found that Aboriginal youth's feelings about parental authority were not generalizable to nonparental institutional authorities such as the police. In fact, the Aboriginal youths had much less positive attitudes toward the police. The researchers state that this finding is related to the conflict between the Aboriginal people and the White police. Many of the children in the study had actually witnessed such conflict and others had been informed of the strife by older Aboriginals or their peers. This finding is similar to that of Waddington and Braddock (1991), who found that in Britain adolescent boys either saw the police as officers of order or bullies and when divided into the racial groups of Asian, Black, or White, their attitudes differed. Individuals in the White and Asian groups saw police in both ways, whereas the vast majority of the Black sample regarded police as bullies.

Changing juveniles' negative perceptions of the police requires making contact with those youths who harbor resentment toward the law. Because these views are usually a result of their community's influence, it is unlikely that any headway would be made in attempting to go into neighborhoods and make a positive impact on young people. Instead, intervening at the school level would allow police an opportunity to make a positive impact on the lives of those children who may not otherwise have positive interactions with the legal system. This idea has lead to the development of Police–Schools Liaison programs. These programs were developed to create a positive view of the police and to decrease the adherence to criminal and delinquent lifestyles. In schools with such a program, a police officer becomes a full-time School–Liaison Officer (SLO). The role of this individual is to improve the police image and to offer young people positive interactions with police and law enforcement. School–Liaison Officers provide many functions in the school including interacting with school officials and teachers about particular students, disciplining and warning pupils, investigating illegal activity such as theft or vandalism, offering supervision, or participating in school assemblies. These varied activities offer a wide array of opportunities for students to have contact with their SLO; however, most students see this individual while they are patrolling school grounds or eating in the cafeteria (Hopkins, Hewstone, & Hantzi, 1992).

Policymakers hope that Police–Schools Liaison programs will change juveniles' negative attitudes toward both the police and criminal offending and in a 1992 study by Hopkins et al., the impact of these programs was investigated. They targeted six schools with SLOs and seven control schools that did not have one. They used a detailed questionnaire to assess a number of factors from the student's point of view including police stereotypes, amount of contact with police, attitude toward the police, and perceptions of crime. These psychologists found that there was a very low level of direct contact between students and their SLO in the target schools. Upon interviewing others in the school it was learned that although the direct contact may be minimal, there was a great deal of police input into the school. In regard to attitude change, there was no significant difference in the attitude development of the students in the target and control schools over the time studied. This could be related to the age of the students (14–16), as it is common for adolescents to develop negative views of law enforcement. The most important finding of this study relates to the students' perception of *their* SLO and police in general. Students in the target schools viewed their SLO more positively than police in general. It seems that students do not perceive their SLO as being a typical representative of the police and therefore do not generalize their positive feelings about their SLO to the entire police force.

This finding is demonstrated by the case of Devon, who attended a high school with a Police–Schools Liaison Program. He had a number of interactions with his school's SLO, Officer Riley, who was present throughout much of Devon's secondary education. Not only did he attend many school functions during which Officer Riley spoke, but Devon also developed an individual relationship with him. He had a habit of missing and being late for class, and Officer Riley took it upon himself to discuss Devon's behavior with him. He became aware of Devon's dislike and fear of police, and he therefore attempted to make a positive impression of law enforcement officials. Even though many of their interactions revolved around Devon's delinquent behavior, such as being suspected of destroying school property and the possession of illegal drugs, Officer Riley and Devon developed a relationship marked by mutual respect and understanding. Officer Riley worked hard to educate Devon about the consequences of his behavior and encouraged him to attend and succeed in school. Devon believed his SLO was not "out to get him" and that he was honest and trustworthy. Unfortunately, this perception did not generalize to other police officers. When Devon came into contact with police in the community, he was defensive, angry, and scared. He thought that he must have done something wrong and that they were looking for him. He viewed his SLO as an exception to the rule, and that Officer Riley was the only police officer whom he could talk to and who might actually listen and believe him.

Forensic Psychology and Policy Implications

Community policing and problem-solving policing are law enforcement strategies designed to promote the positive role of policing in the community and which may be successful at instilling a positive attitude in juveniles toward the police. Community policing involves the development of a working partnership between the community and the police to better citizens' lives by addressing issues of crime and disorder. Community members work with officers to identify problems and find workable solutions (Schmalleger, 1997). These solutions often have a significant affect on children and their view of the police. For instance, the efforts of community policing has involved making the law enforcement system visible through school activities, antidrug and alcohol programs, and sporting events. By encouraging parents to support these positive efforts, children become educated about the positive role of police. It is important that juveniles not only become aware of a specific police officer such as their School–Liaison Officer, but that they are aware of other members of the police force and are able to develop a positive view of police in general. This may be enhanced by ensuring that minority police are highly involved in demonstrating a positive role and that they reflect the entire department. Minority juveniles may be inclined to view the police negatively because they are formed by another group of people who are different from themselves. Dispelling this point of view may engender benefits for both the juveniles and the community.

Problem-solving policing is a style of policing that involves addressing the underlying social conditions or social problems that relate to crime, as it assumes that many crimes are a result of specific social conditions in a community. Through this type of policing, community members are educated about issues related to crime prevention and the police make use of community resources such as counseling centers or job-training facilities in their efforts to control crime (Schmalleger, 1997). Imposing this type of policing would allow officers to target the conditions that cause juveniles to espouse delinquent attitudes and activities. Understanding the root of these behaviors would also help curb younger children from engaging in these same activities as they get older.

Suggestions for Future Research

In addition to the results previously mentioned, Rigby and Black's (1993) study also demonstrated that Aboriginal youths living in rural areas had more positive attitudes toward their parents than those youths living in more urban areas. Urban environments tend to have a greater level of stress associated with living and also to push children toward a delinquent lifestyle as compared to children living in rural areas. This environment may cause strain on the parent–child relationship and may therefore induce more negative attitudes of juveniles toward their parents. This negative attitude, along with a more delinquent lifestyle, may in turn cause these young people to have a negative view of the police as another representative of authority. This has not been investigated and it would be helpful to find out if juveniles living in urban areas are more prone to have negative views of the police. In addition, whether there is a difference in attitude toward authorities along racial lines in urban and rural areas is an area warranting investigation. This information would help to target those populations which have the most negative views of the police and could subsequently be addressed with community policing or educational programs. Moreover, the effectiveness of Police–Schools Liaison programs should be further investigated. The results of one study do not necessarily generalize to all programs, and future studies could examine the differences between how different programs are implemented. Some programs may require more direct contact with the police than others, which may certainly effect program efficacy. This type of program evaluation and comparison would allow for ineffective programs to adapt their model, hopefully increasing their level of effectiveness.

ADOLESCENT FEMALE PROSTITUTES: CRIMINALS OR VICTIMS?

Introduction

The criminal justice response to juvenile prostitution is composed of distinct departments with conflicting philosophies. Varying aspects of child exploitation are handled by different divisions of law enforcement. Typically, the juvenile division works closely with child protective service agencies and handles child abuse and neglect cases or those cases that involve intrafamilial abuse (Weisberg, 1985). Sexual exploitation cases such as adolescent prostitution are usually assigned to the vice division. While juvenile divisions generally embrace a rehabilitative model, viewing these prostitutes as victims, the vice division police officers tend to favor a punitive approach, perceiving these juveniles as criminals.

Flowers (1995) defines teen prostitution as the "use of or participation of persons under the age of 18 in sexual acts with adults or other minors where no force is present, including intercourse, oral sex, anal sex, and sadomasochistic activities where payment is involved" (p. 82). Jesson (1993) explains that payment is not only defined by money but with anything of exchangeable value such as drugs, food, shelter, or clothing. Although adult female prostitution is being explored as a form of work in feminist theory, the adolescent prostitute is still excluded from this perspective. She is viewed as a victim of deviant adult behavior and frequently of her own past.

Often, these individuals have suffered physical, emotional, and sexual abuse within their family unit. The ranks of juvenile prostitutes abound with runaways or "throwaways." According to Weisberg (1985), intervention by officers usually occurs in the form of an arrest or harassment with little regard for treatment or rehabilitation. Although these individuals engage in a variety of other criminal or delinquent behaviors, they have very complex mental health needs that are not being adequately addressed through the juvenile justice system. Consider the following case illustration.

> Kara is a fifteen-year-old Caucasian female living in a large metropolitan area. Kara comes from a single-parent household, her father having left before she was born. She has never met or spoken with him. From as far back as she can remember, her mother has had various "boyfriends" living with them in the two-bedroom apartment that also houses Kara's two younger brothers. As Kara's mother has been employed infrequently, and her various "boyfriends" have contributed little financially to the family, they have often been confined to modest, if not altogether poor, living circumstances. At times, they have nearly been evicted as rent money has not always been available.
>
> Beginning in early childhood, at age 5 or 6, Kara was subjected to hurtful and psychologically devastating verbal abuse. While her mother rarely struck her physically, her violent outbursts were often directed at Kara. Starting at age 7, she was sexually molested by her mother's live-in "boyfriend." Perhaps the most damaging element of his attacks was her mother's refusal to believe the sexual abuse was occurring.
>
> At the age of 13, Kara took to the streets to "get away" from her troubles at home. Having no money, shelter, or food, Kara was quick to accept the help offered to her by other young girls living on the streets. These girls gave Kara the sort of friendship and "care-structure" that was not available to her at home. As Kara would come to find out, however, these girls were prostitutes, utilizing the only resource they believed they had to survive. At the age of 14, Kara began prostituting herself.
>
> Now Kara has been discovered by the local police. While she has had no prior contact with the police and is otherwise a "good citizen," she has nonetheless engaged in activities that are illegal. Kara assures the police that she has chosen this way of life both knowingly and in a rational manner. She insists that she will continue to prostitute herself, as it allows her to "get the things she wants" and "not have to go back home." What are the police to do in Kara's situation?

Literature Review

Cases like Kara's illustrate the conflict facing law enforcement when dealing with adolescent prostitutes. They are faced with an individual breaking the law, yet what options are available to this child? Despite the abundance of research and various perspectives on adult female prostitution, adolescent female prostitution is an entirely different phenomenon. For example, with regard to adult prostitution, feminist theories look at issues such as power relationships between men and women and the lack of opportunities in the labor market for these women (Jesson, 1993). Sereny (1984) explains that juvenile prostitution addresses the power differential between adults and children who have not yet entered the work force. Although the literature available on policing adolescent prostitution in the United States is sparse, it is clear that the behavior of these juveniles cannot be appropriately considered using theories of adult female prostitution.

The scope of juvenile prostitution in the United States is alarming. Cases like Kara's are far too common. Police figures have estimated between 100,000 and 300,000 prostitutes under the age of 18 (Flowers, 1998). Nonofficial sources claim that for children under the age of 16, the numbers are around half a million "with the numbers doubling or tripling when including 16- and 17-year-old prostitutes." Approximately two-thirds of these prostitutes are female.

The research suggests a variety of contributing factors and motivations that lead to adolescent prostitution. The literature overwhelmingly suggests that prior to entering prostitution, the vast majority of these girls suffered physical, emotional, or, most frequently, sexual abuse (Flowers, 1998; Jesson, 1993; Schaffer & DeBlassie, 1984; Weisberg, 1985; Widom & Kuhns, 1996). The story of Kara illustrates how many teenagers flee from a dangerous household to a dangerous lifestyle on the streets as a prostitute. The Huckleberry House Project concluded that 90% of the adolescent female prostitutes studied were sexually molested (Harlan, Rodgers, & Slattery, 1981). Widom and Kuhns (1996) found that childhood neglect was also a risk factor for entry into juvenile prostitution. These researchers indicated that the children on the streets alone are more vulnerable to the lures offered by pimps or other juveniles. "Early childhood abuse and neglect appear to place children at increased risk of becoming prostitutes, which reinforces the importance of viewing prostitution in a victimization context" (p. 1611).

Jesson (1993) reports that sexual abuse leads to running away and the combination of the two is critical in the juvenile's risk for entering prostitution. Researchers agree that there is a strong correlation between running away and juvenile prostitution. Many of these girls who leave home to escape abuse or to seek independence and excitement quickly become prostitutes to pay for drugs, food, shelter, and the like (Flowers, 1998). Some are lured by the sweet-talking pimp offering love, protection, and companionship. Benson and Matthews (1995) suggest that the majority of women enter street prostitution when they are "vulnerable and impressionable." Other studies suggest that the primary reason these adolescents become involved in prostitution is to support a drug habit (Bagley & Young, 1987).

According to the U.S. Department of Justice, Federal Bureau of Investigation's *Uniform Crime Reports* for 1995 (1996), 504 females under 18 years old were arrested for prostitution and commercialized vice and approximately 108,840 females under the age of 18 were arrested as runaways. Far more female adolescents were arrested for loitering (34,011), vagrancy (313), and suspicion (322) than for prostitution and vice. Research shows that officers will arrest these adolescent girls under various other status offenses in order to prevent stigmatizing them as "prostitutes." In addition to prostitution, these girls frequently engage in diverse criminal and delinquent activities. Flowers (1995) found that the crimes most typically committed by these juvenile prostitutes include theft, robbery, drug dealing, and the use of drugs. Greater than 80% of the arrests of both females and males were between the age range of 15–17 years of age.

Overall, officers exercise a great deal of discretion in their decisions to arrest or not arrest and on what charge (Flowers, 1998). The literature is consistent in that the overwhelming majority of juvenile females arrested for prostitution are Caucasian (Flowers, 1998; Weisberg, 1985). African Americans compose a distant second-largest category of juvenile prostitutes (Weisberg, 1985). Juvenile prostitutes can come from all socioeconomic backgrounds. Flowers (1998) maintains that studies with smaller samples have found that they are overrepresented in lower socioeconomic classes. However, research with larger samples indicates that the majority of juvenile prostitutes come from middle- and upper-class backgrounds.

A number of pieces of federal legislation have been enacted since the 1970s to crack down on the sexual exploitation of children. According to Weisberg, states are creating "criminal statutes that fail to punish adolescent prostitutes either by omitting any mention of sanctions or specifically excluding adolescents involved in prostitution from any liability" (as cited in Flowers, 1998, p. 152). Weisberg (1985) further explains that in civil legislation, many states look at adolescent prostitution as a form of child abuse/sexual exploitation than as a result of delinquent behavior. In both cases, the adolescent prostitute is viewed as victim, not as an offender.

As previously mentioned, most cases of juvenile prostitution are handled by either a police department's vice squad or juvenile division. According to Weisberg (1985), the various units and police officers involved in a juvenile prostitution case create the lack of a coordinated response. He maintains that vice squad officers perceive these juveniles as troublemakers as a result of their involvement with various types of crime and their "streetwise" demeanor. In addition, he explains that frequently officers are unaware of the resources available in the community to help these adolescents. Their typical response is to arrest. In contrast, Weisberg suggests that the juvenile division officers are much more in tune with a rehabilitative approach and have the capability to make the appropriate referrals to community organizations and treatment programs. He levies the criticism that officers who simply arrest are failing to provide any long-lasting solution to the problems posed by juveniles.

Some researchers suggest that it is not an officer's lack of knowledge about community resources for adolescent female prostitutes but rather their belief that these programs are not effective in making either short- or long-term changes in the lives of these juveniles (Weisberg, 1985). All too commonly the same youths are being rearrested on charges related to prostitution time and time again. Weisberg suggests that these officers are left with a lack of faith in the courts and treatment programs for these individuals. The literature suggests that officers are also frustrated by the quick release of adolescents from juvenile hall who are arrested for status offenses such as running away. In Kara's case, she is blatantly telling officers that she will return to prostitution as soon as she is released. Officers are regularly left with the discretion to treat the adolescent female prostitute as either a criminal or a victim. In both instances officers are habitually dissatisfied with the outcome, as the same juveniles are cycled through the system.

Forensic Psychology and Policy Implications

Adolescent female prostitution is in many cases an unfortunate result of abuse or neglect. Young women with various emotional scars are left feeling worthless, degraded, and depressed. Research shows that 10–20% of these teenagers have been in psychiatric hospitals, many on multiple occasions (Johnson, 1992). Studies have shown that almost half of these girls have attempted suicide. Many of these juveniles enter prostitution with a variety of emotional problems and few have sought professional help (Flowers, 1998).

This is clearly a population that would benefit from mental health services. Unfortunately, the link between officers and mental health professionals is not es-tablished in many cases. Some officers are not aware of the available resources or do not recognize the juvenile prostitute as having been victimized. Forensic psy-chologists would be particularly able to see the underlying psychological correlates to the criminality of these juveniles. The plethora of emotional and psychological problems often experienced by adolescent female prostitutes are not being addressed and the cycle of crime and arrest is perpetuated.

Schaffer and DeBlassie (1984) suggest that when in contact with the criminal justice system, these juveniles are exposed to practices that suggest they are mainly being punished for sexual promiscuity. They maintain that treatment is at best sec-ondary. According to Schaffer and DeBlassie, those in authority in law enforcement are "security-oriented" and the law enforcement personnel who are interested in rehabilitation are no more than tolerated, having very little impact on policy. Pro-grams to address these needs could be implemented, with the critical factor being adequate training and education for line officers to recognize those in need of these services. The training offered to both juvenile division officers and vice officers could be more uniform. Although vice squad officers are extensively trained in the different components of prostitution, the special needs of the troubled adolescent often go unrecognized. Officers who see these juveniles on the street committing various crimes could easily miss the child victim that many of these teenagers used to be.

Future Research

There is a paucity of research regarding policing female adolescent prostitution. While the research on adult female prostitution is abundant, more research must consider the unique aspects of juvenile prostitution. The literature overwhelmingly suggests that there are special emotional and psychological issues that must be considered with this population. However, there is no research indicating what differences occur between those adolescent prostitutes who receive psychological services from their contact with the criminal justice system and those who do not. Program evaluations comparing police departments that take a more rehabilitative approach with juvenile prostitutes in comparison with those who take more of a retributive approach are needed. Recidivism rates and suicide rates could be compared. Additional research on how officers view juvenile prostitutes, as criminals or victims, would also be of great value. Research is needed on those juvenile prostitutes who come from middle- and upper-class backgrounds. This is a growing phenomenon with seemingly different precipitating factors. Overall, female adolescent prostitution is an area needing further research.

CHAPTER 3

Civil Forensics

OVERVIEW

The overlapping fields of policing and psychology are not limited to crime and justice controversies afflicting adult and juvenile offenders. There are also many issues that impact society in general. The domain of civil forensics and law enforcement encompasses those topics in which the relationship between the police and the public is called into question and more closely examined. There are many facets to this relationship. Psychology is one medium that allows us to understand where and how the police and the public interface.

In this chapter, six controversial matters are investigated. These topics include (1) public attitudes toward the police, (2) exploring the police personality, (3) police and the mentally ill, (4) community-oriented policing, (5) police training in communication skills and conflict resolution, and (6) policing minority populations. These subjects represent a limited set of issues confronting the civil forensic arena of law enforcement. However, as with each chapter in this textbook, a wide array of concerns is presented highlighting the breadth of the field.

The public's perception of law enforcement is substantially informed by the media, especially popular television. How does the mass media influence public perceptions and how do these sentiments affect societal attitudes toward the police?

Patrol officers can, on occasion, confront dangerous citizens, aggressive suspects, and agitated groups. How, if at all, do exchanges such as these relate to the development of a police personality? Are officers susceptible to psychopathology? Can preemployment (mental health) screening of officers assess for such characterological traits? Does cynicism and violence, as dimensions of law enforcement, draw certain individuals to this line of work?

The police increasingly find themselves responding to citizen encounters with the mentally ill. What preconceived notions, if any, do officers harbor regarding the psychiatrically disordered? How do officers deal with the mentally ill? Does police academy training sufficiently prepare cadets to interface with the psychiatrically ill?

Recent strategies designed to improve the law enforcement presence in various urban, rural, and suburban neighborhoods have relied upon community-oriented policing techniques. What are these techniques? Is this strategy a viable solution to fighting crime? Is it a law enforcement trend with limited effectiveness? How does the public perceive community-oriented policing?

Police departments find that communication skills and conflict resolution training are integral dimensions to effective police–citizen encounters. What kind and degree of training do officers receive? How do these skills affect victims and offenders?

Officers exercise a wide range of discretion in different contexts. This discretion is operative when making decisions about racial and ethnic minorities. What attitudes do police officers engender toward such constituencies? Where do these sentiments come from, and are they institutionalized within the organization of policing?

The sections within this chapter reveal several important civil forensic areas where the psychological sciences and law enforcement are significantly linked. While certainly not exhaustive, it is clear that a societal dimension to the police–psychology interface does, in fact, exist. It is also evident that forensic psychologists schooled in organizational analysis, social psychology, race relations, and similar domains of inquiry would offer the public a uniquely trained specialist who could meet the changing and pressing needs within the civil arena of law enforcement. In addition, more and better research at the crossroads of psychology and policing would help educate future generations of forensic experts with interests in these and related issues. Indeed, if forensic psychology is to affect the organization, culture, and practice of policing in society, then responding to crime and justice controversies such as those canvassed in this chapter is not only necessary but essential.

PUBLIC ATTITUDES TOWARD POLICE

Introduction

The public's perception of police can be broken down into a variety of separate entities. For example, the "public" may be considered the everyday citizen, who has had their own dealings, either positive or negative, with local police departments.

Alternatively, attitudes toward law enforcement and policing practices may stem more from secondhand accounts from neighbors, family members, or friends' encounters with police. Perhaps the largest influence on public perception of any topic is the mass media. It has a powerful, and in some ways monopolizing, control over the public's perception of virtually all topics in popular culture, including that of police decision making. While many scholars have debated the media's influence on these domains, one need not be a scholar to understand the everyday influence and clout the press has on the public's perception of forensics in general and police in particular. The following case scenario illustrates one of the many mechanisms of how the public come to perceive law enforcement.

> Imagine you are sitting at home and hear a tremendous commotion occurring outside in the street. Intrigued, you go outside to investigate and discover that a roadblock has been set up right outside your house in the street and that a police car, lights flashing and siren blaring, is pursuing a car in front of it. Thwarted by the roadblock, the pursued car stops and the police surround the car. A young man of about 25 is virtually dragged from his car and thrown onto the hood of a police vehicle. By this time, a rather large crowd has gathered around the scene, making for an interesting spectacle. The police gruffly yell some incomprehensible statements to the young driver, who at this point is not resisting in any way, and throw him into the back of a squad car. All the police eventually leave, with one remaining officer yelling to the surrounding onlookers that "the show is over" and that "everyone must leave the scene and return to their houses immediately."

Your opinion of the situation may be somewhat clouded. What exactly did the young man do to deserve such reprehensible treatment? Were the police justified in their handling of the situation? Why didn't an officer inform the onlookers of what was going on? Confused and intrigued, you are forced to come to your own conclusions, feeling somewhat frustrated at the lack of information given to you, and with, perhaps, a distorted view of what just occurred. Issues such as these are discussed in the following section, as are other aspects of the public's perception of police and criminal justice. Theoretical views of public perception are examined, as are ways in which the police deal with media and cooperative relations between police and media, including practical implications law enforcement establishments use to effectively deal with media relations in hopes of establishing good public relations patterns.

Cases such as these and many others influence how the public generally view police and their practices. Often, police are forced to deal with situations that are sensitive and therefore cannot reveal information that may be sensitive to a pending case or which may violate someone's Fourth Amendment rights (the right to privacy). A good example of the way in which the public's view of police is influenced by the media is through popular television.

Literature Review

It has been argued that television shows portraying policing have all but dominated prime-time television for quite some time. In fact, detailed analyses have been conducted examining the effect the media and its influence on popular culture has had on public views of criminal justice. For example, Newman (1990) describes how a variety of popular cultural mediums provide a framework for public perception of the criminal justice system. More specifically, he describes the history and role of television detectives, soap operas, nonfiction television, advertising, popular/rock music, comics, movies and their detectives, and westerns in shaping this public perception. He concluded that the content and media of popular culture are ways of understanding the kind of consciousness it represents and that various themes involved in this medium should be understood since we are all, in essence, elements of criminal justice, particularly that of criminal punishment.

In keeping with the theme of popular culture, media, and criminal justice, perhaps no better example exists which exemplifies the positively growing relationship between these forums as do television shows such as "Cops" and "Real Stories of the Highway Patrol." Series such as these are the epitome of the blending between police practice and media portrayal of law enforcement work. In fact, in one case (*United States v. Sanusi*, 1992), a suit was initiated involving nine defendants who were charged with credit card fraud. In preparation of his defense, the defending attorney subpoenaed a CBS videotape filmed during a search of one of the defendant's apartment; CBS refused to turn over the videotape. In turn, a variety of issues were brought into the public eye involving First and Fourth Amendment issues and controversies. In other words, had the press' rights been violated when asked to return the tape or had the defendant's rights to privacy been violated when a media source obtained a copy of his personal affairs? As a result of this case, a number of legal controversies were clarified. Most of these related to policy matters that are discussed in the following pages.

A review of the discussion thus far, however, may lead the reader to believe that all public perception of crime and legal control have been through the influence of the mass media; this is not necessarily the case. Ericson (1991), for example, describes a series of other sources that are also influential in the establishment of this process. He cites research that has shown that the mass media are only one of many sources in which the public obtains its views on police and criminal justice. Further, he states that there are certain types of approaches, one of which is termed the "effects" approach, that holds certain assumptions regarding the public influence of the mass media and crime, law, and criminal justice. Some other assumptions of this view include the notion that the mass media transmits distorted information about crime and legal control. He goes on to describe how the effects of the mass media as agency, technology, and institution interact with the criminal justice system.

Naturally, public perception of law enforcement may come from the psychological underpinnings of how officers tend to view themselves. In other words, the officers' attitudes regarding themselves and their profession may elicit certain psychological sets which manifest behaviorally. The public views these behaviors and consequently makes its own judgments regarding police and their practices.

Research has demonstrated that police tend to view themselves and their profession in both an ideological and a traditional fashion. These belief systems were found to be significantly correlated with police worldviews of their profession as a sort of "craftsmanship." In turn, this craftsmanship belief system was found to be associated with favorable attitudes of police toward certain aspects of their jobs, such as antipathy toward the due process system, the police code of secrecy, and the tendency to use "street justice" in resolving conflicts (Crank, Payn, & Jackson, 1993).

The ways in which police handle themselves, from their demeanor at a traffic stop to control of a hostile situation, naturally leads citizens to form opinions regarding police practices. Another question related to this is how police view themselves. In other words, attitudes from police toward their own practices may have important implications for the public's perception of these same practices. It is with this notion that Crank et al. (1993) conducted a research study examining the relationship between police belief systems and attitudes toward law enforcement practices.

Results of the above experimental question revealed that police tend to see themselves as professionals who, like most other professions, engage in a craft. This craftsmanship holds a large degree of influence on police attitudes toward the world in general, and three other traditional police practices in particular. These practices are, as mentioned above, antipathy toward due process, the code of secrecy, and the tendency to resolve citizen confrontations with "street justice."

The results of Crank et al. (1993), tabulated from over 205 members of various Illinois police departments, indicated that attitudes congruent with the described police practices are associated with the police view of themselves as types of craftsmen in a specialized trade. Further, the feelings of police as being professionals contributes a modest relationship to these attitudes.

As a result of these attitudes regarding police and the criminal justice system, what steps can be taken to help alleviate tensions between the media and law enforcement? As mentioned earlier, cop shows which allow cameras to accompany officers in the line of duty help to blur the line between police and society. However, some may argue that this relationship is biased and distorted and that only successful and properly handled scenarios actually make it to prime-time episodes.

The Federal Bureau of Investigation (FBI) has been particularly vocal in its stance to promote healthy and professional relations between media and the police. Francis Dunphy, a special agent with the FBI, and Gerald Garner, a member of the Lakewood, Colorado, Police Department have developed what they believe represent guidelines a law enforcement agency can use to interact effectively with the news media. These measures include everything from making good eye contact with the audience, to "predicting the future," in which an officer tells the press of an upcoming situation or event which may interest them (Dunphy & Garner, 1992).

Implementing programs and educating law enforcement agents regarding the sensitive relations between police and societal views will no doubt help influence the public's perception of law enforcement in a positive direction. In theory, a society in which the public holds a very positive view of police and policing will allow for a more systemic, cooperative, and organized form of implemented criminal justice and law enforcement. This has implications for promoting a more civic-minded society.

Forensic Psychology and Policy Implications

Improving relations between the general public and law enforcement is certainly an area ready for policy reform. Some departments have gone as far as to suggest ways in which police officers can change their outward attitude through verbal and non-verbal communication in their encounters with the public (Pritchett, 1993). Other departments have attempted to revise their policies for filing citizen complaints.

A review by Ericson (1991) revealed that the mass media are more open and influential than most researchers believed. Further, he states that the media does not merely report on events, but participates directly in the processes of world functioning. Therefore, when the media becomes involved within the criminal justice arena, its own injustices are exposed. It is these injustices that must be targeted for further regulation and reform. This concept elicits the need for an increased working relationship between the media and law enforcement, perhaps through a psychological medium. Mechanisms of increasing the efficacy of this medium are discussed within the following paragraphs.

According to Parrish (1993), very few citizens have direct contact or correspondence with the police. Therefore, the public makes its decisions regarding the police and their practices based on what they see, hear, or read. Consequently, it is imperative that the police act in a manner that is the most conducive to appropriate public image building. This is accomplished through the changing of officer attitudes, the recognition that cameras are very present in today's technological society, and that police should operate under the assumption that they are under constant surveillance.

These realities make it necessary for law enforcement agencies to adopt policies that specifically address and attempt to resolve these issues. This will help build more solid rapport between the police and the public. These policies can include mandatory sessions for officers, both in training and those already in service, to undergo classroom instruction in how to deal effectively and in a collaborative manner with members of both the media and society. In addition, police departments can become more visible, hold public rallies, or support television shows exemplifying their own local "heroes."

Since the media can portray law enforcement in any way it chooses, it is wise for law enforcement administrators to establish a meaningful and ongoing working relationship with its representatives. This relationship needs to be one of cooperation and mutual respect. Forging this association can be accomplished through such initiatives as designated police discussion forums or press conferences. An effective working alliance between the media and law enforcement could allow for even more effective crime reduction, prevention, and justice.

Suggestions for Future Research

Research examining the relation between the public and their view of police is surprisingly minimal. Given the amount of attention to police-oriented television shows and detective and true crime novels on bestseller lists as well as portrayals of police and law enforcement in movies, little has been documented on the dynamics of public perceptions of law enforcement. High-profile cases in the media regarding police practices and the inconsistencies or shortcomings of their work are almost always scrutinized by analysts and the public. However, restitution of these attitudes and portrayals of law enforcement are often neglected due to a lack of scientific understanding of how these systems interface. Research examining these interacting systems is clearly needed.

Further research can examine the effects that solved cases have on public confidence in law enforcement. Also, the effects of police interaction with the public, such as those in which local police departments organize charitable events, are yet to be analyzed. Research examining individual differences between police departments is sparse, and what research does exist points to inconclusive findings regarding the public's perceptions of various styles of police department operations.

It is clear that law enforcement is a large part of both popular culture and is under the constant eye of scrutiny. The public's perception of law enforcement is no doubt influenced by the mass media's interpretation of police and criminal justice events. Therefore, all people who are not in regular contact with police systems form their opinions of law enforcement based on a media filter. The public is forced to make individual decisions based on media presentations. Consequently, individuals may be swayed in the direction that the media filter portrays events related to criminal justice. It is not only necessary to understand that these interactions take place, but that examining criminal justice and law enforcement through unfiltered eyes is difficult, albeit necessary, in order to gain a full understanding of the criminal justice system.

EXPLORING THE POLICE PERSONALITY

Introduction

Police officers hold a position that is replete with stress and responsibility. These officers face dangerous situations, aggressive suspects, and agitated citizens. Line officers must comply with their supervisors and uphold the law. These individuals are entrusted with a tremendous amount of power and with a great deal of discretion in how they use that power. As a result, various methods have been employed to assess the personality and any psychopathology exhibited by the officer candidates. Most frequently, psychological tests and civil service interviews are used to ascertain this information. Some researchers argue that this information is only detected by on-the-spot observation of on-the-street interactions (Toch, 1992). With the increasing media attention to cases of police brutality, there is a growing concern about the mental health screening of police officers. Are these cases examples of a few violence-prone men or are they more indicative of a "police personality" that pervades law enforcement? There exists a concern that the screening of officer candidates is insufficient at recognizing those officers who will be unable to cope with the responsibilities of the job. Consider the following case illustration.

> Cameron's father had been a police officer and Cameron admired the "tough-guy" image and excitement that he perceived to be embodied in police work. He had always been outgoing and seemingly fearless. All of his friends and family knew that he would be an excellent candidate for law enforcement. Cameron applied for a job with the local police department. After what seemed like hours of psychological tests and panel interviews, Cameron was relieved to hear that he qualified to be on the police force. Being a new officer on his probationary period, he was eager to belong and to perform his duties to the upmost of his abilities. He had heard countless stories by the "veterans" about the difficulty of gaining compliance from a particular category of civilians. In addition, Cameron was warned that it was best to take a firm, consistent approach in dealing with this group as suspects.
>
> In his second month of duty, Cameron tried to obtain identification from a suspect who fit this description of "difficult" civilian. The suspect met his expectations by being belligerent and threatening. Cameron responded by being increasingly commanding and forceful. The conflict escalated into an altercation between the suspect and Cameron.

Literature Review

Conflicting conceptualizations of "police personality" are found in the literature. Some researchers contend that individuals with certain personality traits are drawn to police work (Cortina, Doherty, Schmitt, Kaufman, & Smith, 1992). Cameron's fearless attitude would seem to have led him to police work. These researchers hold that personality traits or any psychopathology present are detected during their initial screenings for the police academy. Other researchers maintain that although these individuals have similar occupational interests, it is really the police subculture of violence and cynicism that leads to particular actions such as excessive force or police brutality (Graves, 1996). In Cameron's case it is difficult to determine if it was his personality characteristics alone or the influence of other officers that led to the violent interaction with a civilian. Yet others maintain that years of working with hostile civilians, occupational stagnation, and the loss of faith in our criminal justice system lead to personality and attitude changes in police officers. While some believe that one of these scenarios is dominant, other researchers contend that these influences can be interdependent. There is a growing controversy surrounding how to establish whether an individual is suitable for police work.

Researchers maintain that the considerable demands routinely placed on police officers require persons who are not only free from psychopathology, but that are very well adjusted, with good coping skills (Beutler, Nussbaum, & Meredith, 1988). Police officers encounter life-threatening situations, aggressive offenders, and have to answer to the community as well as to their supervisors. It is suggested that officers face the worst of society and then have to handle the most delicate of human crises with sensitivity. The unique stressors that officers face make emotional strengths and weaknesses the focus of screening procedures for officer candidates.

The research indicates that psychological assessment tools have been increasingly utilized in the past 2 decades as a means to screen and select police officer candidates (Beutler et al., 1988). The Minnesota Multiphasic Personality Inventory (MMPI and MMPI-2) is the psychological test that is most commonly used as a screening device in police officer selection (Beutler et al., 1988; Cortina et al., 1992; Kornfeld, 1995; J. J. Murphy, 1972). The MMPI is primarily a test of psychopathology and is used most successfully when testing for this purpose (Graham, 1993). The literature suggests that these instruments are employed to determine which candidates are the most likely to fail during training or probationary periods (Cortina et al., 1992; Inwald, 1988; J. J. Murphy, 1972). In addition, they are used to indicate which candidates are most likely to use excessive force or misuse weapons while on duty. Other researchers maintain that efforts to correlate MMPI scores to job performance have not been effective (Cortina et al., 1992). By identifying personality styles and any psychopathology, police departments hope to save time and money as well as avoid any negative publicity or litigation that would ensue following an excessive force claim.

Cortina et al. (1992) state that police officer candidates exhibit a distinguishable pattern on the MMPI. For example, these candidates' validity scales, which measure the accuracy of the test, usually show defensiveness or an unwillingness to acknowledge distress. The Psychopathic Deviate (Pd) scale is frequently elevated. Interestingly, the elevation of the Pd scale is typically seen in individuals who engage in criminal behavior. Interpretive possibilities for an elevated Pd score include: aggressive or assaultive behavior, substance abuse, or poor tolerance of boredom. A study by Kornfeld (1995), in which the MMPI-2 was administered to 84 police officer candidates, indicated low scores on scales 0 and 2. Male candidates had a low scale 5, while female candidates had an elevated scale 5. For a nonclinical sample, low scale 2 scores suggest individuals who are less likely to worry, to have problems reaching decisions, and to worry about being rejected (Graham, 1993; Kornfeld, 1995). They are also more likely to be self-confident. A low scale 0 on the MMPI denotes an individual who is sociable, extroverted, and friendly (Graham, 1993;

Kornfeld, 1995). A low scale 5 for a male indicates an extremely masculine presentation, with stereotypical masculine interests, and someone who is action oriented (Butcher, 1990; Graham, 1993; Kornfeld, 1995). A females with an elevated scale 5 could be a woman who has rejected the traditional feminine role, embracing more commonly masculine interests. Overall, Kornfeld (1995) found that these police officer candidates were psychologically well adjusted, comfortable with people, free of worry, and self-confident.

The MMPI was not designed particularly for the selection of police officers and some researchers have expressed concern over its use in this context (Cortina et al., 1992). In response to this concern, the Inwald Personality Inventory (IPI) was developed (Cortina et al., 1992). The IPI is a 310-item questionnaire that ". . . attempts to assess the psychological and emotional fitness of recruits as well as some of their job-relevant behavioral characteristics" (p. 20). In a validity study conducted by Inwald, Knatz, and Shusman (1983), the IPI was found to be superior to the MMPI in predicting job-relevant criteria such as absences, lateness, and derelections (disciplinary interviews). However, according to Cortina et al. (1992), neither the MMPI nor the IPI could add much over the Civil Service Exam, a multiple-choice exam testing cognitive ability, in predicting performance ratings and officer turnover rates.

Eber (as cited in Lorr & Strack, 1994) obtained objective psychometric data on 15,000 candidates for positions in law enforcement agencies around the country. Using the Clinical Analysis Questionnaire, one of Eber's objectives was to determine a distinct police personality style that might explain the sporadic occurrence of excessive force or assaultive behavior in typically rational, stable, and professional officers. The Clinical Analysis Questionnaire consists of personality measure scales and 12 measures of psychopathology. Overall, the candidates were found to have very little psychopathology. They were less depressed, less confused, and less likely to engage in self-harm than the general population. However, they were more thrill seeking and had a disregard for social conventions based on these measures. Regarding their personality styles, Eber found that these candidates were self-disciplined, very tough-minded, and slightly independent.

Expanding on Eber's work, Lorr and Strack (1994) divided the police personality profile into three robust profile groups. The largest cluster was reflected as the typical "good" cop or those who are self-disciplined, low in anxiety, extroverted, and emotionally tough. One in four candidates fell into a cluster that had relatively high levels of paranoia, schizophrenia, and psychasthenia as well as high anxiety and lower self-control. Despite their relatively high occurrence compared to "good" cops, these occurrences of psychopathology were relatively low compared with the general population.

Other researchers maintain that adverse psychological changes occur in officers after being on the job. A study conducted by Beutler et al. (1988) using the MMPI looked at 25 officers directly after recruitment, 2 years later, and, finally, 4 years later. These researchers found that the officers presented personality styles suggestive of substance abuse risk and stress-related physical complaints. In addition, they concluded that this risk increases with officers' time in service. Beutler et al. (1998; Beutler, Storm, Kirkish, Scogan, & Gaines, 1985) maintain that overall this group is guarded and will be hesitant to seek mental health treatment. Russell and Beigel (1982) report that the alcoholism and suicide rates among police officers surpass by far those of the general population, suggesting the impact of police work on these individuals.

In a study undertaken by Saathoff and Buckman (1990), the most common primary diagnosis among 26 state police officers who requested or were referred to psychiatric services by their department was adjustment disorder, followed by substance abuse and then personality disorder. The majority of officers believed that there was a stigma attached to receiving mental health services. Despite infrequent occurrences, Saathoff and Buckman stress that the extremes of violence, homicide, and suicide must be taken into consideration with police officers, as they carry guns in the course of their duties.

Some researchers believe that the negative behavior displayed by some officers is related to a personality style that officers have when they join the force. However, other researchers maintain that incidents like police brutality stem from a belief system that forms as they begin to feel betrayed by the system and lose respect for the law (Graves, 1996). These researchers explain that officers see the worst of society on a daily basis and begin to lose faith in others, trust only other officers, and suffer "social estrangement." Some researchers contend that policemen develop a survival personality defined by rigidity, increased personal restriction, and cynicism (Kroes, 1976; Saathoff & Buckman, 1990). Most of the research on police cynicism occurred in the late 1960s and mid-1970s (Graves, 1996). Cynicism is defined as a distrust in human beings and their intentions. According to Graves, ". . . cynicism is the antithesis of idealism, truth, and justice—the very virtues that law enforcement officers swear to uphold" (p. 16). He contends that cynicism is the precursor to emotional problems that lead to misconduct, brutality, and possibly corruption. In addition, he stresses the negative impact on officer productivity, morale, community relations, and even the relationship that the officer has with his own family.

Researchers have found that cynicism is more prevalent in large urban police departments, particularly with college-educated, lower ranking officers, during their first 10 years of service (Graves, 1996). Graves suggests that the heavy demands of law enforcement lead to these incidents of burnout, stress, and cynicism. He contends that these factors also lead to unhealthy emotional responses such as a withdrawal from society and an antipathy to idealism or a loss of respect for law and society.

Toch (1992) explains that there are "violent men" among the ranks of police officers. He further adds that while these men have certain fears, insecurities, and self-centered perspectives with which they enter the force, their brutality is often protected by a code of mutual support among officers. According to Toch:

> In theory, aggressive police officers could be dealt with as dangerous deviants by their peers and by the administrator of their departments. Instead, they are seen as overly-forceful practitioners of a philosophy that comprises themes such as "lots of suspects are scumbags," "one cannot tolerate disrespect," "situations must be (physically) controlled," and "the real measure of police productivity is number of arrests." (pp. 242–243)

Toch suggests that it is a fallacy to believe that the "police problem" is a function of personality disturbances among a small group of officers that can be detected during initial psychological screenings or a function of racial beliefs that can be eradicated by cultural sensitivity lectures. He contends that some officers have a proclivity to escalate interpersonal interactions into explosive situations. In addition, he maintains that this propensity for violence can only be identified through on-the-spot observations of their interactions on the street. Clearly in Cameron's case, early detection of this type of behavior could prevent future abuses of citizens. In addition, his department could recognize the need for additional training in handling hostile situations without resorting to violence.

Forensic Psychology and Policy Implications

Overall, it is clear that mental health professionals need to have a role in police training as well as provide psychological services and evaluations after a critical incident or trauma. Many forensic psychologists specialize in the unique psychological dynamics of police work, the emotional needs of police officers, and the complexities of law enforcement organizations. In order for a mental health professional to be effective within an organization, they must understand the special needs or issues of their constituency, in this case police officers.

Within the police department, Beutler et al. (1988) suggest that departments should enhance coping strategies for officers by including intradepartmental programs for stress management, psychological interventions, and educational programs on the abuses of alcohol. Saathoff and Buckman (1990) recommend that when psychiatrists or psychologists conduct a psychological evaluation of officers, they should not be cajoled by the officer or the department into limiting the scope of their evaluation. Officers' continuing mental health has endless implications for their own safety and the safety of the community. These researchers also suggest including officers' families in the mental health process in order to elicit critical information and increase the level of support for that officer.

It is imperative for police departments to take all possible steps to reduce the stigma attached to psychological services for officers. Police supervisors should receive training to help them identify those officers in need of psychological referrals. These interventions should be encouraged and rewarded by supervisors and even made mandatory after critical events.

Regarding cynicism, Graves (1996) suggests that competent, principle-centered, people-oriented leadership can help to inspire and motivate employees and prevent negativity. In addition, these police leaders need to actively recognize the positive actions by police officers within the department as well as in the community. He also maintains that by having continuous training about the intent of rules of evidence, officers can be empowered within the criminal justice system rather than manipulated by it. Graves contends that a participatory management style that allows officers to have a voice increases their satisfaction with their jobs and reduces cynicism that flows out toward the community. Finally, he suggests that a realistic job preview should be offered to police officer candidates during recruitment.

Toch (1992) suggests that rather than focus only on the individual recruit's personality style, their pattern of social interaction should be examined in order to assess the violence potential. He points out that it should be impressed upon young officers that they need to communicate to civilians the reasons for their actions. For example, Toch cites multiple incidents where police officers demand a certain response from a suspicious civilian and their increasingly authoritative and demanding demeanor contributes to the escalation of violence. Toch recognizes that the ambiguity in the power delegated to police officers frequently results in the abuse of those powers. He suggests that more guidance should be offered in handling discretion. Officers are bombarded with phrases like "reasonable force" without a clear understanding of their meanings or applicability in street situations. In the case illustration, Cameron was faced with a noncompliant suspect and no plan to counter the situation.

In order to confront these situations, Toch (1992) suggests that officers should be provided with criteria of conduct with a realistic preparation for their use on the street. Specifically, he recommends directive, in-service training experiences rather than passive learning experiences. In addition, he suggests that while on their probationary periods, officers should be shadowed. During this shadowing procedure, when violence-producing situations are confronted, a resolution *should be* worked out and errors *should be* open to analysis and correction.

Suggestions for Future Research

The literature called for more objective or qualitative data on the mental disorders experienced by police officers. The categorization of the personality traits identified in the current research does little to elucidate the experience of police officers. Traditionally a guarded group, it is difficult to obtain an accurate indication of psychological functioning. Longitudinal studies of personality and mood changes could help to identify the effect of continued police service on the mental health of officers.

Regarding the psychological assessment instruments used to screen officer candidates, Kornfeld (1995) reports the need for new normative data on the MMPI-2, especially for female and minority police officer candidates, to help promote fairness in the selection process. Overall, more validation research needs to be done on the effectiveness of these various instruments or personality clusters in the prediction of job suitability.

More research needs to be conducted on the notion that principle-centered, person-oriented leadership reduces cynicism among police officers. Program evaluations can be carried out in departments that implement these type of leadership styles and policies reflecting participatory management. Finally, departments that would implement the "shadowing" concept provided by Toch (1992) should be evaluated. This assessment would explore if incidents of excessive force or police brutality would be reduced by more directive evaluations of and preparations for violence-producing situations and training for violence-prone individuals.

POLICE AND THE MENTALLY ILL

Introduction

A police officers's job is one riddled with a variety of pitfalls and potential dangers. As if maintaining control over "normal" populations is not difficult enough, law enforcement agents often find themselves having to deal with populations that cannot, or are incapable of, rational and reasonable thought. More specifically, mentally ill people often find themselves having to deal with law enforcement after having made some specific threat or engaged in some inappropriate or illegal action. Consider the following example of how a mentally ill individual may come face-to-face with the law.

> A police officer receives a call and is told that there is an involuntary commitment request at a large psychiatric institution downtown. The officer calls for an ambulance to arrive at the scene before he arrives. By the time he has reached the institution, he is greeted by a mêlée of interested pedestrians, disarrayed staff members, and a hostile-looking man holding a butter knife he apparently stole from the kitchen. The man in question is pacing and mumbling something to himself, apparently severely agitated. It looks to the police officer like any movement toward the patient may result in a violent outburst. Due to the fact that the patient is in possession of a potentially dangerous weapon, the situation must be handled with extreme caution, diligence, and cunning in order to prevent the patient from hurting himself or anyone else.

The manner in which the police officer handles the above situation is critical for a variety of reasons. For example, would a wrong or inappropriate statement made by the officer invoke some sort of rage response? Would other patients observing the ordeal become agitated as well after seeing such an encounter, thus resulting in other psychotic outbreaks? If the patient refused to submit, how will physical restraints be applied? Will anyone get hurt in the process? These questions and others are faced by officers every day. However, a surprising paucity of literature exists on exactly how an officer should deal with the mentally ill in the line of duty (Patch & Arrigo, 1999). This section attempts to answer these questions as well as address other related issues regarding the public's perception of the mentally ill and law enforcement, how police should handle mentally ill patients, the psychological makeup of the mentally ill lawbreaker, the cooccurring or comorbid diagnosis often given to jailed mentally ill inmates, and public policy implications dealing with the appropriate manner in which to effectively deal with the mentally ill.

Literature Review

Knowledge and attitudes by police officers toward the mentally ill have traditionally been that of ignorance and misunderstanding. Further, police officers have tended to have somewhat cynical attitudes toward this same population (Nunnally, 1961). This is not surprising, considering the tremendous amount of stress experienced by police officers every day. The failure of police academies and training programs to adequately address issues related to mental health have conceivably fostered the ignorance toward this specific population.

While many are led to believe that the mentally ill are no more dangerous, nor cause more crime than the general population, this does not seem to be entirely accurate. Shader, Jackson, Harmatz, and Applebaum (1977) found that 45% of schizophrenics, in relation to only 33% of nonschizophrenics, exhibited "violent" behaviors. These behaviors most often consisted of kicking, hitting, or shoving. The Secret Service are forced to arrest approximately 100 people per year for causing or attempting to cause disruptions at the White House. Gottesman and Bertelson (1989) found that of 328 people attempting to cause problems at the White House, 91% met the criteria for schizophrenia. It is clear from these statistics that the mentally ill do engage in certain behaviors that are likely to bring police action. While often officers are called upon for transportation to acute psychiatric units or emergency rooms, other situations do arise which call for more finite and definitive policing skills necessary to adequately handle the mentally ill.

In an article by Arcaya (1989), a psychoanalytic framework is postulated which describes the essential psychological functioning of the mentally ill patient and the effective means for dealing with such a person. Based on Freud's popular id, ego, and superego models of intrapsychic functioning, the mentally ill patient is believed by Arcaya to be suffering from a number of specific deficits. These deficits are concerned with issues relating to confrontations and power struggles between the id, ego, and superego and their concomitant manifested behaviors. He states that, "in sensitizing the police officer to think of disturbed behavior in terms of competing psychic forces rather than individual traits or characteristics (e.g., 'Crazy people say one thing when they mean another.') psychoanalytic theory focuses the police officer's attention on a potential root cause of the manifest disturbance" (p. 41).

Through these means, a more effective method for dealing with the mentally ill is described which consists of improving the patient's contact with reality, managing the superego, and managing the id. For example, in improving the patient's contact with reality, the officer may wish to use a direct or indirect method of clarifying reality. This may mean describing and defining exactly what is taking place to the mentally ill person during a confrontation.

An experiment conducted by Finn and Stalans (1997) showed that police officers tend to have certain preconceived notions regarding male versus female victims and assailants. Mentally ill assailants in particular were shown to be viewed in a somewhat different light than their nonmentally ill counterparts. The study examined the influence of assailant or victim role, gender, and mental status on police officers' attitudes regarding both assailants' and victims' naïveté, passiveness, dangerousness, future criminality, psychological sickness, responsibility, credibility, blameworthiness, and control over actions. It was hypothesized by the researchers that if mental state was a large contributing factor in officers' inferences, then both male and female assailants who display signs of mental illness would be less capable of understanding the wrongfulness of violence, should be less passive, more dangerous, more likely to engage in future crime, more psychologically sick, less responsible, less credible, less blameworthy, and less in control of their actions than assailants who are not mentally ill.

The researchers found (based on reactions to fictional vignettes) that stereotypes of the mentally ill appeared to shape officers' beliefs and inferences regarding assailants when signs of mental illness were recognized. More specifically, mentally ill assailants were believed to be more dangerous and less in control regardless of their gender. Further, findings suggested that when no mental illness was evident in the vignettes, gender stereotyping did take place (Finn & Stalans, 1997).

Forensic Psychology and Policy Implications

Given the current state of police attitude, inference, and beliefs regarding the mentally ill, what can be done to improve the knowledge base surrounding this issue? Clearly, literature and programs designed to improve police officers' understanding of the handling and treatment of the mentally ill are lacking (Patch & Arrigo, 1999). What information does exist tends to be limited in scope. However, certain programs have been implemented, with varying degrees of success, in an attempt to help bridge the gap between the mentally ill and law enforcement procedures and policies.

Mentally ill persons very often find themselves in jail for committing an act which has broken the law in some way. Often, the mentally ill are incarcerated in a jail setting not because they are criminals, per se, but because there are no other available resources to utilize at the time of the offense (V. B. Brown, Ridgely, Petter, Levine, & Ryglewicz, 1989).

Abram and Teplin (1991) found that the vast majority of 728 severely ill jail inmates met criteria for alcohol disorders, drug disorders, or antisocial personality disorder. Further, these inmates were found to have other comorbid psychiatric disorders. The researchers concluded that codisordered arrestees require mental health policy development in three key areas: improving the treatment of the codisordered when they are in crisis, improving the jails' identification of and response to the codisordered mentally ill, and developing community treatment facilities to address the needs of the codisordered mentally ill. These same researchers concluded that there is little choice but to reform the current health care delivery system in order to accommodate and properly treat the mentally disordered in jail.

Alleviating problems such as those just described may start at a more basic level by invoking mandatory mentally ill training sessions for police officers. These training sessions are designed to keep the mentally ill from initially ending up in jail, as they do currently, making it more difficult to remove them from those conditions after the fact. Educational sessions appear to be a useful concept in this regard.

Godschalx (1984) described a program developed to educate police officers on the various aspects of mental illness in an attempt to have them deal more effectively and efficiently with this population, in addition to helping the officers more accurately understand the psychological processes involved with the mentally ill. A brief questionnaire was given to a sample of officers before undergoing a training session on the mentally ill. After the educational program was completed, the questionnaire was administered again. Officers not attending the program were shown to make no change in their understanding of mental illness. Conversely, those who completed the program understood a statistically significant greater amount about the mentally ill. However, these same officers did not change their inherent attitudes toward mental illness despite the training.

These results beg the question of whether police officers should be mandated to learn more in-depth information regarding the mentally ill so as not to make faulty decisions regarding their treatment. Policy implications relating to these findings are good evidence that programs of this nature should be implemented.

Suggestions for Future Research

Areas related to future research are, not surprisingly, wide open. The few articles described here are valuable contributions to the study of the police and the mentally ill. Virtually any other scientific information which could advance the understanding of police officers' perceptions regarding the mental ill is in need.

More specifically, pre- and post-test evaluations of police officers' training in, and understanding of, the mentally disordered would be of value in detecting the understanding of the police officers' learning curve on the mentally ill. Further, data obtained from mentally ill persons themselves would permit a converse view of the treatment of the mentally ill by police officers or law enforcement in general. This would allow for further understanding of the effective and ineffective manners in which to handle different types of police situations involving the mentally ill.

Finally, research on the effectiveness of various educational programs is sorely needed in order to promote advancement of officers' understandings of the mentally ill. Conceivably, once greater understanding is achieved, better decisions regarding crisis intervention and the physical handling of patients may lead to the deescalation of potentially dangerous situations, thus making the police force's ability to deal with the mentally ill that much more effective.

COMMUNITY POLICING: TRENDY OR EFFECTIVE?

Introduction

The past several decades have witnessed a dramatic rise in crime rates and a growing distrust of police officers. This phenomenon is particularly evident in low socioeconomic communities and among ethnic minorities. According to T. M. Joseph (1994), from 1961 to 1994 the violent crime rate rose over 500% and total crimes rose more than 300%. In addition, he reports that while citizens fear becoming victims of crime, they have a growing tolerance to criminal activity and its impact on their communities. In order to combat crime rates and the deteriorating relationships between police officers and members of the community, many police departments are implementing community-oriented policing (Thurman et al., 1993).

Community-oriented policing is an attempt to move the focus of law enforcement from reaction to criminal activity to prevention of crime. While no single definition of "community-oriented policing" exists, a broad definition is a combination of strategies designed to prevent crime through the establishment of a strong community/police relationship. Skogan (1994) identified various strategies that are utilized with this approach:

> opening small neighborhood substations, conducting surveys to identify local problems, organizing meetings and crime prevention seminars, publishing newsletters, helping form Neighborhood Watch groups, establishing advisory panels to inform police commanders, organizing youth activities, conducting drug educations projects and media campaigns, patrolling on horses and bicycles, and working with municipal agencies to enforce health and safety regulations. (pp. 167–168)

Despite the advantages associated with the cooperation and collaboration between citizens and police officers, the implementation of these strategies has presented many challenges for administrators and officers. The ambiguity in defining community policing has raised concerns. Issues such as the community's willingness to participate and officers' attitudes regarding community policing have caused many to question if this policing strategy is a viable solution to crime prevention or just another ineffective trend in law enforcement. Consider the following case illustration.

Dear Lakeshore Police Department,

   This letter is in regard to the recent change in policing procedures in my neighbor-hood. While I am appreciative that your department has taken notice of the rampant crime in this community, as a resident I have many concerns. Not a day goes by that I do not hear gunshots or see some adolescent on the street selling drugs. Gangs and drugs seem to have taken over our community and many residents do not feel safe in their own homes. Although this neighborhood is full of crime, most people living here are not criminals. I am a single mother struggling to raise two school-age children.

   I have heard on the news and read in the paper that your department is implementing "community policing" in our neighborhood. I have heard of Neighborhood Watch programs and the like but usually in upscale neighborhoods. Having more officers on foot patrol and a substation on our block will make me feel safer and will hopefully reduce crime. However, I would not feel comfortable providing tips about neighborhood crime or testifying in court about any crimes I have witnessed. I have no doubt that some form of retaliation against my children, home, or myself would be inevitable.

   Unfortunately, many residents keep to themselves and frequently distrust the police. I fear that my neighbors would label me a "snitch" if I were to join a police-run organi-zation. While I hope this new approach will make the neighborhood safer, community participation would surprise me. Once again, I appreciate that your department has taken steps toward reducing crime in this neighborhood.

Sincerely,
Sandra

Literature Review

For the past 20 years, the trend in anticrime policy has been to implement com-munity policing. During the 1970s and 1980s, the citizen's role in solving crime was the focus in police research (Rosenbaum & Lurigio, 1994). The fact that pri-vate citizens were often major factors in solving crimes or obtaining arrests was the foundation for community policing. Research found that low clearance rates in most police departments could be attributed to the lack of useful tips offered to officers (Eck, 1982; Rosenbaum & Lurigio, 1994). Residents of a neighborhood are usually the best sources regarding problems in their communities (Pate, Wycoff, Skogan, & Sherman, 1986). However, police departments must consider if citizens like Sandra would be willing to participate. This issue is particularly relevant in areas with high crime rates.

   The first attempt to make law enforcement more community oriented occurred with team policing. In 1967, the police task force of the President's Commission on Law Enforcement and the Administration of Justice suggested team policing as a way to improve the relationship between line officers and the community. Team policing consisted of long-term beat assignments and "walk-and-talk" foot patrols. Problems with implementation led to the failure of team policing. The problems associated with decentralized decision making were credited with the downfall of this approach. It was discredited by the majority of police departments by the end of the 1970s (Rosenbaum & Lurigio, 1994).

However, the 1980s saw the rise of community policing. Despite the ambiguity of this concept, common themes are mentioned by Rosenbaum (1988), which include "an emphasis on improving the number and quality of police–citizen contacts, a broader definition of 'legitimate' police work, decentralization of the police bureaucracy, and a greater emphasis on proactive problem-solving strategies" (p. 334). Typically, this approach has been utilized in specialized units and within specific police districts. It has yet to be implemented departmentwide throughout a large police organization (Rosenbaum & Lurigio, 1994).

According to Cordner (1997), community policing has become the dominant strategy of policing in the 1990s. In fact, the 1994 Crime Bill mandated that 100,000 newly funded police officers must be involved in community policing. However, Cordner points out the difficulty of producing reliable knowledge regarding the effectiveness of community policing. He maintains that most community policing studies have considerable research design limitations that include lack of control groups, nonrandom treatments, and the tendency to only measure short-term effects. While very few studies have used experimental designs and victimization surveys to evaluate the effect of community policing on crime, many studies have utilized before–after comparisons and single-item victimization questions taken from community surveys (Cordner, 1997). Due to methodological limitations, researchers argue that credible evaluations of this approach do not exist, leaving police officers, citizens, and forensic psychologists to debate whether community policing works.

Although the results are mixed, the fear of crime and calls for service are reduced due to the police–citizen contact with community policing (Cordner, 1997). In addition, the overwhelming number of studies suggest that community relations are improved. Residents in Sandra's neighborhood need to obtain a better perception of the police in order to create a productive alliance. According to Skogan (1994), 9 of 14 areas in six cities using community policing demonstrated improvement in the community's perception of the police. In addition, seven areas had a decrease in the fear of crime, six areas reduced their perceptions of neighborhood disorder, and victimization rates were lower in three areas. Critics maintain that these results should be viewed with caution as they only represent short-term results and questionable methodologies.

Studies investigating officers' job satisfaction have generally shown positive results. However, these results do not represent long-term effects or all officers, just those in specialized units (Cordner, 1997). Conflict between officers in these specialized units and those in the rest of the department has been consistently found. Research indicates that many officers who are not working in a substation or on another beat utilizing community policing view these assignments as social work rather than as real police work (Rosenbaum & Lurigio, 1994). T. M. Joseph (1994) maintains that the collapse of social institutions such as the deterioration of the traditional family structure, the lack of affordable housing and health care, and the paucity of residential care for the mentally ill have created the need for a more humanistic, collaborative approach to policing. The perception that community service officers do less work under more favorable conditions adds to the resentment felt by other officers (J. Patterson, 1995). Resentment can also be felt by neighborhoods that are not targeted by community policing.

Another criticism of community policing is that community membership in neighborhood or block organizations usually includes only a small portion of residents and even fewer are active members (Buerger, 1994). In addition, membership is typically ". . . dominated by homeowners and by White residents in racially mixed areas" (Buerger, 1994, p. 412). Research suggests that citizens in neighborhoods that need community policing are frequently the most distrustful of the police. This phenomenon was illustrated by Sandra's letter. The fear of retaliations from drug dealers or gang members as a result of cooperating with the police can also hinder community involvement (T. M. Joseph, 1994).

Forensic Psychology and Policy Implications

The research clearly demonstrates the need for more systematic evaluations of community policing programs. Anticrime policy needs to be supported by social science research reflecting long-term effects and rigorous methodologies. Forensic psychologists can undertake the task of program evaluation and the testing of new policing strategies in order to help identify those which are most effective. Kennedy and Moore (1997) state that,

> [b]y implication, since social science does not now play this role in policing on any large scale, social science, practiced by outsiders, should gradually come to be a considerably more central and influential part of policing than is currently the case. (p. 474)

The forensic psychologist has the benefit of training in research methodologies, criminological theories, and criminal justice administration.

Community policing is an attempt to foster stronger relationships between officers and the community to facilitate crime prevention. In order for this approach to work, police departments must shift the focus of training from paramilitaristic techniques to those that promote cooperation with citizens. Walters (1993) indicates that the highest standards of discipline and professionalism must be exhibited by officers to maintain credibility and involvement from the communities. Careful personnel selection and training is critical, particularly with regard to police discretion. Forensic psychologists can assist this process by utilizing psychological tests and employment interviews or screenings.

In addition, criminal justice administrators must be sensitive to the needs of both the citizens in the community and those of the police officers. Large-scale implementation of this approach is needed. Department-wide training and implementation of community policing strategies will provide more useful information about its effectiveness and reduce the animosity between officers. However, cost effectiveness remains a critical issue.

The cooperation between citizens and officers could lead to more arrests and crime prevention. The more traditional role of officers does not encourage community participation in decision making and strategy in law enforcement. Forensic psychologists can assist police departments and communities in adopting a more social problems-oriented approach to crime prevention. However, whether community policing is an effective means of crime prevention remains to be seen.

Suggestions for Future Research

Much research is needed to determine if community policing works. In additon to finding ways by which to evaluate the approach, new ways of determining officer performance must be created. The traditional means, such as number of arrests and the number of tickets issued, are not appropriate performance measures for community-oriented police officers (T. M. Joseph, 1994). The utilization of proactive techniques for crime prevention and a greater response to community demands has fostered the need for creative ways to answer increasing calls for police service (Walters, 1993).

Another important aspect of this approach is community participation. Research into what encourages this participation and individual expectations is needed (Buerger, 1994). What would convince a resident like Sandra to participate in community policing? The concerns of those residents least likely to trust officers need to be explored in order for this approach to be effective in the communities that would benefit the most. Specific problems within the target areas identified must be carefully examined in order to implement the most effective strategies. Rosenbaum and Lurigio (1994) suggest that the continued use of case study methodology would provide more accurate and complete data on the effectiveness and long-term effects of community policing. In addition, these authors maintain, "[t]he process of working together and the barriers to cooperative relationships are essential for future research" (p. 304).

POLICE TRAINING: COMMUNICATION SKILLS AND CONFLICT RESOLUTION

Introduction

The nature of a police officer's job requires routine interaction with members of the public. Often, these encounters entail the resolution of some existing, or potentially existing, conflict. Through domestic disturbances, communication with victims and offenders, interviewing witnesses, answering citizen questions, making arrests, and giving citations, to name a few, communication with the public and, thus, occasional conflict, is inevitable and potentially harmful in consequence. The police officer, beyond nearly any other profession, must be capable and effective in communicative abilities and processes of resolving conflict. As a result, training and education in matters of conflict resolution and skill in interpersonal communication play fundamental roles in police interactions.

These issues stress the necessity of proper police training and education in effective communication and conflict resolution. In addition, the employment of officers who are capable of assessing the situation, finding the most appropriate tactic, and actually using that technique to benefit the encounter becomes important. This section discusses some of the issues with regard to police officers and conflict resolution skills. Commonly used tactics as well as tactics which are not commonly practiced by police officers, yet would arguably be more effective in some situations, are addressed.

> Two officers were dispatched to [a] halfway house where resident Henry had been causing a disturbance. The staff wanted him expelled. The first officer to arrive gave him an intense lecture. Henry, feeling unjustly chastised, walked off and went outside. The officer grabbed him by the back of the shirt and told him he was not finished talking to him. Henry pushed the officer and the officer pushed back. A backup officer arrived at the scene and stepped in between the two men just before the situation got out of control. Through the use of verbal skills he calmed Henry and helped his fellow officer regain composure. He then persuaded the staff members into allowing Henry to remain at the center. Henry agreed to modify his behavior. The result? Because of good communication skills on the second officer's part, everyone was appeased (Woodhull, 1993).

Literature Review

Police officers estimate that 75–90% of their time is spent in some form of communication (Woodhull, 1993). Training in communication skills, however, has failed to reflect this fact. An estimation of training time allocated to learning communication skills is less than 10%. One officer noted, in addressing the significance of communication in his work, that communication is the basis for all police work and is necessary for the effective enforcement of laws (Woodhull, 1993). Thus, police officers are aware of the large portion of time that is spent in communicating with the public. Further, they recognize the importance of being adequately trained in that area. Administrators and educators also agree that police officers need to be trained in interpersonal communication (Woodhull, 1993).

The necessity of communicative abilities, and failure of existing training programs to acknowledge the importance of communication and conflict skills, is illustrated in current training programs. Woodhull (1993) notes that police officers "undergo more intense training than perhaps any other professionals" (p. 4). Officers are extensively trained in the use of firearms and subsequently required to demonstrate proficiency in firearm use. Most officers, however, will rarely, if ever, use their weapons in the line of duty. In contrast, officers will inevitably spend most of their time communicating, but are not as extensively trained in such skills. This contradiction was alluded to over 2000 years ago by Aristotle, who claimed that people should not train themselves in fist-and-weapon tactics while neglecting to train themselves in verbal tactics (Woodhull, 1993). As communication characterizes the human being, effective communication can develop understanding, while ineffective communication can result in violence (Woodhull, 1993). Thus, even before the day of the modern police officer, the importance of communication versus physical tactics in human encounters was well understood. Given the extent of communication in a police officer's job, and the significance of effective skills, we need to examine some of the reasons why conflict occurs between police and citizens.

The police are asked to maintain public order, including defusing volatile or potentially volatile situations. As noted earlier, these situations may involve criminal, disorderly, intoxicated, and/or mentally ill citizens; individuals who are angry about more general police practices or motivated by political views; and a host of other situations. The instability of citizens in these encounters creates significant risk to the officers, the citizen, and the bystanders (L. Wrightsman, Nietzel, & Fortune, 1994). Often, these disputes between police officers and the public exist because of differing opinions about the duties of police officers. The *role* of police officers is an area where there has been much disagreement among scholars, the public, and the police. There is general agreement that the police officer's job consists of multiple duties, including situations where no crime has occurred. In addition to law enforcement practices (crime detection, making arrests, questioning individuals about criminal activity, etc.), the police must concern themselves with keeping peace, maintaining order, and servicing the public in general. While the disagreement often revolves around exactly what duties the police are responsible for, there is little debate that the job includes dealing with many different types of problems (Brooks, 1997).

Public encounters may result in conflict when the officer's perception of his or her duties or role differs from the citizen's perception (Bennett & Hess, 1996). A prime example is the otherwise upstanding citizen who is cited or ticketed for a traffic violation and replies, "Why are you bothering me when there are real criminals running around on the streets . . . Don't you have anything better to do with your time?" Such complaints are common in police work and often open the door for conflict. Once one understands the motivating factors behind conflict situations, the next step is to understand the other side. In other words, what are some basic tactics of conflict resolution and how are they employed by police officers?

Tactics of conflict resolution include a large group of behaviors which are intended to either gain compliance in an interaction or resolve the interaction in a way satisfactory to both parties (C. Wilson & Gross, 1994). Such tactics are necessary when two parties have goals or desires in an encounter which are incompatible, yet the interaction must end in some sort of compromise. This scenario describes the great majority of interactions involving the police and the public. The question becomes, "What tactics do police officers generally employ in public situations, and what other (better) options are available to them?"

C. Wilson and Gross (1994) note that the tactics officers use are dependent upon the citizens' socioeconomic status, gender, ethnicity, and age. Chosen tactics have also been related to the degree of citizen compliance and perception of intoxication (R. Worden, 1989), as well as to the neighborhood in which the encounter occurs and the specific police department's attitude toward tactics for gaining compliance (D. Smith & Klein, 1984). Toch (1985) and others have implied that the attitude of specific officers upon entering an interaction can increase the likelihood of a conflict occurring or even escalating. Some officers, whose chosen goal is to obtain compliance from the citizen, may behave in a way that increases the probability of a negative (confrontative or escalated) interaction. These officers may perceive coercive tactics as the most effective available strategy for dealing with the situation. On the other hand, officers who prefer problem-solving tactics would be less likely to increase the existing tension in the interactions with citizens (C. Wilson & Gross, 1994). Problem solving is one method of *nonconventional* conflict resolution to which we now turn our attention.

Common, or conventional, methods of conflict resolution for police officers include legitimate use of physical force, arrest, coercion and/or threats to arrest, and avoidance (Cooper, 1997). These tactics are commonly employed in conflict situations and admittedly are necessary on occasion. The issue is whether more appropriate tactics are available that would allow an officer to address a volatile (or potentially volatile) situation in a more productive and less injurious way. Cooper (1997) refers to methods which do not involve force, coercion, or arrest as *nonconventional* conflict-resolution methods. These methods include mediation, arbitration, third-party negotiation, facilitation, reconciliation, counseling, problem solving, and problem management. He contends that these methods are suitable for addressing situations such as "disputes or conflicts characterized as public, barricade situations, community-based, and interpersonal" conflict (p. 88). Further, the effectiveness of such techniques on a global scale requires not only increased usage, but also perfecting the *manner* in which they are used. A more in-depth discussion of the various methods previously outlined is not necessary here. The point worth noting is that there are a number of conflict-resolution tactics available to police officers which may not be typically employed, but are useful in the appropriate situations.

Forensic Psychology and Policy Implications

Given the extent and nature of conflict between police and citizens, as well as the large majority of time officers spend in communicative encounters, the need for training is undeniable. It is apparent that existing policy for training officers in communication skills, as well as extended training throughout their careers, is currently inadequate in many departments. In the case of Henry, the first officer to arrive on the scene was clearly not effective in communicative abilities. His communication, in fact, escalated the conflict rather than brought it to a peaceful resolution. Based on the story, we can assume that the first officer's attempt to initially communicate with Henry was ineffective for a number of reasons. Namely, his "intense lecture" immediately left Henry feeling like the officer was against him, not with him or for him. Naturally, Henry's perception was that the officer was there to lecture him and punish him rather than peacefully resolve a conflict between Henry and the staff. Later, when Henry felt "chastised" and walked away, the officer responded with an even more authoritarian attitude, bringing threats and physical force into the interaction. At this point, the encounter could have easily become unnecessarily inflated to the point of violence and the arrest of Henry. Luckily, the second officer arrived on the scene in time to calm the situation. The communication and conflict-resolution skills of the second officer became vitally important, and a potentially explosive conflict was controlled.

Approaching a situation as did the first officer in Henry's case will regret-tably create unnecessary consequences for citizens and police. The more aware the public becomes of such behavior and the more communicative conflicts that citizens themselves have with officers, the more likely society is to doubt and disrespect the police. For police to enjoy the kind of relationship it aspires to maintain with citizens, communicating effectively becomes as important as other duties. Whenever possible, resolving volatile or conflict situations without the use of unnecessary force, threat, or arrest should be the goal of every police officer. Consequently, natural communicative ability and effective training become a necessity.

More recently, psychology has made important contributions to police–citizen conflict situations. Generally, psychologists are called upon to educate the police about matters such as dealing with the mentally ill, hostage situations, domestic violence situations, and other crises (L. Wrightsman et al., 1994). Psychology has proven an effective tool for developing approaches to such situations but has more to offer than just training. The knowledge of human relations and general communication skills establishes a place for psychology in the education and training of police officers. Further, psychology avails itself well to the establishment and ongoing evaluation of training programs. Forensic psychology, in its mutual regard for psychological and criminal justice matters, has established a place for itself in police administration and consultation. Recently, more departments are realizing the value that psychology can bring and are beginning to employ psychologists in roles outside of the traditional clinical and crisis situations. Police departments are beginning to realize the importance of officers having the necessary communicative skills (like the second officer in the scenario with Henry) and thus are looking to increase training in such areas in the future.

With regard to policy implications, Cooper's (1997) work on nonconventional conflict-resolution methods has particular relevance for the police administrator and policy maker. Addressing nonconventional conflict-resolution techniques provides information on how and why these processes are appropriate and effective interventions for police officers and where and when they are appropriate for use. Finally, Cooper's work allows us to understand the organizational and professional climate which are essential for these tactics to be effectively taught and administered.

Cooper (1997) addresses more specifically one of the necessary prerequisites for a successful nonconventional approach to conflict resolution. He states that police departments must recruit officers who have either had professional training or are intellectually capable of engaging in professional training in conflict resolution. The objective, he adds, is "to recruit personnel who possess the intellect to become conflict/dispute resolution professionals" (p. 97). Officers must be capable of "diagnosing the dispute, selecting the appropriate response, and employing it" (p. 97). This approach is itself nonconventional, as intellectual capacity of potential police officers is not typically the primary concern of departments. While education is, of late, assuming a more significant role, there still exists a tendency to favor training as more important (Bennett & Hess, 1996).

Turning our attention to why police officers do *not* favor nonconventional techniques, we can examine the traditional concept of the "real job" of police officers. Dating back to the conception of policing, there is a measurement of good policing based on the absence of crime. This measurement of whether police are doing a "good" job does not consider the manner, or specific behavioral ways, in which officers *do* their job. As a result, many officers view their job as getting the criminal element off of the streets. Society and police administration have not traditionally accepted any opposing views. Thus, officer performance is often measured by the number of arrests one makes, not necessarily how the arrest was made or the arrests one didn't have to make because of "good" policing. Consequently, officers are not rewarded for the application of nonconventional conflict resolution skills, as the defusing of a dispute without arrest is not measurable by traditional means (Cooper, 1997).

These considerations may impede the development of nonconventional educational and training programs for police officers. They may further dissuade officers from using such techniques, even if the officer is capable of using them. Though not traditionally practiced in law enforcement, nonconventional conflict-resolution tactics provide police officers with a "toolkit" of sorts for approaching the various kinds of disputes and conflict they may encounter in the field.

Suggestions for Future Research

Given the increasing public awareness and citizen complaints regarding police use of force, brutality, and "attitude," such nonconventional tactics are worthy of additional research and consideration on the policy level. Certainly, additional research needs to be done on the effectiveness of nonconventional tactics and their applicability to various situations. The lack of officer training in nonconventional techniques and communication skills in general makes them difficult to employ and even more difficult to measure in terms of their effectiveness. Situations such as Henry's provide convincing evidence of the positive benefits of communication and nonthreatening and nonforceful measures by the police. The fact that, as of yet, appropriate education and training is often not supplied renders only speculative accounts of the effectiveness and usefulness of these methods.

POLICING MINORITY POPULATIONS

Introduction

Research has demonstrated that police officers are given discretion in enforcing victimless crimes such as traffic violations (Hecker, 1997; Schifferle, 1997). As a result, a police officer's personal biases may have an effect on whom he or she chooses to stop. Research from the 1970s indicates that in predominantly African American precincts in Boston, Chicago, and Washington, over three-quarters of the Caucasian policemen expressed highly prejudiced attitudes (Wintersmith, 1974). More recent occurrences do not indicate that police attitudes toward minorities, particularly African Americans, have changed. Despite ex-Los Angeles Police Department (LAPD) officer Mark Fuhrman's outward expression of racism, making statements such as "Anything out of a nigger's mouth for the first five or six sentences is a f... lie ..." (Texeira, 1995, p. 235), he was not fired from the police department. Instead, Mark Fuhrman was promoted and given the best assignments (Texeira, 1995).

Although not all police officers share the same racist attitudes, many officers say that there is a code of silence to which they must conform, or at least pretend to conform, based on the beliefs of other officers (Texeira, 1995). Police recruits do not necessarily bring a racist attitude to the job with them; they learn it from older, more experienced officers who expect the new officers to conform (Wintersmith, 1974). Because many police organizations foster racist attitudes, it is not surprising that minorities tend to be targeted for traffic stops and for suspicion of criminal activity (Hecker, 1997; Schifferle, 1997; Texeira, 1995). In fact, African Americans are targeted so much more than Caucasians that there is a violation many African Americans refer to as D.W.B., that is, "driving while black" (Hecker, 1997). The following scenario is an example of a traffic stop based on race, which clearly outlines how discrimination occurs in policing and helps to explain why African-American citizens would coin a term such as D.W.B.

> Ben, a 30-year-old African-American man living in Maryland, recently graduated from law school and started working at a law firm. He went and purchased a new red Lexus to celebrate his new job and graduation from law school. One weekend, Ben was driving his Lexus when he noticed a Caucasian police officer following him. He was not wearing his usual suit, as it was the weekend, and was wearing jeans, a T-shirt, and a hat instead. Ben continued to drive and was extra cautious because the police officer continued to follow him. Ben finally came to his exit and turned on his signal to exit right. After he exited, the police officer pulled him over, indicating he violated a traffic law; Maryland law requires a signal be activated at least 100 feet before turning right.
>
> When the officer pulled Ben over, he asked if he could search the vehicle. At this point Ben realized he was the victim of discrimination. Ben told the officer he could not search the vehicle and that the Constitution prohibited the police from searching the vehicle without reasonable suspicion of crime. The officer ordered Ben out of his car and called a unit with a narcotics dog in to search the vehicle. The officer found nothing illegal, left Ben with a warning about the signal law, and drove away (Hecker, 1997).

This section utilizes the case of Ben to explain how current law allows police to use complete discretion in enforcing the law, discusses how this discretion may effect minority populations socially, reviews arguments that suggest police racism does not occur, and examines the policy implications for this controversy. Because most research on this topic has been conducted specifically on the African-American community, racial bias toward African Americans is primarily discussed. This focus does not imply that other minority populations are not discriminated against or are unworthy of discussing; there is certainly a need for research in this field.

Literature Review

Research clearly indicates that police discrimination toward minorities exists. However, the issue is more complex than racism among officers. There are laws that actually allow such racism to occur. There are psychological issues for both the police officers and the minorities affected by discrimination, and there are policies that can be adopted to reduce the likelihood of discrimination. Although the case of Ben is fictional, it is an accurate description of what has occurred to many upstanding African Americans. In 1996, a journalist who interviewed delegates to the Black Caucus convention reported that nearly every delegate he spoke with, including doctors, lawyers, and professors, had been stopped by police on several occasions without being cited a traffic violation (Hecker, 1997).

The Law and Discretion

Selective law enforcement has always been used to oppress minorities (Schifferle, 1997). For example, in 19th-century Oregon, "[c]hinese were more than sixty percent of all persons arrested for violations of city ordinances during the years of 1871–1885" (Schifferle, 1997, p. 4). Although police may or may not use selective enforcement to oppress minorities as they did years ago, they do use selective enforcement. One researcher describes how the jail at the police station in which she worked was filled with Mexican and African Americans, and the watch sergeant never questioned it (Texeira, 1995). Unfortunately, the law allows for such selective overenforcement because there are no guidelines or limitations helping police determine when they should or should not enforce a law. Although there is no specific law that allows it, police have nearly unlimited discretion in deciding whether to enforce a particular violation (Hecker, 1997; Schifferle, 1997).

The traffic code is where many police exercise selective enforcement (Schifferle, 1997). Police are given discretion in determining who to stop for traffic violations or when they suspect criminal activity (Hecker, 1997; Schifferle, 1997). Traffic stops have been used by police officers who suspect criminal activity such as drug trafficking (Schifferle, 1997). Ben was a victim of such selective enforcement. Police officers saw an African-American man dressed in casual clothing driving an expensive vehicle and automatically suspected criminal activity. Much of the justification for such stops are gang and drug-dealer profiles. Police departments have compiled information on what the "typical" drug dealer or gang member looks like (Hecker, 1997; Schifferle, 1997). Such profiles result in stereotyping in which police equate race with criminal activity (Schifferle, 1997). Most likely, police suspected Ben to be a drug dealer and police profiles of drug dealers probably supported their belief. A police officer can pull over any automobile, and if he or she needs justification for such a stop, the officer is allowed to follow a vehicle until a traffic violation occurs (Hecker, 1997). If a police officer has reasonable cause to believe that the individual is breaking another law, such as drug trafficking, he or she may conduct a plain-view search of the vehicle and seek consent for a complete search. If the individual does not consent to the search, a narcotics dog can be brought in to search the vehicle for drugs; this is exactly what happened in Ben's case.

Traffic stops have been challenged in court cases, providing some limits to such stops. For example, in *Terry v. Ohio* (1968), the Supreme Court indicated searches and seizures without probable cause could only be conducted if the officer has a reasonable suspicion of criminal activity (Hecker, 1997; E. Long, Long, Leon, & Weston, 1975). This ruling also indicates that reasonable suspicion requires "specific and articulable facts which, taken together with rational inferences from those facts, reasonably warrant" a search (Hecker, 1997, p. 7). Although this ruling attempted to protect minorities from unreasonable searches, it most likely does little. Police profiles of drug traffickers and gang members provide police the factual information they need to justify stopping and searching vehicles.

Another more recent case that challenged traffic stops was the case of Michael Whren (*United States of America v. Whren*, 1997). Whren and another occupant in his car were driving a Nissan Pathfinder with temporary plates in Washington, DC. Officers in an unmarked car indicated that the driver was not paying full attention to his or her driving and followed the vehicle to investigate. When the officers pulled alongside the Pathfinder, they saw plastic bags that appeared to be drugs. The police then arrested the driver and passenger, searched the vehicle, and found more drugs. Michael Whren was convicted on four counts, all of which were possession of or intent to distribute drugs. However, Whren took his case to the U.S. Supreme court, claiming the stop was unreasonable under the Fourth Amendment and, as a result, the evidence was not obtained legally. However, the court ruled that, although the Constitution does not allow selective enforcement of the law, "the constitutional basis for objecting to intentionally discriminatory application of the laws is the Equal Protection Clause, not the Fourth Amendment" (Whren, as cited in Schifferle, 1997, p. 8). The ruling on Whren only provides that discretion not be based on race. Clearly, it would be difficult to prove whether a stop were based solely on race. In Ben's case, the officer could have claimed that Ben met the description of a drug trafficker, thus warranting a stop. Despite Constitutional protection against discrimination, it appears as though vague laws and stereotypical police profiles prevent true protection for minorities when selective enforcement of the law is considered. Minorities continuously report taking precautions such as wearing conservative clothing, driving conservative cars, and carefully obeying traffic laws to prevent being harassed by police officers (Hecker, 1997).

How Discretion Affects Minorities

Based on research that suggests police tend to target minority groups for traffic stops and drug investigations, it is not surprising that African Americans are disproportionately arrested in relation to their representation in the general population (Schifferle, 1997). In addition, although research does not specifically indicate the impact the high arrest rate has on the African-American population, one could speculate that the arrest rate perpetuates further stereotyping toward this population.

Police discretion effects minorities many ways, both socially and psychologically. Because police tend to single-out minorities for traffic stops, minorities, especially American Americans, tend to fear police harassment (Hecker, 1997). One might question how minorities could be able to perceive police as protectors and helpers in their communities when they are harassed by police officers. In a British study in which 641 Black, White, and Asian men were polled, researchers found that Blacks had worse perceptions of law enforcement officers than Whites and Asians. Although it is difficult to determine why Blacks had worse perceptions, the researchers indicate that Blacks perceived police discrimination. The case of Ben is an excellent example of how a successful, upstanding citizen who values the laws America is based on (he was an attorney) can develop a negative perception of police similar to the perceptions of Blacks in the British study. When Ben was stopped by the officer and forced to allow the canine to search his vehicle, most likely his respect for law enforcement officers deteriorated. As one author stated,

"The belief among a substantial segment of the population that law enforcement officers act with bias or prejudice undermines the authority and effectiveness of law enforcement and threatens law" (Hecker, 1997, p. 3).

Police Racism Does Not Occur

Despite evidence that suggests police discriminate against minorities and this discrimination has a negative impact upon these populations, there are arguments that suggest it is not police discrimination that results in such high arrest rates, there are other factors which account for the high arrest rates of African Americans.

Despite numerous examples of cases in which African Americans have been stopped by police for apparently no reason other than "driving while black," there are arguments against the notion that police officers are racist. Although some of the arguments do not deny that police target minority populations, they justify the targeting of such populations by suggesting that the offense rate among these populations is higher. The arguments defending police are that more minorities are arrested because the areas in which they live tend to be patrolled more, that more minorities are of low socioeconomic status and therefore commit more crime, and that minorities, African Americans more particularly, engage in more criminal activity than the general population, thus resulting in higher arrest rates (Schifferle, 1997; Texeira, 1995).

Wilbanks (as cited in Schifferle, 1997) provides several reasons why minorities are more likely to be arrested. He indicates that minority neighborhoods are subject to more police surveillance, which would lead to higher arrest rates. This argument is supported by other researchers as well (Texeira, 1995). However Texeira (1995) argues that such surveillance results from police racism toward minorities. Still, other researchers could argue that minority neighborhoods are watched more closely by police because minorities commit more crime. This appears to be the belief of Wilbanks who claims that differential offending by African Americans can explain for differences in arrest rates.

Other research indicates that minorities are more likely to be of low socioeconomic status (SES), which leads them to commit more crime (Jefferson & Walker, 1993). Researchers argue that only until SES is controlled in research on police bias will we be able to determine if it is police bias or low SES that results in disproportionately high arrest rates for minorities. While the notion of low SES may adequately explain the disproportionately high arrest rate for minorities, it does not explain for the significant number of minority traffic stops in which no traffic violation occurred (Schifferle, 1997).

There is no way to determine if the final argument, that African Americans commit more crime and are therefore arrested more than Caucasians, is true. Not all offenders are known to police, and an officer's decision not to arrest an offender may not be documented (Schifferle, 1997). Some researchers indicate racial bias plays a role in police decisions to arrest (Schifferle, 1997). Other researchers indicate police may be more suspicious of African Americans because they commit more crime. As a result, police stop African Americans more often, allowing police to uncover criminal activity (Wilbanks, as cited in Schifferle, 1997).

Although it is difficult to determine the actual cause of high arrest rates for minorities, research supports the notion that high arrest rates for African Americans in particular are at least partially due to racial bias of police officers. Although racial bias is apparent, it is difficult to determine if police bias toward minorities is due to institutionalized racism within the police organization or if police target racial minorities because minorities commit more crime. Nevertheless, action should be taken to ensure police are not discriminating against minorities.

Forensic Psychology and Policy Implications

Researchers and legal scholars have made suggestions that could prevent discriminatory traffic stops. Hecker (1997) suggests civilian review boards insist police agencies that have been accused of discriminatory law enforcement on several occasions report statistics on every police stop made. The act of recording the data alone may reduce police discrimination. Civilian review boards should question whether drug profiles are suggestive enough of criminal activity to warrant their use.

Another tactic which has already been used to prevent racism in the police force is to hire more minorities. In the 1980s the Detroit police force shed its reputation as being racist by hiring a police force that was 50% African American (Jackson, 1989). However, with the decreasing popularity of affirmative action, it is likely that a police organization's hiring of all minority and no Caucasian officers would meet with some opposition from the Caucasian communities.

Legal scholars have proposed other methods to limit police discretion. Although many scholars recognize that police discretion is necessary, some argue that discretion needs to be limited. Some scholars recommend judicially mandated internal police rulemaking to govern selective enforcement (Hecker, 1997). Other research suggests that departments develop guidelines for controlling police discretion. Although these guidelines would ideally help reduce the problem, it is questionable that they would be effective in reality, namely because racism is so ingrained in many police organizations.

Governmental policies need to be enacted that specifically constrain police discretion. In addition, police organizations accused of selective law enforcement should be required to report statistics on every individual stopped. Until policies are enacted to limit the amount of discretion police are given and to monitor the amount of race-based traffic stops, minorities will be unable to view police as their protectors.

Suggestions for Future Research

Most of the research on racism in policing focuses on African Americans, yet Latino Americans are also overrepresented in jail and prison populations, and there are reports of discrimination against Asian Americans. There is a clear need for research on selective law enforcement for all minority groups. There is also a need for research that deals with how selective enforcement impacts minority populations. Although the impact of selective enforcement was addressed in this section, much of the information was based on speculation due to lack of extensive research.

The case of Ben exemplified a situation that is a reality to many Americans. The occurrence of police-selective enforcement is unfortunate. Perhaps what is more unfortunate is the law's inability or unwillingness to protect minorities against such selective policing. Despite some research claiming that selective policing does not occur, most research indicates it does occur and on a regular basis. Several policy implications were indicated in this section; however, until action is taken to implement these policies, selective enforcement and racism in policing will continue.

CHAPTER 4

Family Forensics

OVERVIEW

At the crossroads of policing and psychology are controversies that affect adult and juvenile offenders as well as society in general. The previous three sections of Chapter 3 examined a number of crime and justice issues exploring these particular domains. However, another related area of inquiry in the field is law enforcement and family forensics. As developed in this chapter, family forensics refers to how the psychological sciences are or can be used to understand the manner in which police officers address domestic dilemmas in their own lives or in the lives of citizen-suspects.

The following section considers four topics that are squarely in the realm of law enforcement and family forensic psychology. These matters include (1) officers as mediators in domestic disputes, (2) police stress, (3) police work and family stress, and (4) homosexual police officers. While certainly not exhaustive, the four issues investigated in this section represent some of the more controversial concerns at the forefront of the family forensic area of policing and psychology.

Law enforcement personnel are called upon to resolve domestic disputes. To this extent, the police function as mediators attempting to peacefully settle family strife. What police methods are used to mediate family squabbles? What are the prevention strategies officers employ to quell protracted domestic violence?

Police work is stressful. This stress assumes many forms and impacts the family of which the officer is a member. How does substance abuse, the use of a firearm, work violence, and stigma contribute to an officer's experience of stress? How, if at all, do law enforcement personnel express their concerns about these experiences in their home life?

The stress of police work also directly impacts an officer's family members. This is not surprising since crime, suffering, and death are routine components of law enforcement. How do occupational stressors (e.g., shootings) create family trauma and turmoil? What is the impact of an officer's authoritarianism, cynicism, and violence on his/her family members? What support, if any (e.g., grief therapy), is provided to surviving spouses of officers killed in the line of duty? How do family members cope in the aftermath of an officer's suicide?

Increasing numbers of police officers identify themselves as gay or lesbian. Homosexual officers face obstacles that affect their status on the force as well as their role in the gay and lesbian community. In a manner of speaking, affiliations in both represent extended "families" for the homosexual officer. What is the level of stigma for gay versus lesbian police officers in the workforce? How do homosexual officers deal with conflicts on the job with other professionals? How do they deal with conflicts between other gay or lesbian citizens?

The controversies considered in this section suggest that law enforcement and psychology are undeniably linked in matters that affect the domestic life of officers, their families, and the public. As the specific topics collectively disclose, it is also clear that little attention has thus far been given to this important, though underexamined, area of forensic psychology. In an era where much is made about violence, crime, and our law enforcement response to it, it is essential that we not forget or overlook how matters of peace and justice also operate at the intersection of policing and psychology. As described in the pages that follow, the family forensic domain is evidence there is much to learn about the intricacies of this specialized field.

POLICE AS MEDIATORS IN DOMESTIC DISPUTES

Introduction

Domestic violence has occurred, and even been condoned, among certain cultures throughout history. In fact, the often-heard phrase "rule of thumb" actually refers to the old practice that a man could not beat his spouse with an object greater than the width of his thumb. It is unarguable that domestic violence is a pervasive societal problem and effects not only victims and their offenders, but also the police, who must deal with such a delicate, emotionally laden, and often controversial subject.

The following case illustration is a typical yet compelling scenario of a domestic violence situation.

> An officer is patrolling in his squad car when he receives a call from dispatch to respond to a complaint of domestic violence. The officer recognizes the address and mumbles to himself in an irritating manner, "Why, should I even bother to respond?" This address with this same complaint has occurred numerous times since his joining the police force some 13 years ago. This scenario happens about once a month. Typically, a complaint is received from Mrs. Jones that her husband is being verbally and often physically abusive and that she requires assistance immediately. However, each time an officer confronts this situation, Mrs. Jones refuses to cooperate with the arresting or prosecuting procedures, stating that her call to the police was premature, a mistake, and does not wish to prosecute despite her blackened eyes and bruised cheeks. Often, Mr. Jones is not present in the home, making it a waste of valuable time to try and find him.

Situations such as these are commonplace for the police officer who responds to domestic violence calls. Depending on the policy and procedures of the police department's jurisdiction, officers are instructed to deal with these situations differently. Some law enforcement departments have a mandatory arrest policy for the perpetrator as well as the victim. In a time of increased public concern and increased police involvement, officers are faced with the task of having to handle domestic disputes via mandatory arrest or through mediation.

A significant amount of literature exists on the dynamics, causes, prevention strategies, policing methods, and other topics related to this subject. Mediators are most often police officers who deal with these types of situations on a daily basis. The focus of this section is on the role of police officers as mediators in domestic disputes. A variety of aspects related to mediation in domestic disputes is examined including police practices and tactics, existing policies regarding offenders, recommendations, and prevention strategies.

Literature Review

Research indicates that about one-third of all police calls result from domestic disturbances in which intimate partners have engaged in loud or abusive arguments or even physical violence (Bell & Bell, 1991). As a result, police officers are forced to attend to such disputes in an effort to maintain order as well as to protect potential victims from imminent physical injury. Depending on the particular officer, they may or may not feel comfortable assisting in domestic violence calls due to lack of training or knowledge in the area of domestic violence and dispute resolution. Research indicates that police have historically been reluctant to intervene in domestic disputes (Bayley & Garofalo, 1989). It has been the attitude of many officers that social workers are better suited to deal with the social problem of domestic violence instead of law enforcement. Despite the idealism of this philosophy, it is an inherent duty of law enforcement to maintain order as well as to enforce the law.

The police response to domestic violence is regarded as a controversial and ever-changing social problem. Traditional responses to such disputes have several distinct characteristics. They include case screening, avoidance of intervention by police, and bias against arrest. Research indicates that historically less than 10% of domestic violence incidents were reported to the police (Buzawa & Buzawa, 1997). This suggests that due to socioeconomic and racial factors only a small minority of incidents were ever reported. Violence in middle to higher socioeconomic groups was often communicated to medical or religious personnel. The research also suggests that victims of domestic violence were often advised to contact social service entities instead of expecting the assistance of police officers. One study found that in a sample of cases, over two-thirds of domestic violence incidents were "solved" without the dispatch of officers (Buzawa & Buzawa, 1997). Because of the pervasive lack of social concern, these practices were unofficially accepted.

Historically, in regard to police attitudes and perceptions of domestic violence, research consistently shows that most police officers, regardless of individual or departmental characteristics, strongly dislike responding to domestic violence calls (Buzawa & Buzawa, 1997). There are several reasons for this which include organizational impediments, lack of training, police attitudes, and fear of injury.

Prior to the 1970s and 1980s almost all 50 states limited the police in arresting misdemeanor and domestic violence assaults. Police could only intervene with an arrest if they directly witnessed the assault. This policy affected police officers' perceptions regarding their role in domestic disputes. Many felt that their role was merely peripheral. Without being able to make arrests, they were limited in their abilities. In addition to organizational constraints, many officers have experienced a lack of training in the areas of domestic violence and conflict mediation. This further impedes their efforts to effectively combat the issue.

Traditionally, police departments denied the importance of their role in domestic violence because of society's view, organizational and legislative constraints, as well as a general lack of training and knowledge in the area; however, modern policies have changed dramatically. The catalyst to such change involved pioneer legislation in the state of Pennsylvania enacted in 1977. As a result, all 50 states, including the District of Columbia, passed domestic violence reforms. Depending on the jurisdiction, arrests were encouraged or even mandated by legislation. New statutory-specific domestic violence offenses have been incorporated into the criminal code. In contrast to traditional policing, punitive solutions are currently being emphasized.

Today some jurisdictions have mandatory arrest laws in which both the victim and the offender are taken into custody. Mandatory arrest laws have been studied by Mignon and Holmes (1995). Their research indicates that police officers were much more likely to arrest offenders when mandatory arrest laws were in place, particularly in cases of violation of restraining orders. In addition, it was discovered that two-thirds of offenders were not arrested and that physical assaults provided the strongest evidence for arrest. The greater the injury to the victim, the more likely the offender was arrested.

The police officer who responds to a domestic violence call must in some way play the role of a psychologist. Upon arriving at the scene of a domestic dispute, the officer must discriminate between conflicting stories, examine the psychological status of the victim, evaluate the potential dangerousness of the alleged offender, and provide support and comfort to the victim. Quantitatively, it has been found that a variety of factors contribute directly to an officer's decision to make an arrest. In order of importance they are (1) use of violence against police officers, (2) commission of a felony, (3) use of a weapon, (4) serious injury to the victim, (5) likelihood of future violence, (6) frequent calls for police assistance from household, (7) alcohol-/drug-intoxicated assailant, (8) disrespect for police officers, (9) previous injury to victim or damage to property, (10) previous legal action (restraining order), and (11) victim insists on arrest (Dolon, Hendricks, & Meagher, 1986). It is clear that the police officer must consider a large array of factors, either consciously or unconsciously, when faced with a domestic dispute. In addition to these influences, other variables such as personal attributes and officers' perceptions regarding their role in domestic violence will ultimately influence his or her decision to make an arrest.

Forensic Psychology and Policy Implications

The establishment of policies related to domestic violence took center stage in the feminist movement of the 1970s. During this time, it was demanded that policies and laws should be reformed to further protect a woman from her abusive partner (Stalans & Lurigio, 1995a; 1995b). Today, research exists that has attempted to make restitution and has influenced the further reformation of public policy relating to domestic disputes.

Breci and Simons (1987) postulate two basic models. The organizational effects model and the individual effects model. These models examine the influence of the police organization on the police officer's response to domestic disturbance calls and the characteristics of officers that may influence the officer's perceived role as a mediator of domestic violence. Testing of these models revealed that the organizational model relies heavily on the type of training received by police officers in handling such situations. Also, the officer's departmental role was found to be significantly related to the service response. The individual effects model testing revealed that attitudes, values, and perceptions play a major role in determining how police officers respond to domestic disputes. In addition, these attitudes, values, and perceptions are influenced to some degree by peers, education, police experience, and gender.

Research also indicates that mandatory arrest laws, overall, significantly contribute to increased arrest rates for domestic violence offenders. Although about 40 states currently have mandatory arrest laws, this policy should be extended to all states, with strict enforcement, in order to ensure complete protection regardless of geographical location.

Bail reform based on allowing the release of domestic offenders, only after a clarification hearing focusing on the offender's level of dangerousness, is also a possibility for policy reform. Changes in firearm possession restrictions for those who are deemed dangerous, as stated by the plaintiff, is another enhanced legislative procedure that would allow for further safety of abuse victims (Defina & Wetherbee, 1997).

Prevention should be the ultimate goal of any potentially violent situation. In 1991, the Massachusetts Criminal Justice Training Council and the Farmingham Police Department combined with local educators and victim advocacy groups to establish a program which attempted to lower domestic violence rates. This program targeted students in the 7th and 8th grades and educated them in the skills necessary to help them avoid destructive behaviors. The program was incorporated into local schools as part of a health class. Ideally, a female officer and a male teacher would inform the students, based on their own extensive training from experts in domestic violence, of the dangers, consequences, and avoidance methods of violent home situations. The initiation of this program, while too new to objectively evaluate, showed remarkable positive results as measured by students' attitudes toward violence in current or future relationships and other related measures of partner relations and violence (W. D. Baker, 1995).

As mentioned, the establishment of more informed and rigorous training programs for police officers is seen as the most important step in controlling or mediating domestic dispute situations. This, coupled with the implementation of available legal and social resources, is the method of choice for the Albuquerque Police Department. Legal and social resource availability such as domestic violence shelters, medical care, counseling, and even escorted transportation and assistance in the removal of items from the victim's residence, have shown to be powerful in developing immunity from civil liability as well as being a comforting force to the victims of domestic violence (Baca, 1987).

Suggestions for Future Research

There are a number of areas ripe for research in the field of domestic violence mediation. Research is needed that examines public support for different interventions in the criminal justice system. Victim counseling efficacy and financial/legal service usefulness has yet to be examined. Public perception and support for plea bargaining of offenders is under-researched, as are victims' views of the criminal justice system related to domestic violence (Stalans, 1996).

Other research could examine the effects of chronic spousal abuse on victims' psychological symptom development and their refusal to prosecute offenders. Also, more studies are needed that examine the psychological profiles of officers who deal with domestic violence situations.

Police attitudes toward domestic violence have been examined, albeit rarely, in the professional literature. However, comprehensive studies examining the relation between certain police personality characteristics such as cynicism and other possible causal or relational links to domestic violence responses are unstudied. Since domestic violence calls constitute such a large percentage of police responses, the dynamics of domestic abuse can also affect the police officer and not just the offender or victim.

Due to the process of change and controversies in domestic violence, the particular style of policing used by different officers within a department as well as between departments varies to a greater extent than before (Buzawa & Buzawa, 1997). Traditionally, police have avoided responding to domestic disputes, but due to societal change, police have been forced to deal with domestic disputes at increased frequencies. Because of the controversies associated with police responses to domestic violence, it is imperative that they receive adequate training to effectively deal with this issue. When looking at the case illustration of Mrs. Jones, the repeat nature of her domestic disputes and lack of follow-up may become very frustrating for the officers who respond. Depending on the departmental policy, the officer may have certain limitations, which may further frustrate him or her. Training by psychologists as mediators may help the officer learn effective methods to help reduce the frequency of incidents as well as to recommend other options for Mrs. Jones. By utilizing other agencies within the community, the officer may act as a liaison for victims of repeated violence.

POLICE STRESS

Introduction

Many different definitions from many different disciplines have attempted to define the term "stress." However, with such inherent issues as constant danger, severe intensity of job responsibilities, threat of personal injury, grueling shift changes, and a myriad of rules and regulations, police work may in some ways typify the very meaning of stress. Not surprisingly, then, police officers experience a tremendous amount of stress, often leading to tragic circumstances such as substance abuse, termination from the police force, or even suicide.

> Imagine for a moment that you are a police officer. You have been assigned to work the graveyard shift this particular night, a shift you have not worked for about 2 weeks. Your assignment for the night is to patrol a particularly dangerous area of town. You have had only a few hours sleep due to the abrupt shift change, and you are certainly not feeling very alert. As luck would have it, you receive a call over the radio stating that

you are to investigate a complaint of gang activity in the area you are patrolling. Without hesitation, you arrive at the scene, and are greeted by a number of men holding a variety of weapons. As you step out of the car, you cannot help but think that this confrontation may very well cost you life or limb.

Literature Review

Incidents such as that just described may cause feelings of fear, resistance, and acute stress. Researchers have examined the topic of police stress to help us understand the dynamic process involved with a law enforcement officer's job requirements and its association to the amount of stress experienced.

A survey conducted by J. M. Violanti and Aron (1995) demonstrated that police officers experience two basic types of stressors: organizational practices and the inherent nature of police work. Organizational stressors refer to events stemming from police administration, which are found to be bothersome or intolerable to members of the police force. They include such issues as authoritarian structure, lack of participation in decision-making processes, and unfair discipline. Inherent nature stressors refer to those occurrences that may threaten to harm the police officer either physiologically or psychologically. Included in this category are such items as high-speed chases, dealing with crises, and personal physical attacks (J. M. Violanti & Aron, 1993). According to the results of this study, killing someone in the line of duty was found to be the most stressful event one could experience as a police officer. Experiencing a fellow officer being killed was found to be the second most stressful experience. Both of these stressors could be considered inherent to the nature of police work.

In J. M. Violanti and Aron's (1993) study, the highest ranked organizational stressor was found to be shift work, followed by inadequate support, incompatible patrol partner, insufficient personnel, excessive discipline, and inadequate support by supervisors. Interestingly, 7 of the top 20 stressors were found by the authors to be organizational/administrative. The authors further broke down stressors by job ranking and experience. Those with 6 to 10 years of police experience were found to have the highest levels of overall stress (organizational and inherent combined). The ranking of desk sergeant was found to be most associated with overall stress, as were those officers ages 31–35 years, Caucasian, and those who were female.

Substance Abuse

Remembering the vignette described earlier, one can only imagine the cumulative effects that years of police work can have on one's psychological functioning. Given the many varied sources of police stress, it is of little surprise that officers often utilize unhealthy ways of coping with these stressors. One of the most common, yet under-reported, ways police officers cope with these stressors is through the use/abuse of drugs and alcohol.

Of particular interest is the number of officers who abuse alcohol as a means of dealing with their stressful lives. J. M. Violanti, Marshall, and Howe (1985) claim that reported alcohol abuse is underrated due to fear of retribution or demotion within the police department. Further, the authors state that known alcohol abusers are "hidden" in positions where they cannot detrimentally influence the department or the public's interaction with the department.

J. M. Violanti et al. (1985) describe a model of how a police officer may be driven to drink as a result of job-related stress. Job demands can lead to a number of possibilities for the police officer. These demands can be dealt with using various coping techniques, some of which may lead to feelings of stress or alcohol/drug use. Probably most common, rather than a direct route, is a combination of pathways eventually leading to alcohol/drug use.

With proper psychological coping mechanisms, the abuse of alcohol and other substances can be avoided. Indeed, it is the destruction or breakdown of the coping mechanisms available to the officer that most often leads to the abuse of alcohol/drugs. Consequently, alcohol/drug abuse may lead to unsatisfactory job performance, resulting in reprimand, which may then lead to increased use of alcohol/drugs, thus forming a maladaptive cycle of dysfunctional behavior.

The Impact of Using a Firearm

At this point, it is likely that one will ask themselves what the single most contributing factor leading to the abuse of substances within police work might be. As mentioned earlier, there are numerous factors which contribute to police stress. These factors can be broken down into finite categories of stressors. Not surprisingly, research reveals that the use of a firearm by a police officer to kill someone is often the single most stressful event experienced by a police officer (J. M. Violanti & Aron, 1995).

The use of a firearm by a police officer often leads to a number of detrimental psychological states. Much like a soldier using a firearm to defend oneself or others, the police officer may experience flashbacks, perceptual distortions, isolation, emotional numbing, sleep difficulties, depression, or a heightened sense of danger following the event. In fact, it is often after the use of a firearm that many officers decide to leave their profession, due to the traumatic psychological nature of the event (R. Solomon & Horn, 1986). When combining these factors with the hours of paperwork dealing with the rationale for the use of the firearm, the entire impact of such an ordeal burdens the officer with a great deal of stress.

Police as Targets of Violence

Perhaps no other single event is more stressful than the threat of personal bodily harm. Immersing yourself in the imagined scenario described at the beginning of this section may have induced feelings of stress. Considering this, one can certainly understand the level of stress an officer faces when the nature of the profession threatens violence against him or her every day.

A study conducted by McMurray (1990) revealed that of 161 police officers surveyed from the Washington, DC or Newark, New Jersey, police departments, 90% indicated that they felt assaults against the police had increased over the past year. These same officers also felt that support services within their departments were inadequate.

An interesting and distinct pattern emerged when the officers were asked to rank events that most disturbed them following an assault. Seventy-four percent explained that not knowing that the assault was coming was most disturbing to them. This was followed by feelings of powerlessness (53%) and nonsupport from onlookers (48%), from the courts (47%), from police officials (35%), from fellow officers (26%), from friends (23%), and lack of support from family (8%). It is clear that the lack of a support structure on both professional and personal levels are substantial sources of distress for the police officer who has been assaulted (McMurray, 1990).

In addition to these findings, a factor analysis revealed that four basic attitudinal subscales were developed: (1) work-related support, (2) job satisfaction, (3) alienation, and (4) law enforcement. Regarding work-related support, an average of 74.5% of the surveyed police officers did not feel that those who assaulted officers were adequately punished. Further, only 24 officers of the total sample felt that court officials were generally supportive in prosecuting criminals who had assaulted a police officer. Concerning job satisfaction, 18% reported that they disliked going to work since they had been assaulted and 21% were less satisfied with their job. Also, 19% indicated that their being assaulted may have affected their decision to remain in law enforcement.

The subsection of alienation revealed that 44% indicated that police officers were less casual with citizens in their patrol area, while 68% indicated that they took their work more seriously since the assault. McMurray (1990) points out that this may have implications for officers precipitating assaults on others that they may otherwise not engage in.

Finally, the law enforcement category indicated that 90% of officers stated they were as aggressive in law enforcement after the assault than prior to it. Half of the officers surveyed indicated that they would be more likely to use force if a situation called for it prior to their being assaulted. McMurray (1990) further states that while an aggressive officer may cause fewer officer injuries, this may also have implications for placing the community and police department at undue risk if unwarranted or excessive force is implemented against the citizens.

Concluding the discussion on police as targets of violence necessitates a summary of the detrimental effects of being assaulted while on active duty as a police officer. One need not be a psychologist or criminologist to understand that being assaulted, especially unexpectedly, can result in a tremendous amount of stress and emotional turmoil. Everything from recurring nightmares to a "quick-trigger syndrome" may develop as a result of being a victim of assault. Considering that the police officer places him- or herself in a potentially hostile environment every day, it is no wonder that some officers harbor feelings of violation and psychological disarray.

Suicide

There is no doubt that the ultimate and most tragic result of an inability to cope with police stress is suicide. An occupation surrounded with constant death, deceit, antisocial behaviors and personalities, defiance, ridicule, criticism, boredom, rigid hierarchical structures, and lack of social support may result in suicide in some cases. T. E. Baker and Baker (1996) reported that in 1994, 11 New York City police officers committed suicide. However, only two officers were actually killed by criminals in New York City that same year. It is clearly an unacceptable and distressing ratio when police are killing themselves at a rate more than five times greater than that by criminals.

An article by Arrigo and Garsky (1997) investigated a police officer's decision to commit suicide. The authors state that a combination of occupational stress, a nonsupportive family structure, and alcoholism may contribute to suicidal ideation in the police officer. Occupational stress in the police force is what the authors describe first as a contributing factor in police suicide. The inherent and chronically stressful nature of police work accumulates in the form of such feelings as helplessness and hopelessness. Also, organizational stressors such as those described earlier lead to feelings of suppressed hostility, frustration, and a sense of having little influence.

In addition to occupational stress, family strife is cited by Arrigo and Garsky (1997) as being another significant source of stress. A number of important and often undesirable responsibilities such as shift work and disabling injuries occur with police work. These and other factors have a tremendous impact on the officer's family, who must deal with these issues daily. A police officer's job requires a large amount of time and energy in order ensure that he or she is doing their job properly and "by the book." As a result, police officers' spouses are often neglected in the process. Also, police officers' training often attempts to instill such psychological coping techniques as detachment from emotional situations. All too often this detachment is reflected in the personal lives of the officers. This results in a breakdown of family communication and a lack of emotional intrigue, attachment, or romance within the marriage.

The final component described is that of a police officer's use of alcohol and its effects on the decision to commit suicide. It is a well-known fact that many people use alcohol as a means to escape a reality that they would rather not experience or to at least detach themselves from it. As described in the section on police officers' use of alcohol, the typical officer's use is higher than that of the general population. When one examines the nature of police work, it is not difficult to understand this phenomenon.

Alcohol is often used by police officers as a sleep-inducing agent to help deal with biological rhythm disruptions associated with shift work. It is also used to help control deep-seated cynicism, another coping strategy employed by police officers who have become disenchanted with the operation of the police department in which they work.

T. E. Baker and Baker (1996) described the warning signs associated with the police officer who may commit suicide. According to these authors, supervisors should look for clusters of symptoms such as a recent loss, sadness, frustration, disappointment, grief, alienation, depression, loneliness, physical pain, mental anguish, and mental illness. Other signs should also be examined, the most obvious being a previous suicide attempt or other type of self-mutilation.

Stigma in Asking for Help

As with many other occupations, law enforcement includes its own unwritten code of conduct and subculture. A traditionally masculine occupation, many male police officers feel the need to keep psychological distress signs to themselves for fear of being viewed as "soft." Likewise, female police officers often do not wish to display their negative psychological states for fear that they will be viewed as weak in character. Many police officers also refuse to reveal their emotional concerns or disruptions for fear that they will not obtain one of the very few promotional positions available within the department (Arrigo & Garsky, 1997; Shearer, 1993). This often results in a police officer's understanding that asking for help may result in such things as forced leave, demotion, or simply ridicule and lack of respect by colleagues. As a result, emotions, feelings, and sometimes faulty or unhealthy thinking patterns remain bottled up inside for indefinite amounts of time, causing such states as depression.

Depression is characterized as a mood disorder that may encompass a person's entire range of functioning: increased or decreased appetite or sleep, bouts of crying, feelings of worthlessness, guilt, difficulty concentrating, difficulty making decisions, and thoughts of suicide and death. Clearly, this psychological state can detrimentally affect the police officer's ability to competently and objectively perform his or her duties. Realizing this, the police officer often chooses silence as a means of avoiding these issues.

Understanding this, supervisors must take a more active role in identifying problems that officers may have. It is not enough to simply tell the officers that they are available if anyone has a problem or issue and would like to discuss it. Supervisors must actively question the officers and provide periodic check-ups that will give them a better opportunity to assess if an officer is dealing with an issue or experiencing a large amount of stress and is in need of counsel.

Forensic Psychology and Policy Implications

A variety of topics were discussed in this section, and a multitude of policy implications exist for each topic. Police stress is a problem that has existed since the inception of law enforcement and will certainly not disappear any time in the near future. Despite this, however, surprisingly few policies have been implemented in order to not only protect the police officer from the detrimental effects of exposure to stressors, but also to prevent and treat stress-related syndromes.

As discussed earlier, police officers' abuse of substances such as drugs and alcohol are used as a means to escape the stresses associated with their occupation and to escape their harsh realities. Therefore, policy implications surrounding the use/abuse of alcohol and/or drugs within the police force must deal with the very root of the problem in addition to the abuse of substances itself. In other words, helping the officer to utilize more effective coping mechanisms and encouraging him or her to discuss more openly his or her concerns will, in effect, reduce the need to use alcohol or drugs as a means of dealing with these same issues or problems.

It is also surprising that perhaps the most stressful event one could experience as a police officer, using a firearm, incorporates virtually no policies to help the officer cope and deal effectively with the potential psychological trauma associated with this situation. Aside from the hours of paperwork required of the officer after the use of a firearm, the officer is left to him- or herself to cope with the posttraumatic stress associated with this event. Luckily, many police agencies are now incorporating psychological care to assist the officer in coming to an understanding of the psychological consequences of their actions. Still, more formal policies need to be enacted as standard procedure after a police officer uses a firearm to ensure their psychological well-being.

Many policy implications stem from police officers who have been victims of assault. McMurray (1990) described a number of useful policy implications associated with this topic. For instance, he states that supervisors need to be trained to deal with posttraumatic stress associated with assault, crisis intervention, and "how to listen." In addition, assaulted police officers should be allowed time off with pay following an assault until he or she is deemed fit to return to work. Further, the paperwork associated with the event should be performed by another officer familiar with the case.

Many officers interviewed in McMurray's (1990) study claim that the police department only concerns itself with physical, not psychological, injuries. Psychological screening should become mandatory following an event involving an assault. Finally, many officers claim that they are not even sure what resources, if any, are available to them following a traumatic event. This should result in a policy requiring officers to understand at all times what psychological resources are available and encouraging them to use those resources whenever necessary.

Issues surrounding police suicide are lacking and in need of development. Since troubled officers often resist seeking help, supervisors should instill the notion that no officer will suffer economic or promotional consequences. Further, all information given to supervisors must remain confidential, and this policy relayed must be to the officers. In addition, any information given to a supervisor by an officer should ultimately lead to a referral to a professional source, such as a psychologist or other counselor (T. E. Baker & Baker, 1996). Also, psychological interventions should be made available at any time an officer deems necessary. Crisis counseling specifically for police officers is often nonexistent, causing the officer to rely on the same resources available to the public. This may leave officers with a feeling of hesitancy if they believe the treatment will be lengthy or costly. Therefore, the intervention supplied to officers should be made free by the police agency.

Arrigo and Garsky (1997) advocate three main policies which may help deter the officer from engaging in self-mutilation or suicide. The first of these is stress management and stress-reduction techniques. The authors recommend that a special class explaining how to cope with anxiety and stressors, in addition to reducing them, needs to be incorporated into all training programs. The aspects of the course could include such topics as nutrition and dieting, physical health, fitness, humor, play, amusement strategies, and others.

In addition to stress management and stress-reduction techniques, group "rap" or process sessions should be made available to all police officers. This would incorporate group sessions emphasizing peer support dealing with issues such as the death of a partner or the use of deadly force. This training, according to Arrigo and Garsky (1997), should occur early in the candidate's training and regularly while in the police force. The intention of this policy is to help demystify the concept of counseling for the police officers, hopefully leading to more voluntary use of these services.

Finally, Arrigo and Garsky (1997) advocate police mentoring. While some types of mentoring within the police force already exist, this type of instruction may not be governed by a standard of quality. This could lead to negative influences regarding policing, stress build-up, and possibly even suicidal ideation. Skilled mentoring could allow for more disciplined officers incorporating a higher degree of respect for colleagues and others.

Police officers' reluctance in asking for help has already, to some degree, been discussed. With the promise of confidentiality, absence of ridicule, and no detrimental advancement or employment threats, officers should not feel hesitant in asking for help. Inclusion of even a few of these policies would no doubt make for a less dangerous, more psychologically (and physically) healthy lifestyle for police officers. With the opportunity for officers to vent frustrations and use appropriate emotional outlets, better decision making will no doubt take place, resulting in more efficient policing techniques and procedures and fewer inappropriate and dangerously hostile outbursts by officers.

Suggestions for Future Research

The subject of police stress encompasses a large array of topics and information. As a result, many opportunities for future research in this area are available. Police officers' use of alcohol, for example, has been blamed on the rigid structure associated with the police department as well as with often faulty coping mechanisms such as police cynicism. However, others argue that it is within the individual alone that such habits develop (J. M. Violanti et al., 1985).

As discussed, the use of a firearm is judged by many officers as an extremely stressful event. However, a small percentage of officers actually have engaged in such behavior. Future research is needed in order to determine the psychological ramifications associated with the occurrence (or perceived view of the occurrence) of such an event.

Future research is also needed in the area of assaulted police officers. Relatively few studies exist examining issues such as attitudes toward the perpetrator, self-esteem reductions associated with being physically injured, attitudes toward counseling and psychological treatment, and the psychology of anticipating physical confrontations. If officers were able to be trained to anticipate the intentions of a would-be attacker, less injury might result.

Research in the area of police suicide is, by comparison, an area in dire need of additional research. Studies examining the impact of suicide on family members, friends, the community, criminals, and other police officers is clearly lacking. More importantly, research dealing with teaching police officers more effective psychological coping mechanisms is needed. Also, research regarding the inherent elements of police work and how to reduce their detrimental psychological impact is needed in order to help reduce the rate of police suicides.

Police work is by no means a stress-free job. A myriad of potential stressors plague the officer daily. This section attempts not only to enumerate, but to explain some of these sources of police stress and their consequences. Police officers are not immune to the effects of psychological and physical manifestations of stress. A clear understanding is needed in order to allow law enforcement agencies and the officers themselves to function to the best of their abilities.

POLICE WORK AND FAMILY STRESS

Introduction

The precarious nature of police work not only affects police officers, but their families as well. There is ample research suggesting that the job demands of police officers can have an adverse effect on their psychological as well as physical well-being. This is evident when looking at issues such as police stress, police suicide, alcoholism, and cynicism. Based on research of the police profession and the extreme stress officers endure on a daily basis, it is inevitable that this stress will manifest itself within the family structure.

In this entry, the focus is to identify certain stressors, examine the various effects of police work on family members, and present ways in which they can learn to cope with the demands that are placed upon them. Issues examined include various occupational stressors and Posttraumatic Stress Disorder as a result of critical incidents such as officer-involved shootings and police suicide. Research is discussed which addresses these issues. Observations on coping strategies designed to ultimately help police families understand and process stress from law enforcement work are also presented.

> Imagine that you have just received a phone call from the Los Angeles Police Department informing you that your spouse, a seasoned police officer, has been shot and killed in the line of duty. Once the shock wears off, you fade back to reality. An event such as this is one that you have always thought about, yet never expected would happen to you. You begin to think about how you will recover from this traumatic occurrence and how you will continue to raise two small children, while at the same time try to cope with the loss of a loved one.

This tragic example is an extreme illustration of how policing can have an adverse effect on the lives of an officer's family. Research indicates that police officers have one of the highest levels of stress among all occupations (J. Violanti, 1995). Based on what is known about the extreme stressors of police work, it is imperative to recognize how various forms of stress effect officers' family members.

In order to have a better understanding of the extreme stressors of police work and the effects on the family, it is first important to recognize the various forms of stress and how they directly effect the family.

Literature Review

There are several occupational stressors that can potentially have an adverse effect on the police officer. Many of the stressors identified by peace officers as particularly problematic have a direct and immediate impact on spouses and family members (White & Honig, 1995).

A shooting incident is one of the most severe occupational stressors that an officer is likely to experience during his or her career (Blak, 1995). Police officers are trained to use authorized weapons in the event that they might encounter a life-threatening situation at some point in their career, yet every officer hopes that he or she will not have to resort to such an extreme. Shooting incidents will inevitably impact the lives of the officer as well as the lives of his or her family (Blak, 1995).

The clinical research regarding officer-involved shootings focuses on both physical and psychological reactions to the incident. Posttraumatic Stress Disorder (PTSD) is defined as an expected, but functional reaction to an abnormal and trauma-producing situation (Blak & Sanders, 1997). Officers often feel estranged, isolated, depressed, anxious, and emotionally unprepared. They also experience increased irritability (Blak, 1995). Oftentimes these reactions are projected into the home environment of the officer involved, resulting in interpersonal problems.

The spouses and children of officers involved in these incidents naturally experience psychological and physical trauma as well. The stress that they endure is considered "secondary stress reaction," or secondary trauma, which is a common reaction by family members to such encounters (Blak, 1995; White & Honing, 1995). It is not uncommon for there to be a strain on the marital relationship as a result of the emotional upheaval that each spouse is feeling.

According to research on the effects of PTSD on family members, the family system is affected in numerous ways including the following. (1) The family may exhibit their own symptoms such as a lack of self-worth and helplessness. They naturally want to help, but may feel frustrated in the attempt, resulting in a feeling of helplessness. Oftentimes, the officer feels depressed as a result of the lack of support from his or her family. (2) Because the officer often isolates and detaches him- or herself from others, family members feel that the officer is emotionally dead, or uncaring, and they experience defeat and failure. (3) The family may express puzzlement (Blak & Sanders, 1997).

Suicide is a route some officers chose to take as a response to the stress encountered on a daily basis. In the case of officers who commit suicide, it is the survivors left behind who must try to understand and cope with the tragedy.

Families of the deceased officer oftentimes experience emotional anguish as well as feelings of guilt. In the midst of this grieving and mourning process, the families are frequently left to take care of funeral expenses. Because suicide is perceived as dishonorable, families may not be afforded the full honors of a police military-style funeral (J. Violanti, 1995).

In terms of the family receiving any type of support services from the department to deal with the grieving process, police departments often abandon surviving family members after 1 or 2 weeks of condolences (J. Violanti, 1995). This is a harsh reality for many families who experience the aftermath of police suicide.

Stressors are hardships that affect the family unit because of the choice of a policing career by one or both of the spouses (Canada, 1993). As stated earlier, there are specific occupational stressors that are well documented in the research. Several authors have described the stressors that have been found to develop from the burden of police work and from the repetitive facing of crime, suffering, and death (Dietrich, 1989).

Depersonalization is a process where officers learn to become desensitized to the unpleasant conditions to which they are exposed on a daily basis. Through this process, they become emotionally detached. As some authors have stated, peace officers see not only the worst aspects of life, but see everyone at their worst (Dietrich, 1989).

Emotional hardening is a personality characteristic commonly found among many police officers. It is a protective maneuver that may be successful at work, but disastrous in terms of maintaining the intimacy necessary within a family (Kannady, 1993). Numerous authors have documented the tendency of peace officers to demonstrate emotional detachment, emotional blunting, or emotional repression in response to the environment in which they work (White & Honig, 1995). As a result of this personality characteristic, there is an incongruence between job-related activities and real human emotions. This leads to interpersonal problems within the family environment, such as a lack of intimacy between the spouse and the officer. The officer may appear to be distant, withdrawn, noncommunicative, and nonempathetic to the needs of family members.

The occupation of police work fosters a particular culture as well as a particular outlook on the world. This worldview not only develops within the officer, but is also brought home, where it influences the family's perception of reality (Kannady, 1993). The family's understanding of reality, based on the officer's account, is somewhat distorted. They begin to perceive the world as threatening, dangerous, and view others as being untrustworthy. The officer and spouse may become overly protective of each other as well as of their children.

Authoritarianism is a fundamental aspect of the police occupation. The officer must function according to a preset list of legal and organizational guidelines (Dietrich, 1989). It is common for the officer to experience stress related to this aspect merely because they oftentimes feel that they lack the control over decisions that affect their work and their lives. This can have a negative effect on family members in the event that the officer overcompensates at home for his or her perceived lack of control at work.

Many times the officer can be rigid or overly demanding of his or her spouse and children. In a study conducted in 1990, rigid, authoritarian peace officer parents were regarded as being unapproachable and "nonhuggable" (Southworth, 1990). As a result of this perception, children of peace officers were more likely to become rebellious adolescents as well as to have more emotional problems.

Danger Preparation is the realization that an officer is risking his or her life when on duty. This realization invariably affects the family members, resulting in anxiety and psychological stress. Threats to an officer's safety can create emotional fatigue for a spouse (Arrigo & Garsky, 1997).

A majority of the research regarding the relationship between police stress and the impact on the family is dated. Despite this fact, much of the research focuses on issues such as domestic violence and divorce within law enforcement families as well as on a lack of unity and trust between the child–parent relationship. Displacement of anger, decreased communication and conflict-management skills, alienation and withdrawal, and decreased trust all serve to create an environment that can place a law enforcement relationship at greater risk for domestic violence (White & Honig, 1995).

The various stressors presented in this entry are inherent to the police profession. An officer may be regarded as a success on the job, yet not very successful within the family structure. "The traits and dispositions that make exceptional police officers unfortunately make very poor spouses, parents, and friends" (Southworth, 1990, p. 20).

Forensic Psychology and Policy Implications

Stress is common and inevitable among police families. How they cope with the stress will determine the quality of their marriage (Canada, 1993). This determination is contingent upon the coping mechanisms that they choose to employ. Coping mechanisms must be utilized to successfully combat the stressors of police work as well as to learn to become resistant to them.

It is the responsibility of the law enforcement agency to provide the families of peace officers with the resources necessary to successfully cope with ongoing stressors. The first and most important intervention must be at the management and organizational levels (White & Honig, 1995). Education must start within the organizational structure to address occupational stressors and the adverse effects they have on the family structure.

Spouse orientations, training, and workshops must be provided to address issues related to occupational demands and stressors. Orientations provide spouses the opportunity to acclimate themselves with their spouses' job requirements. Ongoing workshops and seminars act as support groups for spouses as new problems surface with the progression of peace officers' careers.

With regard to the stress encountered by family members when an officer is involved in a critical incident, the family members need to be educated in terms of knowing the normal responses to such an abnormal event. If family members are fully informed of the responses they may expect to encounter as a result of such trauma, the disabling impact of the event may be ameliorated significantly (Blak, 1995).

In the tragic event of an officer fatality, law enforcement agencies must go beyond departmental boundaries to assist the families of all deceased officers, including those who take their own lives (J. Violanti, 1995). The department can facilitate the grieving process by offering assistance to the families in terms of financial matters, pension rights, counseling, and maintaining contact with the survivors.

Employers are now slowly beginning to recognize the need to provide more in-depth assistance to the families of law enforcement personnel (White & Honig, 1995). It is imperative for law enforcement organizations to take an active role in recognizing the effect of law enforcement on families and in providing viable interventions and support services for the family members to utilize.

As stated earlier, families of police officers must manage many difficult stressors. Without appropriate resources such as good communication and problem-solving techniques, psychological services, and organizational training and support systems, many families find it difficult to adapt to the demands of the police profession.

Suggestions for Future Research

It is evident that stress associated with police work can and does manifest itself within the family arena, resulting in poor interpersonal relationships with spouses and children, divorce, domestic violence, and emotional consequences. There is an abundance of research which examines the adverse reactions police officers endure because of their jobs, yet there is a paucity of information which specifically examines the relationship between police work and family stress.

As with the case illustration presented at the beginning of this chapter, this situation exemplifies the most severe form of stress a law enforcement family can experience. In order to have a conceptual understanding of the effects of occupational stress upon the family, future research needs to further examine the aforementioned stressors including the direct physical and psychological effects of police work. Law enforcement agencies need to be responsible for program implementation as well as evaluation to gauge the effectiveness of specific programs which address this issue.

HOMOSEXUAL POLICE OFFICERS

Introduction

The face of law enforcement has changed dramatically in the past 4 decades. The late 1960s saw the rise of African American males in the police force followed by women in the 1970s and the 1980s (Leinen, 1993). In the 1990s, lesbian women and gay men have attempted to become police officers. Some acting police officers are coming out, while many more are suspected of hiding their true sexual orientation.

Lesbian and gay officers face ridicule by other officers as well as by the gay community. According to Buhrke (1996), these individuals are sometimes labeled as "fags" or "dykes" by homophobic officers. He further explains that the gay community can also hold great disdain for police officers, who have historically oppressed and harassed them. Some argue that these officers are subject to additional stressors from either hiding or disclosing their sexual orientation.

Although some gay and lesbian officers have received tremendous support from fellow officers, others have been put at risk by partners or colleagues who are unwilling to back them up (Buhrke, 1996). Policies such as the 1964 Civil Rights Act and the 1972 Equal Employment Act were created to protect workers from discrimination particularly on the basis of color or gender. However, antidiscrimination policies that include sexual discrimination are lacking at both the federal and local levels. Some researchers argue that until sexual orientation is federally protected, homosexual officers will be subjected to harassment and discrimination in the workplace (Buhrke, 1996). Despite encouraging trends toward acceptance, many homosexual officers still face tremendous obstacles in the stereotypically masculine profession of law enforcement. Consider the following case illustration.

> In the early 1980s, Mitch Grobeson graduated Number One in his class at the Los Angeles police academy. When he joined the police department it was standard practice to ask the recruits if they had ever had sex with another man. An answer of yes resulted in immediate disqualification. Concealing his sexual orientation, Mitch was an honor cadet and was elected class president. After graduation from the academy, he was quickly promoted. During this time it was common practice for officers to actively harass gays on the streets and to raid gay bars.
>
> In December of 1984, another officer reported to Mitch's superior officer that Mitch was gay. Despite the harassment he subsequently endured from his supervisors and fellow officers, Mitch did not resign. Suffering ridicule, intimidation, and alienation, he was one of the top officers in his division. Officers would glue his locker shut and call him a variety of derogatory names. Many officers refused to work with him.
>
> His colleagues refused to back him up in the field. In one instance Mitch responded to a robbery alarm call (rated in California as the second highest call where officers are killed or injured) and received no backup. On October 6, 1985, he was in foot pursuit of two gang members. After catching and handcuffing the first, he caught up with the second. He had no way to cuff the second suspect and he was surrounded by 30 additional gang members. Fifteen minutes after the pursuit began and after many frantic attempts made by the dispatcher, not one of the 8000 Los Angeles police department (LAPD) officers provided back up.
>
> Mitch's superiors did nothing to curtail the harassment and in many cases encouraged it. Eventually, Mitch resigned from the LAPD, hired a lawyer, and filed the first lawsuit in the country by a police officer claiming discrimination based on sexual orientation. On February 10, 1993, the City Council agreed on a settlement that "included recruitment, hiring, and promotions of qualified gays and lesbians in LAPD." In addition, managers and supervisors would be held accountable for failing to take action to stop the harassment. (Adapted from Buhrke, 1996, pp. 25–32)

Literature Review

Mitch Grobeson's case illustrates the potential for conflict between the police and the gay officer. The image of bravado and machismo that is attached to police officers is diametrically opposed to stereotypes that label gay men as effeminate or weak.

Not only do gay officers face harassment or discrimination from fellow officers, they also face rejection from the gay community. Law enforcement has negative connotations for the many lesbians and gays who experience years of harassment, bar raids, and abuse from the criminal justice system (Buhrke, 1996).

Historically, homosexual acts were considered illegal and resulted in severe sanctions. From colonial times to the mid-1800s, sodomy was punishable by the death penalty (D'Emilio, 1983). During the 1950s only two states did not consider sodomy a felony (Buhrke, 1996). In 1971, 110 men who were convicted of homosexual acts were sentenced 15 years to life (Shilts, 1982).

Although homosexual acts are no longer severely punished, they are still viewed as deviant or criminal. According to D'Emilio (1983), homosexuals have been harassed with charges such as disorderly conduct or public lewdness. He states:

> Vice squad officers, confident that their targets did not dare to challenge their authority, were free to engage in entrapment. Anxious to avoid additional notoriety, gay women and men often pleaded guilty even when the police lacked sufficient evidence to secure convictions. (pp. 14–15)

Buhrke (1996) claims that abuse inflicted by police officers is not rare or a thing of the past. Although Mitch had a close association with his colleagues and an impressive work history, he suffered various forms of harassment and intimidation from his coworkers. This abuse was based on their discovery of his sexual orientation. According to Dodge (1993), the police do not prevent gay bashing and may even engage in it themselves. He maintains that, "[a]ll law enforcement efforts that touch on issues of sexual orientation take place against a background of hostility and mistrust. There is a long history of antagonism between the police and the gay and lesbian community" (Dodge, 1993, p. 302).

In a study conducted by Swerling (1978), 20% of California police officers interviewed disclosed that they would quit if law enforcement began hiring openly gay officers. Researchers have consistently found that gays and lesbians are one of the most disliked categories of people by the police (M. Burke, 1993; P. Jacobs, 1966; Niederhoffer, 1967). Traditionally, the police force is associated with conservative ideals. Some officers view homosexuality as not only morally wrong, but criminal. "From a police point of view then, homosexuality would appear to represent part of the societal disorder that the police officer has dedicated his or her life to eradicating" (M. Burke, 1994, p. 193).

Interestingly, researchers have found that the level of stigma and deviancy associated with male homosexuality in law enforcement is not present with lesbianism. M. Burke (1994) suggests that gay women are more likely to be masculinized than gay men, who are considered weak. In general, gay men as officers encounter more hostility than lesbians (Buhrke, 1996). According to Buhrke, "[s]tereotypes of lesbians as erotic and gay men as HIV/AIDS carriers reinforce existing prejudices" (1996, p. 260). Many lesbians in law enforcement are part of an informal network that serves to protect its members by being invisible (M. Burke, 1994). In some instances, these women are threatened by the attention to homosexual issues in law enforcement (Buhrke, 1996).

Unlike gender or race, sexual orientation can be concealed, making it impossible to actually know how many homosexuals are in law enforcement. In 1981, Sergeant Charles Cochrane of the New York Police Department was the first gay officer to come out while still in the police force (Griffin, 1993). Research has shown that leading double lives creates an inordinate amount of stress on gay and lesbian police officers. Fictional relationships are created by some officers to ward off suspicion of their homosexuality (Buhrke, 1996). The Weinberg and Williams study (1974) found that the fear of exposure was associated with psychological problems such as anxiety and alcoholism.

In a study conducted by Doyle (1996), 58% of randomly selected law enforcement officers in Southern California supported equal job opportunities for gays. However, 71% believed that male homosexuals should not be allowed to claim their partner on employee benefits. The belief that gays should not be allowed to work as police officers was held by 37% of the respondents. Practically half of the officers viewed homosexual acts as deviant.

Cases like Mitch Grobeson's demonstrate the need to examine the willingness of officers to provide backup to on-duty gay officers. Eight of 10 respondents (89%) believed they would help a gay officer having difficulty with a police procedure. Finally, 89% responded that they would check on the safety of a gay officer on a routine traffic stop.

Homosexual officers are constantly bombarded with the heterosexual police officer's viewpoint of them. M. Burke (1994) describes the phenomena of "identity ambivalence." It is identified when these officers cannot embrace their own gay subculture completely, yet they can not completely reject it. He further explains that this phenomenon influences homosexual officers whose stigma is, on average, less visible, to look upon more flamboyant homosexuals, with disdain. These homosexuals, whose characteristics and behaviors embody those that lead to alienation, are depreciated.

Overall, lesbian and gay officers have better experiences in larger agencies that employ a number of openly gay officers (Buhrke, 1996). Locale is also important. Typically, areas like San Francisco, California, would be more likely to tolerate diverse lifestyles than Dallas, Texas. In general, harassment and discrimination are less likely if the criminal justice employee has more power and authority.

Forensic Psychology and Policy Implications

The research and stereotypes that associate gay men with HIV/AIDS present many implications for policy and forensic psychology. In Doyle's (1996) study, 56% of respondents would hesitate to give first-aid to a known homosexual officer. Homosexuals on the police force would raise the personal fears about contracting AIDS of 49% of the officers interviewed. Finally, 74% said they would object to working with people with AIDS.

Will departments make HIV testing a part of the screening process for potential recruits (Blumberg, 1989)? Should HIV-positive applicants be hired? If an officer becomes infected on the job, should they be allowed to continue working (Doyle, 1996)? Doyle suggests that policies to prohibit discrimination based on sexual orientation should be developed. Employees should be educated about homosexuality. Sensitivity and diversity training should be implemented. Gay and lesbian support groups should be created and maintained. Having supportive heterosexual colleagues in the force is instrumental to a comfortable work environment for homosexual officers.

Buhrke (1996) raises the question of what provisions are available for the partner of a homosexual officer killed or injured on the job. As more lesbians and gay men become visible in law enforcement, years of mistrust, stereotypes, and abuse will have to be confronted.

Suggestions for Future Research

Buhrke (1996) highlighted the need for a more detailed analysis of the experiential differences that exist between gay men and women working in law enforcement. Studies that examine the factors that influence greater acceptance of lesbian police officers than homosexual male officers are needed. Currently, there are speculative ideas surrounding this topic but little research exists to support the available theories. Studies need to be conducted to examine the additional stressors that homosexual officers endure and the impact of those stressors. Are homosexual officers more likely to commit suicide or to have an addiction? Due to the relatively small number of gay police officers who are open about their sexuality, qualitative research could be undertaken to explore the experience of being a homosexual police officer. More research is needed on the attitudes and perceptions that heterosexual officers harbor regarding homosexual officers. Research could also be undertaken to look at whether open or latent homosexuality causes greater hostility by heterosexual officers.

PART II

Courts and The Legal System

CHAPTER 5

Adult Forensics

OVERVIEW

The role of psychology in the legal system is both diverse and expansive. In addition, new and/or emerging application areas are being discovered all the time. The adult forensic field is one domain where this particular focus is appreciable. The adult forensic arena encompasses all facets of criminal adjudication, from the pretrial stage to the postconviction phase, where psychology's role in the court process is evident, necessary, and, ultimately, impactful.

In this chapter, six controversies are explored. These topics include (1) plea bargaining, (2) competency to stand trial, (3) jury selection, (4) psychological tests and forensic evaluation instruments, (5) risk assessment, and (6) forensic verdicts. Individually, these controversies demonstrate the breath of specialized roles that exist for forensic psychologists in the court system. Collectively, the issues explored in this chapter explain where and how the adult forensic field routinely relies upon the psychological sciences to inform effective legal practice and sound judicial decision making.

The plea bargaining process is a key dimension to the criminal prosecution of a defendant. How does personal fear and prosecutorial coercion impact the pretrial negotiations that occur? What are the psychological and legal consequences of plea bargaining for individuals, society, and the justice system? In order for a person to be prosecuted, the individual must be competent to stand trial. What is the legal standard for mental competence? What role does psychology play in furthering our understanding of competency? How does the "psycholegal" standard relate to one's capacity to stand trial? Jurors are an indispensable component of most criminal (and civil) cases. The selection process can significantly affect the desired outcome of a case. How do the psychological sciences contribute to the scientific selection of a jury? Is it possible to assemble, through the selection process, an impartial jury panel? How does the pretrial publicity of a high-profile case impact the jury pool? Both prosecuting and defense attorneys increasingly rely upon forensic experts with psychological assessment skills who can testify in court. Do forensic tests provide accurate information about the personality, intelligence, ability, and psychopathology of an offender? Are such instruments and their findings legally admissible? What is the reliability and validity of testimony based on forensic assessments in the courtroom? Relatedly, one type of forensic evaluation is risk assessment. In short, the question posed is whether the defendant presents a risk for future violent behavior. How accurately do risk-assessment instruments predict future dangerousness? Do evaluations tend to be over- or underinclusive and what are the implications for defendants? What is the constitutionality of using risk evaluations in a criminal case? Mentally ill defendants can be found guilty or not guilty. In addition, however, they can be found Not Guilty by Reason of Insanity (NGRI) or Guilty But Mentally Ill (GBMI). How does the legal system understand insanity and mental illness? What are the various tests or standards the court uses for insanity? How do NGRI and GBMI verdicts differ?

The six controversies examined in this chapter, though limited in scope, nonetheless explore several noteworthy subjects that dramatically reveal the interplay of law and psychology in the adult forensic arena. Responses to the problem of crime entail sophisticated, scientific solutions. Whether the questions asked involve mentally disordered defendants at different stages of the adjudication process, the vagaries of selecting jurors, or the psycholegal consequences of plea bargaining, one thing is clear: psychology can and does impact what happens in the criminal courtroom. As the individual sections of this chapter explain, the policy implications for this continued trend necessitate that carefully trained specialists who understand the mechanics of law, the science of psychology, and the geography of human behavior be called upon to assist the legal system. In part, as is suggested in the pages that follow, more and better research are therefore essential to accomplishing this end. Indeed, this level of training will ready the way for future generations of forensic specialists so that they can confront the challenges that await them in the adult forensic field.

PLEA BARGAINING

Introduction

Even those unfamiliar with the criminal justice system have some understanding of the role of plea bargaining in our legal system and its impact on justice. While the popular media likes to portray a courtroom drama involving fanatic lawyers vigorously defending their clients in front of both judge and jury, the reality of criminal proceedings is much different. The majority of criminal cases never reach the courtroom, as they are resolved through the process of plea bargaining. Approximately 90% of all criminal cases are resolved through plea bargaining (Abadinsky & Winfree, 1992; Melton, Petrila, Poythress, & Slobogin, 1987). Thus, fewer than 10% of criminal convictions are achieved through the trial process. These statistics alone illustrate the significance of the role of plea bargaining in the criminal justice system, and this issue has prompted much debate as to the consequences that plea bargaining exerts on individuals, society, and the system of justice. Does plea bargaining serve justice or is it unjust? The following section explores this and similar questions concerning plea bargaining.

> Jim is a 42-year-old ex-professional basketball star. For the past 5 years he has worked as a sportscaster for a major television network. While driving home from the supermarket late one night, he is pulled over and arrested by local police. He is charged with robbery, assault with a deadly weapon, unlawful use of a deadly weapon, and unlawful entry in connection with a residential robbery which had occurred earlier that evening. Jim maintains his innocence, contending that he was home alone all evening before leaving to pick up some groceries. The evidence against him, however, seems strong and he is unable to provide a sound alibi. Upon consulting with his attorney, he learns that if convicted on all charges, he faces a maximum of 40 years in prison plus fines of up to $15,000. His attorney therefore recommends that he enter a plea of guilty to the offense of robbery, which carries a maximum sentence of 15 years and a $5,000 fine. By doing so, the prosecution will drop the remaining charges and recommend leniency in sentencing. Jim now faces a dilemma. He is very emphatic with regard to his innocence, yet if a jury trial ensues and he is convicted of these charges, he faces severe consequences. Regardless of whether Jim actually did commit the offenses in question, he is forced to make a decision that will have a profound effect on his future.

Literature Review

The practice of plea bargaining involves an exchange between the defense, the prosecution, and a judge. The defendant's part of the bargain involves pleading guilty to some offense. In return, the State agrees to one or more of the following: reduction in the number of charges, reduction in the number of counts, a change in charges, recommended leniency in sentencing, and/or promise of alternative sentencing

(Abadinsky & Winfree, 1992). It should be noted that the judge is typically not obligated to follow the prosecutor's recommendation. Thus, if a defendant enters a plea of guilty in exchange for the prosecution recommending a more lenient sentence, he or she should be aware that the judge is the final bearer of all decisions. The judge may decide that the defendant's crime is deserving of the harshest punishment allowable by law, regardless of the plea bargaining agreement. Though judges often do follow the prosecutor's recommendation, there is no guarantee (L. Wrightsman, *et al.*, 1994). Particularly with regard to sentencing leniency, some judges believe that always accepting the prosecutor's recommendation without first considering such issues as seriousness of the crime, harm to the victim, and the offender's background discredits their duty as a judge (L. Wrightsman *et al.*, 1994).

Plea bargaining thus appears to be beneficial for both the prosecution and the defendant. The admission of guilt relieves the prosecution of having to prove that the defendant did indeed commit the crime(s), thereby eliminating the uncertainty of a trial. Further, and perhaps more important, it relieves the prosecution and State of the burden of a lengthy, time-consuming, and expensive trial. For the defendant, the perceived benefit is leniency in one or more of the ways discussed above. The continuing controversy concerning plea bargaining, however, generates questions as to whether the practice of plea bargaining actually does serve justice or is in fact unjust.

Proponents of plea bargaining insist that it is an absolutely necessary component of the criminal justice system. Plea bargaining (1) keeps cases moving through the system without adding to the backlog of cases already present; (2) allows for cases to be settled promptly and with a sense of finality; and (3) spares the victim and/or his or her family, police officers, and others involved in the case from having to spend hours testifying in court and reliving the experience (L. Wrightsman *et al.*, 1994). Proponents of plea bargaining have obtained support from the courts as well. In *Santobello v. New York* (1971) the Supreme Court upheld plea bargaining, agreeing that it was a necessary component of the criminal justice system. Though plea bargaining is arguably beneficial in several ways, it has been equally denounced for not serving justice.

Plea bargaining has been criticized as being unjust for several reasons. Critics feel that it results in improper sentencing, either too harsh or, more often, too lenient (L. Wrightsman *et al.*, 1994). The media's portrayal, and often the public's perception, of plea bargaining is that it is an abuse of discretion and results in serious criminals "getting off easy" (Abadinsky & Winfree, 1992). Others argue that plea bargaining is unjust to the *defendant*. They claim that the defendant's justice is jeopardized in the following ways: (1) by agreeing to a plea bargain, he or she is surrendering his or her constitutional rights; (2) disparity in sentencing is inevitable (all defendants do not receive the same "deals"); and (3) innocent as well as guilty defendants may feel coerced into pleading guilty because they fear the more severe consequences which may result if convicted by way of a jury trial (L. Wrightsman *et al.*, 1994). From these issues, considerations of particular relevance arise for the forensic psychological practitioner. The defendant's competency to enter a plea of guilty, as well as whether the decision is in fact voluntary, are questions which must be addressed.

In light of the fact that the defendant essentially waives his or her constitutional rights by entering a plea of guilty, the Supreme Court has held that the judge must "affirmatively establish on the record" the defendant's competency to plead guilty (Melton *et al.*, 1987, p. 97). In assessing competency, the primary questions that need to be addressed by the forensic psychologist include the defendant's (1) reasons for pleading guilty, (2) understanding of the *specific* rights being waived, and (3) understanding of the charge he or she is admitting to. The judge must therefore determine whether the guilty plea is completely voluntary. In order for a plea bargain to occur, the defendant must be fully aware of the meaning and consequences of his or her plea. Even if the defendant is legally competent to make such a decision, questions arise as to whether he or she reached such a decision by way of a logical, rational process. It is this issue which has generated interest in the role of *coercion* in plea bargaining.

Plea bargains are often perceived by the defendant as a favorable means to resolve the case, as they often result in less aversive consequences than would be risked through a jury trial. The plea, then, may be considered an issue of avoidance rather than a logical decision. The question for the forensic psychological practitioner is whether the defendant is making a voluntary choice based in his or her own best interest or whether he or she is coerced into an involuntary plea by fear. Reinforcing this fear are the common practices of overcharging and overrecommending. Police often charge arrested individuals with every possible crime related to their actions. Overcharging both increases the likelihood of a plea bargain and, if a jury trial ensues, gives the jurors the impression that the defendant committed numerous wrongdoings. In either case, the result of overcharging is an increased chance of the defendant being found guilty, either through plea or by a jury. Overrecommending is a strategic move by the prosecution to increase the level of fear in the defendant. By threatening severe sentences, the chances are much greater that the defendant will concede to a plea bargain to avoid such harsh punishment. Overcharging and overrecommending are both strategies of the criminal justice system employed to immerse the defendant in fear.

The "fear factor" generates an important question as to the voluntariness of the defendant's plea. Truly innocent individuals may also feel coerced into pleading guilty as they fear the consequences of trial. The Supreme Court addressed the issue of coercion in *North Carolina v. Alford* (1970). Alford was charged with first-degree murder, a capital crime in North Carolina. Out of fear of the death penalty, Alford agreed to plead guilty to the lesser charge of second-degree murder, which carried a sentence of 30 years in prison. After the sentencing, Alford claimed that his plea of guilty was not valid because it was the result of fear and coercion. Ultimately the Supreme Court held that his plea was in fact valid, particularly as it was made under the advice of competent legal counsel.

Forensic Psychology and Policy Implications

With regard to plea bargaining, we have discussed some of the psychological and legal issues for both the defendant and the justice system in general. The issue of fear and coercion is only one of many pertaining to plea bargaining. What *is* the impact of plea bargaining on society and the individuals within it? Is it truly beneficial to the defendant, as he or she does in fact receive a better "deal"? Or is the defendant forced to plead guilty by fear of the possible consequences? Is the system of justice letting criminals off "easy" or is it taking more criminals off the streets by ensuring a guilty plea to some offense? The Supreme Court acknowledged in *Santobello v. New York* (1971) that plea bargaining is essential to the justice system and is to be encouraged. While we can assume that an abolition of plea bargaining would exceed the resources of our justice system, chief justice W. Berger's usage of the phrase "properly administered" seems to be a more important consideration. The system of justice in the United States must respond to the controversy by considering all of the issues addressed and determine the most appropriate (and beneficial to all parties involved) way of utilizing the plea bargaining process.

Suggestions for Future Research

Further research needs to be conducted on alternatives to plea bargaining. The effects of abolition of plea bargaining and alternatives to plea bargaining have been debated for some time. An adequate alternative to plea bargaining, however, has yet to be established and implemented. More practical questions may revolve around the improvement of existing plea bargaining policy. To understand how policy may be improved, it is important to understand the psychological impact on defendants faced with the prospect of plea bargaining.

While we know that the majority of cases are plea bargained, future research could address the reasons that individuals choose to plea bargain. For example, do defendants feel that their chances of being found not guilty by a jury are slim? If so, does it depend on the specifics of the case or is there a broad lack of confidence about jury verdicts? Recall that some defendants may feel coerced or fear the undetermined consequences of being found guilty at trial. If jury verdicts were more consistent and external influences (e.g., pretrial publicity) were not a factor, would that change the defendant's decision? What about the defendant's confidence in her or his attorney? Court-appointed attorneys (public defenders) may be perceived as less likely to represent the defendant well at trial and, thus, the defendant may be more inclined to accept a plea bargain.

The fact that plea bargaining will significantly impact an individual's future is well understood. Future research should be concerned with the thoughts that influence defendants when faced with such a decision. The advantage to the legal system is more obvious and was discussed above (e.g., reduce the number of cases); the advantages to the defendant are less understood.

COMPETENCY TO STAND TRIAL

Introduction

Some of the more frequently addressed issues concerning psychology and the legal system involve the concept of competency. *Black's Law Dictionary* (Garner, 1996) defines competency as "the mental ability to understand problems and to make decisions" (p. 117). The precise meaning of competency assumes different forms, however, depending on the context for which it is addressed. In general, there is longstanding agreement that an individual should not be subjected to the processes of the legal system if he or she is unable to understand the nature and purpose of those proceedings (L. Wrightsman *et al.*, 1994). Further, it is important for defendants to be competent in order to ensure accurate results, maintain the dignity of the legal system, and justify the imposition of punishment (Weiss, 1997).

Questions of competency in the legal system can be raised at any point throughout the proceedings of the criminal process. Such questions may be raised by the prosecution, the defense, or the judge. The most frequent application of the competency rule concerns competency to stand trial. In addition, a number of other competency issues may be raised including competency to plead guilty, competency to confess, competency to refuse the insanity defense, competency to waive the right to an attorney, competency to testify, and competency to be sentenced and executed.

What exactly does the legal concept of competence refer to, and what implications ensue from its legal existence? This section explores these questions and looks more specifically at the issue of competence in the legal system. In addition, the issue of competency to stand trial is examined. For further analysis on competency to be sentenced and executed, refer to the section entitled "Incarcerating and Executing the Mentally Ill." The implications for forensic psychology, policy analysis, and practice that surface in light of the concept of competence are also briefly discussed.

> Jenne Foster is a 28-year-old woman who was arrested for felony theft 3 months ago. Jenne has a history of moderate-to-severe psychological dysfunction. She has been hospitalized at various times since the age of 13 for mood-related issues, often accompanied by psychotic symptoms. Though her mental illness manifests only periodically, it is often compounded by her long history of substance abuse. In addition, Jenne has been diagnosed as mildly mentally retarded. Intelligence tests conducted by clinical and forensic psychologists consistently measure her within the 60–70 range.
>
> After initially interviewing Jenne in preparation for her trial, Jenne's defense attorney, John, questions her understanding of the upcoming proceedings and ability to assist him in the trial process. Having genuine concerns regarding these issues, John raises the

question of Jenne's competency to stand trial. In other words, is Jenne mentally capable of being a defendant in the criminal process? If so, what other competency issues might arise? And, if not, what will happen to Jenne?

Literature Review

Stone (1975) referred to Competency to Stand Trial (CST) as "the most significant mental health inquiry pursued in the system of criminal law" (p. 200). Perhaps one reason for the significance of competency applied in this context is the large number of persons found incompetent every year. A study conducted by H. Steadman, Monahan, Hartstone, Davis, and Robbins (1982) found that in the United States in 1978, approximately 25,000 CST evaluations resulted in over 6,000 individuals found incompetent to stand trial. Thus, the sheer number of individuals facing competency evaluations leaves competency to stand trial as one of the most significant issues confronted in the fields of law, psychology, and forensic psychology.

The legal definition of competency to stand trial was put forth by the Supreme Court in *Dusky v. United States* (1960). The *Dusky* standard requires the individual to have (1) "sufficient present ability to consult with a lawyer with a reasonable degree of rational understanding" and (2) "rational as well as factual understanding" of the general proceedings (*Dusky v. United States*, 1960, p. 402). Though competency standards vary somewhat from state to state, nearly every state has adopted some variation of *Dusky* (Grisso, 1996a).

Thus, the contemporary concept of CST concerns not only the presence of mental illness, but also the individual's ability to function as a defendant in light of the effects of his or her mental illness. The primary concern, then, is whether the mentally ill defendant is capable of fulfilling his or her role as a defendant. The knowledge and ability to do those things required by the court before and during the trial process are of primary importance (L. Wrightsman *et al.*, 1994).

Competency to stand trial must be differentiated from the standard of insanity. Competency refers only to a defendant's *present* ability to function. For example, an individual may have been legally insane at the time he or she committed a crime, but perfectly competent to stand trial and be sentenced. Likewise, an individual who was legally sane during the commission of a crime may not be competent several months later when he or she faces criminal trial. Thus, insanity and competence are entirely different legal constructs and, though often confused, must be considered as such.

One important distinction between the two concerns treatment of those found insane or incompetent. Typically, the defendant found insane [i.e., Not Guilty by Reason of Insanity (NGRI) or Guilty But Mentally Ill (GBMI)] faces a sentence in a placement where psychiatric care is available. The NGRI individual may spend a life sentence in a psychiatric hospital. The incompetent to stand trial individual, on the other hand, has not been tried, convicted, or sentenced for any wrongdoing.

He or she is simply treated in an effort to restore his or her ability (if possible) to understand the proceedings and assist his or her counsel in the trial.

How long can an incompetent individual be held in a psychiatric facility? The Supreme Court attempted to answer this very question in *Jackson v. Indiana* (1972). Prior to *Jackson*, it was not uncommon for incompetent defendants to be confined to psychiatric facilities for unlimited periods of time. At times, this period exceeded the sentence the individual would have faced if tried and convicted. Thus, it was not uncommon for the prosecution to raise questions concerning competency to essentially sentence an individual without the time and effort of a trial (L. Wrightsman et al., 1994).

The Court's decision in *Jackson* placed limits on the amount of time an individual who was found Incompetent to Stand Trial (IST) could be confined. Thus, the time afforded to the state to treat defendants and restore their competence was subject to limitations. The proposed limits were defined as "... a reasonable period of time necessary to determine whether there is a substantial probability that [the defendant] will attain the capacity [competence] in the foreseeable future" (*Jackson v. Indiana*, 1972, pp. 737–738). The defendant found IST is not subjected to the trial process. He or she is generally placed in a psychiatric facility and treated until competency has been sufficiently restored. The *Jackson* decision, however, was the first Supreme Court case to place legal limits, though imprecise and not well defined, on the commitment of such individuals.

Forensic Psychology and Policy Implication

The implications of competency issues and developments for the forensic psychologist are profound. Research in the area has shown that the expert opinions of psychologists on the issue of competency are highly valued. It is uncommon for a judge to disagree with a mental health professional's recommendation (Nicholson & Kugler, 1991). Thus, the role of the practicing forensic psychologist is one that assists in defining the future of the defendant whose competency is in question. For Jenne in our case illustration, the opinion of the psychologist conducting the competency evaluation may determine whether she must face the trial process in her present state or be committed for treatment to possibly restore her to a level of functioning that may enhance her ability to assist in her own defense.

For example, if it is determined that Jenne is competent to stand trial when she is in fact incompetent, the ensuing trial may be contaminated and unjust. The reverse, however, is also true. If Jenne is judged to be incompetent when she is capable of standing trial, the public may regard her as "getting off easy" and not receiving due punishment if she were found guilty.

Perhaps even more significant, however, is the very issue of incompetence and the treatment of individuals such as Jenne. One who has been found incompetent to stand trial, for example, is deprived of liberty by being involuntarily confined, without ever being found guilty of anything. The incompetent defendant not only faces the loss of liberty that may eventually follow a guilty verdict, but is also subjected to the loss of freedom, liberty, and sometimes the questionable conditions of the facility where he or she is confined. The very practice of confining the incompetent before they have been convicted raises important policy questions.

Another of the more significant developments concerning competency and policy is that of involuntary medication to restore competency. Often, an individual's competency may be restored following the administration of psychotropic medications. Questions then arise as to whether there is a justified basis for forcing medications on defendants in an effort to restore competency. The issue of right to refuse treatment for both prisoners and civilly committed individuals is explored more fully in other sections of this book.

Suggestions for Future Research

Perhaps the most controversial issue with regard to competency issues is exactly what constitutes a competent individual. Though cases such as *Dusky v. United States* (1960) shed light on the question, no distinct and specific conclusion has been reached by any court of law. This topic continues to receive substantial attention in both legal and social science literature. Given the inherent difference between individuals, forensic psychologists must consider whether it is even possible to adopt a specific standard of competency.

Another area in need of future consideration concerns involuntary confinement of incompetent individuals. Many jurisdictions continue to allow for the automatic confinement of such persons (Melton *et al.*, 1987). Several proposals have been made to place limitations on the conditions under which this commitment should occur. Further, though the Court's decision in *Jackson v. Indiana* (1972) forbade unlimited confinement, it failed to define "reasonable period of time" and "substantial probability" (pp. 737–738). Thus, the Court has assumed some responsibility for the treatment of incompetent defendants. It has not, however, adequately resolved the issues with consideration of the best interest of the individual and the State.

JURY SELECTION

Introduction

The selection of jury members is one of the most important aspects of any given trial. The Sixth Amendment guarantees that "in all criminal prosecutions, the accused shall enjoy the right to a speedy and public trial, by an impartial jury." How then is an impartial jury selected? The last several decades have generated a substantial amount of criticism as to whether a jury can in fact be impartial. Many factors, both sociological and psychological, can influence the means by which a juror reaches a decision about a defendant's guilt. The presumed impartiality of each juror is questionable, and several methods for assuring impartiality have been implemented. Each of these factors and methods must be considered by both the defense and the prosecution in selecting a final jury. This section examines these as well as other important questions concerning jury selection.

> Jen has been arrested and charged with felonious assault in a domestic dispute in which she was recently involved. Let us suppose that Jen has considered her plea bargaining options and decided against them, preferring instead to risk the trial process. She believes that she is completely innocent and that a jury of her peers will also see it that way. Thus, Jen has made the decision to place her future in the hands of the 12 jurors to be selected. Given this, it makes sense that Jen will want the jury to be composed of people most likely to find her innocent. The prosecution, on the other hand, will desire a jury composition that will be convinced of her guilt. Jen and her defense counsel must now be concerned with how the members of the jury are selected and what, if anything, they can do to impact Jen's chance of acquittal. To further complicate matters, Jen happens to be a well-known public figure, and anyone who watches television has heard about her case. What are the defense's chances of finding a jury who has not already developed an opinion about the case? The media has been quick to suggest Jen's guilt, and polls have shown that the majority of the public believes her to be guilty even before the trial has begun. These are important considerations for the defendant in this case which will undoubtedly effect the outcome of the trial.

Literature Review

The process of jury selection spans several stages, involving both the prosecution and the defense. After an initial jury pool is chosen, a panel is selected for a *voir dire* hearing. At this hearing, each prospective juror is questioned by the judge and often the defense and prosecution. The voir dire is intended to identify and dismiss those who would be unable to render an impartial verdict. An individual may be dismissed by the judge alone or *challenged for cause* by the prosecution or defense. Challenges for cause address specific issues, such as the prospective jurors' relation to the defendant, exposure to media coverage of the case, or expressed personal biases about the defendant or case material. In addition, most jurisdictions allow the defense and prosecution a certain number of *peremptory challenges*. These challenges may be used to dismiss a juror without having to provide a specific reason (*Swain v. Alabama, 1965*). Peremptory challenges may not, however, be used to dismiss a prospective juror solely because of his or her race (*Baston v. Kentucky,* 1986). This exception does not, as yet, extend to religion, gender, or national origin (L. Wrightsman *et al.*, 1994).

The voir dire process has been the focus of much interest in the field of forensic psychology. Consider the issue of pretrial publicity. While many questions remain unanswered with regard to pretrial publicity, there is ample evidence that it can effect the jurors' ability to be impartial (Dexter, Cutler, & Moran, 1992). Several remedies for such effects have been investigated, yet their effectiveness has not been well established. One of these remedies is the voir dire, or jury examination, process. The use of the voir dire process as a remedy for pretrial publicity assumes that upon extensive questioning by the prosecution, defense, and/or judge, the impact of pretrial publicity on that juror can be assessed. Thus, each juror could be examined for potential biases resulting from media exposure to the case and discarded from the pool if it is suspected that they will be unable to remain impartial in rendering a verdict. In theory, using extended voir dire to assess for biases should work. However, research in this area has failed to reach a conclusive status. Dexter *et al.* (1992) found that subjects who were exposed to pretrial publicity perceived the defendant as more culpable (guilty) and that subjects who were exposed to extensive voir dire (as opposed to minimal voir dire) perceived the defendant as less culpable. It is safe to assume, then, that pretrial publicity has an impact on juror perceptions of culpability, and extended voir dire may be beneficial in these types of cases.

In the 1970s, the concept of scientific jury selection was introduced. This notion examined whether social scientists could be employed by the defense to select the most favorable jurors in an effort to increase chances of acquittal. Generally, a telephone survey was used to interview people who met the same eligibility standards of prospective jurors. Questions concerning biographical information and general beliefs and attitudes about the defendant which may influence their verdict were posed. The interviewees were also presented a brief description of the case and questioned as to how they would vote if they were part of the jury (Abadinsky & Winfree, 1992). By measuring sociological variables, general beliefs, and attitudes of those who could potentially be jurors, it could be determined how certain types of jurors would vote before the jury selection process began. Thus, the defense would be able to predict how members of the jury pool might vote based on personal characteristics in an effort to increase the probability of acquittal. Lawyer-conducted voir dire could be used to determine whether the potential jurors "fit" their desired profile. The results of scientific jury selection have been noted as modest at best, and it is generally believed that the success of such a process will continue to decrease in the future, as national trends regarding the jury selection process will render scientific jury selection nearly useless (Diamond, 1990).

Forensic Psychology and Policy Implications

When considering jury selection, a number of controversial issues arise. One of the most pervasive concerns in the modern system of justice is whether a truly representative jury is possible. The effects of pretrial publicity, particularly in highly publicized cases (e.g., O. J. Simpson, Theodore Kaczynski, Timothy McVeigh), creates a situation where trying to find jurors who are impartial about the case is extremely unlikely and perhaps even futile. Thus, in many cases, defendants (and their legal representatives) leave their freedom in the hands of jurors who most likely have preconceived ideas or opinions about the case. The legal system permits some exposure to cases through the media, yet attempts to find those jurors who may be less biased than others in the pool. Consequently, the question of whether anyone can receive a truly *fair* trial by an *impartial* jury remains unanswered.

Steps to reduce jury bias, such as voir dire, may have some benefit. They allow for the exemption of jurors who are obviously biased or may show signs of being biased. One of the problems with the voir dire process is that both the defense and the prosecution are entitled to a certain number of dismissals. Consequently, any juror who is presumed to be a detriment to one side's case will be dismissed by the opposing counsel. A policy question arises when we address the voir dire process and the role of the defense and prosecution in that process. If each is concerned with finding jurors who favor, or who they presume will favor, their view, then the final product (selection of jurors) is not truly representative. As noted earlier, a judge may dismiss potential jurors at his or her own discretion. Yet if the judge is presumably unbiased and the defense and prosecution are presumably biased, we would be led to believe that the most unbiased final jury would be selected by the judge alone.

Suggestions for Future Research

Additional research on the effects of pretrial publicity in influencing jury bias is needed. The available research has shown some influence, yet the extent of that influence remains somewhat speculative. If researchers in fields such as forensic psychology are able to determine the type and extent of bias from pretrial publicity, only then can steps be taken to ensure juror impartiality. Further, the voir dire process leaves many questions unanswered. Its effectiveness is questionable, particularly when addressing extended voir dire. Certainly research in the psychology of thought may provide some direction regarding this issue. Specifically, psychology has addressed how biases introduce themselves, why they exist, and why some individuals are able to look past bias-inducing experiences/thoughts while others are not. This information, applied specifically to the legal system, could provide direction for research and possibly a remedy for the issue at hand.

PSYCHOLOGICAL TESTS AND FORENSIC ASSESSMENT INSTRUMENTS IN THE COURTROOM

Introduction

Psychological tests are an objective and standardized measure of a sample of behavior (Anastasi & Urbina, 1997). Typically, psychological tests attempt to shed light on an individual's intelligence, personality, psychopathology, or ability. Traditionally, these tests were normed on clinical or psychiatric populations and were used primarily for diagnosis and treatment. However, with the increasing presence of forensic psychologists in the courtroom, these tests are being used to help determine legal questions or legal constructs. As a result, there is a growing debate over the utility of these tests in the courtroom. Currently, a limited number of forensic assessment tools have been developed specifically for forensic evaluations such as competency to stand trial or criminal responsibility (insanity). Critics argue that the reliability and validity of these instruments have not been sufficiently tested, indicating that future research is needed before these instruments can be used with confidence (Borum & Grisso, 1995).

According to Wakefield and Underwager (1993), the consequences of a forensic evaluation regarding criminal issues such as competency to execute or civil issues such as child custody are potentially immediate and severe. These researchers argue that in a clinical setting if a test is misused or if an inaccurate interpretation of a test is made, the most likely result is a correctable misdiagnosis or an ineffective treatment plan. The controversy over the careful selection and interpretation of assessment tools as well as their legal limits is at the forefront of the debate over the role of forensic psychologists in the courtroom. The following case illustration demonstrates the impact of psychological tests and the responsibility held by forensic psychologists in their administration and interpretation.

> A father in a divorce and custody dispute was accused of tying up his 3-year-old son with a bicycle chain and then sexually abusing him. Both parents were evaluated by a psychologist. The father was tested and interviewed by the psychologist, who left the office, leaving him to finish his drawings. He took them home, finished them with the use of drafting instruments, and brought them to her office the next day.
>
> The psychologist stated that the response style to the projective drawings suggested "obsessive–compulsive tendencies, high defensiveness and an intense need to control . . . [and] his rigidly defensive posture does not adequately bind the underlying anxiety and trepidation of doing poorly" (Wakefield & Underwager, 1993, p. 59). However, his Bender Visual Motor Gestalt Test results were completely normal. His House-Tree-Person (HTP) drawings were careful and detailed. He clearly attempted to do as good a job as possible. Given that his understanding was that these drawings would be interpreted to indicate whether he was an abuser, his choice to carefully complete them at home demonstrates an understandable effort to comply with the instructions and do the best job he could. None of this was noted in the report. There are no scientific data to support the interpretive comment quoted above. It is meaningless jargon with no connection to an empirical base.

Literature Review

Cases like the one presented by Wakefield and Underwager (1993) illustrate the potential for misuse or misinterpretation of psychological tests or other forensic assessment tools. This case illustration demonstrates the great care forensic psychologists must take in choosing, interpreting, and corroborating psychological tests with other relevant archival or third-party information. Forensic psychologists must address the issue of which assessment tools are appropriate in forensic settings. Conclusions reached by forensic psychologists can be challenged during cross-examination and are subject to close scrutiny in the legal arena (Wakefield & Underwager, 1993). Therefore the primary focus of forensic assessment is on accuracy as opposed to a "therapeutic" focus in clinical settings (Heilbrun, 1992). Traditional psychological tests have seen widespread use in forensic contexts. However, their utility is being challenged. Currently, specialized forensic assessment instruments (FAIs) are being developed to address specific legal questions. The rigor by which these instruments have been validated has also come under fire. Forensic psychologists are questioning how to more effectively answer legal referral questions with the available assessment tools.

According to Heilbrun (1992), "the primary legal criterion for the admissibility of psychological testing is relevance to the immediate legal issue or to some underlying psychological construct" (p. 257). He states that the courts typically will not limit the use of psychological tests or forensic instruments if their relevance to the legal standard is shown. Heilbrun explains that relevancy can be demonstrated either by directly measuring a legal construct included in the forensic referral question or by measuring a psychological construct that is considered to make up part of a legal standard. For example, intelligence testing could be used to measure an individual's ability to understand the charges against him or her. He concludes that this relationship could be demonstrated through a written report or testimony (Heilbrun, 1992).

The broad range of legal issues requiring the assessment of a forensic psychologist are subject to a standard that is determined from either statutes or case law. Federal Rules of Evidence, Rule 702 (Melton, Petrila, Poythress, & Slobogin, 1997) considers the admissibility of expert opinions, stating that the primary criterion is whether the opinion will assist the factfinder (judge or jury). Rule 703 indicates that evidence presented by mental health professionals in the legal setting must be "reasonably relied upon" by professionals in the field (Melton *et al.*, 1997, p. 59).

In the past, the majority of courts required that evidence follow the Frye test or that the evidence be based on procedures that have achieved "general acceptance" within that particular profession (*Frye v. United States*, 1923, p. 1013). Critics charge that under the Frye test evidence that is novel yet reliable is excluded while unreliable evidence that has gained general acceptance is allowed (Melton *et al.*, 1997). In 1993 the Supreme Court's decision in *Daubert v. Merrell* shifted the standard for the admissibility of evidence to focus on scientific validity, methodology, and the application of the expert opinion to the facts at issue. Melton and his colleagues (1997) warn that if *Daubert v. Merrell* (1993) were strictly followed, a considerable amount of clinical testimony would not meet this threshold. They maintain that it would prevent the use of novel ways of thinking about human behavior that have relevance to the legal proceeding.

The Supreme Court has upheld rulings that a defendant can present "less reliable" evidence banned by a State statute (*Chambers v. Mississippi*, 1973; *Rock v. Arkansas*, 1987). The Court explained that a defendant's Fourteenth Amendment right to present evidence is paramount to the state's ability to ban such evidence. Heilbrun (1992) recognizes the potential for "... a similar approach to the admissibility of expert mental health testimony based on psychological testing, even if they were inclined to exclude some tests on the grounds of limited psychometric rigor" (p. 261).

Holub (1992) found that in two-thirds of the cases in which clinicians used tests, the Minnesota Multiphasic Personality Inventory (MMPI), the Wechsler Adult Intelligence Scale-Revised (WAIS-R), the Rorschach Psychodiagnostic Inkblots (Rorschach), or the Bender Visual Motor Gestalt tests were used. In a study conducted by Borum and Grisso (1995), 68% of forensic psychologists rated psychological testing as essential or recommended in evaluations for criminal responsibility, with 32% rating it as optional. Of the 94% of forensic psychologists mentioning specific tests, 96% indicated that they used objective personality inventories (typically the MMPI or MMPI-2). Intelligence tests were utilized by 80% of the psychologists followed by neuropsychological instruments at 50% and finally projective tests at 42%. In competence to stand trial evaluations, 51% of the forensic psychologists surveyed viewed psychological testing as essential or recommended and 49% considered it optional.

For criminal responsibility evaluations, 46% of the forensic psychologists in this sample reported they never used forensic assessment instruments (FAIs) and another 20% reported rarely using them. Of the remaining 34%, the break down was as follows: 10% sometime users, 12% frequent users, and 12% almost always users. In competence to stand trial evaluations, 36% of forensic psychologists reported that they almost always use FAIs and 36% reported that they never use them. Borum and Grisso (1995) reported that The Competency to Stand Trial Assessment Instrument and the Competency Screening Test were undoubtedly the most popular FAIs used.

According to Podboy and Kastl (1993), frequent misuse of standard psychological tests include ignorance of the reliability and validity of a particular test, incomplete administration, overreliance on a single test or scale, failure to correlate test results with other available data, and failure to address malingering. Lanyon (1986) notes that in many cases mental health professionals have the awkward task of trying to assess mental state at the time of the alleged offense with instruments that assess current mental functioning. These types of evaluations are done retrospectively and require other sources of data including police reports, medical or mental health records, psychosocial history from friends and family, and the like (Heilbrun, 1992; Lanyon, 1986; Melton *et al.*, 1997).

Melton *et al.* (1997) suggest there are limitations regarding traditional clinical methods in gaining accurate information from forensic populations. These researchers note the potential for malingering, defensiveness, and even normal forgetfulness. Lanyon (1986) maintains that this population is greatly invested in a particular outcome and that attempts will be made to influence the conclusions of an evaluation in their favor.

Forensic assessment instruments have been under development for the past 2 decades. According to Melton *et al.* (1997), these instruments are more focused to specific legal criteria and have been tested on relevant legal populations. However, these researchers acknowledge that many of these instruments are conceptually flawed and lack empirical research. Forensic psychologists are left to determine the methodology of the various psychological tests and forensic assessment instruments available to them as well as their relevance to the legal question.

Forensic Psychology and Policy Implications

Research indicates that traditional psychological tests will continue to be used in forensic assessments. However, as more instruments are developed to address specific legal questions, their role will diminish. Lanyon (1986) points out that years ago traditional psychological instruments were considered adequate to answer all questions in the realm of neuropsychology, specifically, the presence or absence of organicity. He suggests that the area of forensic psychology will also develop its own psychometric instruments specific to legally relevant behaviors.

Some researchers are calling for "... the development of an independent set of standards for the selection, administration, and interpretation of psychological testing in forensic contexts (Heilbrun, 1992, p. 269). The case illustration of the father who is assumed to have sexually abused his child due to his "response style to the projective drawings" demonstrates the need for more accuracy in test administration and interpretation as well as corroborating data if possible in forensic contexts (Wakefield & Underwager, 1993, p. 57). The consequences of a custody dispute as well as accusations of sexual abuse could result in this father's loss of his child and possible incarceration.

Forensic psychologists are continually trying to improve their effectiveness in the legal arena. Unfortunately, many criticisms have been leveled regarding the role of psychologists in the courtroom by legal professionals. The subjective and unreliable nature of the instruments used for assessment is a primary criticism. Techniques by which forensic psychologists can be more effective, persuasive, and credible in legal proceedings are being developed and put into practice.

Suggestions for Future Research

Clearly, the development of methodologically sound forensic assessment instruments is needed. Those FAIs in current use are in need of additional research to determine their validity and reliability. Research is also necessary to determine if these instruments produce any positive trends when used in forensic evaluations.

In general, more empirical data are called for on the uses of psychological tests in forensic evaluations; which are more effective and with which type of evaluation? The many differences between the fields of psychology and law should be continually explored to better prepare forensic psychologists for entry into legal settings.

RISK ASSESSMENT

Introduction

Mental health professionals who work in the arena of forensic psychology are often asked to conduct risk-assessment evaluations. This type of assessment involves making predictions about an individual's likelihood of engaging in future violence. In the criminal justice system, the sentencing hearing is a particularly common time for the court to ask a psychologist to generate an opinion as to an individual's risk for reoffending. In this regard, a psychologist serving as an expert for the court can have a significant influence on the sentence imposed. With a consistent movement toward a more stringent application of the retributive process in the criminal justice system, risk assessments have been utilized more and more frequently in the United States court systems. However, there are a number of very serious issues involved in risk assessment that need to be addressed. Of utmost concern is the lack of accuracy with which psychologists are able to predict future violent behavior. In many instances, a clinician's opinion regarding an individual's likelihood of committing future violence is no better than chance. Based on such knowledge, research in the area of risk assessment is currently focusing on how to improve the predictive models of violence which are utilized by clinicians in making such predictions. The constitutionality of risk assessment, as well as the crucial role that psychologists play in making such predictions, has been examined in such landmark cases as *Barefoot v. Estelle* (1983). The following case illustration summarizes this case as well as the findings by the court.

> Thomas Barefoot was convicted of first-degree murder and sentenced to death by a jury who based their opinion largely on the expert testimony of two psychiatrists. During Mr. Barefoot's sentencing hearing, the jury was instructed to consider whether "there is a probability that the defendant would commit criminal acts of violence that would constitute a continuing threat to society." If the jury found that such a probability existed, they were required to impose the death penalty on Mr. Barefoot. The jury listened to testimony by two psychiatrists, each of whom offered predictions as to Barefoot's likelihood for engaging in future violence. The conclusions by the two psychiatrists that Mr. Barefoot would continue to commit violent acts if he was not executed, assisted the jury in delivering their decision that Mr. Barefoot did indeed deserve the death penalty.
>
> Mr. Barefoot challenged the constitutionality of risk assessment in a appeal to the United States Supreme Court. He argued that the expert testimonies of the psychiatrists were based on unreliable predictions. However, one of the psychiatrists who provided

a risk assessment claimed that the accuracy of his prediction was "100% and absolute." Mr. Barefoot lost his appeal and the presiding Justice White stated that "the likelihood of a defendant committing further crimes is a constitutionally acceptable criterion for imposing the death penalty." (*Barefoot v. Estelle*, 1983, p. 880)

Literature Review

The case of *Barefoot v. Estelle* (1983) has repeatedly been used to illustrate the strength of the influence that psychological testimony has on jurors regarding an individual's perceived risk. While the controversy surrounding the accuracy of risk assessment remains unabated among psychologists and criminologists, certain issues are agreed upon by the vast majority of experts who research and conduct risk assessments. One such issue is that predictions of dangerousness are never 100% accurate. Thus, the psychiatrist who offered an expert opinion in *Barefoot v. Estelle* was misleading jurors at best and perhaps not only made an inaccurate statement, but also an unethical one. This has serious implications given that mental health professionals who provide expert testimony in court regarding a risk assessment carry a great deal of weight in terms of the eventual sentence delivered (Melton *et al.*, 1997).

John Monahan, a leading expert on violence prediction, has examined the concept of risk assessment over the past 2 decades in order to offer some insight as to where this controversial issue is headed in the future (Monahan, 1996). He suggests that years ago, the controversy was centered around the constitutionality of risk assessment. As illustrated by several cases, however, the courts have determined that regardless of the accuracy of the predictions, risk assessments will continue to be allowed in court (*Barefoot v. Estelle*, 1983; *Schall v. Martin*, 1984; *United States v. Salerno*, 1987). With this in mind, Monahan states that rather than focusing on whether clinicians can make accurate predictions about violence, the focus has now shifted to researching ways in which the clinical models of prediction can be improved.

Research has suggested that one way in which the predictive models of future violence can be improved is to use actuarial data as the premise for the prediction as opposed to clinical opinion. M. Miller and Morris (1988) state that clinical prediction is based on professional training and experience, whereas actuarial prediction is based on statistical models used to determine the commonalities between a particular individual and others with similar characteristics who have engaged in violent behavior. Research has consistently shown that actuarial methods are far more sophisticated in terms of predicting risk than clinical methods (McGrath, 1991; Milner & Campbell, 1995). As noted by McGrath (1991), "it is imperative that decisions that can affect the liberty of offenders and the safety of the community are based not only on clinical experience but on empirical findings as well" (p. 331). However, limitations have also been noted with the use of actuarial data. For instance, the court system often has difficulty understanding information that utilizes statistical predictors (Melton *et al.*, 1997). Milner and Campbell (1995) suggest that a combination of actuarial and clinical methods will provide the most accurate risk assessment.

While the literature remains controversial, there are certain factors that have consistently been shown to be significantly related to future violent behavior. Among such factors are the individual's score on the Hare Psychopathy Checklist, a history of criminal behavior, a history of substance abuse, and the age of the offender (G. Harris, Rice, & Quinsey, 1993). Other studies have attempted to develop predictive models for specific types of offenders. Blanchette (1996) states that there are special considerations in conducting risk assessments for sexual offenders, such as assessing the individual's cognitive processes, their general lifestyle, and their history of sexual deviance. Moreover, as noted by Quinsey, Lalumiere, Rice, and Harris (1995), risk assessments vary considerably depending on the specific type of sexual offender. For this reason, mental health professionals who are not trained specifically in the assessment of sexual offenders are likely to draw erroneous conclusions regarding their risk. Another common population for whom mental health professionals tend to conduct inaccurate risk assessments is the mentally ill. It has been suggested that this may be due to the illusory correlation between mental illness and violence or the belief that an individual is more dangerous simply because he or she is mentally ill (Melton *et al.*, 1997). Therefore, it is crucial for mental health professionals to truly have expertise with the specific population on whom they purport the ability to conduct risk assessments.

Melton *et al.* (1997) provides guidelines for the most appropriate ways for mental health professionals to communicate the results of their risk assessments to the courts. These authors stress the importance of refraining from using language which suggests that their opinion is absolute. They also suggest that experts present information to the court regarding the factors which have been empirically shown to enhance an individual's risk for violent behavior. Finally, these researchers encourage mental health professionals to provide the court with a statement as to the poor validity of violence prediction. These suggestions are in stark contrast to the method employed by the psychiatrist who testified in the *Barefoot v. Estelle* (1983) case.

In California, even those mental health professionals who are not accustomed to their work entering the legal system have been faced with the issue of conducting risk assessments. In 1976, the landmark case of *Tarasoff v. Regents of the University of California* delivered a decision that requires therapists to take preventative measures if any reasonable therapist would believe that their client is likely to harm an identifiable victim in the near future. Currently, most jurisdictions have a statute similar to that of Tarasoff in California (Melton *et al.*, 1997). Thus, this statute brought the issue of risk assessment into the lives of all therapists. In so doing, controversy exists among mental health professionals concerning the damage that this form of risk assessment has on the therapeutic process and the ethical principle of confidentiality between a therapist and his or her client.

Forensic Psychology and Policy Implications

Experts have consistently agreed that predicting risk for future violent behavior is an extremely difficult task (G. C. N. Hall, 1990; McGrath, 1991; Monahan, 1981). However, it is likely that the courts will continue to turn to psychologists to provide risk assessments, despite the difficulties noted in providing accurate predictions. The courts have repeatedly ruled that expert testimony is permissible regarding the predictions of violent behavior (*Barefoot v. Estelle*, 1983; *Schall v. Martin*, 1984; *United States v. Salerno*, 1987). With this in mind, it is crucial for the mental health professionals who provide risk assessments to the courts to uphold their ethical duty and acknowledge the limitations of their expertise in making such predictions.

As illustrated in the case of *Barefoot v. Estelle* (1983), there are decisions that juries make which require the risk assessment to be a primary consideration in their final decision. Perhaps there are legislative and policy reforms that need to be considered, given the overwhelming evidence that risk predictions are unreliable. Suppose for a moment that Mr. Barefoot was in fact sentenced to death because of the testimony by a psychiatrist who claimed to be able to predict with 100% accuracy that imposing the death penalty was the only way to keep Mr. Barefoot from committing another violent crime. There are currently no provisions against an expert witness providing such testimony in court. Given the weight that the judge and jurors give to expert testimony regarding predictions of dangerousness, the criminal justice and the mental health systems would do well to place parameters around the predictions that can be offered in court.

Suggestions for Future Research

To date, no predictive models exist which can predict future dangerousness with a high degree of certainty. Given that risk assessments continue to be commonly requested of forensic psychologists, it is imperative that research continues to explore factors which are associated with future dangerous behavior. The research has grown tremendously in the past 20 years on violence prediction; however, the accuracy of such predictions remains extremely limited. The predictive models that have been established thus far need to be tested in longitudinal studies across diverse populations of offenders.

An additional area of research that has not received as much attention concerns the jurors' decision-making process regarding expert testimony of risk assessments. This would shed light on the impact that mental health professionals have when providing risk assessments to the court. The decisions of jurors could then be compared to the decisions of judges in this regard in order to establish whether the judge is better able to consider the limitations of risk assessments when rendering his or her final decision.

FORENSIC VERDICTS OR PSYCHIATRIC JUSTICE: NOT GUILTY BY REASON OF INSANITY AND GUILTY BUT MENTALLY ILL

Introduction

The insanity defense has long been a debated issue within psychology, the legal system, and society in general. Melton *et al.* (1987) have referred to the defense of insanity as "probably the most controversial issue in all of criminal law" (p. 112). While society and the law have historically been inclined to treat rather than punish mentally ill offenders, there are nevertheless a plethora of arguments that encourage an alteration in the legal system's present philosophy toward insanity and crime. Such strong opposition to the defense of insanity is founded upon several notable cases in which societal perception was that justice was not done. In addition, there are several problems with the insanity defense as it stands. These problems encourage the perspective that such defenses should be at the very least modified, if not entirely eliminated, while other alternatives should be implemented.

One such alternative was established in the 1970s and is referred to as the Guilty but Mentally Ill (GBMI) verdict. Thus, GBMI is not a defense per se, but a verdict that is reached wherein the defendant is found guilty, but his or her need for treatment is acknowledged. The GBMI verdict, however, has also had its critics. In addition to the proposal of a GBMI verdict and in response to the perceived inadequacy of the Not Guilty by Reason of Insanity (NGRI) defense, several states have adopted other alternatives. Montana, for example, has completely eliminated the insanity defense. In this section, we explore the purpose of the insanity defense and the different variations of "insanity" and tests for insanity as well as several of the proposed alternatives.

> On March 30, 1981, John Hinckley, Jr. attempted to assassinate the then-President of the United States, Ronald Reagan. Hinckley was apprehended and, a little over a year later, went to trial for his actions. One of the psychiatrists in the case offered the opinion that Hinckley was unable to control himself (i.e., that he did not know what he was doing). Hinckley's attorneys invoked the defense of insanity. It was argued that Hinckley was driven to action by the movie "Taxi Driver" in which the lead character stalks and attempts to assassinate the President in an effort "win over" the 12-year-old prostitute played by Jodie Foster. Hinckley is said to have seen the movie numerous times and become infatuated with the "hero" of the movie to the degree that he was driven to reenact the events of the movie in real life.
>
> The expert witnesses (mental health professionals) in the case were in general agreement that Hinckley suffered from schizophrenia. Hinckley's defense argued that if someone can be so influenced by a movie as to reenact those events in his real life, he must not be in a rational frame of mind and therefore should not be held responsible for his actions. His attorneys agreed with the prosecution in conceding that Hinckley had planned the attack (therefore establishing premeditation and a presumably "sound" mind), yet they claimed his entire "plan" was based on the movie and that he was acting upon forces that resulted from a diseased mind. Several months later, the jury returned the verdict of NGRI.

Literature Review

The Purpose of the Insanity Defense

It must first be noted that "insanity" does not refer to mental illness alone. It is a common misconception that "insane" equates to "mentally ill" or "psychotic" or "crazy." It is often thought that "the insane" are those seeking (or not seeking) help from the mental health profession. In fact, "insanity" is specifically a legal term that is not used in psychological literature. *Black's Law Dictionary* (Garner, 1996) defines "insanity" as "any mental disorder severe enough that it prevents one from having legal capacity and excuses one from criminal or civil responsibility" (p. 319). Thus, insanity is a legal standard that must be differentiated from the medical and psychological conceptions of mental illness, psychosis, and the like. While the presence of a mental illness is often required for a finding of "insanity," it alone is not sufficient. We explore this distinction later in this section.

The insanity defense is generally invoked by those considered to be of unsound mind at the time they committed their offense. Historically, society tends to hold criminals responsible for their actions. That is, we regard their crimes as having been committed by rational persons who have made a free choice concerning their actions. Naturally, society finds justice in punishing such offenders. In other cases, however, persons committing crimes are thought to be too irrational to have made a sound decision regarding criminal actions. In such cases, we have been reluctant to impose punishment on such individuals. In instances where persons have committed crimes without being aware of what they were doing, why they were doing it, or who may have been unable to control themselves, society often feels that these persons need not be held liable for their actions and, in some cases, are in need of compassion. Thus, the prevailing attitude has been that such persons are in need of treatment rather than punishment.

The American legal system is based upon the notions of morality and blameworthiness (Melancon, 1998). To be criminally responsible and therefore subjected to punishment for one's actions, one must be capable of making a moral decision regarding one's actions to be blameworthy. Theories of punishment are founded upon the idea that human beings are free to make rational decisions concerning the actions in which they engage. Therefore, such individuals are to be held accountable for their actions. Insanity (i.e., mental disease or defect) is thought to interfere with such free and rational decision making. Therefore, the presence of insanity does not allow for an individual to form "criminal intent." Such intent (i.e., *mens rea*) is necessary for a finding of blameworthiness under the American legal system. It is generally held, then, that the insane offender is better served by rehabilitation than punishment. If one is unable to make a rational decision about one's actions, punishment is unlikely to persuade one (or others) not to engage in similar behavior. In light of the questionable value of punishing the mentally ill, rehabilitation through hospitalization and psycho-medical treatment is generally considered to be in the better interest of the individual and society.

The Historical Basis of the Insanity Defense

The case of Daniel M'Naughten is generally regarded as the historical origin of the insanity defense. M'Naughten shot and killed the British Prime Minister's secretary in 1843. The jury found M'Naughten to be insane at the time he committed the offense and acquitted him of the charges. The verdict in the M'Naughten case was somewhat controversial at the time and consequently resulted in an official process of inquiry wherein English common law judges were given the task to determine the precise standards for competency. The first official test to determine a defendant's sanity developed out of these proceedings (Moran, 1981).

The test that came to be known as the M'Naughten Test required clear proof that the individual was, at the time he or she committed the offense, under defect of reason resulting from a disease of the mind and that such defect resulted in the individual not being able to recognize the nature and quality of his or her actions (or not knowing that such actions were wrong). The idea behind such a rule concerns the presence of *mens rea*. It is often thought that insane persons do not possess sufficient *mens rea* (criminal intent) to be found guilty for the crimes they commit. As *mens rea* along with *actus reus* (wrongful act) are the necessary components for criminal liability, the absence of necessary intention on the part of the actor justifies not punishing the individual. The M'Naughten Test for insanity became the official determinant of sanity in Great Britain and its standard was adopted by the United States.

The M'Naughten Test eventually expanded to include an "irresistible impulse" component. In such cases, an insanity defense was raised on the grounds that the person knew the nature and quality of their actions, knew that it was wrong, but whose mental disability resulted in an "overpowering compulsion" which did not enable the individual to resist the actions he or she undertook. The rationale for the "irresistible impulse" provision was that such a powerful compulsion was sufficiently strong that the prospect of criminal punishment would not act as a deterrent and, thus, persons should not be held accountable for their actions.

In 1954, Judge David Bazelon proposed an even broader test for insanity (*Durham v. United States*, 1954). Judge Bazelon opined that "an accused is not criminally responsible if his unlawful act was the product of mental disease or mental defect" (pp. 874–875). In reacting against the cognitive test of M'Naughten and in consideration of the available psychological literature at the time, the Durham Test held that "[o]ur collective conscience does not allow punishment where it cannot impose blame" (pp. 666–667). In other words, we punish those committing criminal acts of their own free will and criminal intent (i.e., *mens rea*). Those persons whose actions are the result of a mental disease are not held to be morally responsible for their actions and, consequently, should not be punished as others.

Like the M'Naughten Test, the Durham Test also sustained its share of criticism. As a result, the American Law Institute (ALI) proposed its own test for insanity. This test would be known as the ALI Test. The ALI Test holds that "a person is not responsible for criminal conduct if at the time of such conduct as a result of mental disease or defect he lacks substantial capacity either to appreciate the [wrongfulness] of his conduct or to conform his conduct to the requirements of the law" (Model Penal Code, Section 4.01, as cited in Melancon, 1998, p. 293). The ALI Test includes both a cognitive component (lack of appreciation for wrongfulness) and a volitional component (unable to control behavior). Thus, it is widely recognized as being advantageous over either the M'Naughten or the Durham Tests. Further, the ALI Test's focus on "substantial incapacity" is thought more realistic than a necessary showing of total incapacity as is necessary with M'Naughten.

Forensic Psychology and Policy Implications

After the verdict reached in the Hinckley case, the issue of insanity assumed one of the more controversial roles in American legal history. The American public generally felt that justice had not been served in what they perceived as letting the man who attempted to assassinate the President "go free" (H. Steadman et al., 1993). In fact, Hinckley's acquittal, as with any successful insanity defense, is not grounds for immediate release back into society. Rather, the offender found not guilty by reason of insanity is confined to a mental hospital for an indeterminate length of time. It is rare that such offenders are released from the hospital short of several years, and many remain there for most (if not all) of their lives. The criteria for release in these cases are far more restrictive than other cases of commitment (L. Wrightsman et al., 1994). In fact, it is not uncommon for an insanity acquitee to serve more time in a psychiatric hospital than he or she would have served in prison had the jury returned a guilty verdict.

The primary beliefs of the public concerning the insanity defense are that criminals often employ the defense; many of these criminals are "set free" by naive juries; those found NGRI are released back into society after the trial; and such persons present a threat to society, as they are dangerous and once again "on the streets" (Melton et al., 1987). Public outcry, however misinformed it may be, places a tremendous amount of pressure on the justice system to revise its handling of these cases. In fact, the reality of the insanity defense is much different than the public generally believes. The insanity defense is employed in only about 1 out of every 200 criminal cases. Of these, it is successful less than 1% of the time (L. Wrightsman et al., 1994).

The basis of the misconception that such acquitees "go free" is, perhaps, the use of the phrase "not guilty" with regard to the insanity defense. In response to such public outcry, some states have implemented the GBMI verdict. The primary difference with regard to the GBMI verdict concerns the finding of "guilty" rather than "not guilty." In states allowing for a finding of GBMI, the defendant generally pleads insanity, but the jury has the option of finding him or her GBMI rather than

NGRI. In such cases, the defendant is sentenced for the crime committed, but spends the sentence in a hospital until sanity is restored. If and when such a time arrives that the defendant is perceived to have regained her or his sanity, the person is transported to prison to serve the remainder of the sentence. Generally speaking, the public is often less likely to oppose a finding of GBMI. Presumably, this perception of justice being served has, to some extent, a relationship to the fact that the offender has been found guilty of his or her crime in one way or another. Thus, had John Hinckley, Jr. been found GBMI rather than NGRI perhaps the public would have rested more content.

One of the more common criticisms of the insanity defense concerns its reliance on expert testimony. That is, the disposition of cases in which insanity is an issue is placed in the hands of psychologists and psychiatrists who ultimately influence the jurors' opinions as to the defendant's mental state at the time of the offense. This controversy raises important issues regarding the extent to which psychology is and should be involved in the legal process. Critics argue that psychologists are often unsuccessful in evaluations of insanity. This criticism often stems from the fact that psychologists are asked to provide opinions, which are potentially extremely influential in court, on matters in which they hold little understanding. In other words, psychologists are often untrained or undertrained in legal matters. This very point, perhaps, marks an intersection for the field of forensic psychology. Justice, it would appear, necessitates an understanding of both the legal and psychological disciplines when treating cases such as those employing the insanity defense. Until recently, this cross-disciplinary training has been essentially nonexistent. With the advent of programs stressing both psychology and law (i.e., forensic psychology), the system of justice may be turning in this direction.

Suggestions for Future Research

Given that criticism concerning the insanity defense often targets the role of psychology in the legal process, it seems necessary to ascertain the effectiveness of such involvement. In other words, are psychologists helping to inform justice or merely interfering with justice? This raises important issues for future research in the field. In particular, it may be helpful to understand to what extent forensic psychologists can improve upon the previous wedding of psychology to the legal system. Does forensic psychology have something to offer that traditional psychology does not?

Additionally, the efficacy of insanity defense reform and proposals for reform must be examined in more depth. As mentioned, several states have adopted alternative policies including the GBMI verdict. Some states have taken it upon themselves to create their own standards for determining sanity. Are such alternatives more successful in the eyes of the law? The public? Justice? These questions are not nearing resolution and must be further examined in light of continuing developments.

CHAPTER 6

Juvenile Forensics

OVERVIEW

The role of psychology in the juvenile justice system brings a different set of pressing and complicated issues to the forensic field than its adult counterpart. As various and recent media accounts depict, adolescent behavior can be no less gruesome and shocking than conduct committed by career criminals. The domain of juvenile forensic psychology examines the conduct of children and explains why they act deviantly and break the law. Although there are many more questions about adolescent (mis-)behavior than there are answers to date, the psychological sciences can help the court system make sense out of what juveniles do and why.

There are four controversies investigated in this chapter. These topics include (1) defining the age of criminal responsibility; (2) juveniles and the reliability of their courtroom testimony; (3) the "best interest of the child" doctrine; and (4) sentencing: the psychology of juvenile rehabilitation. Certainly, many other contested subjects exist in the legal domain of juvenile forensics; however, these four issues represent key areas of considerable debate within the law and psychology communities. In addition, the four issues explored in this chapter demonstrate where and how forensic psychological experts are called upon to assist the court system from the pretrial adjudication phase to the postconviction stage of a particular case.

Adolescents can behave recklessly and deviantly. They can also engage in illicit conduct. What knowing decision-making capabilities do children exercise when breaking the law? How does psychology help us determine when youths are or are not responsible for their (criminal actions)? Is there a definable age of criminal responsibility?

Juveniles can provide testimonial evidence in a court of law. How does the child's age impact the admissibility and/or veracity of his/her testimony? Can youths tell the difference between right and wrong? Do adolescents understand the consequences of giving sworn testimony in a legal proceeding?

Child custody cases involve a decision about the placement of a youth with a particular parent or parental surrogate. Typically, judges rely upon the "best interest of the child" doctrine. What is this standard and how do psychologists interpret it? How, if at all, does the juvenile court system promote it? To what degree does the "best interest of the child" standard aid judges in child custody determinations?

Youths who violate the law can be held accountable for their behavior. Are children who engage in illicit conduct troubled or dangerous? How do the psychological sciences assist the court system in treating at-risk youths?

The field of juvenile justice and the courtroom process are fraught with difficult questions about the appropriate and necessary response to individual acts of adolescent misconduct. The discipline of psychology seeks to provide some worthwhile solutions. As the sections of this chapter demonstrate, there is an important role for forensic psychologists in the juvenile court arena. As a matter of policy, the entire adjudication process remains largely uncharted by mental health specialists. Notwithstanding, therapists, administrators, and advocates in the psychological community are routinely called upon to help address the problems of at-risk youths and to divert them, where possible, away from the formal justice system. Solutions to many of the remaining questions in the juvenile forensic arena require careful and thoughtful research strategies. As the sections of this chapter repeatedly make clear, this is one viable direction by which psychologists can assist those court practitioners who work in the field.

DEFINING THE AGE OF CRIMINAL RESPONSIBILITY

Introduction

> There is evidence . . . that there may be grounds for concern that the child receives the worst of both worlds: that he (or she) gets neither the protections accorded to adults nor the solicitous care and regenerative treatment postulated for children. (383 U.S., at 556, 1966)

The above statement was taken from the United States Supreme Court case of *Kent v. United States* (1966). In this case an intruder entered the apartment of a woman in the District of Columbia, raped her, and then took her wallet. The fingerprints at the apartment matched those of Morris Kent, a 16-year-old. He was soon taken into custody and interrogated from 3 P.M. to 10 P.M. the same evening. The next day Kent underwent further interrogation by the police. Kent's mother did not know that he was in custody until 2 P.M. on the second day.

Kent's mother and her counsel visited Kent, at which time he was charged with housebreaking, robbery, and rape. This section examines the issues stemming from this example, especially the question of when juveniles are responsible for their actions and how juveniles should be treated for their actions. This section examines the respective roles criminal justice and psychology assume in creating, sustaining, and responding to the issue of the age of criminal responsibility. Also examined is the age of criminal responsibility by looking at and providing examples of the juvenile and criminal court systems, reviewing literature, analyzing case law, and discussing current research.

At the turn of the century juvenile offenders were separated from adult offenders because they were seen as treatable. Today, however, there is a general trend in society to hold juvenile offenders accountable (Umbreit, 1995). According to Umbreit, society is moving away from rehabilitation and restorative justice; instead, society is moving toward punishment and retributive justice. In the 1980s many state legislatures passed laws that enacted waivers which transferred juvenile offenders of serious and violent crimes from the juvenile justice system into the criminal justice system. These waivers lowered the age of criminal responsibility and held juveniles accountable, as adults, for their crimes. The Supreme Court said that with the lowering of the age of responsibility, due process should be present in the juvenile justice system (Fritsch & Hemmens, 1995).

The Courts' trend toward punishment creates a need for psychologists to determine when people are responsible for their actions and when they should be punished. When trying to determine the psychological age of responsibility, one cannot base the answer on a decision from a court, like the legal age of responsibility. This creates some tension between these two fields. Notwithstanding, the fields of psychology and law are continually merging closer together. To understand cases like *Kent v. United States* (1966) and the age of criminal responsibility, we examine the relevant legal and psychological literature.

Literature Review

According to Fritsch and Hemmens (1995), English common law held that children under the age of 7 were incapable of criminal responsibility. Children between the ages of 7 and 14 were still incapable unless it could be established that they were able to understand the consequences of their actions. Juveniles over the age of 14 were considered fully responsible for their actions and would receive the same punishment as adult offenders. The *parens patriae* doctrine, which is derived from English common law, allows the state to intervene and act in the "best interests of the child" whenever it is deemed necessary (Reppucci & Crosby, 1993).

What is "in the best interest" of the juvenile? When a 15-year-old girl wants an abortion should the court grant her request? As discussed by Reppucci and Crosby (1993), "in most situations there are several alternatives that may be equally positive or harmful for a child" (p. 4). So, it is important for the court to understand as much as possible about the juvenile in order to increase the odds of a positive outcome. In the case of *Kent v. United States* (1966), the court stated that "the *parens patriae* philosophy of the Juvenile Court is not an invitation to procedural arbitrariness" (383 U.S. 556, 1966).

There is a general trend in society to lower the age of criminal responsibility and to punish rather than rehabilitate offenders. "This move away from rehabilitation has had a marked impact on every level of the criminal justice system, from the police to the courts to corrections" (Fritsch & Hemmens, 1995, p. 17). Legislatures responded to the public's desire to "get tough" on crime by passing laws that have toughened the adult criminal justice system. These laws included making prison sentences longer, eliminating "good time" credits used toward an earlier parole, and replacing indeterminate with determinate sentencing. The trend of holding the offender accountable carried over from the adult criminal system into the juvenile justice system with the rise in adolescent crime. The juvenile courts then shifted away from rehabilitation and moved toward punishment. This shift caused a large increase in the use of waivers by judges (Fritsch & Hemmens, 1995). Judges use waivers to place juveniles into the adult justice system so that youth offenders can receive a more severe punishment. This procedure or waiver is also referred to as "certification," "transfer," "reference," "remand," or "declination" (Kinder, Veneziano, Fichter, & Azuma, 1995).

In the 1980s many state legislatures passed laws that enacted waivers. These certifications transferred juvenile offenders of serious and violent crimes from the juvenile justice system into the criminal justice system. The legislatures believed that the juveniles would then receive a greater punishment for their offenses. In one research study this intention of greater punishment was found only to be true in a small number of cases (Kinder *et al.*, 1995). In fact, the juvenile cases transferred to adult courts were far more likely to be pending or unresolved (see below for the results of a comparison study done by Kinder *et al.*, 1995). Waivers are usually attached to the more serious and violent crimes like murder, rape, and aggravated assault because these offenses need more severe sanctions than the juvenile justice system can impose (Fritsch & Hemmens, 1995).

> *A Comparison of the Dispositions of Juvenile Offenders Certified as Adults with Juvenile Offenders Not Certified*
>   In 1993 a study was conducted that tracked a group of juvenile offenders certified to adult court with a noncertified adjudicated sample of juvenile offenders to compare the two groups. Its primary purpose was to determine whether those certified as adults

were treated more punitively by the criminal justice system than those adjudicated for felonies in juvenile court. The two samples were taken from St. Louis, Missouri. The total sample consisted of 111 male juveniles ranging in ages from 14 to 17.

It was clear that the cases were moved more rapidly at the juvenile level as opposed to the adult level. For all the 1993 cases, all juveniles in the adjudicated sample had their cases decided. At the adult level, however, nearly two-thirds of the cases had either been taken under advisement or were pending (36.0 and 29.7% respectively). It is clear that for many of the juveniles transferred to general jurisdiction court, there were no immediate consequences. It is also apparent that for most of the cases, transfer to general jurisdiction court did not mean that a "get tough" policy was implemented. Of the sample remanded to adult court, 6.3% were sent to prison. Another 17.0% were placed on probation. Most of the remaining cases had not been completed, and many will most likely be dismissed.

In contrast, nearly one-half (49.5%) of the sample that went through juvenile court was placed on probation, and 20.7% was placed with the Division of Youth Services and sent to an institution. Cases determined at the juvenile court level were thus more likely to receive the services provided by the juvenile court. It was found that youths are treated as first-time offenders when they reach adult courts. The results suggest that most juveniles transferred to adult court are not given longer punishments than if they had remained in the juvenile justice system. Furthermore, it is not clear that at the adult level they will receive the services for youth potentially available to them if they had gone to juvenile court. General jurisdiction court might be the only solution for a small number of youthful offenders who have committed very serious crimes, but this policy appears unlikely as implemented at present to either have a deterrent effect or to deal with the problems facing juvenile offenders. (Adapted from Kinder *et al.*, 1995, pp. 37–41)

There are several types of waivers, but the two most common are the judicial waiver and the legislative waiver (Fritsch & Hemmens, 1995). The judicial waiver is popular because it allows the juvenile court judges to use their discretionary power to waive jurisdiction and send the case to adult court. The juvenile court may decide on its own to use a waiver or base its decision on the prosecuting attorney's motion. The legislative waiver is sometimes called the automatic waiver because this waiver can cause some juvenile offenders to completely bypass the juvenile justice system and go directly to the adult criminal justice system at the time of the arrest. For example, if a 14-year-old juvenile in Idaho is arrested for the possession of drugs and/or firearms near a school or at a school event, the youth is automatically sent to a criminal court (Fritsch & Hemmens, 1995). The judge in Idaho has no power of discretion in this case because the juvenile meets one of the requirements of the Idaho state government legislative waiver. In the example of *Kent v. United States* (1966), the juvenile court judge ordered a judicial waiver to place the 16-year-old Kent into the criminal court system and he was tried as an adult. Kent's counsel filed a "question of waiver" motion. This motion was filed in the juvenile court asking for a hearing to present reasons why Kent should be tried as an adult and his motion was refused.

Juvenile offenders who appear before a judge in juvenile court are no longer seen or treated as immature children who deserve protection from the juvenile justice system. Instead juveniles who are accused of serious crimes are held accountable and punished (Fritsch & Hemmens, 1995). This has led to treating juvenile offenders the same as adult offenders, especially those charged with violent crimes. This begs two questions: If you are going to hold a juvenile accountable as an adult, then should the juvenile receive the same rights as an adult? Second, what are the relationships that exist between children's responsibilities and children's rights? The Supreme Court said that with the lowering of the age of responsibility, due process should be present in the juvenile justice system (Fritsch & Hemmens, 1995). A major reason for the courts granting juveniles more rights is the belief that because of their age and inexperience they lack the ability and/or capacity to protect their own best interests (Reppucci & Crosby, 1993).

In *Kent v. United States* (1966), the Supreme Court outlined the procedures for using waivers and extended several due process rights to juveniles that are involved in the waiver process. The waiver hearing must be a full hearing in which the juvenile has the right to have counsel present (Fritsch & Hemmens, 1995).

When determining the psychological age of responsibility, one cannot base the answer on a decision from a court, such as the legal age of responsibility. The age of responsibility differs from state to state, but federal law regards juveniles as adults at the age of 16. In *Thompson v. Oklahoma* (1988), the Supreme Court ruled that the Eighth Amendment to the U.S. Constitution prohibited the execution of a person who was under the age of 16 at the time of the offense. According to *Stanford v. Kentucky* (1989) and *Wilkins v. Missouri* (1989), executions are legal for crimes committed by juveniles ages 16 and 17 years. Sixteen is now the constitutional age of responsibility for capital punishment purposes. According to the Supreme Court, whatever type of environment a juvenile comes from, the legal age of responsibility is still 16 years (L. Wrightsman *et al.*, 1994; *Thompson v. Oklahoma*, 1988).

The law has long recognized that children are less mature and less capable than adults in many legal areas. The law, however, is not clear as to what degree certain capacities of responsibility vary with chronological age. For example, as we get older are we more responsible for our actions? The law is also unclear as to how levels of cognitive and socioemotional development affect levels of responsibility (Woolard, Reppucci, & Redding, 1996). When a juvenile court judge sends a youth to the criminal court, the youth is then supposed to meet the adult standard of responsibility. The adult standard of responsibility includes the ability to make informed decisions. This requires "competence." Woolard and her colleagues (1996) indicate that competence generally refers to the knowledge and abilities of a person to express him-/herself under ideal circumstances. The law, however, is only concerned about the youth's capacities in the context of the particular legal act the juvenile was accused of committing. Thus, the law is more interested in the actions of individuals rather than their competence.

Psychologists maintain that a person can learn from his or her mistakes and succeed in life if placed in the right environment. It would be ideal for the courts, when holding a juvenile offender accountable, to consider if the juvenile had both a cognitive meaning (understanding impact of their behavior on the victim) and a behavioral meaning (taking action to make things right) for their conduct

(Umbreit, 1995). Umbreit also argues that the justice system should start practicing interventions or "restorative justice" in which the victim, the offender, and the community actively solve problems together. Psychologists would then be called in to assist the juvenile justice system with this proactive approach.

Forensic Psychology and Policy Implications

It used to be that when an offense occurred, the offender incurred an obligation to society and/or the victim. Even though public safety was of primary concern, the idea was not to punish the offender; rather, it was to provide opportunities for the offender to offer restitution to the victims and/or community. It is important, however, for the courts to remember that juveniles are still growing and developing. "Our lack of scientific knowledge concerning child development and family functioning renders what is in the best interests of children largely indeterminate" (Reppucci & Crosby, 1993, p. 5). There is no way to guarantee that what psychologists and courts believe is actually in the best interest of a youth. If society is going to hold a juvenile accountable as an adult, then the juvenile should receive the same rights as an adult. Additionally, when the court treats a youthful offender like an adult, does the court protect the youth and society (now and in the future)? In the legal system many unlawful acts also constitute moral violations, therefore we must take into account how moral development affects the ability of a juvenile to understand why a particular action is "wrong" (Peterson-Badali & Abramovitch, 1993).

Suggestions for Future Research

In order to provide useful information for legal decision makers, future psychological research must be conducted with legal issues in mind. In this way, the findings will have a direct impact on the law (Reppucci & Crosby, 1993). We need to continue to examine legal cases like *Kent v. United States* (1966) and integrate psychology's knowledge about children's best interests and capacities to the decision-making process of the juvenile justice system. If research is conducted carefully with the inclusion of legal issues, the relationship between psychology and law can be woven together and will enable judges to make decisions that are in the best interest of the juvenile. Legal standards and their assumptions about children's capacities must be investigated from both legal and psychological perspectives (Woolard *et al.*, 1996). Studying children's capacities and performance in a legal context, however, is difficult because children can only be compared with adults or other "normal" children (Woolard *et al.*, 1996).

Throughout this section, issues of whether to rehabilitate or to punish an individual have continually occurred. It is important to conduct research on the effects of punishment versus treatment so that juveniles who need help can effectively obtain it. It is important to study age-appropriate legal decision making so that juveniles have the freedom to make legal decisions on their own while allowing them the opportunity to understand the law and their rights. It would also be beneficial to do research on the relationships that exist between children's responsibilities and children's rights. Research in this area is difficult because it is hard to determine at what age all juveniles can be allowed to make their own life decisions, when each juvenile is unique. Studying age-appropriate decision making raises other issues: Are we better decision makers as our age increases, and is age the most important factor in determining responsibility? When examining the age of criminal responsibility it is essential to include as many variables as possible such as environment, ethnicity, socioeconomic status, and even IQ. By studying the age of criminal responsibility, forensic psychologists can examine the effectiveness of the current juvenile justice system and make suggestions as to which changes could be made to improve the treatment of juvenile offenders.

CHILDREN/JUVENILES AND THE RELIABILITY OF THEIR COURTROOM TESTIMONY

Introduction

More and more often, children are becoming involved in the legal system to provide courtroom testimony, especially in sexual abuse cases (Ceci & Bruck, 1993). It has been estimated that more than 200,000 children per year are in some way involved in the legal system (Ceci & Bruck, 1995). Frequently, children provide key testimony because their word is the only evidence available in many abuse cases. The court must then determine whether the child is a reliable witness (J. E. B. Myers, 1993a). As is discussed in this section, the court must examine various factors, such as the child's age, whether the child can tell the difference between the truth and a lie, and whether the child understands the consequences of the testimony he or she will provide.

> Martha is a 12-year-old girl who has recently accused her old babysitter, a neighborhood friend named Mitch, of sexually abusing her when she was 8 years old. She never told anyone about this while it was occurring because she said he had threatened to kill her favorite pet dog. However, recently she was behaving in an inappropriate sexual manner, so her parents questioned her about her behaviors until she finally admitted what had occurred several years ago. Her parents pressed charges against Mitch, and they are expecting the case to go to trial because Mitch denied his guilt. Martha is the only witness for the prosecution, and she has been questioned many times about the alleged abuse. Some of the details of her story have changed, and she has expressed great fear about having to be in the courtroom with Mitch. Because of the inaccuracies in her story, the prosecutor wants the judge to determine if she is a competent witness. He has also requested the use of closed-circuit television so that Martha will not be in the room with Mitch when she testifies. The judge must determine whether Martha is a

competent witness by deciding if she can distinguish the truth from a lie and understand the meaning of taking an oath. She also must decide whether allowing Martha to testify via closed-circuit television would be a violation of Mitch's constitutional rights.

Literature Review

As reflected in the case illustration, having a child present testimony in court is not a simple, straightforward matter. There are many factors that need to be considered. Because prosecutors rely so much on children's testimony, especially in abuse cases, it is important to determine if children are competent to testify (Saywitz, 1995). It used to be common practice to have children below a certain age deemed automatically incompetent. Yet, a 1770 case, *Rex v. Brasier*, held that there should be nothing automatic in determining competency, no matter how young the child (J. E. B. Myers, 1993b). *Wheeler v. U.S.* (1895) stated that no age marker should determine competency to testify. However, there are a few states that still use this approach. The approach used in most states today is that everyone is competent, which comes from the Federal Rules of Evidence—Rule 601. Some states also guarantee competence in sexual abuse cases (J. E. B. Myers, 1993b).

Whatever the state's approach, judges are ultimately responsible for determining children's competence, and they have broad discretionary powers. According to J. E. B. Myers (1993b), there are three main requirements that judges use to determine competency. The first is whether children have certain capabilities. For example, they must be able to observe what occurs in the courtroom, not necessarily completely comprehend what happens. They must possess adequate memory. Firush and Shukat (1995) reported that even young children, ages 3 to 6, are capable of providing detailed descriptions of past events after long periods of time. J. E. B. Myers (1993b) described further capabilities that children must possess in order to be deemed competent to testify. Children must be able to communicate. They also must be able to tell the truth from a lie and understand the importance of telling the truth. In other words, they must understand the consequences of lying. K. Bussey, Lee, and Grimbeck (1993) indicated that even 4-year-olds have the capacity to distinguish a lie from the truth and that they are able to knowingly lie or tell the truth. The second requirement described by J. E. B. Myers (1993b) is whether children have personal knowledge about facts pertinent to the case. This comes from Rule 602 of the Federal Rules of Evidence. The final requirement is taking the oath. A. G. Walker (1993) stated that children can be found incompetent if they do not understand the meaning of the wording of the oath. However, some states allow children to forego this element and still testify (J. E. B. Myers, 1993b). In Martha's situation, the judge will have to determine if she possesses the capabilities described above and whether she understands the meaning of an oath.

If the prosecutor wants to proceed with Martha's case and use her as the sole witness, she/he must decide whether her testimony is reliable so that the jury will believe her. According to Jaskiewicz-Obydzinska and Czerederecka (1995), evaluation of a child's reliability is extremely imperative and is determined by the stability of his or her account after consecutive interrogations of the child. The authors conducted a study with juvenile witnesses/victims of sexual abuse, with the majority between the ages of 11 and 15. They found that in half of those examined, testimonial changes occurred. However, they found that the most common reason for these changes was the juvenile's low intellectual level. They concluded that in order to accept a child's testimony as reliable, psychological factors that include intellectual ability, significant fear of social evaluation, and increased self-criticism should be considered.

In addition to Martha's conflicting stories, her age also presents a problem with establishing reliability. Bottoms (1993) reported that younger children tend to be viewed as more reliable than older children and adolescents in testifying about sexual abuse. People believe that children are not cognitively efficient and therefore could not possibly invent such stories, whereas adolescents are believed to be at fault in the sexual abuse or to have fabricated their story.

Another factor affecting the reliability of children's testimony is the stress of the entire situation. Children must face an intimidating courtroom setting and discuss personal, traumatic events while confronting the alleged abuser (Batterman-Faunce & Goodman, 1993). Having this feared person in the courtroom could reduce the likelihood of the child disclosing entire descriptions of the events. Therefore, allowing the child to testify in the absence of the accused may provide more reliable testimony (Pipe & Goodman, 1991). Tobey, Goodman, Batterman-Faunce, Orcutt, and Sachsenmaier (1995) suggested that if a child testifies in front of the defendant, then he or she may be psychologically traumatized because of facing the alleged abuser. They highlighted that this trauma could negatively effect the reliability and thoroughness of the testimony. The authors stated that the use of closed-circuit technology eliminates the need for children to testify in such a traumatic situation. They could provide their testimony from outside the courtroom via television monitors. The opposition to this procedure is that it violates a defendant's Fourteenth Amendment right to due process because it interferes with the factfinder's capabilities of determining witness credibility and it violates a defendant's Sixth Amendment right to confront witnesses directly (Goodman *et al.*, 1998).

The Supreme Court has agreed with this opposition to some extent. In *Coy v. Iowa* (1988), the Court ruled that the use of closed-circuit television did violate a defendant's Sixth and Fourteenth Amendment rights. However, 2 years later in *Maryland v. Craig* (1990), the Court decided in favor of allowing closed-circuit television in child sexual abuse cases where the child would be so traumatized as to be unable to reasonably communicate. The Supreme Court does agree that such technology is a violation of rights but that the psychological effects related to a child's testimony outweigh those rights. In Martha's case, the judge would need to determine if she would be so traumatized as to incapacitate her communication abilities that it would warrant the use of closed-circuit television.

Goodman *et al.* (1998) conducted a study comparing children's testimony both in the courtroom and via closed-circuit television (CCTV). They found that CCTV reduced suggestibility for younger children and that these children made fewer errors related to misleading questions when compared to those testifying in the courtroom. Closed-circuit television overall fostered more reliable testimony in children. The authors also concluded that in the CCTV situation, the defendant had no greater chance of being convicted, and the trial was not identified as being more unfair to the defendant. However, jurors in the study reported that children testifying by CCTV were considered less believable, even though they actually were more accurate, than children testifying in the courtroom.

There are many issues that can affect the reliability of children's testimony. It appears that the stress and trauma of testifying can reduce reliability. In the case illustration, Martha likely has legitimate fears about facing her alleged abuser, and these fears could decrease the reliability of her testimony.

Forensic Psychology and Policy Implications

The issue of whether children are competent witnesses seems to rest solely with judges. This allows judges a great deal of discretion in making decisions that may have psychological implications. The requisite abilities for a child to be deemed competent are psychological in nature, yet judges rarely involve mental health professionals in their decision-making process (J. E. B. Myers, 1993b). Forensic psychologists should become involved in these types of cases, especially when a judge is uncertain. If they do not provide expert testimony, they could at least educate the court on psychological issues relevant to competency for child witnesses. In the case illustration, a forensic psychologist could offer the judge information as to whether Martha possesses the necessary abilities to testify.

Another important implication is to reduce the level of trauma and stress that children endure when they must testify, especially in abuse cases. One approach offered is to prepare children by providing a tour of the courtroom and teaching them information about the legal system. This would need to be conducted in age-appropriate language and may reduce their anxiety and thus increase the reliability of their testimony (Saywitz, 1995). Policies need to be developed to ensure that these children are not further traumatized, while at the same time keeping in mind the constitutional rights of the defendant. Although closed-circuit television appears to be one possible solution, it is not currently standard procedure due to constitutional dilemmas. However, more solutions like this must be implemented so that children can provide reliable testimony.

Suggestions for Future Research

Much of the research on children's testimony has focused on suggestibility of child witnesses, yet an important area related to reliability that should be examined is whether increased levels of suggestibility influence children's capability to offer reliable testimony (Ceci & Bruck, 1993). Since children are increasingly being relied upon to provide testimony. Research must find the optimal techniques that limit the emotional stress that could compromise the reliability and credibility of their testimony (K. Bussey *et al.*, 1993). Research on this topic should also examine which of these situations will provide a fair trial. It seems that closed-circuit television is a step in that direction, yet there has not been enough empirical analysis to reach any definite conclusions (Batterman-Faunce & Goodman, 1993). Continued research needs to be done on CCTV as a possible solution to the problem of traumatizing children and whether it provides a fair trial. Another focus of research should be how to prepare children to testify more competently and with minimal stress (J. E. B. Myers, 1993a). If it is found that closed-circuit television is an unfair procedure, then children will have to continue to face their alleged abusers in court and will have to provide reliable testimony.

BEST INTERESTS OF THE CHILD DOCTRINE

Introduction

The Best Interests of the Child doctrine was established in the legal system to determine the components of child custody that will provide the best environment for a child's adjustment and development (Kelley, 1997). According to Mason (as cited in Skolnick, 1998), approximately 50% of children born in 1990 will become involved in a child custody case. The Best Interests of the Child doctrine is typically invoked during an adversarial divorce, which is the reason for most custody disputes (Kelley, 1997; Skolnick, 1998). Divorce can have significant consequences for the child, and the purpose behind the best interests doctrine is to consider which adult can provide the most positive relationship with and the best environment for the child (G. Miller, 1993). Although positive aspects of the doctrine have been noted, including the idea that every decision can focus on an individual child's need and that it permits society to address shifting morals, values, and situations (Kelley, 1997), much of the literature highlights the standard's limitations.

> Joe and Sarah have three children, ages 6, 10, and 13. The two youngest are girls, and the oldest is a boy. The parents have abused both drugs and alcohol. In addition, Joe went to prison several years ago for committing a sexual offense against a 12-year-old girl. Sarah remained married to Joe during this time but began having an affair with a coworker by whom she became pregnant. While Joe was in prison, their children were

temporarily removed from Sarah's custody because of her drug use. However, she was able to straighten herself out and they were returned to her. When Joe was released from prison, he and Sarah did not initiate divorce proceedings; they shared joint custody of the two girls while the boy lived solely with his father. Joe does not have steady employment. He works odd jobs as a mechanic and lives with his girlfriend in a trailer in his parents' backyard. Sarah does not work at all and lives with her new fiancé in a one-bedroom apartment. They both claim to be drug free. Recently, Joe and Sarah became angry with one another, and Sarah filed for a divorce. In an effort to hurt Joe, she has sued for sole custody of the two girls, stating that Joe is a threat to them because of his prior sex offense. The question before the court is which parent will provide the best environment for the children.

Literature Review

When deciding between Joe and Sarah as sole custodians of their children, many people might feel that neither should be awarded custody. However, the question before the court is to choose between these two individuals, and the judge must make the decision. In times past, a judge may have based his or her decision on very different criteria. For example, prior to the mid-19th century, children were perceived as property, and therefore fathers were entitled to such property. Courts then turned to the idea that children of young ages should be allowed to stay with their mothers until they were weaned. This was commonly referred to as The Tender Years presumption (A. S. Hall, Pulver, & Cooley, 1996). It was not until 1925 that the Best Interests of the Child standard was initially proposed. This occurred in the case of *Finlay v. Finlay* (1925). A father was suing for custody of his child, and the court ruled that the concern should be for the child's welfare, not for the argument between the parents. However, the Tender Years presumption continued to prevail until 1970, when it was officially supplanted by the Best Interests of the Child standard (A. S. Hall *et al.*, 1996).

A major complaint lodged against this relatively new standard is that it is very vague, allowing for judicial bias that leads to different results in similar cases (Skolnick, 1998). Dolgin (1996), for example, reported that many criticize the standard because it does not provide enough substantial guidance for courts to follow regarding child custody decisions. The author also suggested that using the Best Interests standard could lead to opposing decisions in child custody cases, depending on the presiding judge. Part of the problem is that there appears to be no widely recognized operational definition for the standard (Banach, 1998). Indeed, one study found that the codes and statutes in all of the states had very little in common regarding guidelines for this standard (A.S. Hall *et al.*, 1996).

The criticisms about vagueness extend beyond the problem of judicial bias. There also appears to be a lack of agreement among mental health and legal professionals about the necessary requirements for the best interests of a child, which leads professionals to arrive at conflicting decisions in particular cases (Kelley, 1997). On an even broader level, the standard has been criticized because societal agreement about what is in the best interests of children does not exist (Goldstein, Solnit, Goldstein, & Freud, 1996; Skolnick, 1998).

Dolgin (1996) suggested that the lack of guidance may lead judges to focus on the interests of the parents rather than on the interests of the child. A judge may do this by basing his or her decision on protecting the constitutional rights of the parents. G. Miller (1993) stated that courts often examine other factors in addition to the best interests of the child. These factors include the constitutional rights of those involved. Miller indicated that Supreme Court decisions reflect the idea that constitutional rights precede the Best Interests standard. This leads other courts to examine the interests of the adults over the children. In the case of Joe and Sarah, a judge may have to consider Joe's constitutional rights of losing his children because of a crime he may never commit, even if this supersedes the best interests of the children. Kandel (1994) suggested that the best interests standard "does not rise to constitutional dimensions; it implicates neither substantive nor procedural due process rights. Further, it is subject to limitation in the interests of the state, the interests of the parents, and the interests of children themselves" (p. 349). He also indicated that the standard is more of an infringement on the rights of children than parents because a judge substitutes his or her opinion for the choice of the children.

In forming such an opinion, the judge does not have to consider psychological suggestions. In fact, G. Miller (1993) indicated that the Best Interests standard is defined differently both legally and psychologically, leading to further complications. For mental health workers, the best interests of the child is the conclusive factor in recommending an appropriate placement, while for the courts, it is not; constitutional and legal factors rank higher than the Best Interests standard. According to Kandel (1994), when the court does request psychological assistance, it does so to justify its decision. It appears to create "scientific validity" (p. 348) that this is the best choice; however, often the court asks mental health professionals the wrong question.

Another factor that appears to bias judges' decisions is that since the early 20th century mothers have been given preference with regard to custody of their children, even though this has never been statutorily recognized (Kandel, 1994). Skolnick (1998) suggested that though the Best Interests standard prevails, most custody decisions still are made in favor of the mother. There are four explanations provided by Warshak (1996) for this phenomenon: (1) women by nature make better parents and are more essential to children, (2) most mothers are better parents, not because they possess innate superiority, but because they have more experience than fathers in raising children, (3) custody should be a reward for the types of contributions a mother has made to her children, and (4) mothers suffer more emotionally than fathers from the loss of custody. Warshak also indicated that only 1 in 10 children resides with their fathers, and this has been a steady proportion for decades. Despite evidence showing that divorced fathers can provide nurturance for their children and can handle the responsibilities of child rearing, those who desire custody "must still prove mothers grossly negligent or abusive" (p. 399). If a judge believes that mothers are better caregivers for children, then it can be fairly simple to favor a particular parent by highlighting the negative behaviors of the other parent (Dolgin, 1996). In the case of Joe and Sarah, if the judge preferred that mothers retain custody, then the judge could focus on Joe's prior sexual offense as evidence that he would be an unfit caregiver.

Forensic Psychology and Policy Implications

Based on the arguments against the best interests of the child standard, there should be some type of uniformity in the guidelines (A. S. Hall *et al.*, 1996). Kelley (1997) suggested that a consensus be created detailing what critical guidelines should be included. Banach (1998) indicated that creating more specificity for all professionals involved may decrease the bias associated with decision making. She also suggested that an operational definition be included in state statutes to create some uniformity. In addition, professionals should not rely solely on their own judgment but evaluate their decisions with other professionals to avoid biases.

Skolnick (1998) provided some suggestions to create more uniform criteria. She stated that a child's psychological well-being should be one consideration. This would include examining emotional ties the child has with the parents and the child's need for stability. Also, rules should be provided that prevent a judge from considering lifestyle choices or parental conduct that does not directly damage the relationship with the child. In Joe and Sarah's situation, this could be a difficult task to accomplish because they both engaged in behaviors that were potentially harmful to their children.

Goldstein *et al.* (1996) offered the notion of changing the Best Interests of the Child term to the Least Detrimental Alternative because it is more realistic and less subject to a magical idea of finding the best interest. They also suggested that child placement decisions should remain as free as possible from state intervention and be as permanent as possible because continuity is critical for children. The state should interfere only if it can provide the least detrimental alternative.

Creating new guidelines for this standard should include cooperation between legal and mental health professionals. Wall and Amadio (1994) indicated that child custody decisions must consider the entire family and the needs of each member to provide the most beneficial and continuous relationships between parents and children. They stated that if legal and mental health professionals could cooperate, this task would be easier to accomplish and the best interests of the family would be ascertained.

Suggestions for Future Research

Research needs to focus on exactly which factors to consider when making custody decisions based on the best interests of the child. Before specific guidelines can be proposed, however, they first have to be discovered. Conducting research on those areas of development and functioning most appropriate for children, at various ages, should be pursued by mental health professionals, specifically child development specialists. Also, studying various decisions made by judges and determining which constitutional factors are important in these situations is warranted, especially since courts are not going to let psychological issues prevail over constitutional ones. There needs to be some clarification regarding those factors regularly considered and how different conditions change the factors that are deemed important (Banach, 1998). Once these are learned, they can be incorporated into guidelines for those making child custody decisions.

In the area of gender bias decision making, further research should be conducted on fathers who are awarded sole custody of their children in order to verify that they can be appropriate caregivers. Although findings exist in this area, additional studies are needed because courts continue to favor mothers in their decisions. This bias can adversely impact someone like Joe, who may have made a horrible mistake but could still be a good caregiver.

SENTENCING: PSYCHOLOGY OF JUVENILE REHABILITATION

Introduction

The controversy surrounding the most appropriate way to deal with juvenile offenders remains unabated today. There are two opposing viewpoints which pervade the sentencing of youthful offenders. There are those who advocate a rehabilitative model when addressing juvenile crime and those who advocate a retributive model. The rehabilitative model is based on the premise that youthful offenders are amenable to treatment and, if treated properly, will age out of criminal behavior. Those who promote the retributive model believe that juveniles who commit crimes are treated too leniently by the system and should receive more stringent punishment for their crimes. While rehabilitation used to be the primary goal of the juvenile justice system, over the past decade there has been a shift to ensure retribution (Melton *et al.*, 1997). The following case illustration depicts a recent notorious case in which a juvenile committed a heinous crime which left many individuals throughout the nation wondering what to do with a boy like Kip. While some individuals perceive individuals such as Kip to be troubled teens in dire need of treatment, others think such youths deserve capital punishment.

On May 21, 1998, a 15-year-old freshman named Kipland Kinkel allegedly committed a series of heinous crimes. The young boy walked into his high school cafeteria and opened fire on a room full of students. He fired a total of 52 rounds which some have described as sounding like fireworks. Kinkel's rampage left two people dead and another 22 injured. As if his killing spree at school was not tragic enough, Kinkel shot and killed both of his parents prior to arriving at school that day.

Reviewing the boy's history reveals that Kinkel announced to his literature class that he dreamed of becoming a killer and he expressed his admiration for the Unabomber. Additionally, the day before the shootings, Kinkel was arrested for possession of a gun at school. Rather than being incarcerated or receiving any psychological counseling or treatment, Kinkel was released to the custody of his parents the same day.

Literature Review

As illustrated in the case of Kinkel, juveniles commit crimes every bit as heinous as adults. However, determining what constitutes the most appropriate sentence for juvenile offenders is highly controversial. The execution of one's parents coupled with the mass murder Kinkel allegedly engaged in would make any adult eligible for the death penalty. However, imposing a sentence for a 15-year-old oftentimes requires a great deal more consideration than imposing a sentence for an adult. The case of Kipland Kinkel highlights the numerous issues that ensue in the juvenile justice system. The overarching issue is whether juvenile offenders should be treated any differently than adult offenders.

When the juvenile court was initially established, one of the salient features of the system was its focus on rehabilitation. Inherent in the rehabilitative model was the notion that the disposition would be made based on its appropriateness for the offender, not the offense (Melton *et al.*, 1997). Therefore, when the juvenile justice system was established as a separate entity from the adult system, it was presumed that the juvenile offender was indeed different from the adult offender. However, the differences that were recognized between adult and juvenile offenders had both positive and negative impacts on the juvenile justice system and led to a series of reform measures.

In landmark cases such as *Kent v. United States* (1966) and *In re Gault* (1967), juveniles were recognized as deserving many of the same constitutional rights that adult offenders were granted, and were therefore entitled to many of the same due process protections that adults received during criminal proceedings. On the one hand, these cases acknowledged the rights of juveniles. On the other hand, they highlighted the commonality between juveniles and adults, thereby making the position that the two should be treated fundamentally different in the legal system something of a double standard. After the decision rendered in *In re Gault*, the juvenile court repeatedly encountered challenges to the due process clause as it pertains to juvenile offenders (*McKeiver v. Pennsylvania*, 1971; *In re Winship*, 1970). As a result, Grisso (1996b) notes that lawmakers became more and more supportive of retribution and less tolerant of any efforts to rehabilitate juvenile offenders.

Following the reforms aimed at protecting the due process rights of juvenile offenders were the initiatives geared toward promoting determinate sentencing (American Bar Association, 1980). Thus, this period of reform sought to reduce the arbitrariness inherent in the previous era of juvenile justice, which allowed for discretionary sentencing of youthful offenders. The move to determinate sentencing was temporarily supported by individuals with vastly different philosophies concerning the appropriate way to sentence youths. Grisso (1996b) states that individuals who supported the retributive philosophy endorsed the determinate sentencing reform because, from their perspective, juvenile offenders received their just desserts. Likewise, individuals who advocated the rights of children supported this reform because it prevented the abuse of discretionary decision making by juvenile court judges. Grisso's final example acknowledges support by clinicians who recognized the therapeutic effect of teaching juveniles responsibility for their actions.

The current reform efforts are aimed at increasing the severity of the determinate sentencing for youths. As a result, the treatment of juvenile offenders is becoming more and more consistent with their adult counterparts. This shift is largely a reflection of societal views. A national survey was conducted in 1991, which revealed that 99% of the public advocates punishment for violent offenders (Schwartz, 1992). The public's attitude is reflected in action by the legislature as new laws are created to implement stiffer punishment for juvenile offenders. The 1992 Attorney General for the United States, William Barr, clearly stated that serious juvenile offenders are beyond rehabilitation and laws need to be enacted which provide the justice system with the flexibility needed to prosecute these youths as adults (Barr, 1992).

As a result of these views, legal reforms in the juvenile justice system have primarily revolved around prosecuting juveniles in criminal court (Grisso, 1996b). By waiving the youth to the adult system, the juvenile essentially faces the same sentence as would an adult charged with a similar crime. Moreover, the process by which a juvenile is waived to adult court has been reformed over the years. Initially, in the course of a waiver, the juvenile court took into account the juvenile's individual characteristics and the youth's potential for rehabilitation. However, currently there are laws in some states which require a juvenile to be waived to adult court based solely on the crime committed (Grisso, 1996b). Thus, the flexibility and discretion that was once used in determining sentences for juvenile offenders is becoming increasingly less popular and, in some cases, nearly impossible.

Despite the movement toward retribution, a number of individuals remain in support of rehabilitation for youthful offenders. Weaver (1992) discusses a program in Florida designed to provide services to serious violent juvenile offenders. This program has successfully operated without incarcerating juveniles. The program is composed of three phases during which the juveniles engage in hard work, education, and learn job skills. The program has a behavioral component in which the youths receive "points" based on the degree to which they perform their daily tasks. The points can then be traded in for various privileges. The violent offenders in this program have more significant criminal histories, yet lower recidivism rates upon completion of the rehabilitative program as compared to juvenile offenders in Florida who did not participate in the program. This initiative is one of many in which rehabilitation demonstrates effectiveness in altering the criminal lifestyle of juvenile offenders.

In a similar fashion, policy makers in some states realize that community-based programs for juvenile offenders are more effective than facilities and institutions designed to incarcerate them (Melton *et al.*, 1997). This is perhaps due to the fact that juvenile detention facilities frequently do not offer services aimed at rehabilitating the offender. Moreover, from a fiscal perspective, community-based programs are much more cost effective for juvenile offenders (Weaver, 1992). Furthermore, Straus (1994) presents a theoretical basis for diverting youths away from incarceration in the justice system. Straus reports that many individuals who advocate diversion programs believe that they will reduce the stigmatization associated with incarceration. Therefore, according to Straus, juvenile offenders can be better helped within their respective communities while being spared the detrimental effects of being labeled a delinquent.

There are numerous community programs which currently exist designed to provide juvenile offenders with an alternative to incarceration in a juvenile institution. These programs are often structured to address problems within the families of juvenile offenders as well as psychological issues affecting the youths. Straus acknowledges that there are a variety of programs available to meet the different needs of juveniles. Some of these programs include the following: peer support groups, work training programs, church-based programs, drop-in treatment centers, youth shelters, and inpatient treatment facilities. This list highlights the numerous opportunities for rehabilitative services that are available for youthful offenders. Thus, the dilemma concerning the most appropriate sentence to impose upon a particular juvenile remains at the discretion of the court judge. It is highly likely that the controversy surrounding rehabilitation versus retribution of youthful offenders will continue to spark debate among the legislature, the media, and individuals in the fields of mental health and criminal justice.

Forensic Psychology and Policy Implications

The issues involved in the sentencing of juvenile offenders raises numerous implications for the field of forensic psychology. With the gravity of offenses committed by young persons, such as Kipland Kinkel, the public is intent on "solving" the problem of juvenile crime. Forensic psychologists are needed on both sides of the sentencing debate. On the one hand, those who promote rehabilitation of juvenile offenders must be able to account for the recidivism rate among those who do receive such services. Perhaps the rehabilitative services that are currently available do not meet the comprehensive guidelines suggested by Straus (1994) in targeting social and structural changes in the families as well as in the juveniles. Without data unambiguously documenting how rehabilitative programs serve to protect the community from future acts of violence, it is unlikely that the communities and the legislature will refrain from imposing more stringent retributive sentences on juveniles.

On the other hand, those who support the retributive model in sentencing juvenile offenders must be able to offer explanations as to why, in an era of severe determinate sentencing, young boys such as Kip Kinkel continue to commit heinous crimes. Since 1992 there have been 16 publicized cases of juveniles shooting people on school grounds in the United States [National Broadcasting Corporation (NBC) Research, 1998]. These cases do not provide evidence that determinate sentencing is reducing the severity or frequency with which juveniles commit crimes. Moreover, those who support the retributive model need to provide evidence that determinate sentencing does in fact curb recidivism among juvenile offenders. However, some current literature refutes this position by showing that youths who receive alternative dispositions to incarceration have lower rates of recidivism (Weaver, 1992).

Suggestions for Future Research

The literature lacks longitudinal studies comparing the rehabilitative approach to juvenile sentencing with the retributive approach. Such studies are difficult to conduct due to the legalities involved in obtaining juvenile records; however, these inquiries are imperative for drawing conclusions regarding the effectiveness of either approach. Moreover, there are currently no studies which attempt to detect the bases for the discretionary decisions made by juvenile court judges. It is crucial to understand why judges are sentencing some juveniles to life in prison, while others are sentencing juveniles, with comparable crimes, to juvenile detention facilities or treatment programs.

Additionally, research needs to be designed to examine existing rehabilitative programs. These analyses would include program evaluations, examining the scope of treatment services offered; the provision of specialized treatment programs; and the nature and quality of treatment juvenile offenders receive in such programs.

CHAPTER 7

Civil Forensics

OVERVIEW

The legal system assumes an important role in the adjudication of noncriminal matters impacting the lives of persons with mental illness. In addition, nonadjudicatory remedies affecting parties injured by offenders or those emotionally suffering because of the pain they may have caused the public represent alternative societal responses to the problem of crime and violence. Broadly defined, these are efforts designed to produce civil justice. Psychologists assist the court system or other administrative boards in determining how best to realize specific outcomes in this forensic area.

There are six civil justice issues examined in this chapter. These particular topics demonstrate the variety of avenues wherein forensic psychologists, invested in the effective operation of the formal and informal court system, influence overall decision making. Subjects investigated include (1) defining mental illness, (2) the right to refuse (medical) treatment, (3) the "least restrictive alternative" doctrine, (4) duty to inform versus client confidentiality, (5) victim compensation programs, and (6) victim–offender mediation. Similar to other chapters in this textbook, emphasis is placed on presenting a breadth of topics to canvass. This allows one to consider the broader justice implications for the field (i.e., civil forensics) in relationship to the various roles of the psychologist or expert practitioner.

Persons with mental illness can be, under specified conditions, hospitalized against their will. What is the meaning of mental illness for lawyers and psychologists? Can mental illness be defined with any precision, and, if not, what are the civil justice consequences for individuals so confined? How is the mental illness construct employed for purposes of involuntary commitment? Persons identified as psychiatrically disordered can, under the law, exercise their right to refuse (medical) treatment. To what extent can the mentally ill invoke this right in the context of antipsychotic medication? What role does one's informed consent play in the decision to refuse treatment? How do the legal and psychological communities endorse the individual autonomy of a mentally disordered citizen in the wake of one invoking a treatment refusal right? The law requires that the psychiatric care persons receive must occur in the most nonrestrictive environment possible so that the individual's liberty (e.g., freedom of movement) is protected. How does the "psycholegal" establishment operationalize this standard? In addition to the locus of care, the Least Restrictive Alternative doctrine refers to the type and quality of medical intervention and whether it is the least invasive form of psychiatric care. How, if at all, does the Least Restrictive Alternative doctrine protect a person's freedom from unnecessary, unwanted, and harmful treatment?

In addition to formal courtroom outlets and legal mechanisms for advancing the aims of civil forensics, psychologists are called upon to promote the interests of justice in the informal legal system as well. Mental health clinicians are, on occasion, presented with clients who may act violently toward others. Psychologists are also entrusted with safeguarding the confidentiality of what their clients describe to them. What are the legal and ethical obligations and limits of mental health professionals when a client poses a threat to a third party? Are there circumstances in which client confidentiality can (and must) be breached? Persons victimized by crime suffer personal and financial injury. Do victims have legal rights? How does psychology help us understand victims? How do victim impact statements affect the outcome of a particular case, and what meaning do such statements hold for the victim? Can forensic psychologists determine the degree of "emotional suffering" victims experience for purposes of their financial (or other) compensation? Increasingly, jurisdictions around the country are adopting the philosophy of restorative justice at the postconviction phase of a case. A key dimension to restorative justice is reconciliation through victim–offender mediation (VOM). How does VOM work? How can forensic psychologists assist in the restorative justice process? How does VOM promote the interests of reconciliation for offenders, victims, and the community of which both are a part?

The legal system has a vested interest in the resolution of noncriminal disputes that affect citizens who are users of mental health services or are victims of crime. When the tools of the psychological sciences are relied upon to address these matters, forensic experts are responding to issues of civil justice. The six controversies presented in this chapter reveal the degree to which psychologists influence outcomes in both the formal and informal court system. Clearly, this chapter demonstrates that citizens are impacted by the legal system in a number of noncriminal contexts and that trained forensic specialists assume vital roles in the process of determining how best to address these concerns. As a matter of policy, then, the civil forensic field, in relation to the legal system, presents the skilled practitioner with a different set of issues to understand and/or interpret than its adult and juvenile counterparts. In brief, at the core of this forensic subspeciality is a commitment to making peace with crime and restoring justice to all those (mental health) citizens (potentially) harmed or victimized within society.

DEFINING MENTAL ILLNESS

Introduction

What exactly *is* in mental illness and what is the significance of the concept for issues in law and psychology? While the mental health community has generally used the term "mental illness" somewhat haphazardly for purposes of diagnosis and treatment (B. Winick, 1995), it assumes greater significance when its legal relevance appears in a wide variety of contexts. Perhaps, most importantly, it is a prerequisite for civil commitment (as in the case of Gina below) and for the insanity defense. In these legal contexts, a precise definition of mental illness (or lack thereof) can have profound effects on individuals within the legal system. Mental illness is also used for determining competencies, such as competency to stand trial, to execute a will, or to manage property (B. Winick, 1995). The definition of mental illness further becomes an issue *after* an individual is found incompetent or legally insane. The continued confinement of incompetent individuals or those found Not Guilty by Reason of Insanity (NGRI) is only permissible by law if a continued manifestation of mental illness exists.

Given the importance of the concept of mental illness in issues such as those described above, its legal definition and operationalization have significant consequences for psychology and the criminal justice system. The concern, however, is that the very definition of mental illness is rarely (or perhaps never) made precise by legislators, often resulting in broad, general descriptions. Consequently, issues that rely on a finding of mental illness become confounded—it is difficult to find something when one does not know what it is he or she is looking for. Likewise, it is also *easy* to find something when one does not know what one is looking for. Despite the continuing controversy over the meaning of mental illness as a legal concern, legislators and courts have done very little to clarify the issue. We now turn to the concept of "mental illness" in more detail; specifically, within the context of civil commitment and insanity defenses.

Gina Hampton is a 27-year-old musician in a large metropolitan area. Gina has a history of mental instability, with diagnoses of narcissistic and antisocial personality disorders as well as severe depression and occasional suicidal ideation. Recently, she was exposed to several stressful events, including the death of a close friend and the break-up of a 5-year relationship. Her friends and family have noticed her mental state worsening over the past few weeks and fear that she may present a danger to herself or those around her. Some suggest that she be placed in a psychiatric hospital for further observation. Gina, however, insists that she is "fine" and resists any attempt at psychological intervention. Unconvinced, her friends and family wonder under which conditions Gina may be hospitalized against her will, as they feel it would be in her best interest at this time. The involuntary hospitalization of Gina, however, requires a finding that she is "mentally ill" and presents a danger. Given that she has recently engaged in several dangerous behaviors, jeopardizing her own safety as well as that of others, the primary question is whether she is "mentally ill" in the eyes of the law.

Literature Review

Civil Commitment

The first substantive criterion for civil commitment is the presence of a mental impairment. Most jurisdictions define this as the existence of a "mental illness" or a demonstration that the individual is suffering from a "mental disorder" (Reisner & Slobogin, 1990). Consistent with basic due process, the Court has held that an individual who is not mentally ill cannot be involuntarily committed for civil purposes (see *Foucha v. Louisiana*, 1992). Since the existence of mental illness is a necessary prerequisite for civil commitment, the primary interest is then in the constitution of mental illness. What exactly must be found if an individual is to be hospitalized against his or her will?

Despite the involuntary commitment reform movements of the 1970s contesting that mental illness is a "bankrupt term easily manipulated" (Melton *et al.*, 1987, p. 217), many legislative attempts to define and operationalize the term create only vague and circular meanings (see Levy & Rubenstein, 1996; Melton *et al.*, 1987). The law has imposed only minimal limitations on the term, often using broad and general definitions (B. Winick, 1995). Melton *et al.* (1987) cite one of the most specific of legislative attempts to define mental illness as:

> "Mental illness" means a substantial disorder of thought, mood, perception, orientation or memory, any of which grossly impairs judgement, behavior, capacity to recognize reality, or ability to meet the ordinary demands of life, but shall not include mental retardation. (p. 221)

Such a proposal is far more precise than another statute, which reads, "a mentally ill person means a person whose mental health is substantially impaired" (Melton *et al.*, 1987, p. 221). It is, however, still controversial, as it relies on equally vague terms such as "substantial," "grossly impaired," and "ordinary demands of life." Many statutes have, however, attained some degree of success by excluding conditions such as mental retardation, substance abuse, and epilepsy (Levy & Rubenstein, 1996; Melton *et al.*, 1987). Additionally, alcohol and substance abuse problems are generally not considered a mental illness for legal purposes. Thus, by excluding some mental impairments the law has limited the scope of mental illness to some degree. The meaning of mental illness nonetheless remains open to individual interpretation. Who, then, interprets?

The consistent imprecision with and neglect for operationalization by the legislature has left the courts to "fashion a definition for the words 'mentally ill'. . . thereby fill[ing] the void in the statutory hospital law" (*Dodd v. Hughes*, 1965, p. 542). With the responsibility of defining and assessing potential mental illness as it stands before them, the courts have further deferred to the profession of mental health (i.e., expert testimony by psychiatrists and psychologists) (Arrigo, 1993; Melton *et al.*, 1987; Reisner & Slobogin, 1990). This power given to, or, more appropriately, *dependent on*, the medical and mental health communities in the decision-making process persists, even though substantial research has documented lack of consensus among professionals in matters of diagnosis (Arrigo, 1993). Research has shown that psychologists and psychiatrists are not necessarily any more in agreement about what mental illness is than anyone else. Thus, the failure to legally define mental illness may be, in part, a function of psychology and medicine's lack of precision in defining and describing it.

Insanity Defense

The various insanity defenses (tests) can only be used by individuals suffering from a mental disease or defect. In order to be "excused" from criminal behavior, the individual must not only be mentally ill, but the mental illness must directly cause a dysfunction which is relevant when the offense was committed (Melton *et al.*, 1987). Again, the meaning of "mental illness" becomes the key issue. Melton *et al.* note that with mental illness being imprecisely defined, it would seem that "any mental disability that causes significant cognitive or volitional impairment will meet the threshold [of mental illness needed for insanity defenses]" (p. 199). Historically, however, the successful insanity defenses have generally arisen from individuals who were suffering from a psychosis or mental retardation. Studies suggest that 60–90% of defendants acquitted for reasons of insanity have been psychotic (Melton *et al.*, 1987).

Very few case opinions attempt to define mental disease or defect. The few cases that have, however, define the concept narrowly. In other words, the courts have shown a general disapproval of many conceptions of insanity including mildly psychotic individuals, dissociative disorders, and drug- and alcohol-induced insanity (Melton *et al.*, 1987). Further, the American Psychiatric Association (APA) has defined "mental disease or defect" in a narrow sense, suggesting it should only include "severely abnormal mental conditions that grossly. . . impair a person's perception or understanding of reality" (APA, 1983). Other evidence, however, would suggest that, in reality, the conception of mental illness by the courts is more elastic. In

Connecticut, for example, between 1970 and 1972, 40% of insanity acquittals were classified as "personality disorders" (APA, 1983). Thus, the definition of mental disease or defect for purposes of insanity defenses varies from state to state and is probably more broadly defined than some have suggested.

Foucha v. Louisiana

The Supreme Court shed some light on the meaning of mental illness in the case *Foucha v. Louisiana* (1992). While the case considered the extent to which an individual could be confined *after* being found NGRI, it has some important implications for the meaning of mental illness in civil commitment and insanity defense matters. The Court held that it would be unconstitutional to detain an individual who was diagnosed only with antisocial personality disorder. The primary issue was whether it was constitutional to continue to detain an individual who had been acquitted but had recovered from his or her illness. The short answer from the Court was "no." The more relevant issue, however, is the meaning of "mental illness." While for purposes of involuntary commitment an individual must be shown to be mentally ill and dangerous, the *Foucha v. Louisiana* case found that dangerousness and antisocial personality disorder were not sufficient. Thus, the implication is that personality disorders, at least antisocial personality disorder, do not constitute mental illness for purposes of involuntary confinement. The Court did not justify this finding, leaving the issue still unresolved. Thus, the impact of the Court's decision in *Foucha* may be more apparent in future decisions.

Forensic Psychology and Policy Implications

The longstanding failure of the legislature and the courts to adequately define "mental illness" leaves a number of issues for forensic psychological analysts and practitioners. Most importantly, it leaves the decisions as to what constitutes mental illness and who is mentally ill to the attending forensic examiner. Regardless of the specific (or general) reasons arguing for or against psychology's involvement in the courtroom, its "expertise" is judged central to civil commitment and mental illness affairs. Thus, the *legal* meaning of mental illness has been "passed on" by the courts, only to be adopted by the "expert(s)" attending to the particular circumstances of individual cases (i.e., the treatment team) (Arrigo, 1993). In all likelihood this will continue. Thus, the meaning of mental illness becomes a significant issue for forensic psychologists above all else.

Despite the disagreement among mental health professionals defining what mental illness is, the legal system finds it appropriate to leave the decision in the hands of a select few individuals in the mental health and/or medical field. The individuals who are part of this defining, then, would differ depending on the case in question.

Thus, two individuals with identical mental conditions may be found "mentally ill" and "not mentally ill" depending on the definer. Unfortunately, since the courts rely almost entirely on disagreeing professionals to define mental illness, someone like Gina may be involuntarily hospitalized in one city or by one treatment team and not in another city or by another team. In general, however, the medical community has shown a preference for presuming mental illness. Given the medical community's favor for *presumption* of illness when confronting uncertainty (Arrigo, 1993), it is not unreasonable to assume that borderline cases are frequently labeled "mentally ill" for legal (i.e., involuntary commitment) purposes. Thus, it would seem that forensic psychological practitioners are overinclusive in these matters. In other words, more nonmentally ill individuals are being involuntarily hospitalized than the truly mentally ill who are not.

The forensic psychology implications, then, are profound for individuals like Gina who are facing (potentially) legal intervention. While we must recognize individual freedom, liberty, and self-determination, we must also be concerned with more general matters of public safety and health. The line between the two is not clear, as evidenced in the law's failure to define mental illness. Thus, it is left to forensic psychology practitioners and policy analysts to determine where this line should be drawn. At this point, there is no correct answer. There is no determined future for Gina or others like her. If we know, however, that the legislature and the courts cannot define mental illness, psychology should at the very least assume the task of creating a *consistent* definition, one in which we could know what mental illness stands for in the legal context.

Suggestions for Future Research

As the future of mental illness in the legal system depends to a large degree on establishing an adequate definition of mental illness, it is necessary that research be directed in such a way. While many attempts have been made by legislatures, courts, and even the American Psychological Association to define mental illness, none seem to have proposed any conclusive interpretations. Thus, the varying definitions of mental illness across psychologists, psychiatrists, statutes, courts, and the like necessitate comparative analyses. Research may be directed at establishing commonalities between proposed definitions in an attempt to establish a single, definitive concept of mental illness. More importantly, perhaps, the effects of cases such as *Foucha* need to be analyzed to assess their future impact on other court and legislative decisions regarding mental illness and the law. Defining mental illness, however, is one problematic area of research. It is an area where a significant amount of inquiry has already been conducted; however, these studies have failed to solve the controversy. Thus, future case decisions and their implications in this area must be evaluated.

RIGHT TO REFUSE TREATMENT

Introduction

The concept of personal liberty is, perhaps, the most treasured of all human rights in contemporary American society. The longstanding contention that lies at the historical core of American legal and social thought holds that the individual should have the right to decide what does or does not happen to his or her body and mind. If one becomes physically ill, for example, one can often choose not to receive medical treatment. The same should arguably apply to mental illness. The legal reality is, however, that this freedom from unwanted intrusion is not always enjoyed by the mentally disordered citizen. In fact, in some situations, individuals are subjected to psychological treatment against their will. This is the controversy surrounding the "right to refuse treatment."

Although questions of treatment refusal are relevant when considering the legal ramifications of *any* form of treatment, such questions are generally raised regarding psychotropic medications. The question of right to refuse antipsychotic medication has been called "the most important and volatile aspect of the legal regulation of mental health practice" (Perlin, Gould, & Dorfman, 1995, p. 111). Issues including personal autonomy of the mentally ill to refuse medication, subjection to drugs which occasionally cause irreversible neurological side effects, and questions of "informed consent" and "competency," as well as the "least restrictive alternative," all potentially become significant when confronting the right to refuse treatment. This section explores these concerns in the context of the right to refuse treatment.

> Alyssa is a 34-year-old woman who has been diagnosed by her psychiatrist as suffering from a thought disorder. Her symptoms, including delusions and occasional auditory hallucinations, have become progressively worse over the past year-and-a-half. While there is no dispute as to whether Alyssa is mentally ill, she shows no signs of dangerousness to herself or others. Alyssa has been able to maintain a reasonably "safe" lifestyle and, although she is in a state of obvious mental discomfort, she is not a candidate for involuntary commitment at this time.
>
> Following her diagnosis, her attending psychiatrist recommends that she be placed on Thorazine, an antipsychotic drug that may help to alleviate her symptoms. Following extensive consideration by Alyssa, she asks that the recommended treatment *not* be implemented. In other words, she asks not to be placed on Thorazine. Alyssa reached her decision after learning about the drug, finding that it often causes severe side effects which may be permanent. Alyssa decides that the risk is too high and she wishes to seek alternative treatment(s).
>
> Upon learning of Alyssa's request, however, her psychiatrist questions her competence to make such a decision. He questions whether a reasonable person in need of psychiatric treatment could reach such a decision, as it would clearly not be in her best interest at this time. In light of her wishes and his concern, does Alyssa have a right to refuse medication? Does her psychiatrist have a right to involuntarily treat her as he sees fit? And, how exactly does the issue of competence come into play?

Literature Review

The right to refuse treatment is considered the "most controversial issue in forensic psychiatry today" (Perlin *et al.*, 1995, p. 111). To fully understand its impact, one must consider the issue in light of a number of other important legal concerns; namely, the Least Restrictive Alternative (LRA) doctrine, competency issues, and the doctrine of informed consent. We briefly discuss each of these matters as they relate to the right to refuse treatment.

Least Restrictive Alternative Doctrine and Right to Refuse Treatment

For individuals in need of psychiatric attention, the right to refuse treatment becomes relevant within the context of the LRA doctrine. The LRA doctrine holds that individuals be placed in the least restrictive setting when their condition necessitates state intervention. This doctrine also implies that the least restrictive *method* of treatment be employed. Thus, the goal is to treat the individual in a manner that is least intrusive upon his or her personal liberty.

Without question, the administration of any treatment could be regarded as an intrusion on personal liberty if the citizen did not wish to receive the treatment. For example, the administration of psychotropic medication(s) to alleviate symptoms may be regarded as necessary, but may also significantly effect the individual's mental functioning. In this instance, one may not wish to be subjected to certain primary effects and side effects of medication. Thus, if a less restrictive alternative is available, it must be considered.

Doctrine of Informed Consent

The doctrine of informed consent requires that persons be supplied adequate information concerning treatment prior to consenting. Thus, the individual is able to make a well-informed decision regarding the suggested treatment they may be receiving. Generally, adequate information consists of the risks and benefits of treatment, the potential side effects, the chance of improvement both with and without the treatment, and any other treatments that may be available. The doctrine applies in a number of situations, including administration of medication, tests, and surgical procedures (Levy & Rubenstein, 1996).

While the doctrine of informed consent applies to the general adult public, it also applies to the mentally ill to the extent that they are competent to make such decisions. Thus, the existence of a mental disability alone does not take the right to make treatment decisions away from an individual. In order for such a right to be lost, the individual must be found incompetent by a court of law. While this seems simple enough, some controversial issues arise concerning the incompetent or civilly committed mentally ill and their right to refuse treatment.

Competency

A competent consent to treatment requires that the individual makes a reasoned decision to accept or refuse a proposed procedure. As noted, this generally means that the individual understands the treatment, its risks and benefits, and the potential alternatives. Thus, weight is not placed on the final decision itself, but rather on the manner in which the person came to such a conclusion.

An individual is not regarded as incompetent simply because his or her decision is not consistent with the majority of patients, is irrational, is not in the person's best medical interest, or is not consistent with the psychiatrist's recommendation. In the case of Alyssa, her refusal of antipsychotic medication, given the potential side effects, is not an incompetent decision for the reasons mentioned above. Her choice must be assessed in light of what she considers a better quality of life (Levy and Rubenstein, 1996).

Thus, the standards for competency concerning the right to refuse treatment are similar to other competencies. While there is currently no standard test to determine competency, it generally follows that the individual must understand the implications of the treatment and be able to make a rational choice based on this understanding. If the individual is not competent to make such a decision, another important controversy arises. That is, who makes the decision in his or her place? Generally, this decision is made by a panel of psychiatrists who must decide if, in fact, the individual is not capable of making such a decision and whether the proposed treatment is in the individual's best interest.

Following the Court's decision in *Washington v. Harper* (1990), however, no finding of incompetency is necessary if the individual is judged to be "mentally ill" and either "gravely disabled" or poses a "likelihood of serious harm" to self or others (Slobogin, 1994, p. 687). Thus, similar to civil commitment law, individuals may not have a right to refuse treatment if it is in the state's best interest to protect the community. For further information, see the section "An Offender's Right to Refuse Treatment."

Forensic Psychology and Policy Implications

One of the prevailing controversies regarding the right to refuse treatment concerns its theoretical application versus its actual or practical application. In theory, the right was intended to place final decisions regarding the type and extent of treatment in the hands of the citizen rather than the medical or mental health professional (Arrigo, 1996). In practice, however, the patient merely has the right to object to treatment decisions made by the attending clinician. In such cases, the decision may be reviewed by a team of clinicians to determine the appropriateness of the chosen treatment. Thus, in practice, the final decision concerning treatment of the mentally ill and its consequent effect on the individual's personal liberty ultimately remain in the hands of the clinician or forensic expert. While the intention of the doctrine was to consider individual interests in the name of unwanted intrusions on personal liberty, the practice of mental health treatment essentially disregards this perspective and reinforces the power that the medical community holds over those judged to be mentally ill.

Similarly, questions of competency are often raised only when acceptance or refusal of treatment differs from the opinion of the medical community. Decisions that are consistent with the psychiatrist, for example, are rarely questioned. In the case of Alyssa, the psychiatrist recommended Thorazine to treat her thought disorder. Had Alyssa concurred with the psychiatrist's recommendation, there would have been no issue regarding competency. Psychiatrists often accept a patient's consent without further considering if it is consistent with the physician's opinion. When a patient challenges the treatment recommendation, however, questions of competency are likely to be raised. Often, it is thought that the individual lacks insight into his or her own condition and, thus, is not capable of making rational treatment decisions. In this instance, the individual may be subjected to a competency hearing to determine his or her capacity to make such a decision (Levy & Rubenstein, 1996). Thus, the right to refuse treatment is often not a right at all, but rather a right to object and be subjected to a hearing.

Further, while considerable literature and public attention surround the "antitherapeutic" aspect of the right to refuse treatment, the "therapeutic" aspect must also be considered. Examples of the beneficial nature of the right to refuse treatment include judicial or administrative hearings (following the citizen's refusal of recommended treatment) to ensure that the mentally ill individual has the opportunity to fully present his or her case in a formal legal setting; the consequent procedures that help to prevent the inappropriate use of medications (e.g., for punishment or convenience); and the hearings that ensure that psychiatrists are not prescribing the wrong medication, wrong dosages, or ignoring concerns of the patient regarding side-effects (Perlin et al., 1995). Thus, in addition to the negative or "antitherapeutic" aspects of the right to refuse treatment, forensic psychology must also consider the beneficial or therapeutic aspects of such a right.

Suggestions for Future Research

Some research has been conducted exploring treatment outcomes of refusers and differences between clinical and judicial reviews of petitions for involuntary medication (Perlin et al., 1995). Overall, however, there is a lack of quality research concerning the various "therapeutic" and "antitherapeutic" effects of the right to refuse treatment (Arrigo & Tasca, 1999). Thus, research on quality of life, impacted after a decision to accept or refuse treatment, may be beneficial. As noted above, there is no standard test for competency. While competency to accept or refuse treatment stands as a major legal issue, it seems that a more direct confrontation of this issue is necessary.

LEAST RESTRICTIVE ALTERNATIVE DOCTRINE

Introduction

One of the most significant developments in mental health law and policy over the past 20 years concerns what may be regarded as the third substantive criterion for commitment. The Least Restrictive Alternative (LRA) doctrine requires that individuals be placed in the least restrictive setting when their condition necessitates state intervention. In situations involving persons who are considered dangerous to self or others and are, thus, candidates for involuntary commitment, the restrictiveness of the setting must be a consideration. In addition to setting, however, the doctrine also requires the least restrictive method of treatment. The ultimate goal, then, is to protect the individual's freedom from "unnecessary and harmful treatment" (Arrigo, 1993, p. 152), while serving the individual's interest in receiving effective treatment and services.

Given that the restrictiveness of a setting and the type of treatment administered becomes a concern of the state, several issues arise. First, the concept of restrictiveness (like the concepts of mental illness and dangerousness) must be adequately defined and operationalized. In other words, what settings and treatment plans constitute less restrictive ones than others? The traditional assumption has been that hospitalization is the most restrictive setting and that other settings such as community-based programs become progressively less restrictive. This assumption, however, has been the subject of much debate. In particular, this debate hinges on the issue of what is truly in the best interest of the individual. Like many forensic controversies, this matter becomes a common point of disagreement between psychology and law. This section will explore some of the key issues with regard to the LRA doctrine.

> John is a 42-year-old librarian with a history of mental illness. Though prone to bouts of mental deterioration, his functioning has historically returned to "normal" within a few weeks. John is currently single with no children and no living family members. During this particular week, John's functioning has been markedly poor. He is unable to perform his work-related duties and is clearly unable to care for himself. While he represents no danger to himself or others, he is unquestionably in need of psychiatric care. John's coworkers concern for his well-being prompted him to seek help. After examination by several mental health professionals it was decided that John be required to participate in some treatment program. Thus, John is a candidate for commitment. The question for John is such: what is the best placement and treatment for John given that he represents no danger to himself or others? Is involuntary hospitalization really the best alternative given John's individual needs?

Literature Review

The legal basis for the LRA doctrine is rooted in First Amendment rights. The First Amendment states that the state may only impose on individual liberty to the extent that it is necessary to ensure state interests (Melton *et al.*, 1987). Thus, since civilly committing individuals is a significant imposition on individual liberty, the argument posed by the LRA doctrine is that the state may only commit persons to the extent that it is absolutely necessary to protect the individual, the community, and provide treatment (Melton *et al.*, 1987). Therefore, if release to the care of family or friends, community outpatient services, or a stay in a supervised community facility are all that is necessary to effectively treat an individual and protect state interests, this form of release becomes a less restrictive alternative than hospitalization, and is in the best interest of individual liberty. In such cases, commitment to a state hospital would arguably be unconstitutional.

The first case to apply the LRA concept to mental health (the commitment process) was *Lake v. Cameron* (1966). In this case an elderly demented woman opposed her commitment to a hospital. Though disoriented and prone to wandering, her danger was not significant enough that it demanded confinement in a locked psychiatric facility. Thus, while supervision may have been necessary for Ms. Lake, involuntary confinement in a hospital was clearly unnecessary (Munetz & Geller, 1993). Judge Bazelon wrote that "deprivations of liberty solely because of dangers to the ill persons themselves should not go beyond what is necessary for their protection" and that ". . . an earnest effort should be made to review and exhaust available resources of the community in order to provide care reasonably suited to [Ms. Lake's] needs" (*Lake v. Cameron*, 1966, p. 657). Such efforts are the duty of the court when deprivation of liberty is at stake. The court implied this by stating that it had an "affirmative duty to explore alternatives to hospitalization before committing Lake to an institution" (Melton *et al.*, 1987, p. 224). Thus, the concept of "least restrictive alternative" should be employed in situations involving commitment for mental health reasons.

After the *Lake v. Cameron* decision, a number of states began to implement the concept of Least Restrictive Alternative into their commitment laws. By 1977, two-thirds of the states incorporated it, in some way, into their laws (Hoffman & Faust, 1977). Shortly after the Hoffman and Faust study, the President's Commission on Mental Health (1978) stated that the concept of LRA concerns the "objective of maintaining the greatest degree of freedom, self-determination, autonomy, dignity, and integrity of body, mind, and spirit for the individual while he or she participates in treatment or receives services" (Munetz & Geller, 1993, p. 967). Thus, by the late 1970s the LRA was a significant national concern. And by the early 1990s, the mental health laws and policies of nearly every state included the concept (Munetz and Geller, 1993).

Perhaps the most fundamental and disputed matter with regard to LRA centers upon the question "what is restrictive?" According to Bachrach (1980), several assumptions are employed when considering "restrictive" in individual cases. First, that certain environments (e.g., hospital, halfway house, etc.) are inherently good or bad regardless of the individual in question. Second, that there is a correlation between the quality of restrictiveness and the class of the facility in question. The last assumption identified by Bachrach and, perhaps more of a summary of the first two, is that a continuum exists in which a hospital is the most restrictive environment and living in the home would be the least restrictive. This final assumption places importance on the type of facility rather than those within a specific type. In other words, there is an assumption, for example, that all hospitals are more restrictive than all halfway houses. According to Bachrach, this is a false assumption. In reality, it is entirely possible that what is commonly regarded as a more restrictive type of residential facility may, in fact, be less restrictive than a poorer quality facility that is of a lesser presumed restrictiveness. Thus, the type of facility appears to be of less significance than the individuals' needs and the quality of the particular facility.

Several proposals have been made with regard to what determines the restrictiveness of a given residential facility. Perhaps the most informative is that of Carpenter (1978), who notes that, in addition to the type of facility, we should consider the

> location, staffing, specific programs, treatment provided, patient mix, emphasis on reha-
> bilitation, degree of expectations of patients' performance, degree of autonomy granted
> to patients, extraresidential programs for patients, limitations on length of stay, and the
> facility's track record of success and its specified and unspecified goals. (Munetz & Geller,
> 1993, p. 969).

With each of these variables, as well as others, equally contributing to the level of restrictiveness, it is easy to understand how a given type of institution may be only one consideration. Thus, a more restrictive type of facility (e.g., state hospital) that ranks high on several of these variables, may in fact be less restrictive than a facility that is presumed to be less restrictive (e.g., halfway house) that ranks low on many of the aforementioned variables.

As mentioned earlier, one of the commonly used alternatives to hospitalization is commitment to outpatient treatment. A considerable amount of clinical research has addressed the issue of outpatient commitment since the late 1980s and several attempts to establish clinical guidelines have followed (R. Miller, 1992). The problem, however, is that no standard definition or consensus among states exist, outlining what practices are consistent with involuntary outpatient commitment (Arrigo, 1993).

Proponents of involuntary outpatient commitment argue that mentally ill persons benefit from such practices as their freedom and autonomy increase. For a majority of the time, they are not subject to the impositions that may be present in hospitals. At the same time, some structure remains. The mentally ill enjoy the benefits of hospitalization (i.e., treatment, rehabilitation) while their lives are not being governed to the extent that they would in an inpatient facility.

Though initially a recommendation by legal scholars as an alternative to involuntary hospitalization, there has been an increasing focus of late by the legal field concerning the efficacy of such an option. Two common concerns voiced by legal scholars are that involuntary outpatient commitment will (1) lead to broader social control over persons who are not subject to hospitalization and (2) contribute toward the depletion of already-scarce community resources (R. Miller, 1990). Availability of community resources continues to be the primary obstacle to effective employment of outpatient commitment.

Forensic Psychology and Policy Implications

The LRA doctrine, as with most mental health law and policy, is not without significant controversy. One of the major concerns with the LRA doctrine is similar to those identified with the criteria for civil commitment. First, the statutes are imprecise. As Munetz and Geller (1993) note, "physicians and other mental health professionals are mandated to choose the least restrictive treatment alternative for psychiatric patients without necessarily understanding what the mandate means or how to carry it out" (p. 967).

Second, and related to the first, statutes often specify only treatment in the least restrictive environment. The doctrine's intention was to ensure that hospitalization occur only as a last resort, when absolutely necessary (Melton *et al.*, 1987). The legal concept, however, has essentially been understood as treatment "anywhere but in the state hospital" (Munetz & Geller, 1993, p. 968). Thus, the treatment setting has often been the only basis for measurement. In light of this, there is a presumption that hospitalization is the most restrictive alternative (setting) with progressively less restrictive settings available (e.g., community). As Melton *et al.* (1987) note, however, such a presumption fails to consider that treatment modalities are also restrictive. Thus, certain types of treatment in the community may be more restrictive than the physical constraints of a hospital under different treatment modes.

For example, is community-based treatment accompanied by long-term psychoactive medication less restrictive than hospitalization not requiring the use of heavy medications? This question alone has been the topic of considerable debate. In fact, in *Guardianship of Richard Roe III* (1981) the court noted that it was unable to answer such a question. Thus, when the issue of least restrictive environment includes a decision assessing whether forced medication is more of an intrusion on personal liberty than hospitalization, even the court has not been able to reach a suitable conclusion. In this sense, treatment modalities are important when considering the extent of state intervention, the least restrictive of which is the ideal.

Another important consideration regarding the LRA doctrine was raised by Arrigo (1993). He notes that decisions regarding the individual's best interest are often left to state mental hospitals. Thus, mental health professionals are the primary figures in LRA decisions. It is, however, unlikely that such professionals would opt against drug treatment or confinement in psychiatric hospitals when questions arise concerning treatment. Doing so would essentially require mental health professionals to admit that their current methods of treatment are, perhaps, ineffective or only marginally effective. Thus, it seems unlikely that recommendations by the very people in charge of the decisions would include options other than the conventional restrictive settings and treatment methods.

In general, then, much of the disagreement concerning the LRA doctrine can be regarded as a fundamental difference in perspective. The legal goal is to minimize intrusions of liberty, while the clinical goal is to determine the most effective treatment available for the mentally ill individual and, subsequently, to implement that treatment plan (Munetz & Geller, 1993). Thus, the goals of the legal system and the mental health system may often be in conflict with one another. The concept of LRA requires involvement by the mental health field, ascertaining what the least invasive and most effective psychiatric intervention is, as well as deciding what the least restrictive environment is for that treatment. Thus, effective policy analysis and implementation of new policy requires the insight of both psychological, medical, and legal scholars. Forensic psychology, perhaps, provides this insight by addressing both mental health and legal issues from within one framework.

Suggestions for Future Research

Based on the literature concerning the LRA doctrine, several important considerations are apparent when questioning its future status. First, it is necessary to determine exactly what "restrictive" implies. As discussed earlier, there has been considerable debate questioning what settings and treatments (and combinations thereof) are, in fact, less restrictive. The answer depends on the needs of the individual in question. Thus, methods of relating "least restrictive" to the specific necessities of the individual become crucial in the future employment of the LRA doctrine. In this sense, psychology and law must realize that the resolution of the issue requires joint cooperation. Future research must explore the differences inherent in each of these disciplines and calculate ways to reach mutual agreement on what the LRA doctrine implies for given individuals.

Second, and related to the first issue, is the need for more empirical research concerning individuals who have been affected by the doctrine. In other words, what are the experiences of individuals who have been subjected to commitment (both hospitalization and outpatient) compared to those in community facilities and the like? Are there fundamental differences in individual well-being, treatment effectiveness, and feelings of self-determination? While legal and mental health scholars continue to debate the issue, the input of the very persons affected by the doctrine have been somewhat neglected. Additional research in these two areas may

help resolve some of the controversy surrounding the LRA doctrine and its implications for individuals and forensic psychological practice.

DUTY TO INFORM VS CLIENT CONFIDENTIALITY

Introduction

Duty to inform versus client confidentiality stands as one of the more nebulous areas
of forensic psychology today. The controversy generally involves a mental health
professional's ethical and legal obligation to protect client confidentiality and his or
her duty to warn third parties to whom the client may pose a threat. While the
concept of confidentiality stands historically as one of the primary underpinnings
of psychology, the legal ramifications of the duty to warn have caused substantial
debate as to the limits of confidentiality. In short, the question is "when must and
when should confidentiality be breached?"

The legal limits imposed on confidentiality are the result of the California
Supreme Court's 1976 decision in *Tarasoff v. Regents of the University of California*.
Generally, *Tarasoff* imposed an additional obligation on mental health professionals
to consider the potential consequences of *not* releasing confidential information
under certain circumstances. Thus, the ethically bound psychologist not only has
the responsibility to uphold the value of confidentiality in his or her client relationships, but also must consider the interests of *other* individuals, organizations, and
society in general in the process.

In this section we explore more fully the concepts of confidentiality and duty to
warn. We consider, in detail, the decision rendered in *Tarasoff* and its implications
for psychological and forensic psychological practice. Further, we address a more
recent controversy with regard to duty to warn: the implications of duty to warn
for psychologists treating clients infected by the HIV virsus or diagnosed with
AIDS.

> Peter is a 32-year-old man who recently began a therapeutic relationship with Dr.
> John to address issues of reported depression. Peter's depression appeared to Dr. John to
> revolve around several interpersonal issues that seemed to be common to all of Peter's
> relationships. After approximately 2 months of therapy, Peter told Dr. John that he
> was beginning to feel very secure in their therapeutic relationship and that there was
> something he needed to address. Peter then confessed that he was bisexual which, because
> he had not told anyone, caused him a great deal of stress. Peter further reported that his
> first homosexual encounter was about a year ago and he had since engaged in several
> short-term relationships with other men. While Peter enjoyed the company of men,
> he stated that he had every intention of continuing to date women. In particular, Peter
> noted an 8-month relationship with a woman named Michelle.
>
> Dr. John and Peter continued to address this issue over the course of the next several
> months. One day, seeming particularly tense, Peter confessed to Dr. John that he had

been diagnosed as HIV positive. He maintained that he had been tested "just to be safe" about a month ago and had been informed of the results about 2 weeks ago. Peter told Dr. John that he was concerned, but "it hadn't quite sunk in yet." Further, Peter stated that he was continuing to have unprotected sex with several of his companions because it was unlikely that he could infect others in such a short time. In particular, Peter said he did not want to inform Michelle. He had come to the conclusion that Michelle would end the relationship upon hearing the news, and Peter did not want this to happen.

Literature Review

The ethical principles of the American Psychological Association (1992) emphasize the psychologist's obligation to respect the privacy interests of the client. Maintaining confidentiality (assuring that a client's privacy will be protected) over the course of a relationship ensures that clients will feel free to engage more fully (i.e., fully disclose) with the psychologist (Kagle & Kopels, 1994). Further, the establishment of confidentiality standards serves to protect the client from the negative effects of stigmatization (Stanard & Hazler, 1995). Thus, confidentiality, from its original intent to foster therapeutic relationships to its expanded consideration as an ethical responsibility, assumes a significant and necessary role in the effective psychologist–client relationship.

Confidentiality includes most information obtained over the course of a psychologist's contact with a client. Revealing confidential information is ethically acceptable only upon consent of the client or upon consent from the client's legal representative. Undermining the trust that is often difficult to build in the first place, violating standards of confidentiality may result in termination of the relationship, poor outcome, and/or malpractice suits against the psychologist (Kagle & Kopels, 1994).

Recently, however, confidentiality has become more difficult to maintain. The ability of the psychologist to protect privacy through confidentiality has been curtailed by a number of issues. Namely, these issues revolve around the court's expanding interest and involvement in professional decisions (Kagle & Kopels, 1994). Clients must be made aware of the limits of confidentiality at the outset of the relationship and, additionally, must be made aware of the process of breaching confidentiality. Thus, psychologists are often forced into onerous decisions which necessitate the weighing of confidentiality against third-party interests in obtaining that information. This issue is, perhaps, most profound when clients who are violent or potentially violent are involved.

The "duty to warn," which has more recently invoked limits on client privacy and confidentiality rights, stems from the 1976 California Supreme Court case *Tarasoff v. Regents of the University of California*. In *Tarasoff*, client Poddar informed psychologist Dr. Moore over the course of their therapy that he intended to kill a woman when she returned from vacation. Taking the threats seriously, Dr. Moore consulted with his supervisors and campus police. Poddar did not meet the

California standards for involuntary civil commitment and, thus, was not hospitalized. Further, the campus police detained Poddar briefly, yet released him after deciding that he presented no imminent and immediate harm. Two months later, after Tatiana Tarasoff returned from vacation, Poddar killed her. Tarasoff's parents initiated lawsuits for wrongful death against Dr. Moore, his supervisors, campus police, and the Board of Regents, claiming that their daughter should have been made aware of the danger that Poddar posed. The defendants claimed that Tarasoff was not their patient and that warning her would have breached confidentiality. The California Supreme Court, in response to their defense, would forever change the way psychology and related fields view confidentiality. The Court held that

> when a therapist determines, or pursuant to the standards of his profession should determine, that his patient presents a serious danger of violence to another, he incurs an obligation to use reasonable care to protect the intended victim against such danger. (*Tarasoff v. Regents of the University of California*, 1976, p. 34)

The Court added that this duty would entail warning the intended victim or others who may alert the victim to the potential danger, notifying the police, and/or taking any other steps that may be necessary under the circumstances to protect the victim.

Following *Tarasoff*, a number of similar cases began to emerge in other parts of the country. In general, *Tarasoff* was used as the precedent case in the courts' rulings that therapists had a duty to warn third parties under certain circumstances (Kagle & Kopels, 1994). Thus, the dilemma posed by confidentiality versus duty to warn has profound nationwide implications at this time. While some states had statutes that provided for the protection of confidentiality, *Tarasoff* caused many of these statutes to be amended, allowing for exceptions in cases where a danger to a third party was a factor. Thus, it generally stands that confidentiality should or must be breached when a therapist believes that disclosing information is necessary to protect others from a "clear, imminent risk of serious physical or mental injury, disease, or death" (Kagle & Kopels, 1994, p. 219). The precise implications of the duty to warn, as are presented in the following section, remain somewhat vague.

Forensic Psychology and Policy Implications

Before discussing the implications of Peter's case, let us examine several of the issues more broadly related to the "duty to warn." First, while courts have generally ruled that therapists have a duty to warn, the specifics of this duty have not been clearly elaborated. Court rulings have ruled inconsistently as to whether the duty is limited to specific victims or more generally to all third parties. In other words, exactly which third parties the therapist is responsible for protecting varies widely among jurisdictions (Kagle & Kopels, 1994). Several states and federal jurisdictions have even extended *Tarasoff* to include violence against property, and have extended therapist responsibility to include violent acts where the therapist "should have" known that a danger existed. Further, courts have generally not specified what this protection entails. What, exactly, a therapist must do to protect third parties remains extremely vague (Oppenheimer & Swanson, 1990).

Moreover, questions remain about dangerousness and its prediction. One of the greatest difficulties pertaining to this is determining when a client is truly dangerous to a third party and when he or she is merely fantasizing (Oppenheimer & Swanson, 1990). Is it asking too much of psychologists to be able to identify when a client may "really do" what he or she has brought to therapists' attention? If the therapist remains "on the safe side," he or she may be unnecessarily violating another's confidentiality rights. If that person does the opposite, he or she risks being held legally responsible for harm that may be inflicted upon another individual.

Additionally, how can we hold therapists responsible for the violent behavior of their clients when predicting whether a client will engage in a violent act is beyond the current ability of psychology (*Barefoot v. Estelle*, 1983; Monahan, 1981)? Studies have shown that psychology's success rate in predicting dangerous behavior is a mere 33–40%. Thus, we must ask ourselves if holding the therapist legally responsible is justifiable when the toss of a coin could better predict such acts.

Let us now return to the case of Peter. One of the most controversial aspects of the duty to warn involves the potentially violent sexual behavior of those infected with HIV. There are varying professional opinions as to the implications for psychologists of duty to warn with regard to client HIV infection. Some authors have pointed out that the sexual activity, not the person, is responsible for the risk (Kain, 1988; D. Martin, 1989). Thus, because different types of sexual activity create different risks, the level of danger must be addressed with specific regard to the activity. For example, the therapist must consider whether the activity involves the exchange of bodily fluids and whether preventive measures (e.g., protected sex) are being taken (Stanard & Hazler, 1995).

Others have suggested that the fatal nature of the disease creates a duty to warn which surmounts any ethical obligations to confidentiality. These commentators recommend directly informing the client's sexual partners if the client refuses to do so, and, where unidentified partners are at risk, informing the appropriate authorities (Gray & Harding, 1988). Regardless of the varying opinions, the majority of professionals seem to agree that HIV-positive clients engaging in high-risk behavior with uninformed partners are subject to *Tarasoff* (Stanard & Hazler, 1995). In other words, they are dangerous and steps must be taken to assure that, if a substantial threat exists, third parties are warned. Kain (1988), however, states that with regard to unidentified third parties, the "identifiable victim" criterion of *Tarasoff* is absent. Given this, he believes that breaching confidentiality in such situations is "highly questionable" (p. 224).

Thus, with regard to HIV and duty to warn for psychologists, several important issues must be addressed. First, the nature of the threat—whether specific, identifiable third parties are present; the exact nature of the sexual behavior; whether there is an imminent danger to others; and which third parties or authorities to notify. Next, given our undeveloped knowledge about HIV and AIDS, defining which behaviors put an individual at risk is difficult. Further, identifiable victims are often difficult to identify because the virus can lay dormant for many years (Stanard & Hazler, 1995). As Lamb, Clark, Drumheller, Frizzell, and Surrey (1989) note,

> Given the incomplete knowledge about the diagnosis and transmission of AIDS, there is little agreement as to who is likely to contract the disease from infected persons. Such a lack of certainty about the conditions under which the disease can be contracted make it even more difficult to identify a potential victim. (p. 40)

Thus, while cases such as Peter's may seem reasonably clear, others are far more controversial. As with the transmission of most illnesses, it is nearly impossible to identify potential victims and make a risk assessment. Thus, HIV poses yet another difficult ethical and legal concern for psychologists to confront.

Suggestions for Future Research

Many fertile areas for future research have been addressed thus far. Generally, psychology is not efficient in assessing dangerousness or determining under which conditions dangerous behavior is likely to occur. Like other areas of civil forensics, methods for more accurately predicting dangerousness are necessary if psychology is going to remain in the position of interfering with individual civil rights. Further, we must better understand which third parties are best to contact if such a decision is reached. Clearly, as in the *Tarasoff* case, contacting certain third parties is often not enough to ensure that an individual will be protected from potentially violent acts. With regard to HIV, as our knowledge of the disease continues to grow, we must continue to adapt our strategies for dealing with it in clinical and/or forensic situations. As previously noted, to identify potential victims and potentially violent behavior, we must know which individuals are at risk and under what conditions.

VICTIM COMPENSATION PROGRAMS

Introduction

In 1960, there were just over 2 million crimes reported in the United States. In 1990, there were 14.5 million. Of the various roles that the government plays, it "guards one's physical well-being and safety" (Chandler & Plano, 1988, p. 108). This role, of course, is performed effectively by "providing a safe society in which to live..." (Marion, 1995, p. 419). There now appears to be some contradiction between the latter statements and those concerning the rate of crime in the United States. If we define "victim" as one who is harmed by a crime and we then consider the vast amount of crimes being committed in this country every day, we must realize that not only are the crimes of today more violent and greater in number than at any other time in history, but there are also more victims than at any other time in history. Fourteen million crimes in 1 year could mean at least 14 million victims in a given year. It is arguable, then, that if one of the functions of government is to provide a safe society in which to live, the government is not successfully fulfilling its role.

For this reason, and others, the past several decades have produced a number of important changes concerning the government and its relation to victims of crime. There has been legislation passed at both the state and federal levels allowing for victims of crime to be financially compensated for their suffering. In this section, we explore such legislation; its development generally results in "victim compensation programs."

> Regina Palmer was a 26-year-old college student who was nearing graduation and in the process of applying to graduate schools to continue her education in animal sciences. She had hopes of becoming a veterinarian. One night, while walking home from a class that had ended at 10:00 P.M., she was abducted by a 33-year-old man. She was forced to engage in various sexual acts and was repeatedly beaten by him while being held as a prisoner in his basement for a period of no less than 2 weeks. Upon receiving information linking the young man to a similar crime that had occurred several weeks prior to Regina's abduction, the police apprehended the young man and Regina was subsequently given medical attention. Regina spent the next 3 weeks in the hospital as she tried to physically recover from the abuse. Perhaps more significantly, Regina suffered emotional scarring from which she will never recover. Unfortunately, as a result of the incident, Regina was not able to complete her studies and a year-and-a-half later was still emotionally unable to return to school. In addition, Regina was forced to relive the traumatic experience in the recitation of her experience to the police and, subsequently, to an unsympathetic attorney in a court of law. What compensation does our system of justice have for a woman such as Regina whose entire life was turned upside-down, in part, because of a system that was unable to apprehend a serial criminal before he struck again?

Literature Review

History of Victim Legislation

The latter part of the 20th century witnessed an increase in the rights afforded to criminal suspects and offenders. While the violators of criminal law were enjoying added protections and benefits at the hands of the law, society began to approach the issue from the other side. As a result, movements concerned with the rights of victims emerged. Society began to question if the victims of crime were not being relegated to third-party status (L. Wrightsman *et al.*, 1994). In other words, throughout the criminal process, victims were often forgotten as the state and the offender were of primary concern. Even today it is not unusual to think of a criminal as having broken a law rather than as having victimized another human being. Consequently, the rights of victims began to receive greater attention.

A concern for victims' rights emerged from the civil rights and women's movements of the 1960s (B. Smith, Sloan, & Ward, 1990). Initially, the victims' rights movement was successful in lobbying for financial compensation and restitution. These demands and successes have expanded in recent years to include lessening the often traumatic effects of court appearances by victims and the implementation of laws that allow victims to influence the disposition of the case (i.e., sentencing and parole decisions regarding the offender).

Early demands of the victims' rights movement were generally focused on changing the way that victims were treated by the justice system. The very concept of criminal justice itself has been attacked, as it often neglects the notion of victim justice that must, it is argued, be a part of the administration of justice (B. Smith et al., 1990). Thus, one of the primary concerns of victims' rights advocates is "secondary victimization" (Hagan, 1982), which occurs when victims are mistreated by the police, attorneys, judges, and so on while the case progresses through the system (B. Smith et al., 1990).

As for allowing victims to impact the sentencing of offenders, there are generally two ways in which this occurs: victims' impact statements and victim allocution or formal statements made by the victim regarding his or her loss or injury (B. Smith et al., 1990). A majority of states have passed legislation allowing (or, often requiring) victim impact statements, while slightly fewer have passed laws allowing victims the right to make a statement at the sentencing phase of the justice process.

The first government initiative to drastically alter the way in which victims of crime were treated was California's 1965 victim compensation program. Initially, California was to provide financial compensation to victims of violent crimes and to the dependents of murder victims (McCormack, 1991, 1994). Shortly thereafter, New York (1966), Hawaii (1967), Massachusetts (1968), and Maryland (1968), and New Jersey (1971) all passed similar legislation. By 1991, 45 states had established some sort of program for the compensation of crime victims (McCormack, 1991). For the most part, these programs reimburse victims for the losses they suffered as a result of their victimization. These losses may include medical expenses, long-term care for serious injuries, burial expenses, and other services.

Nearly all states have established victim compensation boards that function to reimburse victims for financial losses they incur as a result of crime. Additionally, all states provide some sort of assistance to victims of sexual assault and domestic violence. Victim compensation has remained, for the most part, a state issue. While the federal government has consistently supported victim assistance, its perspective has remained: "public safety and assistance to crime victims are ultimately state concerns" (McCormack, 1994, p. 214).

The most significant federal involvement in victim assistance is its 1984 Victims of Crime Act (VOCA). The VOCA established a federal office that was responsible for developing the general rights of victims. In particular, it would provide a degree of federal funding for state agencies and programs that dealt with victim assistance through the Crime Victim Fund. In addition to the federal funding, state governments generally pull from taxes and penalty assessments to fund their own victim compensation programs (Greer, 1994).

Forensic Psychology and Policy Implications

Criminals vs. Victims: Where Should the Focus Be?

As noted at the beginning of this section, there is an ever-present relationship between crime and victims, between crime and government, and, thus, between victims and government. Were it not for crime, victims of crime would not exist. If the government's attempts to decrease the rate of crime in the United States were more successful, perhaps the need for victim assistance would cease to exist. Nevertheless, crime is a reality and victims of crime hold an equal place in the present day debate. Where, then, should our efforts be focused? Have we reached a point where we are willing to concede that there is no easy solution to crime and, thus, contribute to victim assistance? Questions such as these have important implications for policy.

The first criticism of some victims' rights advocates addresses the government's efforts to combat the problem of crime in contemporary America. Congress has created numerous laws to deter crime. The laws that have been implemented to decrease the rate of crime, however, have generally focused on the offender. That is to say, the goal of the government with regard to victims of crime seems to be to reduce crime itself and, in the process, the problem of victimization. By the 1970s the government began to implement law and policy that dealt directly with the victim rather than merely the offender. Regardless of such changes, the majority of activity at the governmental level, however, remains focused around the offender. The question here becomes to what degree should the government contribute valuable resources to assisting victims as opposed to fighting or preventing crime itself? This is an important question at both state and federal levels. Given the inadequacy of funding efforts for both preventing and combating crime, as well as compensating victims of crime, resources become increasingly valuable.

Recalling the case of Regina, would the financial and human resources of the state and the county have been better spent on compensating Regina for her losses or, rather, on apprehending the offender before he had the opportunity to strike? Like many issues in justice, there is no easy answer. The reality is that only a limited amount of resources are available and each of these problems requires far more than what is currently being afforded them.

Are We Really Compensating Victims?

Despite all of the reform efforts over the past several decades, questions still linger as to whether victims are really being compensated as they should. With the expansion of policy-related activity on both state and federal levels, one would expect that victims may finally be granted the attention they arguably deserve. This, however, is not a shared perception of victim compensation. Many still feel that victims are not receiving the recognition that they deserve (Marion, 1995). The reality of the situation is that victims receive only minimal aid, compensation programs being one example. Further, the extent of such aid to victims varies significantly from state to state. Perhaps the biggest problems include the lack of funding for such programs and the lack of information available for victims of crime.

It is likely that many persons have never heard of victim compensation programs. It is even less likely that, if victimized, these persons would know how to go about applying for compensation. In fact, the actual application information is often difficult to obtain and victims are rarely made aware of such programs upon their entrance into the justice system (Elias, 1986). As a result, few victims apply for benefits. McCormack (1991) reports that only about 6% of violent crime victims apply for compensation. The number that actually receive compensation is closer to 4%.

Given that very few victims are aware of the presence of compensation programs and even fewer actually receive compensation, we must question whether everything possible is being done to aid the victims of crime. We have already noted that such programs, despite being funded in part by the federal government, are drastically underfunded. Certainly funds do not exist to compensate all victims of crime. The question, then, becomes where do we draw the line? Certainly persons such as Regina Palmer, whose entire lives have been devastated as a result of their victimization, should be compensated. As we consider less severe crimes it becomes increasingly difficult to draw the line. Many persons may suffer far more from being the victim of a minor crime than others would from being the victim of a more serious crime. These psychological differences are difficult to ascertain, even for the trained psychologist. The role of the forensic psychologist in determining "emotional suffering" for the purpose of compensation is one of the more highly debated areas of law and psychology today. Again, we must ask ourselves where the line is drawn and how we are to determine who suffers and to what extent.

General Welfare Perspective

As McCormack (1994) notes, the victims' movement has always been influenced by a retributive philosophy. That is to say, the offender has been the primary concern. Victims' rights essentially mean harsher punishments and the like. This philosophy has caused a great deal of debate within the general field. In particular, strong statements are made by those favoring reform of the entire system. The "general welfare" perspective argues that attention should also be paid to "offender/victims," in other words, those offenders who are also victims "of discrimination, racism, poverty, and related conditions" (McCormack, 1994, p. 216). Thus, programs that assist such high-risk persons are arguably consistent with the more general goals of the victims' rights movement and victim advocacy in that they prevent victimization. In short, the general welfare perspective encourages us not to forget that offenders are often themselves victims.

The general welfare perspective offers a position that undoubtedly causes some substantial debate. To remain true to our efforts to support victims and advocate for victims' rights, we must also support those offenders for whom victimization played an important and decisive role in their lives. If the young man whose repeated assaults on Regina Palmer was abused himself for the majority of his childhood, should we then support him as a victim as well? This, of course, is not to suggest that such persons should not be punished for their crimes, but that we should not overlook the reality that many of today's offenders are or were themselves victims. As such, closer attention to victims before they progress to the status of offender is, perhaps, an effort that could significantly reduce the number of persons victimized at the hands of these individuals. Again, we must make some preliminary choices between compensation for those existing victims and preventative efforts to reduce the number of future victims. This is a debate that haunts all sectors of the system of justice today.

Suggestions for Future Research

Our efforts toward research in the increasingly significant areas of victims' rights and victim compensation must lead us to new and more effective practices. The previous section discussing the general welfare perspective encourages us to determine where our resources are best allocated. This is a question that remains unanswered. While there is certainly research that attempts to determine the effectiveness of crime prevention techniques, this research is far from complete. It remains to be seen whether employing human and financial resources in programs that are aimed at prevention and rehabilitation are worthwhile. Certainly, this is an area open to those interested in forensic psychology and the relationship between human behavior and the system of justice.

Additional concerns were raised by the process of compensation itself. Recall that we previously discussed exactly where the line should be drawn. Current decisions delineating to whom we deliver compensatory aid are far from conclusive. Should such programs be better publicized? If so, where would the necessary resources come from that would assist the increased number of persons asking for relief? These and other questions represent important concerns for our system of justice and those inquiring into how such an institution could and should be improved.

VICTIM–OFFENDER MEDIATION

Introduction

Victim–offender mediation programs were created and are utilized in nearly 100 jurisdictions throughout the United States (Umbreit, 1993). There are more than

290 additional programs in development (Umbreit & Bradshaw, 1997). Mediation programs for victims and offenders offer the victim an opportunity to play a role in determining the offender's punishment, explain to the offender the impact the crime had upon them, and give the victim closure after being violated. The program gives offenders an opportunity to voice their personal problems and explain their crime, avoid a possible harsher punishment such as imprisonment, and allows them to personalize their crime; that is, see first-hand the impact it had upon another human being. This personalization could ultimately reduce recidivism (K. L. Joseph, 1996; Reske, 1995; Umbreit & Bradshaw, 1997). The goal of mediation programs is to provide a conflict resolution that is fair for both parties involved and to develop an acceptable restitution plan (Umbreit, 1993).

Despite a variety in victim–offender mediation programs, most programs aim to achieve the same goals and have principles based on the concept of restorative justice (Severson & Bankston, 1995). Restorative justice is an age-old concept emphasizing that crime should be perceived as an act against individuals within the community, not only as an act against the state (Umbreit & Bradshaw, 1997). Most mediation programs are based on the same principles and follow the same process for mediation. First, either a victim or offender is referred to a mediation program. Second, each party is seen individually by an unbiased mediator who informs them about the process and the possible benefits of participating in such a program. Third, after each party agrees, the mediator schedules a joint meeting between the two parties. During this phase, both the victim and the offender are given the opportunity to talk to each other without interruption. Finally, some programs may have a follow-up phase in which the referral agency approves the restitution agreement and closes the case; approving the agreement may include making sure payments or services that were agreed upon are fulfilled (K. L. Joseph, 1996; Umbreit, 1993). The types of offender mediation programs and how they differ are discussed later in this section.

The following case illustration is a real situation in which victim–offender mediation was successfully utilized. This section uses this case to describe the types of victim–offender mediation programs and how they differ; to discuss the effectiveness of victim–offender mediation programs; and to address arguments against the appropriateness of such programs, including examples of how the following case could have been unsuccessful had circumstances been different.

> Geiger was working as an auditor on the 11 A.M.-to-7 P.M. shift that summer night when five men ages 18 to 21 entered the motel and demanded money. Geiger was punched and kicked, followed quickly by a pistol-whipping that knocked him to the ground. He jumped to his feet when he thought the crooks had left. Then he heard an explosion. The bullet tore into his chest, penetrating his right lung, breaking two ribs, and lodging in his stomach muscles. At the time of the robbery Geiger was a nationally ranked sprinter. Before the shooting he could do 100 meters in under 11 seconds; afterward, he could barely walk the distance. Facing unwanted publicity, motel management fired him.
>
> At the trials of the black defendants, Geiger, who is white, was accused of racism and drinking and made to feel guilty. He felt left out and angry at a system that had

victimized him a second time. He was depressed and he needed answers. He wanted to confront his shooter and tell him about the damage he had done, and he wanted an apology.

Geiger found answers to many of his questions in mediation. He found that the offender was a substance abuser, out of work, and on parole. He had planned a simple robbery. He hadn't intended to shoot Geiger but instead wanted to fire a warning shot. At the end of his session, Geiger shook hands with the man who shot him. "I saw the burden of guilt lifted from him and the anguish from me." Geiger testified on behalf of the man last February at his parole hearing. He was granted parole after serving 12 years of a 12- to 25-year term for first-degree robbery. (Reske, 1995, pp. 1–3)

Literature Review

Types of Victim–Offender Mediation Programs

In the Middle Ages, a criminal act was punished by the criminal making reparations directly to the victim; this is the basis upon which victim–offender mediation programs are utilized today (Severson & Bankston, 1995). Currently, there are various types of mediation programs, which can differ in several ways. Some programs offer mediation after conviction of a crime but prior to sentencing, while others offer mediation upon parole and make restitution a condition of parole. In some programs the victim and offender meet face-to-face while in other programs they do not (K. L. Joseph, 1996; Roy, 1993). In addition, programs may differ on the cases they accept; some programs may only accept juvenile cases while others accept adults. Some programs only accept cases of violent crimes, while others accept nonviolent criminal cases (Severson & Bankston, 1995). Finally, programs differ in who they use to mediate the cases, the model they utilize to run the program, and in their administration. Most programs use trained volunteers as mediators; however, other programs may use social work professionals. Although many mediation programs are supported by religious agencies, some are run and financed by probation departments and private foundations (K. L. Joseph, 1996; Severson & Bankston, 1995).

The most popular model used to run victim–offender mediation programs is the Victim/Offender Reconciliation Program (VORP) model. The VORP model was developed in 1974 by the Mennonite Central Committee in Kitchener, Ontario, Canada (Roy, 1993; Umbreit & Bradshaw, 1997). In 1978, the United States' first victim–offender program was put together in Elkhart, Indiana (Reske, 1995). The Elkhart program, like most victim reconciliation programs nationwide, is based on the VORP model. Programs based on the VORP model provide face-to-face meetings between the victim and offender (Roy, 1993). Also, the VORP is usually a postadjudication program in which the offenders and their victims explore reconciliation and build a plan together for reparation (Roy, 1993; Severson & Blackston, 1995). Most likely, the program Geiger went through utilized the VORP model because he had a face-to- face meeting with his offender and because the mediation took place after the offender had served time in prison (postadjudication). According to Severson and Blackston's 1995 article, 30 states have reconciliation programs and most of them utilize the VORP model. In addition, more recent research suggests that the number of programs utilizing the VORP model is increasing (Umbreit & Bradshaw, 1997). Despite the majority of reconciliation programs that utilize the VORP model, there are successful programs that do not. A restitution program in Kalamazoo County, Michigan, is operated by the Juvenile Probate Court, is a preadjudication program, and does not provide face-to-face meetings between the victim and offender; however, it does offer restitution to the victim similar to the VORP model (Roy, 1993). Despite the differences between the Kalamazoo program and the VORP model programs, Roy found that the Kalamazoo program was just as effective as the Elkhart, Missouri VORP program.

There are clearly many different types of victim reconciliation programs. A discussion of every type of program is beyond the scope of this section. However, it is important to be aware of how such programs differ, and how these differences can have an impact on the effectiveness of the program. Because there are so many victim reconciliation programs and because many of these programs differ, it is difficult to assess the effectiveness of these programs as a whole. However, research on the effectiveness of individual programs, as well as on the effectiveness of programs have utilizing the VORP model, have been conducted.

Effectiveness of Programs

Effectiveness of restitution programs is generally measured by program completion rates, the impact of restitution on lowering recidivism rates, and by victim satisfaction with the program (Roy, 1993; Umbreit & Bradshaw, 1997). For example, in the Geiger case, the mediation was considered successful because the offender and Geiger came to an agreement, the offender showed compassion, and Geiger felt satisfied by the meeting. However, program completion percentages vary from program to program. Roy (1993) conducted a study in which two programs were compared on recidivism rates and program completion. One of the programs was the Elkhart VORP program and the other was the Kalamazoo probate program described above. In his study, Roy found 59% of the offenders in the Elkhart program and 62% of those in the Kalamazoo program failed because of financial hardship. In addition, the researcher found that 41% of the offenders in the Elkhart program and 38% in the Kalamazoo program reoffended. Despite the high rate of program failure in Roy's research, other studies have found successful completion rates as high as 98% (Fishbein, Davis, & Hamparin, 1984). In an evaluation of a restorative justice program implemented by the Vermont Department of Corrections for nonviolent offenders, data suggest that the program is working. According to one researcher, the program is no less effective than the traditional retribution model of corrections and is freeing up space and resources to deal with more violent criminals (Hansen, 1997).

Research that has focused on victim satisfaction with the process has found high rates of victim satisfaction with reconciliation programs (Umbreit & Bradshaw, 1997). When Geiger met his offender, it provided him closure to an occurrence which had a negative impact on his life. When an offender shows compassion, as in Geiger's case, many victims are satisfied with the program. In a 1994 study, Umbreit found 90% of victims were satisfied with the mediation outcome. However, no research was found on the satisfaction rate among offenders; arguments against victim–offender mediation suggest that offenders are often less than satisfied (J. G. Brown, 1994). However, other researchers posit that when a victim's needs are met, the offender's needs will be met as well (Evers, 1998).

Despite a need for further research on victim–offender mediation programs, it appears as though some of the programs are successful at satisfying the victim, providing restitution, and preventing recidivism. In addition, proponents for victim–offender mediation programs suggest that restorative programs are successful at alleviating the problem of prison and jail overcrowding. Currently, more than 1 million people are behind bars and many are held in overcrowded facilities (Evers, 1998). The man who burglarized and shot Geiger may have been in prison for 25 years instead of 12 had he and Geiger not met through the reconciliation program. This illustrates how such programs can reduce the number of incarcerated offenders.

Advocates for restorative justice believe that there is a reason people commit crime again and again. One of these reasons is a lack of empathy for victims. With restorative justice, offenders are held accountable for their crimes, while the needs of the victim are met (Evers, 1998). Geiger needed an apology, and he received that and much more (Reske, 1995). In addition, his offender showed empathy and regret for what he did, which could have ultimately reduced the likelihood he would commit another crime of this nature. According to advocates for mediation programs, one of the benefits of mediation is that it allows offenders to become aware of the impact of their crimes and to see their victims as people rather than as objects (Reske, 1995). When offenders are able to see their victims as people and possibly have empathy for them, the likelihood of recidivism is reduced (Umbreit & Bradshaw, 1997). As a result, less offenders circulate through the prison system, helping to alleviate overcrowding. Also, mediation programs such as the one implemented in Vermont may aid in overcrowding simply by providing an alternative response to jail or prison.

Proponents for mediation programs suggest that prisons have become nothing more than "colleges for crime," which return to the public "meaner" and "craftier" criminals (Evers, 1998; Severson & Bankston, 1995). These advocates suggest that the United States spends more on punishment and less on programs to prevent crime, and indicate that restorative justice is a program designed for prevention (Evers, 1998). Restorative justice programs not only benefit victims, they benefit offenders as well. Proponents note that offenders need to be punished, but also need help; restorative justice can do both (Evers, 1998). However, other researchers are not so optimistic about restorative justice programs. They suggest that offenders often feel pressured into coming to an agreement during mediation and indicate such programs often do not benefit the offender (J. G. Brown, 1994; K. L. Joseph, 1996).

Arguments against Victim–Offender Mediation

Although most research is supportive of victim–offender mediation programs, some researchers note problems with the programs, resulting in debate about whether such programs should be utilized at all. The primary argument against mediation programs is whether true voluntariness exists for the offenders involved in the program (J. G. Brown, 1994; K. L. Joseph, 1996). Because many offenders are referred to mediation programs from the court, they participate because they feel it is required (K. L. Joseph, 1996). In addition, offenders may come to an agreement that they cannot afford or cannot complete because they fear if they do not come to an agreement in mediation they will be punished for noncompliance (J. G. Brown, 1994). In response, researchers who support victim–offender mediation programs suggest that giving the offender the opportunity to have a say in his or her punishment will more likely result in a punishment with which he or she can comply (Reske, 1995).

There are also arguments against restitution programs. J. G. Brown (1994) argues that such programs are a disservice to both victims and offenders. Victims may experience an injustice because reconciliation programs stress reconciliation before the victims "have the vindication of a public finding that the offender is guilty" (J. G. Brown, 1994, p. 3). However, this is not true for all programs; in Geiger's case, the offender was not only found guilty, he served 12 years in prison. Victim–offender mediation programs may pressure the victim into suppressing his or her anger and sense of loss through the assumption that his or her feelings can be expressed to the offender in merely a period of hours. These programs underserve the offender in several ways as well. First, the selection criteria are not related to the goals of the program. Second, such programs eliminate procedural protections, including the right to counsel. Third, programs attempt to gain advantages for the victims by using the threat of a pending criminal trial.

Although Brown makes some important assertions against victim–offender mediation programs, a number of the problems she addresses could be alleviated by changing programs, not eliminating them. For example, in the Geiger case, there may have been some pressure for the offender to mediate because he was due for parole. In other cases, there may be coercion because the process is prior to adjudication; however, if programs are postadjudication and the mediation does not occur prior to a parole hearing, it is doubtful that the offender would feel pressured to come to an agreement as a result of fearing punishment.

Other arguments against victim–offender mediation programs could also be alleviated by changing or restricting programs. Some researchers argue against the use of victim–offender mediation programs for certain offenders such as sex offenders and wife batterers. Women's rights advocates believe restorative justice may reduce progress battered women have made. However, the appropriateness of victim–offender mediation programs for certain populations does not appear to be much of a debate. Even Mark Umbreit, the director of the Center of Restorative Justice and Mediation does not recommend mediation for some sexual assault cases and for all domestic violence cases (Evers, 1998). Proponents argue that in some cases, mediation can be beneficial for sexual assault incidents, and many programs require that sexual assault cases be victim initiated.

Despite evidence which supports victim–offender mediation programs, these programs have not gone without dispute. There are few examples of cases which went wrong; however, they are sure to exist. For example, imagine if Geiger met the man who shot him and the man showed no remorse, guilt, refused to apologize, and did nothing but make excuses for his behavior. It is questionable whether Geiger would have experienced the closure he desired. In fact, such a meeting could have forced Geiger to relive some of the pain he had dealt with over the past 11 years. Clearly, there will always be problems with mediation programs, and there will always be instances where the program is unsuccessful. The question is whether the problems warrant giving up completely on such initiatives or warrant changing programs to be more effective. Because restitution programs threaten to alter the way in which some criminals are punished, there are clearly some policy implications for the existence of such programs.

Forensic Psychology and Policy Implications

A problem with victim–offender mediation programs is that they are run by many agencies. As a result, there are no set criteria about who can mediate, how offenders will be selected, and how the process of mediation should take place (Severson & Bankston, 1995). Currently, most mediation programs rely on trained volunteers who know little or nothing about psychology or sociology. Several researchers suggest using trained professionals as mediators for these programs and that laws are needed to require mediators to have advanced training (Severson & Bankston, 1995). In addition, there is a need for policies based on research to be adopted for victim–offender mediation programs. Although some researchers have suggested policies that should be adopted, there is a need for research to be conducted in order to determine what guidelines create the most effective programs. One policy that most researchers do agree upon is a provision against mediation for domestic violence cases (Evers, 1998). It is essential that research on mediation programs and procedural guidelines be adopted immediately; the concept is becoming more popular and lawmakers are passing legislation to create restorative justice programs in states such as Vermont and Maine. The programs, however, are diverse and there are few guidelines that indicate how the programs could be successfully run. As demonstrated by the opponents of restorative justice programs, the negative effects of unsuccessful programs can be huge. Without guidelines based on research, it will be difficult to minimize the negative effects.

With prison overcrowding, it is more likely that many states will look for alternatives to traditional sentencing. States may begin to implement legislation for the development of restitution programs; they may be met, however, with opposition from the general public, whose current attitude is that punishment equals imprisonment (Severson & Bankston, 1995). The public must be educated about the deficiencies of prisons and how these institutions financially impact them. Before legislation can be changed, society must become informed about alternatives to incarceration. As long as society equates imprisonment with punishment, politicians will continue to build prisons instead of invest in prevention programs. Perhaps the beginning of public education could occur through research results on the effectiveness of restorative justice programs. Because of the diversity of such programs, it is difficult to determine which aspects of various programs do or do not work.

Suggestions for Future Research

Further research on the effectiveness of victim–offender mediation programs is needed (Severson & Bankston, 1995). Although some studies have reported recidivism rates and program completion rates on individual programs, there is a need for research which examines the benefits and consequences of all restorative justice programs in order for recommendations to be made for program guidelines (Roy, 1993; Severson & Bankston, 1995). Also, there has been little research on long-term recidivism rates for those who participated in a mediation program (Roy, 1993). These data are essential when states are enacting legislation to develop initiatives. If program developers do not have findings indicating which programs have successful long-term effects and therefore would serve as models to develop, then the development of these mediation programs will be no more successful than our overcrowded prisons at reducing recidivism.

The case of Geiger is a clear illustration of how victim–offender mediation programs can benefit the victim and offender. However, the outcome of this case is not known. Quite possibly, the offender recidivated after his parole, perhaps this time shooting and killing an individual. There is no way to know this information for most cases that have completed mediation programs, simply because long-term research on effectiveness is limited. Various studies indicate that victim–offender mediation programs do work. Studies demonstrate a high victim satisfaction rate and a recidivism rate no worse than those criminals who went through the traditional sentencing model. With prison overcrowding and the United States spending less on prevention and more on imprisonment, mediation programs appear to be promising.

CHAPTER 8

Family Forensics

OVERVIEW

This chapter examines selected controversies and issues in forensic psychology impacting families. For purposes of this chapter, the use of the term "family" is broadly defined. When the legal and psychological communities promote policies and/or therapeutic interventions that affect how parents and their children are to interact, then the structure and process of what it means to be in a family are called into question.

Several subjects investigated in this chapter explore the way in which the legal system, with the aid of psychologists, make decisions about parents, their children, and the family unit. In addition, other sections consider how trauma and violence affect the behavior of family members and how the court's respond to such abuse. In total, six subjects are examined. These topics include (1) family trauma and the cycle of crime, (2) family violence and homicide, (3) the role of paternalism and *parens patriae* in mental health law on the family, (4) family law and the "emotional rights" of children, (5) domestic violence, and (6) gay/lesbian rights and definitions of the family. While the issues reviewed in this chapter do not exhaustively canvass the family forensic field, the topics chosen are, nonetheless, controversial, significant, and demonstrate the pressing need for skilled practitioners in this subspecialty area of law and psychology.

Repeated exposure in childhood to family trauma and abuse can be devastating for young boys and girls. How does exposure to such violence affect a person in adulthood? What are the behavioral and situational risk factors involved in cycles of crime? What prevention strategies, as developed in forensic psychology, exist to break the intergenerational cycle of abuse? People are at a greater risk to be victimized by a family member than by a stranger. Several manifestations of family violence include infanticide, parricide, and spousal abuse. What are the causal factors leading to these (and other) forms of family violence? How can law and psychology help us understand the phenomenon of family homicide? The field of mental health law affects the behavior and rights of individuals in families. The doctrines of paternalism and *parens patriae* are two legal principles demonstrating the power that the state possesses and exercises in the lives of persons suffering from psychiatric illness. How do paternalism and *parens patriae* work? What influence do these doctrines exert on families? How are these legal principles used in relation to civil commitment? The experience of divorce and adoption can be traumatic for families, especially when children are involved. How are children impacted by these events? What is the emotional impact of the custody dispute for children? How does family law, if at all, protect the emotional rights of children in custody disputes when divorce and/or adoption are at issue? Domestic violence, particularly when physical, sexual, and emotional battering is involved, can be extremely painful for families. How does domestic violence impact couples, their children, and the family unit? Are there patterns to abuse in domestic violence cases? If so, can such patterns be traceable to one's family of origin? What is the role of the forensic psychologist in the area of domestic violence? In today's society, gay and lesbian citizens have redefined the meaning of family life and the family unit. Are children of nonheterosexist couples at any greater psychological risk when growing up in homosexual families? How does law and psychology assist us in our understanding of gay and lesbian family rights?

The legal system has a vested interest in protecting the rights and ensuring the responsibilities of families and their respective members. The domain of forensic psychology examines those situations where questions persist about the behavior, attitudes, and beliefs of parents and/or children in the family context. Some of these concerns are extremely serious in that immediate trauma, abuse, violence, and crime are at stake. On other occasions, the issue is about understanding how the law, with the assistance of psychology, can better address the changing and emerging needs of different families. In both instances, the forensic specialist assumes a pivotal role in the intervention and policy process. As the individual sections of this chapter make clear, the field of family forensics requires additional research into the nature of family life in general and the social, psychological, and legal factors that limit parents and their children from experiencing the joys of such a healthy existence in particular.

FAMILY TRAUMA AND THE CYCLE OF CRIME

Introduction

An increasing number of children are living in chaotic familial and communal environments. Conservative estimates indicate that over 1 million children are abused and neglected each year in the United States alone (National Center on Child Abuse and Neglect, 1994). These children are often exposed to exorbitant levels of trauma characterized by parental neglect, physical abuse, sexual abuse, domestic violence, and inconsistent discipline from parental figures. The biological, psychological, and social repercussions of children growing up with such trauma are numerous. Of particular interest, however, is the significance of family trauma and its relation to intergenerational cycles of antisocial and criminal behavior. The relationship between one's traumatic upbringing and the perpetuation of criminal behavior in adolescence and adulthood has been clearly noted in the literature. Empirical evidence does suggest that the growing numbers of adolescent and adult criminal offenders come from backgrounds plagued with varying levels of trauma. However, currently there are no concentrated efforts made to address this issue in terms of prevention and effective intervention measures. The following case illustrates how a young male, who lived in a chaotic familial environment, resorted to violence.

> Fifteen-year-old Arnold was arrested and incarcerated after he fatally stabbed his mother's boyfriend of 2 months. As a young child, Arnold had been exposed to numerous distressing events. On many occasions he observed his biological father physically assaulting his mother. Arnold's father physically abused him and often used objects such as belts, electric cords, and wooden planks. As a young child, Arnold was left alone in the house for days at a time without any guidance or supervision. Subsequently, Arnold began having numerous difficulties both at home and at school. His teachers reported that during class, he seemed distracted and irritable and he would often engage in physical altercations with other classmates. He began to exhibit increasingly dangerous and reckless behaviors; spoke perseveratively about weapons, stabbings, and the physical abuse he had witnessed; and expressed vague fears that he himself would come to harm others. The night of the stabbing, Arnold witnessed his mother and her boyfriend arguing in the living room. Arnold was unable to tolerate his mother's boyfriend's argumentative behavior and, hence, Arnold impulsively reached for a kitchen knife and proceeded to stab him. Arnold was charged with assault with a deadly weapon and is currently awaiting sentencing.

Literature Review

As a result of Arnold's case and those that are similar, it is apparent that the perpetuation of violence within families needs to be thoroughly examined and, ultimately, prevented. The results of exposure to severe familial violence is not randomly distributed within the population. Some children are substantially more likely to have such experiences associated with where they reside and with whom they live. Children who have risk factors in their lives such as domestic violence, parental substance abuse, and living in poverty are certainly at an increased risk for exposure to trauma and violence. Children can experience such violence within a number of different contexts; however, it is likely that the family, and especially a child's relationship with caregivers, is one of the most important of these contexts. The following literature review explores the risk factors involved in the cycle of crime. Preventative measures geared toward breaking the intergenerational cycle of crime are also discussed.

A common setting for violence is the home. Problems of parental abuse, neglect, and spousal abuse account for a major component of the physical and emotional trauma suffered by children. It is therefore not only important, but necessary to examine the effects of familial violence, abuse, and neglect on the development of children who live within these contexts. In Helfer and Kempe's (1986) study, 82% of a group of adolescent offenders were found to have a history of abuse and neglect and 43% recalled being knocked unconscious by one of their parents. Their sample of violent adolescents were victims of, as well as witnesses to, severe physical abuse. The sample provided a clear indication of how extreme physical disciplinary practices in the home correlated with aggressive and destructive delinquency.

McCord's (1991) study came from a larger longitudinal investigation of males who had been in a program designed to prevent delinquency. McCord (1991) examined families in which fathers were criminals and those in which fathers were not criminals, and found significant differences that help explain the cycle of violence among sons of criminals. Results indicated that sons of criminals were more, rather than less, likely to become criminals. The data suggested that aggressive parental models increased the likelihood that their sons would be involved in criminal activities. Furthermore, maternal affection, self-confidence, and consistent nonpunitive discipline or supervision helped protect their sons from engaging in criminal behavior. This discovery leads to the tentative conclusion that intervention techniques designed to develop competence among parents may be particularly effective when the targets are children at high risk (McCord, 1991).

Who are the children at high risk and how do these risk factors perpetuate a cycle of violence? One longitudinal study, completed by Widom (1992), looked specifically at the cycle of violence. Widom (1992) tracked 1575 cases from childhood through young adulthood and compared the arrest records of the two groups. One group contained 908 subjects who experienced some form of substantiated childhood abuse or neglect and a comparison group of 667 children who were not officially recorded as abused or neglected. Both groups were matched for age, race, sex, and socioeconomic status. Clear and succinct operational definitions of abuse and neglect allowed for a separate examination of physical abuse, sexual abuse, and neglect.

Results indicated that children who had been abused or neglected were 58% more likely to be arrested as juveniles, 38% more likely to be arrested as adults,

38% more likely to be arrested for a violent crime, and 77% more likely to be arrested if they were females. Abuse and neglect cases on average were nearly 1 year younger at first arrest, committed twice as many crimes, and were arrested 89% more frequently than the control group. A noteworthy conclusion was that a child who was neglected was just as likely as a child who was abused to be arrested for a violent crime. The aforementioned study further exemplifies how childhood abuse and neglect can precipitate violent behavior in adolescence and adulthood.

Researchers have also explored the familial and communal backgrounds of criminal offenders. Briscoe (1997) examined the familial histories of youths who were committed to the Texas Youth Commission (TYC). The TYC is a state agency which is responsible for the most seriously delinquent and disturbed youths. The findings indicated that the vast majority of the youths in TYC had histories of abuse and neglect. A majority of youth offenders had family members with histories of violence, substance abuse, criminal behavior, and mental impairments. Approximately 71% of these delinquent youths came from chaotic environments and 80% of the subject's parental figures lacked adequate disciplinary skills. This youth offender study further highlights the relationship between traumatic childhood experiences and the likelihood of engaging in delinquent behavior.

A similar study (A. Levinson & Fonagy, 1999) examined 22 male patients in a prison sample and matched them with a group of psychiatric controls. Their crimes included attempted burglary, theft, property damage, car theft, gross indecency, importation of drugs, armed robbery, kidnapping, rape, and murder. They were interviewed with a structured clinical interview for Diagnostic and Statistical Manual of Mental Disorders (1983), Third Edition, Revised (DSM-III-R) disorders. They all had at least one clinical disorder and 91% had at least one personality disorder; 50% had a DSM-III-R diagnosis of Borderline Personality Disorder. The average Global Assessment of Functioning (GAF) score for the group was 47. The GAF was generally indicative of serious symptoms or serious impairments in social and occupational functioning. A number of striking findings indicated that among this group of 22 criminals, extreme deprivations in childhood, severe physical abuse, and neglect were commonly and convincingly reported. Although this was only a pilot investigation, the results are promising to the extent that they link histories of abuse with the perpetuation of criminal behavior and psychopathology.

Forensic Psychology and Policy Implications

The crisis of family trauma and the perpetuation of violence affects tens of thousands of families nationwide. Increasingly, children are not only witnessing but experiencing varying degrees of violence in their homes and communities. This exposure to violence changes the way children view the world and may change the value they place on life itself (Groves, Zuckerman, Marans, & Cohen, 1993). It can certainly affect their ability to learn, to establish and sustain relationships with others, and to cope with life's stressors. Yet there is a general lack of knowledge and understanding in terms of how growing up in such chaotic environments affects young children's social, emotional, and cognitive development. Factors such as the public's lack of understanding about the effects of family trauma only serves to hinder efficient and effective intervention methods.

The literature clearly points to a link between family trauma and an intergenerational cycle of violence and crime. Children who grow up in unstructured, chaotic, and abusive homes are at an increased risk of engaging in violent or antisocial behavior. Thus, it is imperative that policy makers endorse services for children and families which interface with police, schools, courts, community programs, and health care settings. Solutions must encompass preventing trauma, early intervention, and swift and clear repercussions for chronic or violent behavior. It is crucial to reach children who experience such trauma long before they arrive at an age where they act out their experiences in a violent manner. Another inherent component to helping traumatized children is to provide information and counseling to the caregivers in the children's lives.

Suggestions for Future Research

Future investigations of family trauma must investigate how familial trauma affects children, and how it impacts communities and society in general. The present findings provide some important insights into these issues; however, a great deal of research still needs to be conducted. If family trauma perpetuates itself producing a vicious cycle of violence, then it is imperative to explore what interventions can break this cycle. Studies are needed which elucidate more fully the range and effects of familial trauma and, more so, assess the effects of early treatment measures. We therefore need a closer look at the extent to which some interventions may be more effective than others in terms of differences between parental education, counseling for families in crisis, or stricter accountability measures for perpetrators of such violence. In addition, a gamut of preventative measures needs to be explored and utilized in order to thwart the cyclical nature of family trauma and violence.

FAMILY VIOLENCE: HOMICIDE

Introduction

When most people think of violence, they think of an innocent victim being attacked by a total stranger. The media exacerbates these fears by depicting the perpetrator as an unknown, unidentifiable sociopath that sneaks around hunting for prey. An obvious means of avoiding contact with such a person is to stay away from the "bad" neighborhoods where such crimes are more likely to occur. The safest place appears to be the confines of your own home, behind locked doors and set alarms. The reality, though, is that the risk of dying at the hands of an acquaintance or family member far exceeds the threat of being killed by a complete stranger.

Familial violence, more specifically familial homicide, is much more common than most people would like to believe. This section explores the various forms of familial homicide such as battered women, infanticide, Munchausen disorder by proxy, parricide, familicide, and the causal factors that lead to such incidents.

According to the 1994 Bureau of Justice Statistics report focusing on murders within families, 16% of all murders committed in 1988 were committed against family members. The breakdown of these findings indicated that 6.5% of the victims were murdered by their spouses, 3.5% by parents, 1.9% were killed by their children, 1.5% were victims of sibling violence, and another 2.6% were victimized by other family members (Dawson & Langan, 1994). The following vignette is an illustration of family violence.

> After an exhausting day of caring for the children, cleaning the house, and working at her part-time job, Carla was laying down for a quick nap. Sleeping a bit longer than expected, Carla was late preparing dinner. When her husband Charlie came home, he was infuriated by her tardiness, laziness, and insensitivity to his needs. He had just lost a big contract at work and did not appreciate her lack of consideration. Feeling it his obligation to set her straight, which he had continually done in the past, Charlie picked up a pot of boiling water from the stove and threw it in Carla's face. Screaming for help, Carla charged toward the door where Charlie proceeded to hit her over the head with the pot. Carla died 3 days later from a subdural hematoma.

Literature Review

Domestic homicides are one of the most common forms of familial violence. According to the Presidential Task Force on Violence in the Family, in 1996 as many as 1300 battered women were killed by their abusers (Ewing, 1997). Forty percent of all homicides in the United States are the result of domestic violence (K. Browne & Herbert, 1997). Domestic violence is nothing new to society but has gained public attention due to the shift in opinions regarding domestic relations. In historical context, women were seen as the property of their husbands and, therefore, occasional beatings for their disobedience were expected. Rarely, if ever, were men charged with a crime for beating or killing their wives.

Even with the increased awareness of domestic violence, many women were left legally powerless and vulnerable to the abuse. Women who sought the protection of law enforcement found themselves beating against closed doors or, if they were helped, it was only with the granting of a restraining order. In reality, though, a piece of paper will not be effective when an angered spouse has a mission (Snow, 1997). In all fairness, the elevated number of domestic violence cases is not entirely due to shortcomings with a faulty system. At times, battered women refuse to press charges against their abusive spouses, given the ramifications they face once the assailant is released. Because of the way our legal system is structured, a person is rarely detained for attempted murder if he simply makes threats. If the victim presses charges, the perpetrator will experience at most a night or two in jail, which will more than likely enrage him even more.

In recent times, shelters and special interest groups have been organized to help women in battering relationships. Unfortunately, as the number of shelters has increased, so too have the number of domestic homicides. Once the perpetrator targets his victim, there is little that law enforcement is able to do to prevent the crime from eventually occurring (Snow, 1997).

Considering the lack of effective support available for victims of domestic abuse, the victims themselves have begun to take matters into their own hands. Although husbands are more likely to be the perpetrators in domestic homicides, wives commit a substantial portion of these murders. The percentages vary according to race. According to one study, in white couples, 38% of the victims were husbands while 62% were wives. These results were significantly different in comparison to Black couples. In Black couples, the disparity between victim gender was slim. "[Forty-seven percent] of the victims of a spouse were husbands and 53% were wives" (Dawson & Langan, 1994). No meaningful explanation for this racial difference has been supplied thus far.

The fate of women who kill their abusive husbands has become the topic of many debates in recent years. Some would consider these women to be acting in self-defense, while others would argue that there are other avenues that battered women should take. In terms of Carla, the women in the vignette presented above, if she grabbed a knife to protect herself prior to Charlie reaching for the pot of water and Charlie died as a result of his wounds, should she be charged with and convicted of murder?

In situations such as this, women have tried a variety of strategies for defending their fate during trial. Some have pled insanity, self-defense, guilt, and more recently, battered woman's syndrome. It has been hypothesized that women who are the constant recipients of physical and verbal abuse by their spouses suffer from a mental disorder known as battered woman's syndrome. Several expert psychologists and psychiatrists have defended this theory. Their testimony enables jurors to "understand why the women endured such allegedly serious abuse for so long, why they did not leave their abuser, and why they felt it was necessary to use deadly force at a time when she was not being battered" (Ewing, 1997, p. 34). Of course, those women who have killed their abusers at the time of their abuse are more likely to find success in a self-defense plea as opposed to women who kill while not in immediate danger. Although battered woman's syndrome is becoming increasingly popular in the mental health arena, it has yet to receive substantial support in the courtroom.

In the case of *People v. Aris* (1989), Dr. Lenore Walker, a clinical and forensic psychologist, testified in Ms. Aris' defense on the premise of the battered woman's syndrome. The jury found Ms. Aris guilty because her husband was sleeping at the time of the offense and therefore her actions could not be considered self-defense (*People v.*

Aris, 1989). There is no consistency in the sentencing of these women and verdicts depend largely on the jury of each particular case and the differences from crime to crime. Currently, few women are acquitted based upon battered woman's syndrome.

Another form of homicidal violence that occurs within the family is the killing of children by their parents. Fifty-seven percent of the murders of children under the age of 12 have been committed by the victims' parents (Dawson & Langan, 1994). In October, 1994, Susan Smith and her husband stood in front of media cameras and pled for the return of their two sons who had reportedly been kidnapped by a Black man with a gun. For 9 days the country prayed for the safe return of the Smiths' children. It was later discovered that it was the tearful mother the public had seen on the news who was the actual killer. It was hard to imagine that a mother could drive her car into a lake with her two young boys strapped into their seats. As outstanding as it may seem, infanticide, the killing of children by their parents, and neonaticide, the killing of one's infant, is a common cause of childhood deaths (Dawson & Langan, 1994).

Pitt and Bale (1995) highlighted the characteristic differences between parents who commit infanticide as opposed to neonaticide. The results indicated that mothers in the neonaticide group were significantly younger than the mothers in the infanticide group. The mothers in the infanticide group were more likely to suffer from depression or psychoses and have histories of attempted suicide. "Eighty-eight percent of the infanticide mothers were married, while eighty-one percent of the neonaticide mothers were unwed" (Pitt & Bale, 1995, p. 378).

There are a variety of reasons that parents kill their children. Explanations range from postpartum depression to schizophrenia. Postpartum depression is a mental disorder that occurs with new mothers shortly after they give birth. According to the American Psychiatric Association's Diagnostic and Statistical Manual of Mental Disorders, Fourth Edition (DSM-IV) (1994), postpartum depression often presents with episodes of delusions in which the mother feels that the infant is possessed or of hallucinations that tell her to kill the child. Not all incidents of postpartum depression present with delusions or hallucinations, but there are suicidal ideations, obsessional thoughts of violence toward the child, and psychomotor agitation.

Postpartum depression has gained the acknowledgment of many in the mental health field but little is known about its causes. Some have hypothesized that environmental stressors associated with becoming a parent, along with the immediate demands required of the parent, can overwhelm and cause this disorder in even the most psychologically sound mother (Ewing, 1997). Hormonal changes have also been reported to be a factor in explaining the incidence of severe depression and unusual actions by some mothers after the birth of their children (Ewing, 1997). Postpartum depression is more likely to occur in women who have experienced it with previous children.

Schizophrenics have been found guilty of infanticide. Depending on the defense team's strategy, many of these women will plead insanity due to their disorder. Most likely, these women would not be considered the victims of postpartum depression considering their past and/or current history of schizophrenia, although the symptoms are similar.

Another explanation for why a mother would kill her child is Munchausen syndrome by proxy (MSBP). Munchausen's is a disorder found in the DSM-IV as an appendix to factitious disorder. It differs from factitious disorder in that a person with Munchausen syndrome has a psychological need to feign certain illnesses but for no external purpose, as is found with factitious disorder. Patients with this syndrome have been known to inject themselves with poisons, urine, and feces so that they will become ill and be admitted to a hospital or otherwise receive medical attention. Munchausen's occurs when parents cause illness in their children through these means, requiring constant medical attention. Although the incidences of MSBP are rare and not researched enough to stand alone in the DSM-IV, there have been enough cases to support its existence. In most of the known cases, death is the ultimate fate of the children because the parent will stop at nothing to fulfill their own need (Pitt & Bale, 1995).

Just as it is odd to conceive of a mother killing the life to which she has given birth, it is difficult to fathom a child killing the parent who gave him or her life. Nevertheless, parricide, the killing of one's parent(s), is more common than one would expect. Parricide was highly publicized by the Menendez trial in Southern California where Eric and Lyle Menendez were charged with killing their wealthy parents for the purpose of receiving their inheritances. The defense team claimed that the boys killed their parents in an act of self-defense, given the continual abuse they received from their father. Nevertheless, after much debate, the boys were charged with the murders but spared from the death penalty.

Similar to battered women, some children kill their parent(s) because of a history of abuse suffered by them or witnessed toward the other parent. Further, some youths kill in self-defense during an episode of their abuse; others kill on random occasions as a result of their continual abuse. In terms of Carla, the scenario may have had a different conclusion had her son entered the kitchen and witnessed his father beating his mother as described. Out of fear and anger, the son could have run into his parents' room, grabbed the loaded gun from his father's nightstand, and returned to the kitchen to shoot and kill his father. Heide (1992) claims that "these children, typically adolescents, were psychologically abused by one or both parents and often witnessed or suffered physical, sexual, and verbal abuse as well" (p. 3).

Other factors associated with parricide are mental illness, antisocial personalities, and greed. These can be sole factors but are most likely exhibited as combinations. Greed is rarely found to be a full explanation for why children commit parricide, although some cases have been reported. Children whose immediate motivation for killing their parents is greed will most likely have evidence of antisocial characteristics, abusive pasts, or mental illness. In these instances, the child is usually convicted on terms associated with insanity. In those cases where greed was found to be the sole determinant for the murder, other determinants such as antisocial personality were most likely not effectively explored or not accepted by the jury

(Ewing, 1997). This does not mean, however, that the children were not suffering from some sort of disorder in addition to greed.

The killing of one's entire family, though rare, is not unknown. Familicide is most often committed by White men between the ages of 30 and 40 and almost always ends in suicide (Ewing, 1997). Motivations for such homicides vary, but most commonly, the killer is controlling and domineering yet is dependent upon his family. The killer attacks when he feels that his control over his family is being threatened or when he feels he is a failure. There have been incidences where abusers killed members of their family so that the abusers could maintain ultimate control over them.

Familicide, although more common among middle-aged men, has also been committed by juveniles (Ewing, 1997). Some of the factors leading to juvenile familicide are similar to those for the adult perpetrator. Invariably, however, it is a reaction to abuse. Many of these juveniles have no record of a mental disorder, yet this could be due to the fact that they are too young to be diagnosed. People familiar with these juvenile perpetrators describe them as being disturbed and troublesome (Ewing, 1997).

Forensic Psychology and Policy Implications

A consistent theme throughout most of the above forms of familial homicide is the issue of abuse. For some, the killing of their abuser becomes the only means of protection from receiving further abuse. The legal system has provided little help for victims of abuse. Even if the victims are fortunate enough to receive legal intervention through documentation or incarceration of the abuser, the reality is that the system provides little to no protection once the abuser is released.

There is little that can be done to stop the obsessed abuser from continuing to harm or eventually killing their victim. Yet, this does not mean that law enforcement should not treat abuse as a priority. The fact that domestic violence calls are common should not be a justification for not responding to calls. Instead, the increased number of domestic violence calls should indicate that a special domestic violence unit is needed to deal with this escalating problem. With the push of special interest groups advocating victims' rights, many police and sheriffs' departments have organized units to specifically combat this epidemic.

Child abuse has received a great deal of public attention because society currently views it as its responsibility to care for those who cannot care for themselves. Policies have been established so that fewer children will have to experience abuse from their parents. Programs exist, but they are so crowded and understaffed that too many children are "falling through the cracks." This partially explains why many homicides committed in this country are parricides.

Being abused should not be a justification for killing someone. Much of the debate surrounding sentencing for these perpetrators has centered on this issue.

There are mixed feelings about how to punish someone who takes another's life but does so for the purpose of saving their own. If there were effective programs, community outlets, and judicial supports for victims of abuse, then murder would not have to be the end result. Currently, the mental health field provides support for the plea of self-defense in relation to abuse cases, but it has been faintly accepted by the judicial system. There are several cases and articles that address this phenomenon; more research on policy implications needs to be provided.

Suggestions for Future Research

Research needs to be conducted so that more effective programs are established to decrease the occurrence of abuse and possible murder. As it stands, programs are not necessarily the problem, but the lack of funding and inadequate staffing inhibits these programs from being as effective as they could be. Frequently, money is hard to raise when benefits are not immediate or apparent. Abuse intervention at crucial moments will help to decrease the number of familial homicides because it will eliminate murders by abusers as well as retaliations by the abused.

Many victims who kill their abusers are sentenced to prison terms similar to those of other violent offenders. They are placed in the same units as the other predatorial offenders simply because their crime was murder. This can create many problems for the individual as well as environmental problems within the prison. The individual sentenced to prison for self-defense tends not to have the same predatorial personality as other violent offenders and may encounter unnecessary problems. With the increase of mental health care for inmates in the state of California, for example, special groups have been developed specifically for incarcerated individuals whose crimes involve issues of abuse (*Coleman v. Wilson*, 1995). More programs such as these need to be instituted on a national level and further research needs to be conducted regarding the effects of incarceration on these individuals.

An additional area that needs continued research is Munchausen syndrome by proxy. Without the proper understanding of this form of familial homicide and how it originates, the risk of more unnecessary deaths is inevitable.

IMPACT OF MENTAL HEALTH LAW DOCTRINES ON FAMILIES: PATERNALISM AND *PARENS PATRIAE*

Introduction

At 6 years of age, a child was admitted indefinitely to a state hospital. The child's parents sought treatment for their son because of his aggressive and uncontrollable behavior. His diagnosis was "hyperkinetic reaction of childhood." Four years later, the parents relinquished their parental control to the county, whereupon the boy was placed in a mental hospital. Not long after, the youth filed a lawsuit requesting that the court "place him in a less drastic environment suitable to his needs" (*Parham v. J.R.*, 1978).

This example demonstrates the ramifications of what may occur when a person is deemed incapable of making his/her own decisions and placed under the guardian-ship of the state. The majority of these individuals are juveniles, elders, and persons who are found to be "out of sound" mind/mentally ill. This is the basic premise at work in the doctrines of *paternalism* and *parens patriae*; namely, that the interven-tion of the state in the life of an individual determined to be a serious threat to him/herself and/or others is warranted and necessary. Within this framework, this section explores the development of *parens patriae* and paternalism in the realm of civil commitment and how, specifically, it has influenced the role of the family in such issues.

> In the 1860s, E. P. W. Packard was committed to a mental institution by her husband. Mrs. Packard, who was not in need of such care, was nevertheless institutionalized due to an 1851 Illinois statute that stated:
>
> > Married women and infants who, in the judgment of the medical superintendents of the state asylum . . . may be entered or detained in the hospital at the request of the husband of the woman or guardian of the infant, without the evidence of insanity required . . . (J. E. Myers, 1983–1984, p. 376)
>
> > Upon her release, Mrs. Packard began a nationwide campaign to adjust this law and others like it. Through her efforts, several bills were eventually passed that restricted the institutionalization of any person not found to be "insane or distracted by a verdict of a jury . . ." (J. E. Myers, 1983–1984, p. 376).

Literature Review

Much of Western civilization perceives the family as a unit in which its members have a duty to protect those who cannot care for themselves. This perception rests upon the assumption that adults, due to maturity and experience, are more knowledgeable than children and are better equipped to make decisions for their offspring. This concept was fundamental in establishing the historical notions of *parens patriae* and paternalism, whereby the state, similar to knowing family adults, is entrusted with the responsibility of caring for those persons in need of mental health care.

Analysis of parental obligation to care for family members depicts a different picture. In reality, as the increasing number of child and elder abuse cases indicate, this familial belief system is not always practiced. "Some parents may at times be acting against the interests of their children" (*Bartley v. Kremens*, 1975, p. 1041). Specifically, in terms of commitment, some parents, or other family members, may not have the desire or energy to care for their unruly children or senile parent. In addition, there are instances in which family members are motivated by financial gain, such as inheritance or property control, culminating in the institutionalization of another relative. Hence, they request that the individual child or elder be admitted into a mental hospital despite the consequences that may transpire. Essentially, commitment may not be the most appropriate treatment for a given individual.

To demonstrate the susceptibility of civil commitment, one can analyze the first-mentioned case of J.R. As unmanageable as J.R. may have been, placing him in an institution was not appropriate for his needs, according to the court's opinion (*Parham v. J.R.*, 1978). However, as a juvenile, J.R. was not able to overcome the request of his parents and psychologists when the initial decision to commit him was made. Prior to the Parham decision, there was virtually no judicial input that existed to insure that the liberties and rights of the mentally ill were considered when a relative requested the hospitalization of a child family member.

Before the 1970s, civil commitment was an informal arena that was perceived as medical, not legal (Reisner & Slobogin, 1990). Hearings questioning whether a person should have been committed rarely occurred, if at all, until after the person had been confined. Since the mentally ill were considered incapable of knowing what was best for them, their opinions were not weighed heavily in court. In other words, if a family member requested a relative's commitment and there was a doctor's consent, then regardless of the wishes of the individual, he/she would most likely be committed. Once committed, the person was labeled mentally ill and it became difficult to cast off the stigma. Consequently, the probability of wrongfully or erroneously committing an individual to a mental institution was highly likely, given the nature of mental health policies defining commitment.

Provisions in the mental health field regarding the issue of commitment have only been developed within the past few decades. Previously, questions were not raised regarding the intentions of the family members who suggested it. Now that the courts are more actively involved in the process, there is a more watchful eye over family members, hospital administrators, and their motivations for civil confinement. Public defenders and specialists are assigned by the court to defend those individuals who are evaluated for commitment. This procedure is essential in those instances when family members do not look out for the best interest of a specific relative (e.g., as we have seen in cases such as *Parham v. J.R.*, 1978).

Currently, a judicial-type hearing is held prior to confinement during which time decisions surrounding commitment and the best medical care are addressed. These judicial guidelines are necessary, considering the unjust institutionalization some individuals faced as a result of past unethical standards for commitment. Yet, some major problems have developed with these new restrictions in relation to *parens patriae* and paternalism.

One difficulty with this transition can be observed when families that act in the best interest of a given member are penalized due to the actions of other members who harmfully suggest the commitment of a certain relative. New policies can marginalize the voices of good-intentioned families when deciding what is best for their relatives. Currently, psychologists and judges make judgments with respect to the rights of individuals who are committed. However, these individuals place a professional standard on civil commitment determinations. Ultimately, these decisions lack a more personal understanding from those family members who represent the true needs of the committed patient.

There are aspects of familial relations that are beneficial for determining what is best for an individual. For example, family members may possess a better awareness about the type of programs and activities to which an individual could respond. This is because family members have a personal connection with the individual. Court-appointed servants, however, lack this subjective knowledge about the committee. Thus, their decisions often do not embody all of a given situation's dynamics, and solely reflect documented information.

Despite the obvious advantages, good-intentioned family members, representing the interests of another individual, have often found it virtually impossible to get the care they feel would be most effective for their relative. As a result, the voices of invested family members frequently have been silenced. For these family members, in order to obtain the care they deem proper, several legal barriers must be hurdled. Then, too, there is the risk that the courts will not respect the wishes of family members for a variety of political and economic reasons (e.g., the case of Mrs. Packard).

Many debates exist which argue over whether the current implementation of *parens patriae* and paternalism in the civil commitment arena is any better than it was decades ago, considering the effect it has had on the family. In the process of protecting the mentally ill from family members who did not represent the best interests of the patient, relatives who are genuinely concerned now have to prove their well-meaning intentions to commit a relation in order for that person to receive proper care. This practice is far removed from the historical assumption that family members will look out for the best interest of their relatives.

Forensic Psychology and Policy Implications

It is difficult to balance the views of the individual, family, and the state when dealing with the issue of mental hospital commitment. First and foremost, the individual should always have his/her liberties protected, yet, in most instances, the individual is incapable or too young to fight for such rights. This is why the doctrines of *parens patriae* and paternalism were established. However, when the state is given the power to act as a parent for an individual, the decisions made are going to reflect the politics and economics of that time. There needs to be some consistency in how these doctrines are implemented and what foci should be taken. As it stands, we have come to a point where the interests of the mentally ill are determined by public defenders and specialists. These specialists need to be appointed by the courts and not by advocates on either side of the debate. The experts, whether psychologists or doctors, need to be impartial to the situation at hand. Furthermore, the family needs to be recognized when decisions are made regarding an individual. In providing more protection for the mentally ill, the impact of the family has become less of a force in the entire process. It seems that while trying to protect the individual from family members with ill intentions, others are categorized as being guilty of exploiting the mentally ill when they are not.

Suggestions for Future Research

When the doctrines of *parens patriae* and paternalism were first introduced, our society was very different. Since then, we have been trying to fit these antiquated notions into our modern values and beliefs. It seems as though we have done a successful job, considering the slim probability of pleasing everyone. Yet, it appears as if we have gone too far in making generalizations about the role of the family in this process. Some would argue that it is better to be pessimistic than optimistic in regard to predicting the motivations for people's actions. We have become so paranoid with this new system that we have drifted from making decisions based on human factors and are more concerned with making choices based on the judicial system.

Further research is needed to determine if current legal proceedings regard the patient as the most important figure. Along with that, since the family has become less of a voice in this process, it may be beneficial to investigate the ramifications of losing such a personal figure in the decision-making process.

FAMILY LAW AND EMOTIONAL RIGHTS

Introduction

Children are involved in custodial disputes every day. In 1991, it was estimated that approximately 1 million children experience parental divorce every year in the United States (M. Bussey, 1996; Short, 1998). Other children are involved in disputes between their biological and potentially adoptive, or psychological, parents (Bracco, 1997; Oppenheim & Bussiere, 1996; Wynne, 1997). Both divorce and adoption are events that are lifelong processes affecting the mental well-being of children (Lee, 1997; Oppenheim & Bussiere, 1996; Wertlieb, 1997; Weyer & Sandler, 1998; Wynne, 1997). Children of divorced parents are more likely to have lower levels of social competency, poor academic performance, conduct difficulties, and self-esteem than children from intact homes (Crockenberg & Forgays, 1996; Katz & Gottman, 1997; Lee, 1997; Short, 1998; Wertlieb, 1997). Laws have begun to recognize the emotional impact custody disputes can have on children, especially for custodial decisions for divorce. However, children's emotional rights are not always considered in legal decisions, especially for custody decisions in which spousal abuse occurred in the home or in those cases in which adoption went wrong. Laws vary from state to state and while some states apply the best interest of the child standard for custody issues, others do not. Even when such standards are applied, some researchers indicate they may not, in reality, protect the child's emotional rights (Kurtz, 1997).

In most states, the best interest of the child standard is applied for child custody cases (Kurtz, 1997). In fact, states are mandated to consider the best interest of the child in making custody decisions for divorce cases (Bracco, 1997; Oppenheim & Bussiere, 1996). Rather than allowing divorcing parents to make whatever decisions they want regarding the custody of their children, judges are now required to consider what portions of the divorce will affect the children and make certain their needs are met (Bracco, 1997). However, despite the Best Interest of the Child mandate for divorce custody decisions, a child's right to a loving family and emotional support is not always considered. For other custody decisions, courts may use the Parents Rights standard (Wynne, 1997). This standard does not even acknowledge the emotional rights of the child. The following vignette gives a case example of such a ruling.

> Jessica Deboer was 2 when she was taken away from the only parents she had ever known. Baby Jessica's biological mother, Cara Clausen, signed away her parental rights to the Deboers only 40 hours after the birth of her daughter, despite the Iowa law bars against signing a release before at least 72 hours after the birth of a child. When the Deboer's attorney called and asked Cara who the father of the child was, she lied and named Seefeldt, an ex-boyfriend who signed away what he thought were his parental rights.
>
> Two days after the Deboers received custody of baby Jessica, Cara told Dan Schmidt that he was really the father of the baby. When Jessica was 3 weeks old, Cara sued to have her parental rights restored, and Dan made a legal claim later the same month. The Deboers refused to give Jessica back without a fight, and when Iowa courts continued to rule against them, they took the case to Michigan, hoping to win on the question of the child's best interest. The Deboers won the case in Michigan, but the ruling was appealed when Iowa argued that Michigan did not have jurisdiction. The Iowa court did not consider the child's best interest, arguing that it was not required under Iowa law. By the time the court had determined a ruling, Jessica was 2 years old and did not know her biological parents.
>
> Psychologists argue that nothing is more devastating than losing both parents as a toddler. Nevertheless, baby Jessica was returned to her biological parents. In August, 1993, the Deboers packed baby Jessica's things and tried to explain to her why she had to leave. When the van arrived to pick Jessica up, she began crying and screaming and continued to do so as the van drove away. Follow-up reports indicate baby Jessica, now named Anna, has adjusted well and is happy; however, there is no way to determine the long-term effects this court decision may have on her psychological well-being (Cowley, Springen, Miller, Lewis, & Titunik, 1993; Hansen, 1994b; Ingrasia & Springen, 1993, 1994).

Literature Review

In some states, family law clearly does not focus on the child's best interest when it comes to custody disputes between biological family and the custodial, psychological parent. Wynne (1997) indicates that the case of Baby Jessica illustrates "that as a nation, Americans do not think enough of their children to consider their rights or interests, or to discuss even if they have rights or interests" (p. 187). In fact, most states make a primary effort to give biological parents custody of the child as long as there is no evidence of parental unfitness (Oppenheim & Bussiere, 1996). Even in states where the child's best interest standard is applied, there are different statutory orders of preference for the placement of the child. These preferences do not always take into consideration the child's emotional rights. For example, in California, the child is placed with a relative unless the court determines that such placement is not in the child's best interest. However, the law does not necessarily specify what the best interests are. Although some states do provide factors which should be considered in the best interest determination, much discretion is left to the judge (Oppenheim & Bussiere, 1996). As a result, the child's emotional well-being is not necessarily considered.

Bracco's (1997) examination of Canada's Best Interest test illustrates the court's difficulty in determining the best interest of the child. Bracco explains that the test is a change in mentality from "every parent has the right to a child" to "every child has the right to a family". However, Bracco explains the difficulty with assessing the best interest; she poses the question of whether it is truly in the best interest of the child to keep adoptions in secrecy. In Canada, there is to be no contact between the adopted child and his or her biological parents.

The issue of children's emotional rights and family law is complex because laws differ from state to state (Oppenheim & Bussiere, 1996). However, most researchers agree that family law does not adequately acknowledge children's emotional rights (Bracco, 1997; Oppenheim & Bussiere, 1996; Shapiro, 1993; Wynne, 1997). There tends to be a bias toward biological parents in determining custody between biological parents and a third party (Shapiro, 1993; Wynne, 1997). This bias was evident in the Baby Jessica case. Wynne (1997) argues that the courts need to recognize and support a child's need for a "stable relationship with his or her psychological parent" (p. 189). In addition, Wynne asserts that in order for family reunification attempts to work, the courts need to reassert what they consider real family relationships. According to Wynne, the family reunification policy using a biological definition of family has resulted in abuse, neglect, and even the deaths of many children. Perhaps Wynne's argument can be best illustrated by the statement of Kimberly Mays, a 14-year-old girl who was switched at birth and whose biological parents sought custody. At a news conference, she stated "Biology doesn't make a family" (Shapiro, 1993, p. 13). Mays clearly identified her "psychological" father as her family and wanted to divorce her biological parents.

Fortunately, family law's shortcomings in addressing the emotional well-being of children have not been ignored. The National Task Force for Children's Constitutional Rights has begun to write a children's amendment to the constitution which would afford children certain rights (Wynne, 1997). The amendment would grant children many rights which include the right to a safe home and "the right to the care of a loving family or a substitute which approximates such a family as closely as possible" (Wynne, 1997, p. 187). This amendment would effect every state, which could potentially help protect children's emotional rights by forcing every state to consider the child as a person, rather than the property of his or her biological parents, as Wynne suggests. However, the amendment will do little for cases such as Baby Jessica's when both families appear to be loving. Although the changes in family law are underway for third-party custody disputes, laws already exist for custody disputes between biological parents. These laws and the degree to which they consider the emotional well-being of children are discussed next.

Some specifications have been outlined for custody decisions in divorce cases. The Uniform Marriage and Divorce Act of 1970 provides a list of factors judges should consider in child custody cases (Crosby-Currie, 1996). Because laws in every state differ, the factors vary from state to state. One factor that is considered in custody decisions in every state is the child's wishes. Despite the indication that utilizing the child's wishes in a custody determination was designed to protect the child's emotional best interests, research indicates asking a child about his or her wishes regarding a custody dispute has a negative impact on the child's well-being (Currie-Crosby, 1996). In fact research indicates custody disputes, regardless of whether the child is asked about his or her wishes, are detrimental to children (M. Bussey, 1996). Bussey used a systems perspective to examine the detrimental effects of divorce on children. Some of the systemwide interventions for children of divorce have included legal reform. Because of the abundance of psychological literature that indicates divorce has long-term detrimental effects on most children (M. Bussey, 1996; Crockenberg & Forgays, 1996; Lee, 1997; Short, 1998), some states have begun to change the legal process for divorce (M. Bussey, 1996). For example, parent-targeted interventions are often mandatory instead of voluntary, and some states such as California have court-mandated mediation for all disputed cases. Family law has begun to work with psychologists in an effort to reduce the negative impact divorce has on children's emotional well-being. In 1992, a program to help children cope with divorce was established, and referrals were primarily from a family court judge, who posed the question of whether such programs should be mandated on a statewide or nationwide basis (M. Bussey, 1996).

Although research indicates that law and psychology have begun to intersect when it comes to custody disputes between biological parents, there have been criticisms regarding the adequacy of the law for such disputes. As discussed previously, states use the Best Interest of the Child standard when determining custody cases between biological parents. Kurtz (1997) argues that the Best Interest standard may be detrimental to both the child and the parents in cases of spousal abuse. Judges are not required to take spousal abuse into consideration when determining the custody of the child. When the laws changed to the Best Interest of the Child standard, courts were no longer required to assess parental behaviors. As a result, the courts are less concerned with the parental relationship as long as the relationship does not appear to have a physical impact on the child. In fact, because statutes do not require a judge to take parental abuse into account when determining custody, an abuser may be granted custody. Oftentimes, the abuser is the financial supporter for the family, and the judge may see it in the best interest of the child to be placed with a parent who can provide for him or her. Kurtz (1997) argues that legislation "must create a statutory presumption against awarding a spousal abuser custody of a child. Only then will the best interests of the child truly be met" (p. 2).

Family law has begun to take into consideration children's emotional well-being and their rights of emotional stability. However, the law has been criticized for not protecting the emotional interests of children in all situations. From the literature, it is apparent that the law has progressed further toward protecting children's emotional rights when it comes to custody disputes between biological parents than it has for custody disputes involving third parties. Possibly, the changes in law for custody disputes between biological parents is further advanced because such disputes have existed longer and the detrimental effects to children have therefore been more publicized. Prior to the 1960s adoptions were closed. As a result, no disputes between biological parents and potentially adoptive parents existed. Now such cases are more common, and activists have proposed legislation that they believe would protect the child's emotional interests.

Forensic Psychology and Policy Implications

Activist groups for children's rights have begun to propose amendments which could potentially help protect children's rights (Wynne, 1997). The National Task Force for Children's Constitutional Rights began writing an amendment to the United States Constitution that would grant children rights such as the right to a safe home, the right to adequate health care, the right to an adequate education, and the right to the care of a loving family or a substitute that is as close to a loving family as possible. In addition, the amendment would provide children with the right to an attorney in an any legal matter affecting their interest (Wynne, 1997). The amendment is clearly a starting point toward protecting children's rights; however, the wording in the amendment is ambiguous. What one may consider adequate health care or a loving family may be quite different from another's opinion. Children's emotional rights cannot be protected unless amendments consider psychological research that indicates what children need emotionally. Had psychologists' opinions been considered in the Baby Jessica case, it is doubtful that she would have been taken from the only parents she knew.

Other researchers suggest defining the child's Best Interest standard more clearly and consistently (Oppenheim & Bussiere, 1996). The ambiguity of the Best Interest standard allows for the court to be flexible and meet the needs of each individual child; however, it does not protect children against the biases and prejudices of judges. To reduce the ambiguity, Oppenheim and Bussiere suggest the importance of blood relationships on children's well-being be assessed and coherent laws based on the findings be enacted. In order to establish coherent laws, several questions such as "how much weight should be given to blood relationships in determining custody" and "under what circumstances should relatives be able to maintain a relationship with their kin following an adoption by a non-relative?" (pp. 480–481), need to be considered. Not only do Oppenheim and Bussiere address specific questions that must be answered prior to policy change, they provide guidelines with which each question should be answered. The researchers argue that the child's best interests should be considered more important than the interests of the adult parties, the court should protect the continuity of personal relationships, and the court should respect the importance of the child's relationships with the extended biological family that will encourage connections to family history and culture. If Oppenheim and Bussiere's policy recommendations had been accepted prior to the Baby Jessica case, the judge may have ruled that she remain in the Deboer s home and receive regular visits from her biological parents; it is difficult to determine the effects such a ruling would have had on the child.

Family law experts are proposing measures which could help protect children from the negative emotional impact that results from unsatisfactory family law (Cowley et al., 1993). In an effort to prevent adoption custody disputes, some activists have proposed to make adoptions closed, despite research indicating that positive ties to biological family can be beneficial for adoptees (Bracco, 1997; Oppenheim & Bussiere, 1996). An open adoption could have prevented the Baby Jessica custody dispute completely. Perhaps if the biological mother was granted regular visits with her daughter, she may not have felt as if she were missing out on her daughter's life. Bracco (1997) suggests that the law redefines what is considered family. She argues that adoption law is based on patriarchal child development theories and the current perception of the nuclear family may be too rigid. Bracco argues that policy changes in Canada should be made in which an adopted child's biological parents can have a role in raising the child. Although Bracco's arguments are primarily for adoption considerations and not necessarily custody disputes, her argument for redefining familial considerations relates to policy suggestions made by other researchers. Wynne (1997) suggests that courts work to redefine what are considered "real" family relationships. He argues that children's emotional needs will not be met until courts define family according to a psychological definition. This definition would place more emphasis on psychological ties with parents rather than on blood ties.

The analysis of policies concerning custodial disputes between biological parents and third parties is difficult because the policies concerning custody are confounded with adoption regulations. One cannot examine policy concerning custodial disputes without examining adoption law. A thorough examination of adoption law is beyond the scope of this section; however, the issue is important for the protection of children's emotional well-being and merits further examination.

Family law appears to be more adequate for custodial disputes involving biological parents. Psychological research has indicated that conflict in divorce situations is what is most detrimental to children (M. Bussey, 1996; Katz & Gottman, 1997; Lee, 1997). States have changed statutes regarding custody to protect children emotionally. Although there is still room for family law to change in order to protect children to an even greater extent, the fact that courts and psychologists have begun working together to help determine the best interests of the child is promising. Only when special circumstances such as spousal abuse are considered do researchers make bold suggestions for policy change.

Kurtz (1997) argues that statutes need to be created that would prevent abusive fathers from receiving custody of their children. She argues that even joint custody should not be allowed because this forces the abused parent to maintain contact with his or her abuser. Kurtz argues that the Best Interest standard is inadequate when it comes to spousal abuse cases and that policies must be more specific to prevent further abuse of the spouse and to prevent the child from emotional trauma. Spousal abuse is only one circumstance that may require a change in certain statutes regarding child custody. There are certainly many other circumstances in which current custody laws are insufficient; however, an examination of each circumstance is beyond the scope of this section. Spousal abuse provides one example of how current policies may not protect children's emotional well-being in every given situation.

Suggestions for Future Research

The ambiguity of the law suggests a lack of consensus among experts on the importance of blood ties versus psychological ties (Oppenheim & Bussiere, 1996). Research is not consistent regarding what the best interests of the child are. While some research indicates that blood relationships are more important, other studies indicate that psychological relationships take precedence. Further research needs to be conducted to determine the psychological impact of not knowing one's biological parents, being raised by adoptive parents but maintaining a relationship with biological parents, and of being removed from one's psychological parents as a toddler and placed with biological parents. Psychologists have speculated about each of the above, but longitudinal research to determine the impact of each has not been undertaken. Such research will also provide social scientists with individual characteristics of children that may result in more or less emotional stability after living through a custodial dispute and possibly being taken from psychological parents. For example, research on divorce has shown that gender, degree of conflict in parental relationship, and the child's IQ all have an impact on the extent to which the divorce will have a negative impact on the child; however, research on adoption custody disputes of this nature has not been conducted.

There is ample research on the impact of divorce on children. This research has begun to contribute to change in family law regarding custody disputes. In fact, programs have been implemented such as the Children Cope With Divorce Program (M. Bussey, 1996). Although research has been conducted with 2-year follow-ups of children who have passed this program, longitudinal research to determine the long-term effects of attending such a program would be useful for future policy implementation. The judge involved in the program questions whether it should be mandated across the nation; determining the long-term effects of this program and others like it would help legislatures assess if making such programs mandatory would be worthwhile.

DOMESTIC VIOLENCE

Introduction

Domestic violence is a pervasive social problem which plagues couples and families nationwide. A disproportionate amount of heterosexual domestic violence is male to female and generally affects anywhere from 2 to 28 million women. This variability may be attributed to the ambiguity regarding what constitutes spousal abuse or battery. Hence, definitions of domestic violence are likely to vary among existing counties, states, and nations.

It is readily apparent that women are at an appreciably higher risk in their homes due to the potential volatility that exists in their relationships with their intimate partners. The preponderance of research literature aims to tease out distinct characteristics of the abusers. However, perpetrators cannot be succinctly typified into one global category because they are essentially a heterogeneous group. There is an increased likelihood for partner-assaultive men to report childhood histories of physical abuse. Furthermore, the laws and policies pertinent to domestic violence offenders are continually evolving and are subject to change with new legislation. Currently, limited efforts are being made to address issues such as prevention, intervention, and the implementation of new laws and policies. The following case studies were selected to illustrate the seriousness of this issue.

> On March 23, 1991, Margaret Ann Malott shot her estranged, common-law husband and took a taxi to his new, live-in girlfriend's trailer. She subsequently pulled out a gun and began firing at his girlfriend, Carrie Sherwood, hitting her in the finger and head. Margaret Ann Malott was a classic battered spouse. In her 19 years with Paul Malott, a hulking, tattooed man who often carried a knife on his belt, she was subject to abuse in every form imaginable: physical, sexual, emotional, and psychological. He pushed, slapped, hit, punched, choked, whipped, and threw knives and an arrow at her and he twice broke her nose. He told her she was a terrible mother and a terrible sexual partner.

Subsequently, a jury of eight women and four men rejected Ms. Malott's claim of self-defense based on battered woman syndrome and convicted her of second-degree and attempted murder. She was sentenced to life in prison with no possibility of parole for at least 10 years (Bindman, 1991).

On December 26, 1993, Marsha Brewer Stewart was found with a knife in her chest. Police say she was murdered by her husband, Gregory. Just 7 months earlier, Marsha had defended her husband in a suburban Chicago courtroom by testifying that he had not attempted to murder her. She had dismissed the episode as a drunken fit of rage. Police and prosecutors begged her not to post his bond or move back with him. Like many other women, she forgave him. On December 26, Marsha called the police in a desperate plea for help. By the time a squad car arrived, Marsha was dead. Hours later, her husband was charged with murder (Shalala, 1994).

LITERATURE REVIEW

Cases such as Ms. Malott's and Ms. Stewart's exemplify that domestic violence all too often leads to disastrous consequences for the couple and their children. Early intervention can be facilitated by neighbors, community members, and a legal system that implements stringent arrest policies for the accused perpetrators. However, how can victims, police officers, and the courts identify such abusers? As alluded to earlier, a plethora of research has been geared toward identifying characteristics of male spousal abusers. Thus far, researchers have been unable to consistently identify a profile which is inclusive of most abusers, in terms of personality, psychopathology, and demographics. In this section the predominant patterns of abusers and their families of origin are discussed. Furthermore, issues pertinent to court mediation and legal interventions regarding the deterrence of abusers are explored. The primary objective is to provide clarification on the preceding issues.

The increasing prevalence of cases such as Ms. Malott's and Ms. Stewart's has engendered vast research regarding the incidence of such abuse and the characteristics of abusive individuals. In the United States alone, 4 million women of all races and classes are battered by a spouse or intimate partner (Mills, 1996). Battery by a spouse or intimate partner is the single most common reason for women entering emergency rooms, exceeding the rate of childbirth, automobile accidents, muggings, and all other medical emergencies (Mills, 1996). Cross-cultural research indicates that American women are not alone in this regard. A cross-cultural study of family violence found that domestic abuse occurs in over 84% of the 90 societies examined (D. Levinson, 1988). In countries such as Canada, Guatemala, Chile, Columbia, Belgium, and parts of Europe, domestic violence figures range from 4 to 60%. These alarming statistics have mobilized a number of battered women and feminists nationwide to address the issue of domestic violence.

In an effort to reveal theoretical and treatment implications, vast research has focused on describing the characteristics of abusers. Hastings and Hamberger (1988) suggested that the preponderance of identified male batterers showed evidence of a personality disorder. These researchers found that in comparison to age-matched, nonviolent males, batterers showed higher levels of dysphoria, anxiety, and somatic complaints. The batterers in their sample presented as more alienated, moody, labile, and passive-aggressive. Alcoholic batterers showed the highest levels of pathology, followed by non-alcohol-abusive batterers. Both batterer subgroups showed a greater disadvantage in terms of higher unemployment rates; lower education; and higher rates of reported, experienced, and witnessed violence victimization in the family of origin. In general, their findings provide support for the notion that batterers are a heterogeneous group and cannot be adequately explained by a unified "batterer profile."

Current literature on psychopathology and anger suggests that both significantly contribute to interpersonal violence. Greene, Coles, and Johnson (1994) conducted a cluster analysis with data gathered from 40 court-referred abusers. The Minnesota Multiphasic Personality Inventory-2 (MMPI-2) and the State-Trait Anger Expression Inventory (STAXI) were utilized as measures of personality functioning and the expression of anger among abusers in the sample. The MMPI-2 scores demonstrated that domestic violence offenders indicated some degree of depression, antisocial attitudes, distrust, anxiety, and other psychopathology. Results confirmed four clusters of violent offenders, with the most pathological cluster having the most anger. Furthermore, these results were also consistent with the literature in that there was not a single, homogeneous "abuser" profile (Hastings & Hamberger, 1988).

Researchers have also emphasized the importance of traumatic childhood experiences such as severe physical abuse in an effort to classify abusers. C. M. Murphy, Meyer, and O'Leary (1993) examined associations between family of origin violence, levels of current abusive behavior, and self-reports of psychopathology in a clinical sample of male abusers. Compared to nonviolent men in discordant and well-adjusted relationships, partner-assaultive men were significantly more likely to report childhood histories of physical abuse and physical abuse of the mother in the family of origin. When compared to batterers without such histories, those who were severely abused in childhood displayed more evidence of psychopathology on the Millon Clinical Multiaxial Inventory-II (MCMI-II), and expressed higher levels of aggression directed toward their current partner. These results suggest that violence in the family of origin, in particular a history of severe childhood physical abuse, can differentiate partner-assaultive men (C. M. Murphy et al., 1993).

Literature on the legal attempts to punish perpetrators of domestic violence has become more prevalent during the past 2 decades. Some of the legal responses include an increased reliance on civil protection orders and numerous options for prosecuting batterers, including, most notably, mandatory arrest. Police officers are more likely to arrest the perpetrator when the victim is visibly injured or when there is probable cause to believe a crime has been committed (Mills, 1996). Although mandatory arrest tends to reduce domestic violence, abusers' high recidivism rates continues to adversely affect the lives of many women.

Civil protection orders, which enjoin a batterer from further violence, may curtail domestic violence. In most states, civil protection orders can be used either in conjunction with criminal proceedings or in civil court (Keilitz, 1994). However, Mills (1996) contends that the problem with civil protection orders, prosecution, and arrest policies is that they require women to terminate their abusive relationships and subject them to even more serious attacks by their batterers. Many studies show that battered women who attempt to leave the abuser may be at a higher risk of being harmed or killed. Ironically, criminal strategies which aim to curb abuse and violent relationships through legal interventions may instead place victims in more dangerous predicaments.

Although several studies have examined public views on mandatory arrest policies and civil protection orders, few have examined public opinion about how the criminal justice system should intervene in domestic violence situations. Stalans and Lurigio (1995b) asked adult residents in Georgia to respond to brief scenarios involving their spouses and intimate partners. Results indicate that participants preferred dismissal when their spouses acted unintentionally and when they did not incur injuries. Not surprisingly, both women and men preferred counseling significantly more than jail or probation. More than half of the subjects indicated that they preferred court-ordered mediation to handle their disputes. The subjects' desire to hold abusers accountable for their physical violence by means of counseling, jail, and court mediation further indicates that individuals are becoming less tolerant of domestic violence.

Forensic Psychology and Policy Implications

Domestic violence is a widespread problem that affects families from every socioeconomic level in our society. Psychologists, judges, and lawmakers have struggled with devising an efficient means of preventing, assessing, and deterring perpetrators of such violence. While studies have undoubtedly placed an emphasis on identifying the primary characteristics of abusers, the research suggests that batterers are a relatively heterogeneous group. The heterogeneous nature of the batterers unequivocally hinders efforts geared toward prevention and rehabilitation.

The literature also clearly indicates the increased likelihood of abusers to endorse psychopathological symptoms and express bouts of anger and hostility. Hence, it is readily apparent that domestic violence offenders are likely to need extensive counseling for varying degrees of psychopathology and anger management interventions to modulate their intense feelings of anger. Also, victims are at an increased risk to develop psychopathological symptoms, including mood disorders and posttraumatic stress. Accordingly, group or individual counseling is likely to be a necessary component when working with victims of domestic violence.

Mandatory arrest laws and civil protection orders are currently being utilized by many states to reduce domestic violence. There is, however, an implicit precursor within these statutes which requires women to end their relationships with their abusers and subsequently places them at an increased risk of being attacked. It remains evident that battered women need to be provided with information about arrest policies and protection orders. If battered women decide to take steps to ameliorate their difficulties with violent partners, it is imperative that they are provided with adequate protection from their abusers. If issues such as these are thoroughly considered and implemented, scenarios like that of Ms. Malott's and Ms. Stewart's may be avoided. Conversely, if domestic violence continues to be underprioritized, the issue is likely to go unabated and remain an intractable problem.

Suggestions for Future Research

Over the past 2 decades, research on domestic violence offenders has expanded. However, relatively scant research exists which assesses the legal and psychological impact of the victims in question. Further research is needed to learn what legal and psychological interventions can be implemented to better serve those who are victimized by such abuse. The studies will need to ascertain the efficiency and effectiveness of such interventions and analyze the feasibility of devising remedial methods which can also be implemented.

As research on the profiles of abusers gains more validity, treatment studies can be included to ascertain what type of treatment works best with what type of abuser. It would be beneficial to study if varying treatment modalities differ in terms of effectiveness and, if so, more efficient interventions may evolve. Furthermore, researchers are also encouraged to examine more closely the options available for handling domestic violence situations including mandatory arrest, protection orders, and options for prosecuting batterers. For example, states which utilize mandatory arrest laws or any other laws pertinent to domestic violence can be compared to those which do not. Studies such as these are likely to enhance the opportunities and resources available to victims of domestic violence.

GAY/LESBIAN RIGHTS AND DEFINITIONS OF THE FAMILY

Introduction

The dynamics of contemporary families have shifted away from the "ideal" context of the nuclear family. Single-parent households are becoming increasingly commonplace and, more importantly, there has been an increase in the formation of gay and lesbian families. However, little attention, if any, is paid to how parental rights have often been denied to lesbian or gay individuals. Common misconceptions about gay and lesbian families only serve to hinder the development of laws and policies which favor artificial insemination, adoption, and foster care. For example, many people believe that children of homosexuals are apt to acquire parental sexual proclivities as well as to be subjected to additional sexual harm. Concerns also arise as far as children in nonconventional families experiencing difficulties with gender identity, gender roles, and having an increased likelihood of moving toward a homosexual orientation. A second category of concerns is that children living with homosexual parents may be stigmatized, teased, or otherwise traumatized by peers. Some courts have expressed fears that children in the custody of gay or lesbian parents will be more vulnerable to psychological maladjustment or will exhibit interpersonal difficulties and subsequent behavior problems. These are just some of the pertinent issues which are discussed within the context of gay and lesbian families. The following case illustrates the family dynamics of a young girl raised by lesbian parents.

> Sarah is a 10-year-old in the fourth grade. She is healthy, bright, curious, and determined. She was born to Marsha into a White family consisting of two parents, Marsha and Jane. The donor of the sperm, Bill, is a heterosexual man who is a friend of Marsha and Jane and liked the idea of physically participating in helping his friends create a family. Marsha and Jane have all along chosen to counter external threats to their family by being out as lesbians. They live in a large city in a part of town friendly to lesbian-headed families. Marsha is active at Sarah's school, working to educate the teachers about lesbian and gay parents and the needs of the children. They belong to a local lesbian-and-gay parents group and attend gatherings as a family. In addition, they have consciously tried to give Sarah tools for interacting with the larger world. They talk to her about homophobia, helping her recognize it so she can learn to separate someone else's prejudice from a statement about her personally. However, to her parents' dismay, Sarah is signaling a need to know about her biological roots. Her parents have feelings in common with many parents whose families are created through adoption or donor insemination. They want Sarah to be only their child. Sarah's parents want to protect her from the pain and confusion that may be generated by needing to integrate the complex roots of her identity. On the other hand, her parents want Sarah to feel whole and integrated. They want to do all they can to prepare Sarah by giving her the support and the skills to maneuver through a complex process (Barrett, 1997).

Literature Review

Sarah's case elucidates some of the dynamics which may arise in gay and lesbian families. For example, gay and lesbian families have to continually struggle with prejudicial notions which include homophobia and gross stereotyping. On the basis of their sexual orientation, homosexual parents are continually labeled as unfit parents who are incapable of rearing well-adjusted children. Yet there is an absence of literature indicating any significant difficulties experienced by children brought up in households of lesbian or gay parents relative to those experienced by children growing up in comparable heterosexual households. The existing body of research suggests that gay and lesbian parents are as likely as heterosexual parents to provide home environments that are conducive to positive developmental outcomes among children growing up within them. The following literature review further exemplifies the preceding premise and counters many commonly held misconceptions of gay and lesbian families.

In the United States, the number of lesbian mothers is estimated to range from about 1 to 5 million and gay fathers from 1 to 3 million (Gottman, 1990). Many lesbians and gay men who became parents within heterosexual marriages before adopting homosexual identities are also becoming parents after coming out. Therefore, it is likely that the preceding estimates minimize the actual number of homosexual parents. Thus, it is imperative for social scientists and the general public to take a closer look at the dynamics of gay and lesbian families. Tasker and Golombok's (1995) longitudinal study of 25 young adults from lesbian families and 21 young adults raised by heterosexual single mothers revealed that those raised by lesbian mothers functioned well in adulthood in terms of psychological well-being, family identity, and relationships. The commonly held assumption that lesbian mothers will have lesbian daughters and gay sons was not supported by the findings.

Furthermore, young adults from lesbian family backgrounds were no more likely to remember general teasing or bullying by their peers than were those from heterosexual single-parent homes. With respect to teasing about their sexuality, young adults from lesbian families were more likely to recall having been teased about being gay or lesbian themselves. No significant differences were found between young adults from lesbian and heterosexual single-mother households in the proportion who had experienced sexual attraction to someone of the same gender. Moreover, the majority of young adults from lesbian backgrounds identified themselves as heterosexual. No significant difference between young adults from lesbian and heterosexual single-parent homes were found for anxiety level as assessed by the Trait Anxiety Inventory. The groups did not differ with respect to depression level as assessed by the Beck Depression Inventory. The study clearly indicates that this sample of young adults who were raised in lesbian households did not experience any detrimental effects as a result of their familial upbringing.

On the basis of a literature review on the children of lesbian and gay parents, C. Patterson (1994) concluded that the development of these children was well within normal limits. Patterson studied 37 4- to 9-year-olds and found only two differences between children of lesbian and heterosexual parents: (1) children of lesbian parents reported more symptoms of stress, but also (2) a stronger sense of well-being. Lesbian mothers who did not conceal their sexual orientation and who maintained supportive relationships with extended family members and adults in the community were better able to protect their children from prejudicial experiences. The author concluded that the common misconception that children of gay men and lesbians were more likely to adopt a homosexual orientation was completely unfounded.

Flaks, Ficher, Masterpasqua, and Joseph (1995) compared 3- to 10-year-old children born to 15 lesbian families through donor insemination with those of 15 matched heterosexual families. The families were White, well educated, and drawn from a fairly affluent population. As demonstrated by their performance on a broad range of parent and child outcome measures, couples of both sexual orientations were assessed in terms of parental awareness skills and child-care problems and solutions. Compared with fathers but not with mothers in heterosexual couples, lesbian couples exhibited more parental awareness skills and identified more child-care problems and solutions. The results of this study should generalize well to young children of affluent, stable, and committed lesbian couples who have used anonymous donor insemination. The traditional hypothesis that the healthy development of children requires two heterosexual parents is certainly called into question. The results within this sample show few differences among children of lesbian and heterosexual couples in terms of their psychological and social adjustment.

How important are family structural variables, such as the number of parents in the home and the sexual orientation of parents, as predictors of children's development? Chan, Raboy, and Patterson's (1998) study of 80 families, all of whom had conceived children using the resources of a single sperm bank, included 55 families headed by lesbians and 25 families headed by heterosexual parents. Children averaged 7 years of age and biological mothers averaged 42 years of age. Results showed that children were developing in a normal fashion and that their adjustment was unrelated to structural variables such as parental sexual orientation or the number of parents in the household. Variables associated with family interactions and processes were, however, significantly related to children's adjustment. Not surprisingly, parents who were experiencing higher levels of stress, higher levels of interparental conflict, and lower levels of love for each other had children who exhibited more behavioral problems. The results are consistent with the general hypothesis that children's well-being is more a function of parenting and relationship processes within the family than the function of household composition.

Forensic Psychology and Policy Implications

To many individuals, getting married and raising children are central aspirations; however, these basic rights have been denied to lesbian and gay citizens in many states across America. Common misconceptions allude to the notion that lesbians and gay men are unfit parents or that children suffer irreparable harm if brought up in the households of lesbian or gay parents. Evidence from recent research indicates otherwise and suggests that children raised within lesbian- or gay-headed households are generally well adjusted. In cases such as Sarah's, her parents countered external threats to their family by educating Sarah and providing her with the support and encouragement that she needed.

A question then arises as to why half of the states in America consider parental sexual orientation relevant to child custody, visitation rights, foster care, and adoption rights? State laws on child custody, visitation, and adoption are based on what is in the "best interest of the child." Unfortunately, this particular clause opens the door to consideration of a parent's sexual orientation and may introduce a certain level of subjectivity as far as court decisions about child custody, visitation rights, and adoption cases. Most states, however, utilize the Best Interests standard by considering the parent's homosexual conduct, only as far as it can be shown that this has some adverse effect on the child. Indeed, the evidence to date suggests that home environments provided by gay and lesbian parents are as likely as those provided by heterosexual parents to support and to enable children's psychosocial growth (C. J. Patterson & Redding, 1996). Accordingly, social scientists can work to expand the body of research on lesbian and gay families and can make efforts to ensure that the results become available to the public and policy makers through appropriate publications. Not only can scientific evidence help alleviate misconceptions about lesbian- or gay-headed households, it can also facilitate changes in judicial or legislative decision-making processes. Thus, as certain elements change within the legal system, securing child custody cases and gaining adoption rights may eventually be a less arduous process for gay or lesbian families.

Suggestions for Future Research

Research on lesbian and gay families is still relatively new, and additional work is needed if we are to expand our understanding of the lives of homosexual parents and their children. Future research which explores the predominant child-rearing styles of such families and their effects on children's adjustment in comparison to heterosexual families is certainly needed. Less research is conducted on children of gay fathers than on children with lesbian mothers. There is a lack of research assessing the development of children of gay or lesbian parents during adolescence and adulthood. Longitudinal studies which follow gay or lesbian families over a certain time period are also needed. However, the costly and time-intensive nature of such studies have, to date, hindered such efforts. Nonetheless, longitudinal studies of representative samples of homosexual and heterosexual families, including observational as well as questionnaire and interview assessments, would be better able to enhance our understanding of parents and children within these contexts. Research in this area would help expand our understanding of families such as Sarah's and many others headed by gay fathers and would elucidate more fully the dynamics of such families.

PART III

Corrections and Prison Practices

CHAPTER 9

Adult Forensics

OVERVIEW

The adult prison population presents society with a complex set of issues and controversies requiring thoughtful, manageable, and effective responses. The assorted tools of the psychological sciences and the law are increasingly called upon to makes sense out of difficult correctional questions affecting the lives of prisoners and the community of which they are a part. Thus, not only are the skills of the forensic professional utilized for purposes of evaluating, diagnosing, and treating inmates, they are also employed for purposes of understanding the correctional milieu itself.

This chapter describes a limited number of topics that are of considerable concern for psychologists working in prison settings or responding to matters of confinement for offenders. While certainly other subjects could have been investigated in this chapter, the issues explored represent some of the more controversial matters affecting correctional psychology today. These topics include (1) an offender's right to refuse medical treatment, (2) incarcerating and executing the mentally ill, (3) sex offender treatment, (4) technology and electronic monitoring, (5) prison violence, and (6) the underground economy of prisons.

The legal system has acknowledged that persons civilly committed for psychiatric treatment have, under specified conditions, the right to refuse medical intervention (see Chapter 7). Is the right to refuse treatment for persons criminally confined any different? What types of involuntary treatments do inmates typically refuse? What constitutional protections exist for offenders exercising their right to refuse treatment? Persons experiencing mental illness can be incarcerated and sentenced to death. What are the constitutional limits to executing the mentally ill? What role does a psychological competency evaluation play in a decision to carry out an execution? What moral and ethical dilemmas do psychologists confront when finding that a person is competent to be put to death? Some incarcerated individuals are convicted of various sex crimes, including molesting or otherwise violating children. Psychologists are relied upon to treat sex offenders. Do sex offender interventions work? Is the treatment beneficial? What impact, if any, does sex offender treatment have on recidivism (i.e., the prisoner's potential for future victimization).

In addition to the important role forensic psychologists assume regarding mentally ill prisoners, they also help determine how best to address related correctional dilemmas. With advances in technology, prisoners can be electronically monitored when placed in community settings. What do we know about the effectiveness of such surveillance and management efforts? To what extent does the public experience a concern for safety and security given the electronic technique of monitoring offenders? How, if at all, are prisoners psychologically impacted by the use of electronic surveillance and monitoring? Violence is a part of prison life. How do substandard correctional conditions impact prison violence? How is institutional life psychologically stressful for inmates? What is the relationship between prison violence and overcrowding? Reading the behavior of prisons entails understanding how the formal and "informal" economy operates while controlling and constraining penal institutions and practices. What illicit activities are a part of prison life? How is the underground economy linked to gang behavior in prisons? What is the association between prison gangs, correctional guard relations, and the underground economy?

The adult forensic field of corrections is replete with an assortment of controversial issues or topical themes affecting prisoners and the institutions that house them. Psychologists help provide solutions to a number of these more vexing matters. Not only are forensic experts called upon to assess how best to deal with offenders who are mentally ill and in need of some form of therapeutic intervention, they help correctional facilities interpret the overall climate in which institutional problems surface, are resolved, and can be altogether avoided. As the individual sections of this chapter demonstrate, by its very nature there is a profound psychological dimension to any criminal confinement. Thus, well-trained correctional psychologists are sorely needed if the challenges that confront the adult prison population are to be thoughtfully, effectively, and efficiently addressed.

OFFENDER'S RIGHT TO REFUSE TREATMENT

Introduction

The basic rights provided to citizens under most of the constitutional amendments have been extended to the inmates in our prisons. The source of the right to refuse treatment can be traced to case law beginning in the mid-1970s. In the mid-1970s, U.S. civil rights advocates, after successfully arguing for the rights of minorities, turned their attention to psychiatric patients. They argued for a greater recognition of the general rights of involuntary patients and for the specific right of these patients to refuse treatment. Since a voluntary patient cannot be treated against his or her will unless found incompetent to make treatment decisions, they reasoned that an involuntary patient should have a similar right. Since the late 1970s, an increasing number of state courts have recognized this common law principle as the doctrine of "informed consent." The state courts have not been receptive to countering arguments, namely, economic considerations about lowering treatment costs and the need of mentally ill patients to be treated. Involuntary competent patients are allowed the right to refuse treatment because state courts are creating laws that provide them with a review board or court to make treatment decisions in their best interest.

An offender's right to refuse treatment raises significant questions in terms of constitutional law (Arrigo & Tasca, 1999). When treatment is focused at changing the mind of the offender, the right to refuse treatment is based on the First Amendment right to free speech. The cruel and unusual punishment associated with experimental drugs and unstable treatment programs used on inmates has generated the controversial issue of the Right to Refuse Treatment doctrine. Inmates suffer from severe psychological problems when involuntarily given experimental drugs. The *Washington v. Harper* (1990) case exemplifies this controversial issue.

> In the case *Washington v. Harper* (1990), a prisoner's right to refuse treatment was in question. The Supreme Court decision considered the right of inmate Harper to refuse antipsychotic medication. The Department of Corrections for the state of Washington maintained a Special Offender Center to diagnose and treat convicted felons who were state prisoners and had serious mental disorders. Under the Washington Special Offender Center's policy, if a prisoner does not agree to treatment with antipsychotic drugs ordered by a psychiatrist, the prisoner is entitled to a hearing before a committee consisting of a psychiatrist, a psychologist, and another prison official, none of whom can be, at the time of the hearing, involved in the prisoner's treatment. Also, the prisoner can be subjected to involuntary treatment with the drugs only if the committee determines that the prisoner suffers from a mental disorder and is gravely disabled or poses serious harm to him- or herself, others, or their property.
>
> Walter Harper had consistently taken antipsychotic medication for 6 years to curb his aggression and to silence voices he was hearing. In 1982, he refused his medication because of it's side-effects. In 1988, the Washington Supreme Court agreed with inmate Harper ruling that antipsychotic drugs could only be given to an involuntary

inmate following a court hearing at which time the state was required to show that the medication was both necessary and effective. The Washington Supreme Court held that under the Fourteenth Amendment a state prisoner's interest in avoiding the groundless administration of antipsychotic drugs is not insignificant, since the forcible injection of medication into an unwilling person's body represents an indisputable interference with that person's freedom. Antipsychotic drugs can have serious, even fatal, side-effects, such as a severe involuntary spasm of the upper body, tongue, throat, or eyes; motor restlessness, a condition which can lead to death from cardiac dysfunction; and a neurological disorder characterized by involuntary, uncontrollable movements of various muscles.

The Washington Supreme Court's ruling was reversed and remanded in 1990 when the U.S. Supreme Court decided that the constitution does not require a court hearing prior to a prisoner being involuntarily medicated. The Court held that the Fourteenth Amendment Due Process Clause permits the state to treat a prison inmate who has a serious mental illness with antipsychotic drugs against his will, if he is dangerous to him- or herself or others and the treatment is in his medical interest. The Center's policy agreed with due process requirements because it protected others from potentially dangerous mentally ill inmates. The U.S. Supreme Court held that the Center's policy was acceptable because it applied exclusively to potentially dangerous mentally ill inmates who were gravely disabled or posed a threat to others. The Court held that the drugs could be given only for treatment and under the direction of a licensed psychiatrist. Therefore, the Due Process Clause did not require a judicial hearing before the state could treat a mentally ill prisoner with antipsychotic drugs against his or her will.

In the case of *Knecht v. Gillman* (1973), the court questioned the extent to which injections of the drug apormorphine could be used as an unwilling stimulus. The injections were oftentimes administered by a nurse without the presence of a doctor or specific authorization from a doctor. The United States District Court for the Southern District of Iowa, Central Division, dismissed the complaint and Knecht appealed. The Court of Appeals held that administering a drug which induces vomiting to nonconsenting mental institution inmates on the basis of alleged violations of behavioral rules constituted cruel and unusual punishment.

Written consent from the inmate, however, may obviate this situation's unconstitutionality. This applies if the written consent specifies the nature of treatment, purpose, risk, and effects as well as advises the inmate of his or her right to terminate consent at any time. The inmate must also be given the opportunity to cancel consent at any time, and the injection must be authorized by a physician and administered by a physician or nurse. Also, the fact that civil rights statutes do not specify the scope of judicial relief available in actions successfully sustained under them does not preclude federal courts from fashioning an effective equitable remedy.

Literature Review

One way to consider the issue of the right to refuse treatment is to examine the problems occurring with experimental drugs and involuntary treatment on inmates. For example, behavior modification is one such program that centers on the modification of an offender's actions (Allen & Simonsen, 1989). One type of behavior modification is aversive conditioning for deviant sexual behavior. Territo (1989) indicates that aversive conditioning is the reduction or elimination of behavior patterns by associating them with unpleasant stimuli. Nausea-inducing drugs were used extensively in early experiments in aversive conditioning. The drugs were primarily given by injection to induce vomiting during an undesirable behavior. This procedure is very unpleasant and traumatic to the offender. Territo also explains that in later experiments electric shock replaced drugs as an aversive stimulus. Behavior modification is a highly criticized program. It can make excessive claims about results, use inmates as guinea pigs, and increase the use of behavior modification programs that are actually thinly disguised initiatives for furthering institutional objectives at the expense of prisoners. As a result, proponents of behavior modification are now using more sophisticated and humane treatment techniques with inmates. Nevertheless, as a protection, numerous institutional authorities have dropped the term "behavior modification" from the names of their treatment programs, knowing that the term carries negative connotations.

A program that applies learning theory with the aim of altering criminal behavior is the contingency management program. A contingency is something that may or may not happen and management involves increasing the chances that it will happen. Lillyquist (1985) found that with contingency management in a correctional setting, the aim is to increase the likelihood of occurrence of certain kinds of desired behaviors by reinforcing the behaviors when they occur. For example, participation in educational or vocational training programs, conforming behavior, and prosperous interviewing for jobs are some of the behaviors that have been dealt with in contingency management programs. Territo (1989) suggests that tangible reinforcements such as candy, soft drinks, cigarettes, and snacks can be increased with access to desired activities such as watching television, making phone calls, exercising, and receiving extra visits from family members.

Forensic Psychology and Policy Implications

When an inmate's right to refuse treatment is legally quashed to the point that the prisoner becomes involuntarily medicated, as in the *Washington v. Harper* (1990) case, cruel and unusual punishment occurs. However, if an inmate is involuntarily medicated and a problem occurs with the medication, then the prisoner would have favorable grounds to initiate a lawsuit against the correctional facility. Therefore, public policy makers must create stringent and safe testing requirements before an inmate is medicated. As mentioned earlier, the *Knecht v. Gillman* (1973) case is one example of involuntary treatment leading to cruel and unusual punishment. The psychological problems associated with experimental treatments cause adverse effects on the correctional system. Correctional facilities need to increase their treatment programs to care for inmates that are psychologically damaged from previous experimental and involuntary interventions. Raising the number of treatment programs means an increase in a prison budget. Therefore, public policy makers would be required to develop an appropriate budget plan to accommodate this dilemma in correctional facilities. Today, there are still problems occurring with medication and treatment practices on inmates. Unless research is directed at this area of corrections, the continuing pattern of problems will occur in the future and the correctional process will appear more ineffective with regard to treatment and medication of inmates. Legal standards involving mental health care provisions are among the most composite regulations affecting jails, jail policy, and public policy today. Court decisions regarding the provision of medical care to jail detainees, criminal responsibility for an illegal act, and treatment of the mentally ill in jail play a vital role in legal standards related to the administration of mental health treatment and medication of prisoners. These matters also need to be considered.

Suggestions For Future Research

More research needs to be directed toward implementing safe regulations and procedures regarding inmate treatment administration. For example, a therapist has the ability to exert a high level of control over a prisoner. Experimental methods such as drug therapy and electric shock can change the behavior of an inmate in dramatic and often harmful ways. Unnecessary adverse side-effects may occur when these procedures are administered. Unstable and unpredictable treatment procedures continue to overwhelm prisons. As mentioned earlier, the *Washington v. Harper* (1990) case is one instance of an inmate receiving involuntary treatment and suffering as a consequence of that treatment.

One example of an unstable and unpredictable treatment procedure is when the prison's needs are placed in priority over the needs of the inmate, and treatment programs are temporarily withheld because of prison activity or disciplinary behaviors. For instance, offenders who violate institutional rules may be placed in solitary confinement for a period of time without intervention. Treatment can be terminated when the needs of the institution are more important, causing the treatment to lose its effect and assist the offender. As a result, inmates lose confidence in the prison's therapeutic programming. In these instances, prisoners do not have faith in the correctional facility's promise to provide effective treatment because it can be discontinued based on the needs and financial status of the institution. The lack of prison industry and the presence of enforced inactivity have led to the development of treatment programs that fill time. The long-term value of such programs is questionable at best, and they are a topic of heated discussion, requiring further research.

Unless some highly effective treatment programs are installed and supported by solid evaluation, intervention initiatives will be seriously jeopardized. As a result of failing to improve intervention programs for offenders, future appeals by the offender will not be aimed at the specific actions that brought the person to prison but, rather, will be targeted at the treatment programs themselves. Clearly, still more research and testing need to be conducted in order to ensure that prisoners receive safe and effective treatment programs today and in the future.

INCARCERATING AND EXECUTING
THE MENTALLY ILL

Introduction

On any given day, over 100,000 mentally ill individuals are incarcerated in prisons and jails throughout the United States (Penner & Oss, 1996). The deinstitutionalization of state hospitals has led to an influx of mentally ill persons in the jail and prison systems, as many individuals who were once hospitalized are now incarcerated for their behavior (Belcher, 1988). Despite the prevalence of mental illness in the criminal justice system, it is not uncommon for the mentally ill to receive little or no treatment during their incarceration. Perhaps even more disturbing is the staggering number of mentally ill individuals on death row. Although it is unconstitutional in the United States to execute a mentally ill person who is unaware of the nature or reason for his or her punishment, such individuals continue to be executed (Arrigo & Tasca, 1999; Jacobs, 1998). In addition to the legal issues that are raised by the unconstitutionality of such a practice, a number of psychological issues are raised as well. In order for the court to determine whether a particular mentally ill inmate is fit for execution, a mental health professional must conduct a competency for execution evaluation and provide an expert opinion as to the inmate's understanding of the nature and reason for his or her punishment. Psychologists who conduct such evaluations are often faced with numerous ethical and moral dilemmas due to the literal life-and-death nature of their decision. The following illustration of Horace Kelly depicts the most recent case involving the execution of a mentally ill person.

> There is evidence that Horace Kelly suffered brain damage at birth. He was born over 2 months premature, weighing less than 2 pounds. By the time he was 18 months old he had endured chronic physical and sexual abuse at the hands of his father. By the age of 4 his mother reported that he frequently was observed shivering in a trance-like state. His childhood was further characterized by horrific headaches, terrible nightmares, and seeing and drawing demons.
>
> When Mr. Kelly was 24 years old he murdered three people over a 6-day period, crimes for which he is currently awaiting execution. During the course of his trial, Mr. Kelly reportedly spent weeks in the corner of his cell curled into a fetal position, sleeping under the sink, and crying frequently. Horace Kelly appeared for court looking extremely disheveled with an odor of urine and visible lice in his hair.
>
> Mr. Kelly had virtually stopped talking by the time he reached death row. There are many documented accounts of his bizarre behavior, delusional thoughts, confused state, severe distortions of reality, enuresis, nightmares, and suicide attempts. During his time on death row he has been prescribed numerous different psychotropic medications; however, his psychological decline has persisted. When asked about the meaning of execution, Mr. Kelly stated that it was the day that the payrolls would be processed.
>
> Although several psychologists have diagnosed Mr. Kelly with schizophrenia and mental retardation and a number of neurologists have reported severe brain damage, Mr. Kelly has been rendered competent to be executed. Once the decision of competency

was delivered, numerous attempts were made to spare Mr. Kelly from the death penalty. However, despite appeals, letters to the governor, and public outcry, the state of California has denied clemency for Mr. Kelly.

Literature Review

The case of Horace Kelly is not an anomaly. It has been estimated that approximately 10% of the incarcerated population are mentally ill (Penner & Oss, 1996; H. J. Steadman, McCarty, & Morrissey, 1989). Moreover, according to the National Coalition for the Mentally Ill in the Criminal Justice System, an estimated 40,000 prisoners suffer from schizophrenia (Penner & Oss, 1996). As depicted in the case illustration, schizophrenia is a psychotic disorder which is characterized by a detachment from reality, odd or eccentric behavior, and delusional thinking that is often accompanied by paranoia (American Psychiatric Association, 1994). While schizophrenia is a chronic mental illness, it can often be less debilitating and kept somewhat under control when properly treated. However, in Los Angeles County jails, an investigation by the Department of Justice revealed that inmates who suffer from mental disorders such as schizophrenia oftentimes have to wait dangerously long periods of time before medication will be prescribed and frequently the medication will be improperly administered (Sherer, 1998).

While it is common for inmates with mental illness not to receive proper treatment in jail or prison, it is also far too common for mental illness to remain undetected in this population. H. J. Steadman et al., (1989) report that the method by which jails evaluate for mental illness is insufficient. These researchers state that typically a brief questionnaire administered at the time an inmate is booked is used for the purposes of detecting mental illness. In addition to the fact that a simple questionnaire is an inadequate means for assessing mental illness, many inmates become mentally disordered as a result of the stressful environment of their incarcerated setting (H. J. Steadman et al., 1989). This suggests that ongoing evaluations are necessary in order to adequately assess for mental illness throughout a detainee's period of incarceration.

While incarceration of the mentally ill is controversial in and of itself, the issue is further complicated when mentally ill individuals commit capital offenses and face the death penalty. Every state that has a death penalty acknowledges that it is inhumane to execute an individual who is mentally incompetent and has adopted a law prohibiting such executions from occurring (K. S. Miller & Radelet, 1993). In the landmark case of *Ford v. Wainwright* (1986), the United States Supreme Court ruled that it was unconstitutional to execute a mentally ill death row inmate who did not understand the nature and reason for his execution. Despite such prohibitions, executions of the mentally ill continue to occur.

In addition to the unconstitutionality of executing mentally ill inmates, there are a number of psychological issues that are raised as well. If a death row prisoner's sanity is questioned prior to his or her execution, a psychologist is called upon to conduct a competency-for-execution evaluation. Such an evaluation is requested in order to assist the court in determining whether the inmate has a mental illness which prevents him or her from understanding that he or she is going to be executed and the reason why. There is oftentimes a great deal of skepticism associated with the reliability of psychologists' clinical diagnoses of mental illness. For example, in *Ford v. Wainwright* (1986), although three separate evaluators found Ford to be competent for execution, they all found him to be suffering from some sort of mental illness; yet, they could not agree on his diagnosis (B. J. Winick, 1992). This illustrates the fact that it is necessary but not sufficient for a death-row inmate to have a mental disorder to be found incompetent. Examination of case law shows that neither mental illness (*Ford v. Wainwright*, 1986; *Garrett v. Collins*, 1992) nor mental retardation (*Penry v. Lynaugh*, 1989) in and of itself renders a person incompetent for execution.

Conducting competency-for-execution evaluations frequently poses a number of moral and ethical issues for psychologists. Melton *et al.*, (1997) caution psychologists to examine whether their own belief systems would interfere with their objective assessment of an individual's competency for execution. Often, psychologists conducting such evaluations find themselves in a difficult position, given that their expert opinion can lead directly to an individual's execution. Moreover, if a psychologist finds a death-row inmate incompetent for execution, the individual's life is not automatically spared. In fact, there have only been two cases in this country where a death-row inmate has been found incompetent for execution (Radelet & Miller, 1992). In one such case, *Singleton v. State* (1991), upon the Court's ruling of Singleton's incompetence, his death sentence was reduced to life in prison.

However, in the second case of its kind, Gary Alvord was found incompetent for execution, yet remains on death row today (K. S. Miller & Radelet, 1993). This case illustrates a second issue that is difficult for many psychologists who encounter death-row prisoners while working in the forensic arena. As in the case of Gary Alvord, if an inmate is found incompetent, he or she is sent to a state mental hospital to be restored to competency. Thus, the primary responsibility of a psychologist rendering treatment to a death-row inmate is to restore the inmate to competency so that the state can execute him or her. As might be expected, the psychologist often has ambiguous feelings about providing treatment under such circumstances.

Similarly, individuals within the field of psychology have mixed feelings about the appropriateness of psychologists' involvement in capital cases. One such argument among those who believe that psychologists should not treat those found incompetent to be executed pertains to weighing the costs and benefits of treatment. Opponents of such intervention believe that it is more detrimental to restore a death-row inmate to competency, since the result will be execution, than it is to withhold treatment from that individual (Heilbrun, Radelet, & Dvoskin, 1992). Second, those opposed to treating individuals found incompetent for execution acknowledge the potential adverse effects that such treatment could have on the clinician when he or she knows that rendering their services may result in the death of another human being (Heilbrun *et al.*, 1992).

On the other hand, those who support treating incompetent death-row inmates believe that everyone has the right to receive psychological treatment if they so desire. However, this begs the question: Are incompetent individuals capable of providing informed consent? For example, suspected or documented mental retardation is commonly used as a reason for examining a death-row inmate's competency for execution. In this country to date, 33 individuals with mental retardation have been executed, including those with the cognitive functioning of a 7-year-old child (Keyes, Edwards, & Perske, 1998). With this in mind it is questionable whether such individuals are even capable of providing informed consent. Last, supporters of treating the incompetent argue that refusing to provide such treatment is nothing more than a protest against the death penalty and although the principle of doing no harm applies in nonforensic settings, it is not as applicable to forensic treatment settings (Heilbrun *et al.*, 1992).

One final issue that is raised in the controversy over treating mentally incompetent death-row inmates pertains to medication. As in the case of Horace Kelly, a psychotic disorder such as schizophrenia is a common mental illness for which a competency-for-execution evaluation may be requested. Psychotic disorders are most commonly treated by some form of psychotropic medication. Therefore, death-row inmates who have been found incompetent for execution may be sent to a state mental hospital to be restored to competency through the administration of antipsychotic medication. A problem that arises in cases such as these is the fact that individuals have the right to refuse treatment, including medication (*Washington v. Harper*, 1990). However, the United States Supreme Court in *Perry v. Louisiana* (1990) failed to resolve whether a death-row inmate possesses the right to refuse treatment (B. J. Winick, 1992).

Forensic Psychology and Policy Implications

There are a number of policy implications for the fields of criminal justice and mental health pertaining to the incarceration and execution of the mentally ill. There was a time in this country when mentally ill individuals were primarily housed in state mental hospitals. However, the deinstitutionalization of the mentally ill has in reality reinstitutionalized such individuals in the local jails and state prisons. As noted by Belcher (1988), mentally ill persons who are homeless or who have been previously hospitalized are particularly vulnerable to subsequent incarceration. Perhaps it is society's lack of appropriate means for caring for the mentally ill that leads to the incarceration of such individuals. Policy reform would do well to introduce alternative services to the mentally ill that would ensure that they received the proper treatment needed in order for them to function appropriately in society.

Execution of the mentally ill holds significant implications for both the criminal justice and mental health systems. From a legal standpoint, the ruling of *Ford v. Wainwright* (1986) perhaps raised more questions than it answered. There is a lack of specificity in defining several issues which cross the divide between psychology and the law. For example, although an individual must have a mental illness in order to be rendered incompetent, the Court has yet to specify which mental illnesses can be used to exempt an individual from execution. As illustrated by several cases, this results in psychologists diagnosing death-row inmates as mentally ill while still rendering them competent for execution. Similarly, the Court has not yet ruled on the appropriate protocol to follow when psychologists disagree in their expert opinions. Finally, although there have only been two cases in which death-row prisoners were found incompetent for execution, guidelines have not yet been established in terms of what to do with those deemed incompetent.

Suggestions for Future Research

There are a number of areas which need further exploration regarding the incarceration and execution of the mentally ill. Research is needed that compares mentally ill offenders who have been hospitalized with those who have been incarcerated in terms of their psychological symptomatology as well as their risk to the community upon release. Such research would assist in understanding which environment provides the most benefit to the individual as well as to society.

Research that assesses the reliability of psychologists' expert opinions on death penalty cases would provide valuable information to the courts in determining the weight that should be given to such testimony. Moreover, it would be helpful to both the criminal justice and the mental health fields to have research available that identifies those factors which account for the discrepancies among psychologists' opinions in capital cases. Finally, research could contribute significantly to operationalizing some of the legal terminology so that the legal standards could be appropriately applied to the practice of conducting competency-for-execution evaluations.

SEX-OFFENDER TREATMENT

Introduction

The most appropriate way of addressing sex offenders continues to be an issue debated among psychologists, criminologists, private citizens, and the legislature. The disposition options for convicted sex offenders are wide-ranging and include life imprisonment, civil commitment, chemical castration, and psychological treatment. Perhaps the area which has received the most attention from the fields of psychology and criminology is whether it is beneficial to provide treatment to sex offenders.

This matter continues to be controversial even among the foremost experts in the field of sex offender research. On the one hand, some believe that sex-offender treatment is beneficial (Alexander, 1997; Marshall, 1996), while there are some who do not (Furby, Weinrott, & Blackshaw, 1989; Quinsey, 1998). The method most often used in determining whether a particular treatment modality has been successful is the measure of recidivism. Recidivism is considered the best measure of treatment efficacy since the primary goal of sex-offender treatment is the reduction of future victimization (R. Prentky & Burgess, 1990). Therefore, in exploring whether treatment of sex offenders is beneficial, it is essential to examine recidivism rates between those offenders who receive treatment and those who do not. The case of Jesse depicts a convicted sex offender incarcerated without treatment for a number of years for child molestation. Jesse knows that he will reoffend if released from prison because he is no better equipped to deal with his deviant behavior now than he was 10 years ago.

> Jesse is a 36-year-old child molester who has been incarcerated for the past 10 years for molesting a 9-year-old boy. As his parole date approached, Jesse acknowledged that he did not know why he committed his offense in the first place and he was afraid that he would commit another offense if he was released. Jesse pleaded with the parole board not to release him.
>
> The parole board recognized Jesse's plea as a sign of remorse and released him into the community. For 1 year, Jesse remained offense-free. Then one day a neighborhood boy visited Jesse for a piano lesson and Jesse reoffended.
>
> When Jesse returned to prison, he learned about sex offender treatment. He wrote letters and spoke with prison officials requesting that he receive this treatment. The only response to Jesse's efforts was a prison chaplain who visited him weekly.

Literature Review

Jesse is perhaps a rare case in that he outwardly acknowledged that he would reoffend if he was released and he believed that the only way to prevent a reoffense was to remain incarcerated. Some experts would disagree with Jesse's position that remaining incarcerated was the only way in which to prevent a reoffense. In the 10 years that he was in prison, Jesse did not receive any treatment. It is possible that Jesse would not have reoffended if he had received the proper treatment to address his inappropriate sexual fantasies and behaviors. Despite the fact that numerous experts have shown that treatment does indeed reduce recidivism among sex offenders (Blanchette, 1996), there has been a decrease in funding for sex-offender treatment programs since the late 1980s (Alexander, 1997).

The lack of funding and available treatment for sex offenders is, in part, due to public opinion that sex offenders cannot be successfully treated. The accuracy of such an opinion needs to be explored and is best accomplished through an examination of recidivism rates among sex offenders. In the most comprehensive study to date on the effectiveness of sex-offender treatment, Alexander (1997) conducted a meta-analysis of 81 sex-offender treatment studies involving 11,350 subjects. The results overwhelmingly show that sex offenders who received treatment while in prison have a lower rate of recidivism than do those offenders who did not receive treatment. Among the sex offenders who received treatment in prison, 9.4% reoffended, whereas those offenders who did not receive treatment had a reoffense rate of 17.6%.

In order to accurately examine the issue of treatment efficacy among sex offenders, it is imperative to differentiate the offenders and not address the entire sex-offender population as a homogenous group. In this regard, numerous studies show that incest offenders have a very low rate of recidivism (Alexander, 1997; Hanson & Bussiere, 1996; Hanson, Steffy, & Gauthier, 1993). Referring again to Alexander's (1997) meta-analysis, the recidivism rate of treated incest offenders was 4.0%, whereas untreated incest perpetrators had a recidivism rate of 12.5%. For the incest-perpetrator population, it is apparent that treatment is quite effective in reducing future victimization. The comparison between treated and untreated rapists, however, does not provide encouraging results. Rapists who received treatment had a recidivism rate of 20.1% while untreated rapists had a reoffense rate of 23.7%. This clearly illustrates the point that treating sex offenders as a homogenous group will lead to erroneous conclusions regarding the effectiveness of treatment. The empirical research shows that treatment is quite successful for incest perpetrators; however, it is substantially ineffective for rapists. Therefore, perhaps the question that needs to be addressed is not whether to treat sex offenders, but rather, for whom is treatment most successful?

Another area that has received a considerable amount of research attention pertains to the type of treatment that is most beneficial for sex offenders. The consensus among those who treat this population is that a cognitive-behavioral program which focuses on relapse prevention is the most effective (Laws, 1989; Marshall & Barbaree, 1990; R. A. Prentky, Knight, & Lee, 1997). Such treatment programs have been referred to as "state-of-the-art" in terms of sex-offender treatment (Freeman-Longo & Knopp, 1992). As mentioned previously, rapists tend to have a lower success rate in terms of reducing recidivism after treatment. However, based on the meta-analysis conducted by Alexander (1997), all sex offenders, including rapists, had a recidivism rate under 11% after receiving treatment that utilized relapse prevention techniques. Thus, instead of asking whether to treat sex offenders, perhaps the focus needs to be placed on which type of treatment program is most effective for this population. There is a considerable amount of current research which lends support to the idea that cognitive-behavioral treatment, particularly when coupled with a relapse prevention component, is quite effective in reducing recidivism among sex offenders.

Despite the amount of psychological literature which illustrates the effectiveness of certain treatment modalities for particular types of sex offenders, the legislature continues to decrease funding for these treatment programs and exerts a great deal of energy supporting the chemical castration of child molesters (Alexander, 1997).

There are a number of reasons why law enforcement, the legislature, and the public disregard the scientific research, demonstrating that rehabilitation of sex offenders is indeed possible. One criticism identified by individuals who believe that "nothing works" is the notion that a large number of sex offenses go undetected and therefore skew recidivism results. However, when addressing the issue of sexual offending, it unfortunately goes without saying that many sex offenders are not brought to the attention of the authorities. This is a commonly held assumption, even among those who believe in the efficacy of sex-offender treatment (Hanson & Bussiere, 1996). Thus, the reported recidivism rates reflecting an underreporting of sex offenses remains a valid consideration. It is important to keep in mind, however, that while the statistics underestimate actual victimization rates, this does not discount the vast discrepancy in the recidivism rates between those offenders who receive treatment and those who do not.

Forensic Psychology and Policy Implications

The issue of whether to treat sex offenders remains controversial. Perhaps one reason why this topic continues to be debated is that there are few subjects that raise as much emotion as the issue of child sexual abuse. It is understandable that many of the foremost leaders in the struggle to obtain stricter punishments for sex offenders are the parents of victims of child molestation. However, from a policy standpoint, it is important to bear in mind that even with the emotional disgust and rage exercised against sex offenders, they too are eventually released from prison. Given the research which supports the effectiveness of treatment for this population, consideration needs to be given to increasing rather than decreasing the funding for sex-offender treatment programs. Withholding treatment from such individuals does not address the issue that is at the core of this controversy. Both those who treat sex offenders and those who seek to punish them have the common goal of reducing future victimization. Within the current criminal justice system, the vast majority of sex offenders are released from prison and returned to communities where potential victims reside. Recognizing this fact, it is important to question whether the public prefers to have sex offenders in their neighborhood who have received treatment or those who have not received any treatment whatsoever and, therefore, have not learned how to control their deviant sexual behavior.

Another issue to consider regarding policy reform is the cost of incarceration versus the cost of treatment for sex offenders. Blanchette (1996) presents data which illustrate that treating the average sex offender on an outpatient basis costs approximately $7,000 per year less than incarceration. As noted by Williams (1996), even if treatment was successful only for a small number of individuals, the cost-effectiveness of treatment is clear. Further, it cannot be overlooked that reducing recidivism by even a small amount spares numerous potential victims from suffering the devastating effects of sexual abuse.

Suggestions for Future Research

In recent years, an abundance of psychological literature has addressed the issue of treatment efficacy for sex offenders. However, the fields of law and criminology have scarcely produced any research on this topic. Perhaps this is because professionals in the mental health arena are those who most often provide the treatment. However, it is essential for individuals working within the mental health and the criminal justice systems to find common ground on the issue if the goal of reducing victimization is to be actively pursued. As noted by Alexander (1997), when agencies become convinced that a cause is worthwhile and urgent, the money will be appropriately allotted. Therefore, it is necessary that research be conducted addressing the reluctance by legislatures to implement treatment programs for sex offenders. Perhaps there is a lack of communication between the respective disciplines, and, thus, research would do well to target educating the public, the legislature, and the prison system on the efficacy of sex-offender treatment.

The current literature on the topic of sex-offender treatment is lacking in certain areas as well. The ineffectiveness of treatment with particular groups of sex offenders clouds public perception on the overall effectiveness of treatment. For this reason, research is sorely needed that addresses those sex offenders who do not respond well to existing treatment modalities. Specifically, limited studies assess how best to treat rapists, exhibitionists, and homosexual pedophiles. As suggested by Alexander (1997), research needs to focus on the heterogeneity of sex offenders in order to present a more accurate picture of what type of treatment works best for whom.

ELECTRONIC MONITORING: TECHNOLOGY AND MANAGING OFFENDERS

Introduction

The public fear of having criminals in our midst has caused a wave of sophisticated techniques to be developed for tracking and monitoring offenders in community corrections programs. Electronic monitoring programs are in a fairly early stage of development. Therefore, there are many questions, the answers to which are yet to be determined. A common inaccurate assumption is that since electronic monitors are a technological advance, they must be an improvement over existing surveillance methods and, thus, the ultimate solution. However, overall equipment effectiveness and limitations have not been clearly defined. As a result, it is not surprising that there is psychological stress related to the public because of emerging misinterpretations, misunderstandings, and misconceptions about electronic monitors. The unknown factors about electronic monitors contribute to the public's psychological uneasiness stemming from perceived safety concerns.

When electronic monitors are used, the probationer's or parolee's sense of identity is in question. Research indicates that numerous offenders report high psychological stress when strangers notice them wearing the electronic monitoring device. The electronic monitoring device creates for the user embarrassment and a loss of a sense of identity. These factors contribute to questioning whether electronic monitoring devices are constitutional. In the landmark case of *Katz v. United States* (1967), the court rejected the defendant's claim that electronic monitoring devices are a violation of constitutional rights. Instead, the court ruled that electronic monitoring devices are constitutionally acceptable.

> *Katz v. United States* (1967) is the modern landmark case in electronic monitoring because it ruled that electronic monitoring devices are acceptable for use in any location. More importantly, the Fourth Amendment right to privacy was ruled as a right to a person rather than to a protected place, such as a house or public telephone booth. Currently, the Katz case has been the foundation upon which recent right-to-privacy and electronic-monitoring cases have been decided. Nearly 40 years after *Olmstead v. United States* (1928) (a decision which found that evidence obtained by tapping telephone wires did not violate a defendant's rights), *Katz v. United States* represented the modern landmark case in electronic monitoring when the Court overruled Olmstead saying that the Fourth Amendment protects people rather than places. Therefore, electronic monitors are constitutionally acceptable in protected places because Fourth Amendment rights cannot reach into the boundaries of a place.
>
> In *Katz v. United States* the defendant, Katz, was convicted under an indictment charging him with transmitting wagering information by telephone across state lines in violation of number 18, section 1084 of the United States Code. Government agents, without the defendant's knowledge or consent, attached a monitoring device to the outside of a public telephone booth and recorded only the defendant's conversation. Overruling Olmstead's trespass doctrine, the Court created a new trespass doctrine holding that the Fourth Amendment applies to not only the seizure of tangible items, but extends as well to the recording of oral statements. The Court reasoned that once it is recognized that the Fourth Amendment protects people and not simple "areas" against unreasonable searches and seizures, it becomes clear that the reach of the Fourth Amendment does not protect places. The court held that Katz's Fourth Amendment rights were not violated because Fourth Amendment rights do not protect an individual in a place, such as a public telephone booth.

Literature Review

The constant growth of electronic monitoring devices in the past few years is related to overcrowded prisons and the costs of housing prisoners. Much of the development in the use of electronic monitoring has occurred in the absence of reliable information about the programs. More recently, reliable empirical studies have been conducted that give psychological insight into electronic-monitoring devices. For example, Lilly (1992) presented a large study on Pride Inc., the non-profit corporation which in December, 1984, set up the first continuously operating electronic-monitoring program (Schmidt & Curtis, 1987). The Pride Inc. Initiative is the most widely publicized electronic monitoring program in the U.S. and the principal model for others across the country. Lilly's (1992) study covered the first 415 cases, which comprise all cases from the inception of the program in 1984 to November, 1989. Ninety-seven percent of the offenders successfully completed their electronic monitoring program. However, many participants found electronic monitoring very restrictive, with high psychological stress attributed to embarrassment about others noticing the electronic monitoring equipment. In addition, psychological stress was linked to time pressures such as traffic delays when heading home close to curfew time. About one-half felt that electronic monitoring was more punitive than being in a halfway house.

In another study relevant to the psychological aspects of electronic monitoring, the Community Control Project (J. Beck, 1990) focused on the operational aspects of home confinement and evaluation of the electronic monitoring equipment. The sample size for this study was 357. Program participants were overwhelmingly older and male offenders. Participants were between the ages of 20 and 72, but approximately 80% were at least 30 at the time of release from prison. Approximately half of the parolees were African American or Latino, 69% were high school graduates, and 30% had attended college. About two-thirds of the sample were classified as "very good" risks by the salient factor score, but all risk levels were represented. The majority of the participants had committed relatively serious offenses. Interviews were conducted with 45 participants who successfully completed the program. About one-half of the interviewees thought electronic monitoring was more punitive than being in a halfway house. The majority of those interviewed stated that the most psychologically stressful part of the program was the time restriction factor. For example, some participants complained about telephone calls from the contractor to check the equipment and about having personal telephone calls interrupted by the computer. Others felt stressed by the curfew when traffic was heavy and it was difficult getting home from work.

In regard to the monitoring equipment, most reported that they expected the electronic device to be smaller. Some of the parolees indicated stressful and embarrassing situations when the electronic device was noticed by strangers. When asked by strangers about the device, the majority of the parolees dealt with the psychological stress by telling the truth, while others stated that it was a heart monitor, pager, battery charger for a video camera, or a fish caller (J. Beck, 1990).

These recent empirical studies help facilitate a forensic psychological and general understanding of the theoretical and practical implications of such electronic monitoring programs, enabling policy makers to make informed decisions based on reliable research.

Forensic Psychology and Policy Implications

The primary goal of current community corrections programs is to alleviate public psychological stress over misconceptions regarding electronic monitoring devices.

Community corrections programs achieve this goal by providing punishment in a less expensive manner while, at the same time, emphasizing public education of electronic-monitoring devices. For example, it costs $14,000 to care for each offender in prison per year. The probation system has estimated the cost of electronic-monitoring programs for each offender to be only about $15 per day (J. Beck, 1990). This figure includes the cost of equipment as well as all other costs of supervision.

The overriding reason for alternatives to incarceration is to reduce prison crowding and the financial burden of incarceration that has led to today's crisis in corrections. With the advent of this crisis, community corrections programs have the responsibility to educate the public on electronic-monitoring devices. For example, there are two basic types of electronic-monitoring devices. Continuously Signaling Devices constantly monitor the presence of an offender at a particular location. Programmed Contact Devices contact the offender periodically to verify his or her presence. A Continuously Signaling Device has three major parts: a *transmitter* attached to the offender sends out a continuous signal. Usually transmitters are attached to an offender's wrist or ankle. Transmitters produced by some manufacturers send an altered signal to indicate to correctional officials that an electronic-monitoring device was tampered with. A *receiver-dialer* located in the offender's home is attached to his or her telephone and detects signals from the transmitter. The receiver-dialer reports to the central computer when it stops receiving the signal and when it starts receiving it again. A *central computer* accepts reports from the receiver-dialer over telephone lines, compares them with the offender's curfew schedule, and alerts correctional officials to any unauthorized absences. The computer also stores information about routine entries and exits of each offender so that reports can be prepared.

Programmed Contact Devices provide an alternative strategy. They contact the offender at intervals to verify that the person is located where he or she is required to be. Programmed Contact Devices use a computer programmed to telephone the offender during the monitored hours either randomly or at specifically selected times. The computer is also programmed to prepare reports on the results of the call. Moreover, each manufacturer uses a different method to assure that the offender is the person responding to the call and is in fact at the monitored location as required. One system uses voice verification technology. Another system requires a "wristlet," a black plastic module which is strapped to the offender's arm. When the computer calls, the wristlet is inserted into a verifier box connected to the telephone to verify that the telephone is answered by the monitored offender. A third system uses visual verification to assure that the telephone is being answered by the monitored offender. Programmed Contact Devices tend to be less expensive and less efficient compared to the Continuously Signaling Devices. By 1989, the growth rate for Programmed Contact Devices had fallen behind that for Continuously Signaling Devices (Renzema & Skelton, 1990).

Who gets the electronic monitor? The use of electronic monitoring is generally reserved for defendants who are considered higher risk and therefore require a more structured supervision plan. Cooprider (1992) found that there is a direct correlation between class of felony and the use of electronic monitoring: on average, the more serious the felony charge, the more likely electronic monitoring will be imposed as a condition of release. Conversely, the less serious the felony charge, the less likely electronic monitoring will be imposed. Also, offenders charged with sex offenses are much more likely to be placed on bond supervision with electronic monitoring than any other category of offense. With the exception of sex offenders, on average all other offense types (property, violent, drug, and public order) were more likely to be placed on bond supervision without electronic monitoring than with it. Public order and property defendants are less likely to be electronically monitored than any other offense category.

Suggestions for Future Research

More research needs to be directed toward creating a rehabilitative aspect to electronic-monitoring programs. Electronic monitors alone are insufficient to enforce a viable home confinement and rehabilitative program. Rehabilitation provides the means to remedy the issue of the inmate's loss of a sense of identity. For example, there needs to be personal involvement with the offender on the part of a parole or probation officer to ensure that the offender is gainfully employed, has a balanced domestic life, is not engaging in prohibited behavior such as alcohol/drug abuse or violence, and is a functioning and contributing member of a community. Also, charity work and donations are rehabilitative tools that can brace electronic monitoring because the offender stays out of trouble and contributes toward improving the community. This type of rehabilitation develops an inmate's independence and sense of identity because of the numerous responsibilities and commitments. A decrease in the amount of offenders each parole/probation officer is responsible for would achieve the goals of offender accountability and public protection because of the increase in offender personal attention.

Another suggestion for future research is that electronic monitoring programs need to provide the context in which the monitoring equipment is to be used. A clear definition needs to be instituted in terms of how a user enters the program, who will make the decision, on what the decision will be based, and how long the person will remain in the program. Unfortunately, there is a public misconception about electronic-monitoring programs. Educating the public would clear this up and help foster an understanding of the particular programs. For example, it is often publicly assumed that electronic monitoring equipment has the capability to track an offender as he or she moves around a community. Realistically, the electronic monitoring equipment can only monitor the presence of an individual at a particular location and verify when the offender has reported in. Another misconception is that electronic monitoring programs can prevent crime. Even when the equipment is functioning properly the offender is free to leave any time he or she decides to do so, and nothing about the equipment will stop the offender from doing anything (i.e., reoffending). In addition, the user can leave as if he or she were going to work and then go anywhere. There is also no information about what the probationer/parolee is doing when he or she is at home. Therefore, more research needs to be directed at making the electronic monitors effective and more restrictive so that an offender is inhibited from taking inappropriate advantage of the freedom allotted by the monitoring system.

PRISON VIOLENCE

Introduction

Christopher Scarver attacked Jeffrey Dahmer while he was cleaning a prison gymnasium bathroom, smashing his head with a metal bar borrowed from an exercise machine. Violence has become a central attribute of prison life. Dee Farmer, as another example, was convicted merely of credit card fraud, yet he suffered a savage attack at the hands of a fellow inmate. When Farmer refused an inmate's demand for sexual intercourse, the inmate punched and kicked Farmer. After threatening Farmer with a homemade knife, the attacker tore off Farmer's clothes and raped him. The attacker threatened to kill Farmer if he reported the incident.

The Dahmer and Farmer incidents represent the controversial issue of poor prison conditions which cause prison violence. Numerous research studies indicate that inmate violence is the product of the psychologically stressful and oppressive conditions within the prison itself (McCorkle, Miethe, & Drass, 1995). Measures of poor conditions, such as inadequate prison management and lack of prison programs due to overcrowding, are associated with high levels of prison violence.

Literature Review

Situations like those previously described are very common in prison life. The Farmer incident raises the question: If poor prison conditions are improved, does that indicate that psychological stress will decrease among inmates, causing a decrease in violence? In response to this question, there is growing consensus among recent research studies indicating that prisons with exceptional conditions, such as efficient prison management, numerous prison programs, and comfortable prison capacity, experience a decrease in prison violence compared to facilities with poor prison conditions (McCorkle *et al.*, 1995). Prison overcrowding and lack of satisfactory correctional management were conditions that contributed to the Dee Farmer attack. In Farmer's case, the assailant reacted to the psychologically stressful prison environment by attacking Dee Farmer. Effective prison management, suitable prison capacity, and programs designed to keep inmates busy contribute to relieving psychological tension in the prison. Research indicates that the social and environmental factors that primarily produce prison violence include inmates' personal histories of violence; the youthfulness of the prison population; the lower socioeconomic class of most inmates; racial conflict between prisoners; inmate norms promoting violent behavior; and the psychological effects of prison conditions suffered by inmates. As mentioned earlier, poor prison conditions such as overcrowding, inadequate prison management, and lack of program resources contribute to inmate psychological stress causing violence. Additionally, reduced security from criminal victimization, the loss of autonomy, and the scarcity of goods and services also add to this stress. To lessen the physical and psychological effects of these deprivations, inmates sometimes undertake different illicit activities such as drug trafficking, murder, gambling, and selling protection from victimization. These illegal behaviors, in turn, require means for resolving disputes and thus invite the use of prison violence. The following vignette best exemplifies this process.

> J.T. owes C.L. several bottles of scotch. C.L. reports that this debt covers gambling losses; J.T. insists he has been paying for protection. C.L. gives J.T. 1 month to settle, but J.T. is unable to do so. The best J.T. can do is supply several packs of cigarettes, which only covers a small portion of the amount owed. At the end of the 1-month period, J.T. is violently assaulted and killed by V.P., who is often used by C.L. to "collect debts."

A recent psychological research prison study by McCorkle *et al.*, (1995) found that poor prison management increases prison violence. Data were collected from 371 state prisons and included measures of both individual and collective violence. In this study, only adult male state correctional facilities were examined; federal prisons, institutions for youths and women, medical facilities, drug and alcohol centers, boot camps, work camps, and community correction facilities were excluded. Of the 371 state prisons, 99 were maximum security, 140 medium security, and 132 minimum security.

Institutions were asked to report major incidents for the period of July 1, 1989 to June 30, 1990. Three types of prison violence were examined: inmate assaults against inmates, inmate assaults against staff, and riots. Riots were defined as assaults with five or more inmates involved, which required the intervention of outside assistance and which resulted in serious injury and/or property damage. McCorkle *et al.*, (1995) found that the average rate of inmate-on-inmate assaults reported by prisons for the year was approximately 2 per 100 prisoners. Staff assaults occurred at a rate of less than 1 per 100 inmates, and 8% of prisons had experienced a riot during the year.

Prison management variables included the guard-to-inmate ratio, guard turnover rate, ratio of White to Black correctional staff, program involvement, and institutional size as reported in 1990. McCorkle *et al.*, (1995) found that several management variables were significant causes of individual-level violence. For example, higher White-to-Black guard ratios were identified with higher rates of both inmate and staff assaults. Prisons in which a major percentage of the inmate population involved itself in educational, vocational, and prison industry programs had a lower incidence of violence against staff and inmates. Therefore, a conclusion can be drawn that prisons depriving inmates of program involvement have a higher incidence of violence than prisons that encourage program involvement.

Both individual and collective violence were more common in medium- and maximum-security institutions than in minimum-security facilities. Large prisons reported slightly lower rates of inmate-on-inmate assaults. This study (McCorkle *et al.*, 1995) found that external conditions play a role in influencing prison violence. For example, prisons in states with high unemployment experienced lower rates of inmate assaults than prisons in states with lower unemployment. One explanation is that when there is high unemployment, parole boards may be more restrained and less likely to grant early release. Under such conditions, there is less turnover in prison populations, a factor proposed by some to be a major cause of prison violence.

The results of the McCorkle *et al.* (1995) study strongly suggest that poor correctional management, such as lack of programs available to inmates, has a significant effect on prison violence. The institutions with inadequate management were found to have high levels of violence and the institutions with relatively good prison administration had low levels of prison violence. DiIulio (1987) suggests that prison violence, both individual and collective, is the result of failed prison management, including security lapses, high staff turnover, a lack of discipline among guards, unsearched inmates, and lack of prison programs. Useem and Kimball (1989) found that organizational and management factors were the most important determinants of prison violence.

The increase in the prisoner population, which now numbers more than 1 million, has been relentless since the 1980s and shows no signs of diminishing. The consistent increase of the prison population since the late 1980s has been staggering. For example, the number of prisoners in America increased by 115% (from 329,000 to 710,000) between 1980 and 1989 (Marquart *et al.*, 1994). Prison statistics such as these raise the psychological issue: How can prison programs be effective to inmates in an overcrowded facility? In response to this question, some researchers engaged in a study focusing on the effects of prison overcrowding on correctional educational programs.

Marquart and his coresearchers (1994) found that prison overcrowding decreases the opportunity for inmates to participate and complete prison education programs. This study examined the Windham School System in Texas. Windham's mission is to raise inmate literacy levels as well as to provide prisoners with vocational skills in order to enable them to join the workforce on release from prison. Windham's academic programs are geared toward raising the functional level of prisoners. The Windham School System regards a one-grade-level increase for an inmate to be a significant personal and organizational accomplishment. The Windham School System measures the performance and effectiveness of the vocational courses by the total number of certificates earned.

Information was collected from two separate state databases—the Texas Department of Criminal Justice Institutional Division and the Windham School System. The types of data collected from the prison system included prison number, average sentence length, and average time served in prison on 73,990 new inmates admitted and on 66,160 prisoners who were paroled or discharged in Texas prisons between 1990 and 1992. The second database consisted of prisoner education files maintained by the Windham School System. Individual inmate information included educational level at time of admission, types of classes attended during confinement, dates of testing, number of inmates who passed and received a certificate, number of in-class participant hours, and unit changes in grade levels. There were 21,388 academic enrollments and 6,919 prisoners who participated in vocational courses.

As a result of an implemented population cap and redistribution of funds in the prison system, a significant amount of problems occurred with the Windham academic program and vocational courses. For example, recidivist-type prisoners ages 17 and above were not given enough time to advance one grade level. Furthermore, first-time offenders over age 25 and habitual-type offenders over age 25 served barely enough time to progress one grade level. Overall, the time it took to advance an inmate's grade level was inhibited by the lack of time served. Compounding this problem was the fact that 27% of the 1991–1992 prisoners required by law to enroll in remedial classes had to wait for an opening due to inmate overcrowding. As a result of prison overcrowding, there was a limited number of vocational courses; thus, inmates were forced to wait a period of time before participating in a particular course. There was a 6-month wait before the actual first vocational class. The data indicated that 974 out of 6,919 prisoners were released from prison while participating in vocational courses. Therefore, 1 of 7 inmates enrolled in a vocational course, started the course, and then left prison before certification.

The results of this study strongly suggest that prison administrative personnel enrolled inmates in Windham's School System programs with the expectation that they would complete them, but those expectations were thwarted by early release practices and prison overcrowding policies. The combined effects of population-control policies and early release severely attenuated the Windham School System's performance measures. Consequently, prison overcrowding caused inmates to wait on a space available basis for educational programs and vocational courses. Arguably, delays for admittance to these educational programs and courses could have a profound psychologically stressful impact on an inmate's life. For example, delays frustrate prisoners and created more idle time for them to get into trouble and commit violence. When inmates are enrolled in educational programs, they are less likely to experience violence (McCorkle et al., 1995).

Forensic Psychology and Policy Implications

Life in prison entails facing a chronically stressful environment with its demanding regimentation, loss of control, and daily potential for violence. Prison educational programs offer inmates an escape from these stressors and a lower risk for violence. However, current criminal justice policies aimed at regulating prison populations have negative consequences for correctional education programs and the public. For example, an implemented population ceiling allows thousands of inmates early release and results in a rapid decrease in time served. Therefore, the opportunity to benefit and rehabilitate from educational programming eludes many prisoners. As a policy matter, returning unprepared and untrained prisoners to the community poses a threat to public safety.

Prison educational programs are the most powerful methods to help advance prison governance, institutional stability, and control over inmate violence. For example, inmates who attend several hours of class each day are occupied rather than idle. Inmates who are busy are not security problems and, as supported by the aforementioned McCorkle et al. (1995) study, present a low risk for violence. However, when prison overcrowding forces policy makers to implement criminal justice initiatives, such as a population cap and a redistribution of funds to other prison necessities (additional cells, clothes, and food), the results can have a disastrous impact on educational programming. For example, depriving prisoners of such assistance creates a psychologically stressful environment. Inmates are not rehabilitated through programs nor kept busy with educational work. Abolition of educational initiatives would mean that other programs to keep the inmates active would need to be created, funded, and staffed. Therefore, prison stability and control over prison violence are hampered when educational programs are cut: inmates have increased idle time, which can produce violence and chaos. Research on correctional educational programs demonstrates that they help prison organizations run efficiently and keep inmates at a low risk for violence.

Suggestions for Future Research

One method for minimizing incidents of violence is to use comprehensive environmental scanning systems to regularly monitor behaviors in prisons and identify potential "hot spots" for violence. The use of advanced scanning systems, such as management support systems, is a relatively recent phenomenon in corrections. The ultimate goal of these systems is to enhance the ability of correctional administrators and managers to better monitor the prison environment on a continuing basis. The environment is monitored by collecting and analyzing a variety of factors that provide information on the morale, behaviors, and perceptions of prison staff, administrators, and inmates. Environmental scanning consists of four steps. First, a process is developed to identify emerging behaviors, such as increases or decreases in typical accepted prison tension indicators including assaults and fights. Second, the findings of the scanning process are organized in an information package and distributed to administrators. Third, upon reviewing the information, the administrators must decide whether the behaviors represent a threat to the prison (threats can emerge from factors such as increases in assaults, drug finds, and inmate misbehavior or decreases in such factors as inmate program participation, counseling contracts, or health care services)? Fourth, they must determine if there is a need for intervention policies and/or procedures to address these behaviors.

Scanning systems have a critical role in prison violence prevention. First, potential prison problem areas can be detected before serious concerns emerge. Second, scanning systems force prison administrators to consider which factors best measure the well-being of their institution, the employees, and the inmate population. Third, scanning systems create a database for prison information and help correctional administrators better detect normal versus abnormal data entries. Finally, scanning systems force administrators to ask questions such as: Why did the trends emerge? Why are the shifting? Did any policy and/or personnel actions influence the trends? Should action be taken? These questions help corrections administrators make informed management decisions (Labecki, 1994). The comprehensive scanning systems enable administrators to better understand, predict, and design for the needs of offenders and programs, staffing, and security demands. Most importantly, a scanning system can help administrators distinguish between a psychologically acceptable and a psychologically oppressive and tension-filled environment.

Program involvement helps inmates stay out of trouble and reduces the violence in prisons. Conflict-resolution training teaches inmates the skills and resources to handle their own and other inmates' anger. It also teaches correctional officers the communication skills needed for positive interaction with inmates. Conflict-resolution training usually requires 15 hours of instruction. The course curriculum is designed to provide special skills in handling conflict with an emphasis on developing and improving skills in listening, problem solving, encouraging positive values, and mediation plus an emphasis on anger control, forgiveness, and nonviolence. The conflict-resolution training objective is to improve communication, promote self-esteem, build relationships, and encourage respect for cultural differences and people's emotions. It also teaches techniques to resolve disputes without emphasizing winning or losing.

Love (1994) found that conflict-resolution training was effective in prisons with highly aggressive and violent-prone inmates. For example, conflict-resolution training was developed at the State Correctional Institution at Huntington, Pennsylvania, which houses some of the state's most aggressive inmates and where staff must deal with violence daily. Of the 2200 inmates, nearly a third are serving life sentences and many have extensive histories of assaultive behavior.

In 1988, Community First Step, an inmate organization at SCI-Huntington, decided to bring the conflict-resolution program to that facility. The course was well received, and after 3 years, Community First Step invited prision officers to participate in a training session with inmates. They believed, correctly, that including officers would improve relationships between inmates and officers. One Huntington inmate who was serving 10 to 20 years for a violent assaultive crime participated in the training with corrections officers. He noted that one of the officers who took part was a strict disciplinarian from a military background who believed that inmates were "nobodies." According to the inmate, after completing the conflict-resolution course, the officer was more humane and professional in his relationships with inmates (Love, 1994). The most powerful example of the effectiveness of conflict-resolution training occurred during the 1989 riots at the State Correctional Institution at Camp Hill. Inmates in the New Values drug-and-alcohol program, who had recently completed a course in conflict resolution, were the only inmates who did not participate in the disturbance. Also, these inmates were credited with helping officers so they would not be violently attacked. More research on the effectiveness of comprehensive scanning systems and conflict-resolution training in corrections is needed.

UNDERGROUND ECONOMY OF PRISON

Introduction

The underground economy of prison refers to any illicit activities associated with prison life. Illicit activity can be defined as any action that constitutes a violation of prison rules and a threat to the orderly operation of a correctional facility. Common underground economies of prison include drug trafficking, weapon sales, prostitution, protection racquets, and gambling. The underground economy of institutions is strongly correlated with prison gangs because many of these illicit activities are controlled by prison gang members. A prison gang is a group, large or small, that has a name, common symbols, and an organization toward criminality. Age ranges in prison gangs vary and members may be male or female. As part of a prison gang, members see themselves as part of an established organized crime syndicate. In addition, members are required to abide by all rules of conduct. To prevent internal anarchy, prison gangs adopt a formal and paramilitary organizational structure. Each rank in the structure has defined authority and responsibility. To ensure longevity, most prison gangs require their members to make a lifetime commitment to the gang. Some common prison gangs are White supremacist gangs known as Aryan Brotherhood or Aryan Nation; African-American prison gangs known as Crips, Bloods, and Black Guerilla Family; and Latino prison gangs known as Mexican mafia and La Nuestra Familia.

Prison-gang-and-guard relations are an important area associated with the underground economy of prisons. Some studies show that the control of drug trafficking and facility overcrowding contribute to the deterioration of prison gang and guard relations. Other studies indicate the relationship between guards and gang inmates is reciprocal, with each side benefitting from each other. In the next section, we consider the research supporting these ideas as well as other ideas on how the underground economy of prison affects the guard-and-gang-inmate relationship.

The underground economies of prison have a significant impact on prison gang life. Drug dealing is one example of how prison gangs can control the daily routines of prison life, such as cell changes, work assignment changes, and many other daily prison procedures. The following case illustration exemplifies how prison gangs utilize the underground economies of prison to change their daily routines.

> John, a member of the Aryan Brotherhood, offered a prison guard drugs for a transfer from one cell block to a preferred cell block where other members of the gang reside and the lights stay on later. The prison guard agreed and called the deputy warden in charge of custody and arrangements were made. A week passed by and John told the prison guard that he had not been moved. After several frustrating attempts, the prison guard informed John that he could get transferred with the payment of 10 cartons of cigarettes to the deputy warden's inmate clerk. Otherwise, the cell change would continue to be overlooked by mistake. John paid the 10 cartons of cigarettes and was moved to the preferred cell block within 24 hours. (Chamelin, 1975)

Literature Review

One way to consider the underground economy in prison is to examine the current research exploring the relationship between prison gangs and guards. For example, a reciprocal relationship can exist between prison gangs and guards. A reciprocal relationship is defined as one in which both sides reap benefits from each other. The case illustration above is one example of such a relationship because both sides benefitted: the guard received drugs in exchange for granting the prison gang member a cell block change. Hunt, Riegel, Morales, and Waldorf (1993) found that some prison guards support and encourage gangs to develop. These researchers conducted a prison study that focused on the culture and underground economies of prison life. In this study, Hunt *et al.* interviewed 39 men who had been incarcerated in California prisons. Forty-six percent of the respondents belonged to a prison gang and 38% were members of street gangs prior to their incarceration. Hunt *et al.* found that the majority of the respondents cited financial incentives as the primary reason a reciprocal relationship existed between prison gangs and guards.

Hunt *et al.* found that one reason why a guard might support gang activity is because of a financial interest related to the gangs' illegal activities, such as gambling, drugs, and weapons. A prison gang might want to conduct illegal activities without the possibility of disciplinary actions from the correctional facility. Therefore, a reciprocal relationship is built in which guards are granted financial percentages of the drugs, gambling, weapons, or alcohol, bartering in exchange for turning a blind eye to the underground activity. Additionally, prison guards play a major role in smuggling drugs, weapons, alcohol, and food into the prison. Consequently, gangs have access to a variety of items from this source of importation and guards reap financial benefits from the sale of these items.

Although it may seem counterintuitive, another economic reason guards might want to encourage gang activity is because it threatens the security of the prison. Consequently, prison administrators might recommend an increase in surveillance and this would lead to overtime work and increased salary for the guards. Additionally, Sykes (1967) suggests that guards may overlook prison gang activities for a survival reason. For example, a guard knows that she or he may someday be a hostage during a riot and that one's life may balance on the settling of old accounts; an investment of goodwill, compiled by a series of past favors, becomes a valuable form of life insurance.

Other scholars, however, argue that the control of drugs and other underground economies can adversely affect the relationship between guards and prison gangs. Knox and Tromanhauser (1991) found that the problem of gang threats to guards is related to how much gangs are felt to control the importation of drugs into the prisons and the extent to which gangs are felt to dominate drug trafficking inside the prison. Knox and Tromanhauser determined that when gangs are reported to have higher control over the importation and distribution of drugs, there is a statistically higher probability of a threat by gang members against guards. This finding indicates that the higher the gang drug problem, the higher the risk of violence to the guard.

Prison overcrowding and more inmates coming in at a younger age have produced a new generation of prison gangs. Current research indicates that prison overcrowding and the younger generation of inmate gangs place guards at high safety risks and adversely affect the traditional guard-and-prison-gang relationship described earlier. Maghan (1997) found that one explanation for this phenomenon is because some gang inmates cannot inhibit their impulses even when it is to their advantage to do so. Other gang inmates perceive an advantage in acting tough and violent. Maghan suggests that much of the reputation building in which inmates engage entails violence toward other prisoners and guards. Psychologically, an enhanced self-esteem can establish an inmate's reputation as tough and help neutralize instances of victimization. This situation alters the viability and style of the traditional reciprocal prison-gang-and-guard relationship. Consequently, guards experience a growing sense of insecurity and safety risks in their working environment.

Hunt et al. (1993) offer another explanation for the change in relations between prison gangs and guards. These researchers found that the new generation of prison gangs differed from "old school" prison gangs in their dress, attitudes, and behavior toward guards. Hunt et al. interviewed traditional prison gang members and determined that they perceived the new generation of inmate gangs as disrespectful of the traditional customs established between prison gangs and guards. Hunt and his colleagues found that the new generation of prison gangs is needlessly violent and unpredictable. Therefore, the behaviors of the new generation of inmate gangs coupled with prison overcrowding has the effect of making prison life more unstable and more difficult for prison guards to manage. This effect is expected to continue into the future. Toller and Tsagaris (1996) found that the number of teenagers 15–19 years of age, a target population for gangs, is predicted to grow 23% by the year 2005.

Forensic Psychology and Policy Implications

When a prison gang begins to dominate drug trafficking, weapon sales, and other underground economies of prison, correctional staff are placed at high risk and the stability of the prison is jeopardized. As mentioned earlier, by the year 2005 there will be an increase in the population of incarcerated juvenile gang members. Correctional facilities need to increase their gang rehabilitation programs and intervention tactics to meet this challenge. Therefore, public policy makers should develop an appropriate budget plan to accommodate this dilemma in prisons. Additionally, public policy makers and correctional administrators need to design programs to help inmate facilities deal with the underground economy of prison.

Another strategy a public policy makers might adopt when addressing the underground economy of prisons is to establish an Inspector General's Office. The purpose of an Inspector General's Office is to review and audit records by officials in the prison. Therefore, gang activity and guard corruption would be documented and subject to review. Public policy makers might design an Inspector General's Office to help alleviate the numerous responsibilities a correctional administrator assumes. Consequently, underground economies in prison might be targeted and eliminated at an efficient rate.

Public policy makers might also consider designing a gang-training program for correctional staff. A gang-training program is beneficial because it reduces the chance that the illicit activities associated with the underground economy of prison would undermine the integrity of the facility. Gang-training programs increase correctional staff awareness of the underground economy of institutions. For example, correctional staff are educated on how drug smuggling is conducted and how prison gangs barter goods and services such as weapons and prostitution. By increasing underground economy awareness, correctional staff have an advantage in quickly identifying underground economies and in taking steps to prevent them from controlling their respective prisons.

Gang-rehabilitation programs might also be developed to help correctional facilities deal with the underground economy of prisons. An effective gang-rehabilitation program should be designed to segregate gang members as well as to provide a step-by-step rehabilitation system. Toller and Tsagaris (1996) suggest that a gang-rehabilitation program should include the following: a period of strict observation; investigation; clinical assessment; an opportunity for the inmates to earn privileges 1 week at a time; and a successful completion of a cognitive-retraining program, using a behavior contract indicating "no further gang activity." After completion of the program, prison staff should meet weekly and discuss individual cases as part of an effective follow-up process. Gang-rehabilitation programs are a valuable method to discourage activities associated with the underground economy of prisons. This may be because inmates are retrained to disassociate with gang members. Thus, prison gangs may disband causing a reduction in illicit activities.

Gang-rehabilitation programs are also important because they occupy most of the inmates' time with educational tasks. This leaves little time for inmates to think about the underground economy of prison in relation to gang life.

Suggestions for Future Research

More research needs to address the limitations associated with a flourishing underground prison economy. A prison which continuously allows an underground economy to usurp the traditional guard/inmate relationship compromises the safety of the facility and creates disorder. Therefore, research examining these types of limitations might make some correctional administrators "crack down" on existing underground economies.

The Green Haven Correctional Facility is one example of how an underground economy jeopardized the safety and integrity of the prison. Green Haven is a maximum-security prison located in a rural area of New York. At Green Haven, the attitude of prison guards toward gang inmates contributed to a breakdown in the security and overall safety of the prison. Prison guards at Green Haven adopted a "let's make a deal" attitude. A system of favors to gang inmates developed and was commonplace throughout the prison. Small favors to gang inmates gave way to larger ones. The underground economy at Green Haven became institutionalized. The guards permitted gang inmates to use and barter drugs and alcohol. Prisoners with organized crime connections, on trips outside of Green Haven for medical or family visits, were able to stop for costly meals, to visit with criminal associates, or to walk off unattended. The escorting officer was paid off in cash, sometimes including hundreds of dollars (New York State Investigation Commission, 1981).

As a result of the institutionalized underground economy, the security at Green Haven began to deteriorate. Prison gangs took advantage of the corruption and the relaxed correctional system. One example is Albert Victory, who payed his guards to drink in a bar while he escaped. Albert Victory's escape prompted many correctional officials to think twice about the unprofessional staff attitude toward the underground economy in prison, and the relationship between prison gangs and guards.

More research needs to be directed at exploring why prison gangs and inmates need an underground economy. A key debate among scholars centers on the extent to which inmate culture is either a product of the prison environment or an extension of the external subculture. Those in the former camp, such as G. Sykes and S. Messinger and R. Cloward and E. Goffman, have argued that the inmate social system is formed as a reaction to the various pains of imprisonment and the deprivation inmates suffer while in captivity. Other scholars challenge this view of prison life, arguing that it tends to underestimate the importance of the culture that convicts bring with them from the outside (Hunt et al., 1993). More research is needed to help bridge the disagreements among scholars and create an effective method of understanding why inmates rely on the underground economy of prisons.

Inmate gangs are the major source of the underground economy in prisons. As mentioned earlier, most prison gangs are a manifestation of youth street gangs. Therefore, more research needs to be directed toward street youths. Research designed to create intervention programs for street youths may be a good investment for prisons. Intervention programs could emphasize recreation activities, such as baseball, football, and other team sports. Educational courses can help stimulate the intellectual ability of many street youths and prevent gangs from developing. Consequently, intervention programs diminish the opportunity for prison gangs to organize and recruit from adolescent street gangs.

CHAPTER 10

Juvenile Forensics

OVERVIEW

Juveniles break the law and find themselves punished because of it. On occasion, this punishment includes some form of incarceration. Psychologists, however, typically raise doubts about the efficacy of correctional punishment for adolescents and argue that juveniles who act delinquently are not criminals but, rather, are troubled youths. The field of juvenile forensics, then, examines whether criminal justice or mental health responses are best suited to the needs and interests of juveniles who engage in illicit conduct. In addition, the domain of juvenile forensics explores the impact of correctional remedies for children who break the law.

This chapter investigates five controversies in the juvenile forensic arena. The issues examined in the pages that follow represent some of the more hotly contested matters at the crossroads of juvenile justice, psychology, and corrections. Consistent with one theme organizing this textbook, while the reader is presented with a limited selection of topics to review and digest, the variety of issues considered demonstrates the breadth of the field and the need for experts trained in this sub-specialty area. The five controversies explored include (1) juveniles in adult jails, (2) juveniles on death row, (3) juveniles in boot camps, (4) suicide among incarcerated youth, and (5) the incarceration of status offenders.

Delinquent adolescents can and do find themselves in adult jails. What type of crimes do juveniles commit and how are they different from their adult counterparts? What psychological problems do children experience when placed in the adult jail system? What forms of (physical and sexual) violence do youths confront while in the adult system? Juveniles can be sentenced to death and a representative minority of convicted youths are awaiting execution. Does the age and/or mental state of the juvenile offender matter for purposes of sentencing determinations? What psychological difficulties do adolescents confront while awaiting execution? In response to the problems caused by adolescent delinquency, correctional experts have recently advocated for juvenile boot camps that prepare youths to engage in productive, prosocial behavior. How do these facilities function? Do juvenile boot camps promote the aims of rehabilitation and treatment or the aims of retribution and punishment? What impact, if any, do juvenile boot camps have on recidivism? Some incarcerated boys and girls commit suicide. What are the links between juvenile delinquency and suicide? What are the links between juvenile incarceration and suicide? What psychological prevention and intervention strategies exist to address the phenomenon of suicide among incarcerated youths? Adolescents can be placed in correctional facilities for violating "status offenses." These offenses include such behaviors as running away from home, truancy from school, incorrigibility, and curfew infractions. Why do these behaviors subject youths to incarceration? What role, if any, does the mental health system play in responding to delinquent children? What mental health services, if any, are available for troubled youths?

The juvenile forensic arena of corrections shows us how the mental health and the criminal justice systems differentially respond to the problems posed by adolescent misconduct. Where the correctional community generally promotes retributive measures of justice (i.e., punishment), the psychological establishment typically advances rehabilitative measures of justice (i.e., treatment). As the sections of this chapter reveal, there are a number of pressing issues affecting the lives of youths caught in the crossfire of "intervention politics." Thus, it is not surprising that forensic psychologists, cross-trained in the areas of corrections, adolescent delinquency, and psychology, are most especially competent to understand how the criminal justice and mental health systems *can* work in concert to meet the best interests of delinquent youths and society. Clearly, as the chapter implies, without such careful and thoughtful interventions developed and implemented by such forensic experts, we risk losing too many children to the devastation of crime and violence. This is a loss that our society can ill afford to absorb or sustain.

JUVENILES IN ADULT JAILS

Introduction

Thousands of children are placed in adult jails each year. The conditions in which these children are held, and the circumstances they encounter, pose serious threats to their physical and mental well-being. Children's advocates have long been aware of the dangers that children face in this environment, and their concerns have prompted litigation to end the incarceration of juveniles in adult jails. Despite many years of litigation to abolish the holding of children in adult facilities, approximately 40 states continue to do so, placing thousands of children in dangerous situations a year. Oftentimes, when juveniles are imprisoned with adults in an attempt to reform their behavior, they leave the jail even less equipped to deal with the outside world than before incarceration (Tomasevski, 1986).

There are numerous cases depicting specific problems of incarcerating juveniles in adult jails. Children are particularly vulnerable to suicide when confronted with the adult jail environment. The following example illustrates the problem of keeping children in isolation.

> Kathy Robbins was a 15-year-old girl who was arrested for running away from home in 1984. She was taken to Glenn County Jail in California, where she was strip-searched and placed in a small dark cell with a solid steel door. She was held in virtual isolation for 4 days until her hearing date. At her hearing, she begged the judge to send her home. The court ordered that her case be continued and that Kathy remain incarcerated in the jail until such time.
>
> That afternoon, Kathy committed suicide by hanging herself with a sheet from the guard rail of the top bunk. Disturbing information concerning Kathy Robbins was disclosed during the case of *Robbins v. Glenn County* (1986). Kathy had physical evidence of previous suicide attempts, yet no measures were taken in jail to supervise Kathy or ensure her safety. She was only allowed one brief visit with her mother and was not given any reading material that her mother had provided. Further, the jail staff had refused to take her phone messages from her mother. Most troubling in this case is the fact that space was available at a local group home while Kathy was incarcerated in the jail.

It should be noted that girls who are so traumatized by the experience of being held in an adult jail are not the only ones who resort to suicide. Every year there are cases of young boys who commit suicide while being subjected to the conditions in adult jails. Oftentimes for boys, suicide follows their victimization in a rape assault by adult inmates. Whereas boys are subjected to rape victimization by adult prisoners, girls are often victims of rape by the jail staff, as can be seen from the following examples.

> In *Doe v. Burwell*, a 15-year-old girl from Ohio had left home for 1 day without her parents' permission. In order to "teach her a lesson," the juvenile court judge ordered her to be incarcerated in the county jail for 5 days. During her 4th night in jail, she was raped by a deputy jailer.
>
> A 14-year-old runaway girl was held in a county jail in Pennsylvania when she was raped by the deputy sheriff as well as by two male inmates. One of the inmates was a convicted murderer who was awaiting sentencing. The sheriff released the inmates in order for them to participate in the rape of the young girl (Chesney-Lind, 1988).

Violence in correctional settings is a common occurrence. When children are intermixed with adults, they become prime targets for such assaults as a result of their vulnerability. The following case illustration demonstrates this disturbing fact.

In *Yellen v. Ada County* (1985), a 15-year-old boy was incarcerated in an adult jail for failing to pay $73 in traffic fines. He was held for a 14-hour period during which time he was brutally tortured by other inmates and eventually beaten to death.

Literature Review

Examining the psychological and criminological literature provides us with a better understanding of the pervasive and severe problems encountered when incarcerating juveniles in adult jails. According to the Annual Survey of Jails in 1989, there were approximately 53,994 juveniles held in adult jails. Of particular concern was the fact that many of them were status offenders (runaways, truants, and children out of parental control). Only a small percentage of the children held in jails were charged with violent crimes (Soler, 1988). Murray (1983) reports that of the nearly half million children in adult jails, only 14% of them had been charged with a serious offense such as homicide, rape, or burglary.

A lawsuit was filed against the City of Long Beach and the County of Los Angeles in *Baumgartner v. City of Long Beach* (1987) when a taxpayer was outraged that the cities incarcerated more than 4000 juveniles each year in the Long Beach City Jail. Nearly 1000 of the children had not been charged with an offense. Instead, these children were victims of abandonment, neglect, and abuse by their parents and, thus, were removed from their homes. While proper placements in foster or group homes were pending for these children, they remained locked up in jail with adult inmates. This environment further placed these abused children in the face of danger. Additionally, a nursery equipped with cribs and toys was located in the jail where infants were placed until such time as proper placements could be arranged (Soler, 1988; Steinhart, 1988). Another 1000 of the youths were status offenders, while less than 10% were charged with violent offenses. All of the children were kept in dark cells behind bars.

The adult jail environment is not conducive to the detainment of juveniles. Tomasevski (1986) presents the results from a comprehensive study conducted by the Defense for Children International in 1983, in an attempt to create awareness about the problem of detaining children in adult facilities. Children who are held in the adult facilities are subjected to circumstances which are direct threats to their emotional and physical health. In order to "protect" children in such an environment, they are often separated from the adult inmate population. The result of this action is isolation, often resembling solitary confinement. Tomasevski's (1986) international study of children in adult prisons revealed that the United States displayed the most evidence of virtual solitary confinement.

When children are required to remain separate from adult prisoners by "sight and sound," they are oftentimes completely isolated from human contact. Adolescents are particularly vulnerable to depression and suicide when they are isolated and fearful. Further, the correctional officers are not trained to identify the signs of depression in adolescents, and, therefore, intervention frequently does not occur in time.

As demonstrated by the case of Kathy Robbins, we see the depression that children suffer and the desperate measures they take when held in isolation. When children in jail are not isolated, they encounter severe problems of a different nature. Juveniles are particularly vulnerable to sexual and physical abuse by staff and adult inmates.

Females in jail are held under more restrictive conditions than males (Chesney-Lind & Shelden, 1992). Often, they are housed in a subsection of a male facility. For this reason, they are rarely granted equal opportunity for recreation, education, or work-release programs as their male counterparts (Mann, 1984). Women will often spend most, if not all of their time inside their cell. This is difficult for adult women, but it is particularly trying for young girls. This is particularly dangerous for girls who often have backgrounds involving sexual and physical abuse. This repeated trauma makes them especially susceptible to depression and even suicide (A. Browne & Finkelhor, 1986). Chesney-Lind and Shelden (1992) report that girls in jail tend to be younger, commit less serious offenses (primarily status offenses), and, despite their less severe offenses, remain in custody for approximately the same length of time as their male counterparts.

Forensic Psychology and Policy Implications

The incarceration of children in adult jails is a social, political, and human rights problem. Despite the litigation efforts to end the incarceration of children with adults, estimates ranging from 27,000 to 500,000 indicate that juveniles are still being held in adult facilities each year (L. S. Wrightsman, 1991). As efforts increase to curb the rate of juvenile crime, the special needs and rights of children must not be ignored. Adolescent detention facilities are especially equipped to address the special needs of youthful offenders. Specialized treatment programs are designed to offer juveniles an opportunity for rehabilitation. To hold youths in adult facilities is to deny them this opportunity, as well as to subject them to severe psychological distress, physical and sexual abuse, and an environment where they are influenced by career and violent offenders. Nevertheless, society apparently supports the stricter, more punitive approach to dealing with juvenile offenders. Tomasevski (1986) described the Canadian Adult Prisoners' association response regarding adult facilities as places that should not house children. Those youths who do not succumb to molestation or get hurt tend to become tougher than when they entered the facility; their young age and their exposure to adult facilities only ensures that they will return.

Suggestions for Future Research

There has not been a great deal of recent research conducted on juveniles incarcerated in adult jails. The long-term effects of such an environment on children needs to be examined from a psychological as well as a criminological perspective.

Specifically, follow-up studies on adolescents who have been held in adult facilities would provide useful information regarding their psychological functioning, as well as their subsequent criminal behavior. Further, such analyses could then be compared to youthful offenders who were held in juvenile facilities. This would provide a clear illustration of the ramifications of incarcerating juveniles with adults as opposed to other adolescents. Additionally, the exploration into alternative placements for juveniles needs to continue. Finally, future research might entail an analysis surrounding the reasons why previous litigation has failed to effectively end the incarceration of juveniles in adults jails, despite cases as tragic as Kathy Robbins.

JUVENILES ON DEATH ROW

Introduction

Capital punishment has remained an unabated controversy for decades. The constitutionality of the death penalty, the cost of capital cases and executions, and the impact the death penalty has on deterring crime in our society have all been repeatedly questioned. This controversy is further complicated by the issue of sentencing juveniles to death. There are currently three countries which allow for the execution of juvenile offenders. The United States is not only one of the three countries permitting adolescent capital punishment, it is the leading country. Fifty-eight juveniles in the United States were serving their sentences on death row as of March, 1997 (Streib, 1998). Moreover, juveniles on death row typically exhibit neurological damage, psychoses, and suffer severe physical and/or sexual abuse as younger children (Lewis *et al.*, 1988). The following case illustrates the complexities involved when a juvenile faces capital punishment.

> James Terry Roach was executed on January 10, 1986, in South Carolina, the same state in which he was born. Terry was raised by an ill mother and a father who was absent most of the time. Terry suffered from mental retardation with an I.Q. near 70. He dropped out of school early, became involved with drugs, and was diagnosed with a personality disorder. When Terry was 16 years old, he lived in a home with unemployed antisocial people who were involved in extensive drug use. Due to Terry's limited mental capacities, he was easily influenced by others. When Terry was 17 years old, he was convinced by an older housemate to spend the day riding around in a car while drinking beer and using marijuana and PCP. The boys came upon a 17-year-old male with his 14-year-old girlfriend, both from prominent families in the community. On a signal from his friend, Terry fatally shot the male three times. The boys then took the girl to a secluded area where they repeatedly raped her. Terry's friend then shot and killed the girl and he later returned to mutilate her body.
> The community was outraged by the crimes, especially given the prominent status of the victims' families. The death penalty was sought and received for both Terry and his friend. It should be noted that Terry's court-appointed attorney was disbarred 2 years after his representation of the case for irregularities in his practice. However, his handling of Terry's case was deemed constitutionally adequate. Despite letters to the governor pleading for clemency from Mother Theresa and former President Carter,

Terry's execution was carried out. Although Terry had reached the chronological age of 25 at the time of his execution, his mental age remained fixed at 12. (*Roach v. Aiken*, 1986)

Literature Review

The case of Terry Roach depicts both the gravity of crimes that are committed by juveniles as well as the tragedy of executing an individual who only has the mental capacity of a 12-year-old boy. This case demonstrates the need to explore the sociological, criminological, and psychological dynamics of capital punishment for juvenile offenders. In March of 1997, juveniles on death row constituted approximately 2% of that total population (Streib, 1998). All of these offenders were males who received death sentences for murder. Of these 58 juveniles, 49% were African American, 17% Latino, and 34% Caucasian. This is consistent with the high percentage of minority executions that are found in adult capital punishment cases as well. Moreover, 59% of the executed juvenile offenders were convicted of murdering a Caucasian adult.

From a criminological stance, punishment for crime serves one of three primary purposes: (1) deterrence, (2) retribution, or (3) rehabilitation. For obvious reasons, the death penalty cannot serve a rehabilitative function. However, rehabilitation is the premise of the juvenile justice system in America. Therefore, the basic assertion of the juvenile justice system (i.e., rehabilitation of juvenile offenders) is inherently incompatible with the death penalty.

Capital punishment has been further examined in its relationship to deterrence of criminal activity. The Federal Bureau of Investigation Uniform Crime Reports indicate that since the death penalty was reinstated in 1976, the number of death-row inmates and executions have increased substantially. There has, however, been virtually no change in the commission rate of murders (FBI, 1997). Furthermore, comparisons between those states which utilize the death penalty and those that do not reveal that the majority of death-penalty states have higher rates of murder. This finding supports those who oppose the death penalty because it shows how capital punishment fails to deter crime (FBI, 1997).

Particularly in the case of Terry Roach, it is highly unlikely that his execution will deter others like him. His attorney addressed the improbability of a deterrence effect, stating that Terry (and those with similar problems) did not have the ability to think more than a few hours in advance and could likely not even conceive of possibilities for his actions such as arrest or execution (Streib, 1987). This is consistent with developmental theory, which acknowledges that adolescents have a deficient understanding of mortality. This furthers the previous discussion on rehabilitation in the juvenile justice system. According to his attorney, Terry lacked the ability to think about the consequences of his actions. This is common among adolescents and certainly to be expected from a mentally retarded adolescent. The public outrage at Terry's sentence illustrates the general perception that the punishment did not fit the offender.

Constitutional law focuses primarily on the fact that the death penalty for juvenile offenders is in violation of the Eighth Amendment. In 1976, the landmark

Supreme Court case of *Gregg v. Georgia* held that the death penalty does not violate the Eighth Amendment to the constitution. Although the essence of this case does not involve the age of the offender, the concern over an offender's age did emerge. In this ruling, the Court maintained that the jury must consider characteristics of the offender that might mitigate against a capital punishment ruling. Among such characteristics mentioned was the age of the offender. Special consideration of the constitutionality of the death penalty for juveniles was addressed in *Eddings v. Oklahoma* (1982). This case involved a 16-year-old defendant who was potentially facing capital punishment. Regarding the age of the offender, the Court found that a person's youthfulness is worthy of consideration as a mitigating factor. In *Eddings,* the Supreme Court avoided making a determination on the constitutionality issue and sent the case back for resentencing; however, Justices Burger, Blackmun, Rehnquist, and White stated that there was no constitutional basis to bar the death penalty for the 16-year-old defendant. The Supreme Court continues to avoid ruling on the federal constitutionality of sentencing juveniles to death; rather, the legality of the death penalty for juveniles remains a determination for individual jurisdictions.

It is interesting to note that these same juveniles who are sentenced to death are not legally old enough to vote, enter into a contract, marry, or sit on the juries like those who convict them (Streib, 1987). Perhaps for this reason, the age of minority for sentencing juveniles to death in many states is 18. However, not all states hold age 18 as the threshold, and some states do not abide by a minimum age for capital punishment at all. In 1962, the death penalty existed in 41 states, in which the minimum age was 7 in 16 states, age 8 in 3 states, age 10 in 3 states, and ages 12–18 in 19 states (Streib, 1987). This has changed considerably over the past 3 decades. Currently, the minimum age for the death penalty is age 18 in 13 states, age 17 in 4 states, and age 16 in 21 states (Streib, 1996).

From a psychological standpoint, it is important to assess the juveniles' perceptions and attitudes toward capital punishment and their death sentence. Streib (1987) reports that younger juveniles on death row experience greater fear as well as a strong sense of abandonment. Streib describes such juveniles as exhibiting uncontrollable crying, severe depression, and "childlike pleas for rescue to a parent or authoritative adult" (p. 158). The case illustration of Terry Roach, the 17-year-old mentally retarded boy, demonstrates how the public viewed him as evil for his heinous crimes. A study conducted by Lewis *et al.* (1988) examined 14 juveniles on death row concerning their psychological characteristics and disorders. The researchers reported that the typical juvenile offender on death row had serious injuries to the central nervous system, exhibited psychotic symptoms, and had been physically and sexually abused.

Forensic Psychology and Policy Implications

The appropriateness of imposing the death penalty on juveniles was explored from a criminological, sociological, and psychological perspective. When combining views from experts representing the American Society of Criminology, the Academy of Criminal Justice Sciences, and the Law and Society Association, the death penalty has not proven itself to be a deterrent to crime (Radelet & Akers, 1995). Therefore, the death penalty has not served its primary function in society. For this reason, policy analysts must question why children are being executed, despite the research showing that the intended effects of the death penalty have failed. Moreover, if the juvenile justice system continues to maintain that rehabilitation is the most appropriate goal for youthful offenders, then the death penalty is obviously incompatible with such a goal. Cases such as Terry Roach illustrate the need for special considerations in sentencing juveniles, particularly when capital punishment is involved. Terry's attorney stated that his client lacked the ability to think about the consequences of his actions. By killing such children, society abdicates its responsibility to teach appropriate ways to control behavior as well as the skills needed to think and understand consequences for one's conduct. Particularly since the juvenile justice system prides itself on rehabilitation, it needs to consider, and explain to the public, why killing a child becomes the appropriate remedy when rehabilitation has not even been attempted.

Suggestions for Future Research

Few studies address the psychological impact of death row on juveniles. This knowledge is crucial in order to provide appropriate services to these children. Research also needs to explore what factors influence the jurors who decide to impose the death penalty upon youthful offenders. The law states that age could be considered as a possible mitigating factor in capital cases. The literature has not established when jurors accept age as a mitigating factor and when they do not. The majority of experts in the disciplines of criminology, sociology, and psychology oppose the death penalty for juveniles. However, research is sparse concerning the reasons for their opinion. In addition, we know little about the effects of sentencing a child to death for society. Investigators need to explore why the majority of the population favors the death penalty when new laws regulating its use for juvenile offenders are not being established.

JUVENILE BOOT CAMP

Introduction

Juvenile boot-camp facilities have become an increasingly popular response to adolescent crime in the United States. Often referred to as shock incarceration, boot camps are based on the premise that instilling regimen and discipline in young offenders will decrease subsequent criminal behavior. Controversy exists as to whether recidivism reduction has actually been achieved with the implementation of boot camps throughout the United States. Some experts argue that the implementation of boot-camp programs does nothing to change the environment from which the juvenile emerges, and, therefore, once the program has ended, the juvenile's return to the same environment perpetuates their engagement in criminal behavior. For this reason, it has been argued that boot-camp facilities do not curb long-term recidivism rates among juvenile offenders. The hypothetical case of Johnny illustrates a common trend among boot-camp participants.

> Johnny is a 16-year-old boy who was recently arrested for the first time. He was caught breaking into a house while under the influence of a controlled substance. Because this was Johnny's first offense, he was sentenced to the local juvenile boot camp which had recently been built in his small town. While at the boot camp, Johnny's day began at 5:00 A.M. and ended at 9:00 P.M. His 16-hour day consisted of rigorous calisthenics, strict discipline, difficult work, job training, and educational programs. Johnny became very comfortable with the routine and was a role-model to new recruits. After 90 days in the boot camp, Johnny was released to his parents. He would remain on probation for the next month, during which time he was not to leave his house except to go to school and meet with his probation officer.
>
> Johnny's first night at home reminded him of what his life was like prior to boot camp. His parents were both intoxicated and began yelling at one another within the first hour Johnny was home. Johnny decided to tell his parents about his experience at boot camp and the changes he intended to make in his life. Johnny's father, irate at his son for interrupting, began to beat Johnny and tell him how worthless he was. The physical and verbal abuse lasted for one hour at which time the neighbors called the police for the disturbance. Johnny, afraid of the police seeing his bloody and bruised body, ran away. The next day Johnny was arrested for violating his probation.

Literature Review

A rapid growth of boot camps for adult offenders evolved in the United States in the 1980s. At the time, there were questions as to whether such programs would be appropriate for youthful offenders. The Office of Juvenile Justice and Delinquency Prevention (OJJDP) sought to explore whether adult boot camps could in fact be adapted to suit the needs of juveniles. The OJJDP funded a study in 1992 to examine three existing boot-camp programs in order to determine the possible adaptations that would be required to make them suitable for juvenile offenders (Bourque et al., 1996). Throughout the 1990s, numerous juvenile boot camps have been developed as an alternative to traditional incarceration.

Boot camp facilities provide a militaristic regimen of strenuous physical conditioning and strict discipline. Specifically, boot camps are intended to provide a cost-effective means of dealing with delinquent youths, instill morality and ethics, strengthen academic achievement, and hold adolescents accountable for their actions while providing them with the tools necessary to prevent reoffense. It is questionable whether boot camps are in fact providing juveniles with the necessary tools to curb recidivism. As illustrated in the case of Johnny, it may not be enough to simply provide these youths with the skills and expect them to leave the boot camp and be able to function in their natural environment.

Peterson (1996) reports that the pilot programs evaluated by the OJJDP reveal that there was no significant difference in recidivism between those in the boot-camp programs and those in control programs. Similarly, in a study conducted by MacKenzie and Souryal (1994), an evaluation of boot-camp programs in eight states revealed that such programs did not reduce recidivism rates for juvenile offenders in five of the eight states investigated. In the three states that did show lower recidivism rates for participants in the boot-camp programs, juveniles were provided intensive follow-up supervision (Reid-MacNevin, 1997).

After examining their meta-analysis, Lundman, 1993; Morash & Rucker, 1990, report that boot camp participants may actually have higher rates of recidivism than those who participate in traditional incarceration. It is difficult to properly determine whether this is due to the increased monitoring that boot-camp graduates receive following their release, thereby increasing their chance for subsequent apprehension. However, supporters of boot-camp facilities suggest that recidivism rates are not appropriate measures of a successful program (Osler, 1991).

Several explanations have been offered describing why boot camps do not have a general effect on recidivism. From a criminological perspective, boot camps are theoretically based on deterrence theory. As noted by Reid-MacNevin (1997), "correctional research has shown time and again that deterrence-based criminal justice interventions do not work" (p. 156). This philosophy of deterrence has been repeatedly tested within the criminal justice system through such programs as Scared Straight. These programs assume that juvenile delinquents can be scared and intimidated into engaging in prosocial behavior and respecting authority (Welch, 1997). Unfortunately, such programs have consistently reported unsuccessful deterrence effects. In 1992, Lipsey conducted a meta-analysis of 443 studies between 1950 and 1992 which revealed that deterrence programs such as boot camps had negative effects on juvenile delinquents. Therefore, research has not only shown that boot camps do not lower the rate of reoffending by juveniles, but more importantly, that youths may be negatively effected by such programs.

From a psychological perspective, research has examined the image of masculinity which is portrayed in boot-camp programs. Morash and Rucker (1990) suggest that the confrontation and demanding nature of boot camps illustrate aggression and thus produce aggressive behavior among participants. This can be explained through social learning theory, which maintains that behavior is acquired through modeling the behavior of others. Such learning is particularly found among adolescents. Therefore, according to Morash and Rucker, the goal of teaching juveniles prosocial behavior is not being achieved in correctional boot camps.

As noted by Correia (1997), boot camps are implemented in an artificial environment and, therefore, any behavioral changes that are made by an offender will most likely not be reinforced when the juvenile returns to his or her natural environment in society. Learning theory maintains that it is essential for a behavior to be performed in one's natural environment for a permanent change in conduct to occur. Furthermore, Correia (1997) explains that criminal behavior is strongly influenced by environmental factors. Thus, if changes are not made to an individual's natural environment, any progress made while at boot camp is unlikely to continue postrelease. In the case of Johnny, it is unlikely that any of his progress made at boot camp will present and sustain itself in his home environment. Within the first 2 hours of being released, Johnny's life returned to what it was prior to his participation in the boot-camp program.

According to Peterson (1996), differences between boot-camp participants and control-group participants did emerge in various arenas. Substantial improvement in academic achievement occurred among participants in the boot-camp program. On average, youths increased their achievement scores in reading, language, spelling, and math by at least one academic grade level. Moreover, a significantly higher number of graduates from the boot-camp program became employed while in aftercare. Aftercare is a dimension of the program that follows one's participation in the residential component of the boot camp and entails stringent monitoring for 6 to 9 months in the community.

In order to ensure maximum effectiveness of boot-camp programs, target populations are selected for participation. The criteria initially established included juvenile males who did not have violent criminal histories. Most juveniles who were selected for such programs had been convicted of property or drug offenses. Therefore, the applicability of boot camps was purposefully limited. The OJJDP maintains that the boot camp focus remains within the rehabilitation model of the juvenile justice system. The lack of positive results emerging from recidivism studies begs the question: Are boot camps truly serving their rehabilitative function?

Forensic Psychology and Policy Implications

Millions of dollars a year are used in funding the development of new boot-camp programs for juvenile offenders each year. With such an investment, it is imperative that programs provide the rehabilitation services they propose. Psychologists have acquired a great deal of knowledge in terms of the family environment and the psychological characteristics of the offender that lead to subsequent delinquency. Given this knowledge, it is apparent that boot-camp programs do not fully address the complexity of the issues involved in juvenile criminality. The environment to which the adolescent will return postrelease from the boot camp is lacking in attention. Developmental theory shows us that children do not adapt well to drastic changes in their environment. This is exactly what occurs when a child does not receive any means of discipline in the home, aside from perhaps physical abuse (as in the case of Johnny), and then is placed in a militaristic, rigid environment for 90 days. When 3 months have elapsed, the child is once again placed in an unstructured environment and expected to maintain the regimen that he or she has "learned." According to behavioral theory, the behavior will not generalize to the natural environment because the ecological cues are completely different and the person's conduct is neither required nor reinforced. For these reasons, it appears that psychologists can provide a great deal of insight into the methods for improving existing boot-camp programs; this would allow for the comprehensive impact of environmental influences on human behavior and child development. Furthermore, criminal justice research has illustrated for years that programs based on deterrence are not effective in reducing recidivism. With the vast amount of literature supporting this notion, policy makers should question why millions of dollars continue to be spent to build new boot camp facilities. Such programs have yet to prove they decrease juvenile recidivism. Indeed, at times, they have deleterious effects on adolescents.

Suggestions for Future Research

Outcome studies would provide a more thorough understanding of the lasting effects of boot camp placement on subsequent offending. Future research would do well to focus on which aspects of existing boot camp programs are working and which are not. In some instances, academic achievement increases among those who participate in boot camps. However, there are no studies examining the psychological well-being of the children when they enter as opposed to when they leave the program. Moreover, no studies exist assessing whether strict militaristic discipline has any negative psychological effects on children's self-esteem or self-worth. Finally, future research needs to explore potential program development including a family and community reunification component so that situations such as Johnny's can be better addressed.

SUICIDE AMONG INCARCERATED JUVENILES

Introduction

Suicide claims the lives of thousands of adolescents each year. Currently, suicide is the third leading cause of death among youths. Moreover, it is important to note that for every adolescent who completes suicide, hundreds of others attempt it. Among the youths at high risk for suicide are those who are incarcerated. The isolation, despair, guilt, and hopelessness felt by many incarcerated juveniles is portrayed through suicidal ideation, nonfatal self-injurious behavior, and, ultimately, the desperate act of taking one's own life. The research and clinical intervention concerning life-threatening behavior among incarcerated juveniles is relatively sparse. The link between delinquency and suicide, as well as between incarceration and suicide, has been clearly documented in the literature. However, currently there are no concentrated efforts to address this issue in terms of prevention or intervention measures. The following cases illustrate the gravity of the situation, depicting both a male and female juvenile who resorted to suicide while incarcerated.

> Within 1 year at Westchester County Jail in New York City, two juveniles committed suicide while incarcerated. Nancy Blumenthal was 17 years old when she hanged herself in her cell from her own bedsheet. She was being held in jail while she awaited trial for robbery charges. Her bail had been revoked. Nancy was placed on a suicide watch while she participated in a court-ordered psychiatric evaluation. Following the evaluation, she was placed in the psychiatric ward where she could be observed every 30 minutes. During the investigation of her suicide, it was discovered that Nancy had been taking the antidepressant Zoloft for 2 years prior to her incarceration. During her month in jail, however, she was taken off of the drug.
>
> Ivan Figueroa was another 17-year-old who committed suicide in the same jail within 3 months of Nancy's death. Similarly to Nancy, Ivan hanged himself in his jail cell. He had been in jail for 4 days and was awaiting trial for rape and assault charges. When he was first arrested, he too was placed on a suicide watch. He was subsequently returned to the general inmate population and soon committed suicide (Anonymous, 1997).

Literature Review

Cases like Nancy's and Ivan's remind us that suicide among incarcerated juveniles exists, needs to be examined and, ultimately, prevented. Adolescent suicide in general has been a focal point of research over the past 2 decades. As a result of such close scrutiny, the mental health field is far better equipped to assess, treat, and prevent suicidal behavior than ever before. It appears, however, that examination of suicidal behavior occurring among incarcerated juveniles is a particular concern that has not received a great deal of research attention. Incarcerated adolescents have unique environmental, social, and interpersonal factors that render them especially susceptible to suicidal ideation and behavior. Yet, as the literature illustrates, this population has not been studied nor has it received the amount of clinical intervention for suicide as has the general adolescent population.

The alarming suicide rate among adolescents has resulted in considerable research regarding the incidence, prevalence, and causes of life-threatening behavior. According to the National Center for Health Statistics (1997), adolescent suicide has more than tripled in the past 3 decades. Some studies incorporate individuals ages 15–24 in their investigations of adolescent suicide. Padgitt (1997) states that within this age group, there are approximately 10,000 reported teen suicides a year and estimates that there are between 100,000 and 200,000 adolescent suicide attempts annually. Further, others note that every 78 seconds an adolescent attempts suicide and every 90 seconds one succeeds (National Center for Health Statistics, 1996). Research has repeatedly shown that boys are far more likely than girls to complete suicide; however, there is little gender difference in terms of suicidal ideation.

Although there is extensive research regarding adolescent suicide, there is relatively little research conducted on suicide among adjudicated adolescents (Evans, Albers, Macari, & Mason, 1996). Within the existing literature, there are conflicting results regarding the prevalence of suicide among incarcerated juveniles. Some suggest that one reason for this may be due to the underreporting of such occurrences by detention facility officials (Flaherty, 1983). Flaherty notes that it is a sensitive and embarrassing issue for officials to discuss, particularly when suicides occur within their facilities. Therefore, many results are skewed in the direction of underestimating the incidence rate.

A distinction needs to be made between completed suicide and parasuicide. Completed suicide refers to the suicidal act resulting in an individual's death, whereas parasuicide refers to nonfatal intentional self-harm. Research has shown that younger inmates are more vulnerable to parasuicide (Ivanoff, Jang, & Smyth, 1996). Others suggest that an increase in the incidence of parasuicide among younger inmates may be attributed to impulsivity (G. L. Brown, Linnoila, & Goodwin, 1992). One study reported that in a sample of 11,000 juveniles in detention facilities, 18,000 acts of attempted suicide, suicidal gestures, or self-mutilation occurred within the institution.

Previous research has linked delinquency to physical and sexual abuse (Albers & Evans, 1994; de Wilde, Kienhorst, Diekstra, & Wolters, 1992). More specifically, studies have reported that incarcerated juveniles are at an increased risk for suicide due to their high incidence of substance abuse as well as physical and sexual abuse (Battle, Battle, & Tolley, 1993). In a study conducted by Evans *et al.* (1996), no difference was found between gang and nongang members in terms of reported physical abuse; however, nongang members reported higher levels of suicidal ideation. In this same study, gang members who had a history of sexual abuse had higher levels of suicidal ideation than their nongang counterparts.

Contrary to the previously mentioned research, results have emerged which conclude that incarcerated juveniles are at less risk for suicide. Flaherty (1983) reported that youths in juvenile detention facilities committed suicide at a lower rate than adolescents in the general population. However, this study also reported that juveniles detained in adult jails were at a far greater risk for completing suicide. Flaherty found that 17 of the 21 suicides were committed by youths who were held in adult jails in complete isolation. This was clearly the situation in the case illustration of Kathy Robbins. As demonstrated by this section's case examples, the most common means of committing suicide among incarcerated juveniles is hanging.

Several characteristics distinguish young offender suicides from the general population of inmate suicides. A study by Liebling (1993) revealed that youthful inmates were more likely to commit suicide after their conviction, but prior to their sentencing. Most suicides among the young inmates occurred during the first month of custody. Additionally, Liebling concluded that young inmates who committed suicide were less likely to have ever received psychiatric treatment.

Previous research found that Caucasian delinquents made more serious and lethal suicide attempts than African American delinquents or delinquents of mixed ethnicity (Alessi, McManus, Brickman, & Grapentine, 1984). Alessi *et al.* further reported that offenders diagnosed with major affective disorders or borderline personality disorders attempted suicide at a much greater rate. These results are consistent with suicidal behavior among individuals suffering from these disorders in the general population. Wool and Dooley (1987) reported the explanations given by younger inmates who attempted suicide while in custody. The most frequent explanations included a close relationship was threatened, a visit did not take place, and the prison environment was intolerable. When these adolescent needs are not fulfilled, many youths enter a state of emotional crisis. Sometimes this manifests itself as a cry for help or self-injury, other times the child literally escapes from the crisis through the desperate act of suicide.

Forensic Psychology and Policy Implications

Juvenile suicide is a tragic end to a young life. Psychologists have studied the predictors and the reasons for suicide for many years. Specific studies have been conducted on adolescent suicide and how it differs from its adult counterpart, as well as on subgroups of adolescents who are at a greater risk for suicide. The research clearly draws a link between delinquency and suicide as well as incarceration and suicide. It should be of no surprise that a combination of delinquency and incarceration places a youth at high risk for suicidal ideation and behavior. In the case of Nancy and Ivan, the two suicides committed within 3 months of one another should alert correctional facilities, mental health agencies, and the public to the severity of suicidal behavior among incarcerated juveniles.

Within the field of psychology there is an increased awareness of suicide prevention strategies and an ability to implement crisis intervention with suicidal individuals. If incarcerated youths are at such a high risk for suicide, why is little being done to prevent such occurrences? Relying on the results of empirical studies, we find that specific youths can be identified who are particularly vulnerable. We also know that adolescents who commit suicide while incarcerated often do so within the first month of custody. Thus, in order to provide the necessary preventative measures, these individuals need to be identified and given counseling and crisis intervention as soon as they arrive in custody. When dealing with a human life and, in particular, a young vulnerable life, the focus must be on addressing the problem of suicidality before it occurs. Society places a strong emphasis on research and intervention with suicidal individuals, yet virtually ignores the issue of suicide among incarcerated adolescents. This suggests that some believe that the lost life of an incarcerated youth does not equal that of a nonincarcerated youth. As long as this bias exists, so too will the problem of suicide among incarcerated adolescents.

Suggestions for Future Research

Over the past 3 decades, research on adolescent suicide in the general population has expanded; however, relatively scant research exists which examines suicidal ideation and behavior among incarcerated adolescents. Suicide prevention programs need to be designed and implemented in juvenile detention facilities. Moreover, these programs need to be empirically studied in order to determine the proper method of identifying those individuals in need, as well as the location and time for the prevention program to be most beneficial. Incarcerated settings for juveniles that have crisis intervention and regular psychological services need to be compared with those that do not offer such assistance. Furthermore, studying the similarities and differences among adolescents who attempt or commit suicide within an incarceration facility with those who engage in suicidal behavior in the community would help provide a more thorough understanding of what treatment needs best serve this vulnerable population.

INCARCERATION OF STATUS OFFENDERS

Introduction

According to the Federal Bureau of Investigation's 1994 Uniform Crime Report, approximately 237,000 juveniles under the age of 18 were arrested for status offenses. A status offense is any offense that is committed by a juvenile that would not constitute an offense if committed by an adult. Examples of such offenses include running away from home, curfew violation, truancy from school, and out-of-parental-control. In 1994, approximately 152,000 children were arrested for running away from home. With the great number of juveniles engaging in this behavior, the question that arises is whether these children are better dealt with through the juvenile justice system or by mental health professionals. Historically, the criminal justice system has dealt with status offenders in the same manner in which other juvenile offenders have been handled. For this reason, juveniles who run away from home are oftentimes incarcerated in the same secure detention facilities as juveniles who commit more serious and violent crimes. However, by definition, status offenders have no victims, and in fact their crimes would not even be illegal except by a function of the individual's age. Many in the mental health profession believe that a more appropriate method of dealing with status offenders is to provide psychological services to the juvenile and to his or her family as opposed to incarceration. Congress has enacted laws which require the deinstitutionalization of status offenders; however, despite such movements, thousands of juveniles continue to be incarcerated for status offenses.

Johnny is 13 years old and currently lives with a foster family. He was 8 years old when his parents were divorced, at which time he decided to reside with his mother. When Johnny was 10, his mother remarried, and he suddenly had a stepfather, Derek. Within the first 2 months of living in the same house, Derek began entering Johnny's room in the middle of the night. Derek sodomized and forced Johnny to orally copulate him an average of three times a week for the next 3 years. After years of enduring such abuse, Johnny ran away from home. Johnny was arrested not even 1 mile away from his home, where he was sitting behind a vacant store. Johnny spent 2 weeks in juvenile hall. Like most children who are sexually abused, Johnny was too frightened to tell anyone about the molestation. Upon release from juvenile hall, Johnny was returned home to his mother and stepfather. One week after Johnny returned home, Derek began the molestations again. Johnny ran away from home two more times before he disclosed the abuse. On each occasion, he was arrested and incarcerated in juvenile hall. Following his report of the molestation, a medical exam was conducted which confirmed Johnny's story. Johnny was removed from his home and placed in foster care, where he remains today.

Literature Review

Johnny's case illustrates the complex psychological dynamics that are involved in the lives of many status offenders. The critical issue for forensic psychologists to address is whether juveniles like Johnny are more appropriately dealt with as delinquents or victims of child abuse. With juvenile crime occurring at an alarming rate in the United States, the legislature and the public are increasingly more inclined to deliver stiffer sentences to juvenile offenders. However, perhaps it is wholly inappropriate to apply a blanket approach to the punishment of adolescent offenders.

The literature surrounding the incarceration of status offenders is extremely scant. The research in this area was conducted primarily in the 1980s. Gary Melton spoke on behalf of the American Psychological Association in 1991, during which time he stated "a search of the PsychLit database failed to uncover a single article on status offenses or status offenders published after 1988" (Melton *et al.*, 1997, p. 438). He suggests that the real issue at hand is a lack of services available to families and troubled youths. Melton concluded his testimony by suggesting that petitions to incarcerate status offenders "are clear exemplars of blaming the victim—subjecting a child who already may have a traumatic history to a quasi-punitive process because of a lack of adequate services" (Melton *et al.*, 1997, p. 439).

Thus, given the dearth of recent research, this review of the literature relies on somewhat dated material. An historical analysis of status offenders reveals that around 1960, New York and California amended their statutes concerning juvenile delinquents in order to differentiate between delinquents and status offenders (Zatz, 1982). At that time it was acknowledged that status offenders were more in need of community-based programs designed to address psychological issues; however, such programs were not established. In 1974, the Juvenile Justice and Delinquency Prevention (JJDP) Act further addressed the issue of dealing with status offenders in the juvenile justice system. According to this Act, states were not allowed to incarcerate status offenders in secure juvenile detention facilities. Yet the Illinois courts strongly supported the incarceration of status offenders as evidenced by the decision in *People v. Presley* (1974). In this decision the court concluded that due to *parens patriae*, the state has the authority to incarcerate children who run away from home. It was not until 1992, with the amendments to the JJDP Act, that status offenders were removed from juvenile court jurisdiction altogether. It should be noted that now, almost 25 years after the JJDP Act was passed, approximately 27% of status offenders continue to be held in secure detention facilities (Krisberg & DeComo, 1993).

In addition to the psychological and criminological debate regarding the treatment of status offenders, is the economic controversy. McIntyre (1996) studied the number of status-offender petitions that were filed over the past 20 years. She reported that there was a 54% decline in status petitions from 1979 to 1995, and that such a reduction saved the American taxpayers approximately 6 million dollars. However, although the decrease in status-offender petitions is cost effective, it remains questionable whether the needs of these juveniles are being addressed. Among those who fought for a distinction between status offenders and delinquents, it was hoped that specific treatment programs would be developed in order to better meet the psychological needs of status offenders (Zatz, 1982). Linney (1982) examined the alternatives to incarceration that have been offered for status offenders. In terms of counseling services availed to these offenders, Linney found that all of the programs reported that counseling was available to the juveniles. Upon closer examination, however, the definition and frequency of counseling varied across programs. For instance, in certain programs, any time a social worker spoke with a juvenile "counseling" took place. Furthermore, when individual counseling was provided, Linney determined that it centered around helping the juvenile adjust to the residential placement, and once this was accomplished, the counseling ceased. It is clear from Linney's study that although community-based programs do exist for status offenders as alternatives to incarceration, they are extremely lacking in terms of the treatment they provide.

Eighty-four percent of the facilities examined in Linney's (1982) study reported the juveniles' families as being the primary causal factor in the commission of status offenses. Similarly, as noted by Melton *et al.* (1997), the behaviors of status offenders are oftentimes attributable to psychological dysfunction within one's family. With this in mind, it is necessary to treat juveniles as troubled youths in need of psychological services. As seen in the case illustration of Johnny, his running away was clearly a function of the abuse that he suffered at home as opposed to the development of a criminal lifestyle. However, if individuals such as Johnny continue to be placed among violent juvenile offenders in detention facilities, it is likely that they will be influenced by the delinquent behavior of their peers. Adolescence is a time when individuals are highly impressionable, and the influences of those with whom juveniles come into contact play a critical role in the shaping of their future behavior (Chance, 1988). Therefore, in addition to the specific psychological needs of status offenders, the removal of these delinquents from juvenile detention facilities is offered as a means to curb their recidivism. The current trend, however, is either to incarcerate the individual, despite laws which prohibit such action, or to place the juvenile in a residential program in which treatment supposedly exists, although the nature and extent of the treatment is extremely deficient.

Forensic Psychology and Policy Implications

There are a number of policy implications regarding the incarceration and handling of status offenders. It is clear that the Juvenile Justice and Delinquency Prevention Act established in 1974 sought to end the incarceration of status offenders in detention facilities. Moreover, the Act encouraged viewing status offenders and delinquents separately in that status offenders were troubled youths in need of special services, while delinquents were those in need of punishment for committing criminal behaviors. It is particularly telling that, although a law exists which mandates the deinstitutionalization of status offenders from secure detention facilities, approximately one in four status offenders remains incarcerated. The fact that the federal government's legislation is not being carried out illustrates that significant policy reforms are needed. Moreover, the purpose of deinstitutionalizing status offenders was to provide the special psychological services these individual youths needed. Research has shown that even when deinstitutionalization is successfully implemented, the treatment services are severely lacking. Thus, it appears that the JJDP Act has not been successful in accomplishing its desired goals for status offenders.

Suggestions for Future Research

Recent psychological and criminological literature in the area of status offenders, and specifically regarding the incarceration of status offenders, is relatively sparse. Studies need to be conducted comparing status offenders who receive treatment with those who do not. A shared goal among those who oppose and those who support the incarceration of status offenders is the reduction of future offenses. With this in mind comparative studies are essential to making a determination about what action best curbs recidivism. In a similar fashion, those status offenders who have been incarcerated need to be evaluated against those who have not, particularly in terms of subsequent commission of offenses. Recidivism among status offenders needs to be explored in a twofold manner. Those who reoffend with subsequent status offenses need to be compared to those who subsequently commit more serious or violent offenses. An additional area of research pertains to the families of status offenders. Most individuals within the mental health and criminal justice fields who come into contact with status offenders agree that dysfunctional families play a central role in the juveniles' behaviors. It therefore becomes crucial to develop and implement comprehensive programs designed to address the specific needs of a particular dysfunctional family. Once these programs are in place, it will then be possible to compare the recidivism rates of those juveniles who participate in such programs with those who receive other sentences.

CHAPTER 11

Civic Forensics

OVERVIEW

Psychologists are called upon to address a myriad of problems that directly affect the adult and juvenile prison populations. In addition, though, psychologists are relied upon to assess other correctional dilemmas regarding the intellectual, personality, and behavioral characteristics of offenders and those who work in the institutions, as well as to interpret society's responses to particular offender groups and general correctional practices. This is the domain of civil forensics and corrections. Unlike its adult and juvenile counterparts, the civil forensic field explores many of the social variables that inform noncriminal inmate behavior, ongoing prison practices, and the public's responses to both.

This chapter includes six topical themes, representing of the breadth of the civil forensic field. It is not possible to present a complete and thorough cataloging of issues and/or controversies contained in this subspeciality area. However, those subjects examined in the pages that follow include some of the more interesting and pressing concerns at the interface of corrections, psychology, and civil justice. Topics investigated include (1) psychological stress and correctional work, (2) community corrections, (3) mentally disabled prisoners, (4) society's response to sex offenders, (5) women working in male prisons, and (6) inmate sexuality.

The conditions under which correctional work occurs are emotionally and physically demanding. Symptoms of chronic fatigue, depression, cynicism, burnout, and the like are non uncommon for many correctional officers. What is the psychological impact of work-related stress for correctional personnel? How do employees cope with it, and what prevention and intervention programs exist to curb the excesses of stress? There are several forms of community corrections. House arrest, electronic monitoring, intensive supervision probation, and work release are just a few of them. What impact do these initiatives have for communities, particularly in relation to their perceived (or real) concerns for personal safety and/or household security? What is the NIMBY effect, and what roles exist for forensic practitioners to address it? A representative minority of prisoners are mentally retarded. How are the rehabilitative and retributive philosophies of corrections managed for prisoners with mentally disabilities? What special services and/or programs exist for mentally retarded inmates? How are prisoners screened and assessed for mental retardation, and what role exists for correctional psychologists to assist in the evaluation process? A number of societal responses have been proposed to address the problems posed by convicted sex offenders. Some of these include chemical castration, community notification, civil commitment, and formalized registration. How, if at all, do these interventions prevent future victimization? What is the relationship between these societal responses and recidivism? Do proposals such as these violate the constitutional rights of sex offenders who paid their debt to society? Increasingly, women correctional officers work in male prisons. How are such officers perceived by their male correctional officer counterparts? How do women COs cope with the hostility, sexual harassment, and discrimination they experience on the job? How do female COs cope with the stress of working in male prisons? Inmate sexuality is not necessarily the same outside the confines of the penal institution. What are the definitions of inmate homosexuality? Are all prison homosexuals gay/lesbian outside the facility as well? What are the roles and functions of nonheterosexuality in prison?

The domain of civil forensics and corrections moves the psychologist into a more social arena in which to investigate noncriminal behavior, attitudes, beliefs, and so on pertaining to prisoners, correctional personnel, institutional practices, and the public's responses to them. As the sections of this chapter disclose, we know very little about the civil domain of correctional psychology. Future investigators would do well to engage in research along these and similar lines of inquiry as it would substantially advance our knowledge of prisoners, correctional workers, and society's understanding of offender behavior.

PSYCHOLOGICAL STRESS AND CORRECTIONAL WORK

Introduction

The American Heritage Dictionary defines stress as "a mentally or emotionally disruptive or disquieting influence" (Berube, 1982, p. 1205). This definition does not fully describe the types of stress that correctional officers experience on a day-to-day basis. They are under continual threat of physical danger. They experience hostility from the inmates and often the public. They respond to political changes in attitudes toward the role of institutional corrections. They work daily in a tedious and unrewarding environment. Finally, they completely depend on their coworkers to provide for their safety (Grossi & Berg, 1991). Working in such an atmosphere every day can lead to some very debilitating consequences, including depression, chronic fatigue, physical illness, and even Posttraumatic Stress Disorder (PTSD). The following illustration describes a stressful situation that officers often must face.

> The day began like any other at the prison. The day staff came in and were briefed on any problems or incidents of which they needed to be aware, and then they began their duties of moving the prisoners through their daily routines. After a few hours, when the work was becoming tedious and the guards began to relax, three inmates attacked a guard walking by and managed to get his gun away from him. They used him as a hostage and demanded that the other guards give up their guns. The officers had to comply to avoid having their coworker killed. The inmates were able to gain control of the prison unit by holding approximately 30 employees hostage. The guards that were able to avoid becoming hostages locked themselves in the administrative offices but could not escape from the prison. This highly intense and stressful situation lasted for over 2 hours with the officers under constant fear for their lives. The incident ended without any serious injuries but with a great deal of property damage (Bergmann & Queen, 1987). The officers who had to endure this hostage situation were exposed to a type of stress that most people will never experience in their lifetime. Even the officers that were not held hostage felt the effects of the stress because they had to return to work in this environment wondering if such an incident might happen again.

Literature Review

Although the above illustration is a severe example, it represents the type of stressful situation that correctional officers are potentially faced with and must learn to accept as part of their job. Research shows that most correctional officers do feel this stress. In a study that asked officers to rate their levels of day-to-day job-related stress, only 26.2% reported feeling low levels of stress. Most of the officers experienced medium to high levels of stress every day, with 10.0% reporting very high levels of work stress (Robinson, 1992). Generally, the type of stress that officers experience is related to the work that they do; that is, guarding the inmates. With overcrowded prisons, officers have a more difficult time controlling inmates, especially when the inmates know that they will be there for a long time and do not fear punishment (Martinez, 1997). The case illustration shows how it is possible for prisoners to become uncontrollable just by outnumbering the guards. Robinson (1992) reported that the most frequently cited source of stress by correctional officers is related to security. Twenty-seven percent of the officers reported a fear of offenders and a lack of security procedures. Their second and third most reported sources of stress were a lack of communication in the prison and a heavy workload. In addition Robinson determined that officers' job commitment was affected by stress. He found that officers who reported higher levels of work-related stress had lower levels of commitment to their jobs.

Martinez (1997) states that there are two different types of stress that correctional officers experience in the course of their duties. The first was described in the previous case illustration. This was an episodic stressor where a traumatic incident happened to or was witnessed by a guard. The other type of stress is what the author refers to as chronic stress. This is stress that officers encounter every day. It is the routine of doing the same thing over and over. This can be very damaging psychologically if the officers do not have the appropriate abilities to deal with it. It may even lead to a psychological disability. For example, in the case of *Fasanaro v. County of Rockland* (1995), the petitioner was a correctional officer who began to suffer from a stress-related disability. The doctor who evaluated him indicated that the pressures from his job had become too much for him and recommended that the officer take a leave of absence. This case arose because he was denied disability benefits. The court ruled in favor of the correctional officer and stated that if stress exists at work, then any stress-related anxiety disorders and disabilities can be causally related to the job and the employee should be allowed to collect Worker's Compensation.

A stress-related anxiety disorder is just one possible consequence for correctional officers. A more serious consequence may be suicide. Kamerman (1995) found that speaking about correctional-officer suicide is a taboo. After examining New York City statistics for a 5-year period, he reported that correctional-officer suicides were at least as great a problem as police suicides, and that the number of suicides were most likely greater than what was actually reported. In little over a year, a correctional facility in New York had three guards commit suicide. Kamerman proposed that the overcrowded prisons and the building of new facilities without the necessary funding for additional correctional officers will only increase the pressures faced by these personnel. Kamerman further indicated that the lack of research on officer suicides reflects the public's diminished concern for the stress that correctional guards confront. However, clearly, the effects will continue to manifest themselves in extreme ways such as mental disability and suicide.

The traumatic events occasionally experienced by correctional officers, as in the case illustration, can also have debilitating consequences. Bergmann and Queen (1987) report that there are three characteristics which must be present for an event to be traumatic. There must be an extremely high level of stress, a denial of the importance of the event or a shock-like response, and a normal set of feelings or consequences following the event. They labeled this normal set of feelings as an acute stress response where individuals may withdraw from important people and activities, reexperience the event through flashbacks, feel depressed, have sleep difficulties and nightmares, feel anxious and hypervigilant, feel guilty, and have difficulty returning to work.

Davis (1995) also described stress related to traumatic incidents. He described a traumatic incident as being a routine day where suddenly a fight breaks out among the inmates, and one inmate cuts the other in the neck and creates a gaping wound with blood spraying everywhere. According to the author, possible consequences for the guards are confusion, sweating, depression, anger, grief, and changes in eating and sleeping behaviors. Both Bergmann and Queen (1987) and Davis (1995) identified long-term side effects from stress, including alcoholism, divorce, unemployment, violent relationships, and suicide if the correctional officers did not receive appropriate mental health services.

These traumatic incidents can also cause Posttraumatic Stress Disorder in certain employees. In the case of *Wertz v. Workmen's Compensation Appeal Board* (1996), the plaintiff worked at a prison during a prison riot. He suffered PTSD and was awarded total disability benefits. When he returned to a modified duty position at the prison, his PTSD symptoms began to increase again, forcing him to leave his job permanently. Despite the fact that there were no riots when he returned to work, he was still awarded disability payments because his psychological stress was related to the workplace.

Although many studies have examined the nature and extent of stress experienced by correctional officers, few have researched ways to reduce this stress. As can be seen from the Worker's Compensation lawsuits, stress can have some serious consequences and lead to additional expenses for institutions. A study that did examine methods for reducing stress researched the benefits of exercise programs for correctional officers (Kiely & Hodgson, 1990). The authors found that the exercise programs were a success, although they relied on self-reports for their data. The staff was able to see how they benefitted from the exercise programs and therefore were in favor of them. They reported higher staff morale, improved attitudes, increased confidence, and greater physical fitness which improved resistance to stress. The authors did find that correctional officers had a difficult time recognizing stress in themselves or others and therefore concluded that heightening their awareness of potential stressors along with preventative actions such as exercise would be the best way to minimize the negative consequences of stress. Their overall findings revealed the benefits of physical fitness as a way of reducing stress and aiding guards in overcoming the effects of stress-related illnesses.

Another variable that intuitively would seem to reduce stress is peer support. However, Grossi and Berg (1991) found that peer support actually increased work stress. They hypothesized that in a prison setting, correctional officers may have to compromise their personal values and integrity in order to obtain peer support, particularly when overlooking infractions made by other officers. This would produce in more feelings of stress instead of less. It may be that other forms of support could be stress reducing, such as the role of administration or family support. However, these variables were not examined in this study.

Forensic Psychology and Policy Implications

After examining the effects that stress has on correctional officers, it is clear that programs need to be developed to help them handle work tension before they burn out. One type of program that has received a considerable amount of attention is critical incident stress debriefing. This is a stage method whereby individuals are taken back through the incident to explore their thoughts and feelings with one another regarding the incident. The group processing of such a fact-finding–thinking–feeling model, combined with relaxation training as well as individual counseling aimed at reducing flashbacks of the incident, can help prevent the development of PTSD or assist in reducing the intensity of the experience (McWhirter & Linzer, 1994). According to "Battle Staff Burnout" (1997), critical incident stress debriefing with correctional staff should be done within 1 or 2 days after the event and should include all personnel. The article also recommended creating a policy for debriefing that includes the following points: clear definitions of debriefing, an outline of what critical incidents would require debriefing, rules of confidentiality, and an outline of responsibilities.

Other recommendations for preventing long-term consequences of traumatic stress were outlined by Bergmann and Queen (1987). Departments should organize their response before a traumatic incident occurs. Psychological responses of survivors should be included in the policies and procedures for handling prison disturbances. Departments should make sure that posttrauma services are only provided by qualified and trained staff. Finally, creative ways must be found to finance posttrauma services.

Another important policy matter that needs to be addressed is correctional officer suicide. Training programs need to be implemented to handle all officers' confrontations with death. There should be institutional training for suicide prevention focused on guards and inmates. The gains from such training initiatives could extend beyond suicide prevention (Kamerman, 1995).

A final policy consideration for correctional officer stress is funding. As mentioned previously, with overcrowded prisons and the building of new facilities, correctional staff have not been able to keep up with the growth. Instead of funneling more funds into building prisons, attention needs to be placed on providing services for correctional officers, including adequate numbers of staff. The problem of crime is not going to disappear with the addition of new prisons, but the problem of stress-related disease and disability could be greatly reduced if correctional officers were to receive the appropriate mental health services.

Suggestions for Future Research

The major area in which research is lacking concerns the benefits of stress-reduction programs for correctional officers. Although exercise was found to decrease stress and provide additional advantages, a more rigorous empirical study needs to be conducted. This could take a holistic approach examining ways to create healthy workplaces in terms of overall organizational structure, as well as expanding personal coping mechanisms such as the exercise programs (Kiely & Hodgson, 1990). Also, a more systematic study of critical-incident stress-debriefing programs, including follow-up investigations (McWhirter & Linzer, 1994) and their direct applications in a correctional setting, would provide further evidence that such programs are beneficial. Other creative ways for reducing the job-related stress of institutional work need to be examined. Finally, more research must be conducted on correctional officer suicide (Kamerman, 1995). This could foster a better understanding of the causes of it and the effects suicide has on those left to deal with it.

COMMUNITY CORRECTIONS

Introduction

The issue of correctional facilities and community programming is a controversial one when viewed from the perspective of the everyday citizen. People differ in their beliefs about the goals of sentencing. Some believe that it should be strictly about punishment while others believe that there should be an element of treatment. Regardless of viewpoint, when the issue of where sentencing should take place arises, the public usually does not want it in their "backyard." This creates many problems in today's society because crime rates are rising, causing an increase in prison populations, which leads to a greater need for correctional facilities (K. A. Carlson, 1992).

Proposing a site for a new prison can produce adverse emotional responses from local residents, creating difficulties and delays for states and counties in building new facilities. Yet there is more involved than just building prisons. With the increase in alternative sentencing, given overcrowded prisons, community corrections are suggested, causing concern for citizens. Community corrections involve programs such as house arrest, electronic monitoring, intensive supervision probation, group homes, and work/study release. These programs put the offender into the community with no bars holding them in or guards watching over them. Agencies that want to implement such programs in the community must obtain support from the public if they are going to succeed. This can be a very hostile and treacherous process. If all does not go well, then problems can arise later, as portrayed in the following illustration.

> Susan runs three group homes for adolescent sex offenders in a mid-size city with a highly conservative population and an increasingly high crime rate. The group homes are each located in ordinary-looking houses in residential neighborhoods. In accordance with the law, Susan informed everyone within a mile radius of the intention of these group homes. She faced some opposition from residents in these neighborhoods, but not enough to prevent the project from going forward. George, who is raising two young girls, resides in the neighborhood of one group home. He was strongly opposed to this home being placed in his neighborhood for fear that the boys would harm his daughters. He tried to start a petition to prevent it from happening, but he could not raise enough signatures. The juvenile detention centers were becoming so overcrowded that the state needed alternative sentencing options for juvenile offenders. The possibility of three new group homes in the area provided such options, hence defeating

any opposition the public might raise. George finally acquiesced because he felt he was promised by the various players involved in running the group home that the boys would be monitored 24 hours a day and would not be permitted free access into the rest of the neighborhood.

Once the group home began its operations, George noted that everyday there were at least two boys that walked to a nearby bus stop by themselves. He never saw an adult supervisor with them. They also returned to the group home in the afternoons by themselves. George was enraged at discovering this because he felt that he was promised something just so he would go along with the project. But now, the promise was never going to happen. This is when George began his relentless attempts to have the group home removed from his neighborhood. He continually monitored the premises for any suspicious or illegal activities, and he frequently contacted the police in order to lodge complaints about "problematic" activities in which the boys were engaged. Susan must respond to each of these complaints with an investigation of the boys' activities followed by a report to the local police. This often takes up a great deal of time and energy for Susan. She wonders what happened to cause George to become so hostile when he agreed in the beginning to allow the group home into his neighborhood.

Literature Review

In the group home illustration, Susan was the only person who seemed to have something significant to lose if the project fell through. Frequently, especially when a prison is involved, there are many people who have a stake in the outcome. Pagel (as cited in K. A. Carlson, 1992) indicates that entire communities, especially rural ones, actually want to have facilities built nearby, given their poor economies. The town needs a large operation, such as a prison, to provide employment, commercial activity, and inmate labor (Lidman, as cited in K. A. Carlson, 1992). Carlson provides an example of this with the Clallam Bay Corrections Center.

Clallam Bay was a small community which recently had a large timber company shut down, leaving high unemployment and emigration from the town. Once the prison moved in, there was improvement in the economy and an increase in the population. The benefits did not come without consequences though, as crime rates escalated, causing residents to worry about their safety. Also, the process of building the prison met with opposition and created frustration with the local citizens, much like the situation with George and Susan.

The first problem arose with naming the prison. The residents of the community had come to an agreement with those in charge of the facility operation not to name it after the town. However, because of communication difficulties the person in charge of naming the prison, unaware of this agreement, named it Clallam Bay Corrections Center. This caused a great deal of resistance by the community, refusing to cooperate with the process. Another major problem arose when many of the local residents were not qualified for jobs the prison was offering. Considering the high unemployment rate in this town, new jobs were a major reason for residential support. A final concern voiced by the community was inmate escapes—a common reason for citizens to oppose local prisons. In its first year of existence, Clallam Bay

Corrections Center had five escapes. Citizen anxiety rose because tracking down these prisoners was not handled well by local law enforcement.

All of these problems, stemming from the placment of a prison into a community, led to several consequences. Employees of the prison were not welcomed into the community; therefore, they established residencies in other communities. There were also arguments and physical confrontations between residents and employees of the prison at local facilities. In addition, employee turnover was high at the prison, in part fueled by the tensions in the community. Finally, long-time residents of Clallam Bay moved away from the town, citing concerns generated by the new prison. K. A. Carlson (1992) points out that "the institution cannot separate itself from its locale, and community problems will have institutional consequences" (p. 67). She also states that in order for a community to accept a prison, the public must believe that the benefits will outweigh the deficits, as they will perceive any assurances made as promises, even if they are not in writing. This is exactly what happened with George. He thought a promise was made that the boys would be under 24-hour supervision, and when he discovered that they were not, he became hostile toward the group home. With the Clallam Bay example, the residents perceived several promises of which none were kept.

Prisons are not the only operations that require community support. Community-based programs must also find supporters within local enclaves. The notion of community corrections began in the late 1970s as an alternative to prison, given a desire for neighborhood-based care instead of institutional treatment. This shift created a negative response by communities and led to active efforts to prevent group homes and the like. (P. Solomon, 1983). At their inception, community programs were less expensive than prisons and seemed to lead to lower recidivism rates, although more refined studies question the latter notion (Sigler & Lamb, 1995). Elrod and Brown (1996) state that "successful implementation of community correctional programs is frequently dependent on either the tacit or overt approval of citizens who are often reluctant to accept offenders within their community" (p. 462). Researchers believe that lack of public support can even harm the ability of community corrections programs to reintegrate offenders.

Although criminal offenders are not the only population requiring community programs, they are among the least acceptable populations, along with troubled adolescents, the mentally ill, and alcohol and drug abusers according to residents. Several reasons for opposing homes for such groups include fears of making the neighborhood more dangerous, worries that these individuals would bother residents, and dislike of such persons or groups in family neighborhoods (P. Solomon, 1983). Other reasons found were fear of a reduction in property values and increased traffic in the neighborhood (Arens, 1993; Cook, 1997; Wahl, 1993).

In several studies examining residential attitudes about group homes located in neighborhoods, it was found that none of the expressed fears occurred and that community members actually experienced no problems with the group home. Arens (1993) found that although over one-third of respondents initially perceived the group home as a negative addition, only 2% felt that way at the time of report. Once the residents actually had experience with a group home in their neighborhood, they felt that its residence made good neighbors. They also found that property values were not affected by the existence of a group home, as people had no problems selling their homes. Wahl (1993) also learned that residents who lived near a group home found the experience satisfactory and reported no impact on initial fears concerning traffic, property values, crime, and neighborhood appearance. In fact, more than one-quarter of respondents were unaware that a group home was located near them. The author actually discovered more dissatisfaction among residents in the control group, who did not have a group home in their neighborhood. Those respondents expected to have problems if a home were to be established. One common complaint concerned the lack of communication with residents during the process of establishing the group home. This was the dilemma with the Clallam Bay Prison situation, and also with George and the adolescent group home.

Cook (1997) reported that residents who did not have a group home in their neighborhood expected the impact to be higher than what was actually experienced by residents who did have group homes near them. They overemphasized potential problems, whereas the latter group was supportive of placing group homes in communities. The author indicated that people with certain demographic characteristics were generally opposed to group homes. These included residents who were older, male, more affluent, educated, married, and homeowners. His study found some support for this idea. His older residents were more likely to oppose government support for group homes, and the more affluent neighbors were more likely to contemplate relocating.

Wenocur and Belcher (1990) identified opposition from certain demographic types. For instance, they found that group homes in single-family-type residences were more likely to face problems than were homes in apartment buildings. They reasoned that renters rather than owners lived in apartments, thereby housing a more transient type of resident. They also found that opposition was more likely to occur if other housing programs were already located in the community. Two court cases in the state of New York addressed this opposition.

The City of Albany opposed a housing facility for mentally disabled persons because their neighborhood already housed several group homes for various populations. The court ruled that the facility would not substantially change the character of the neighborhood, so it was allowed (*Jennings v. New York State Office of Mental Health*, 1997). The town of Gates, New York also opposed a home for developmentally disabled adults in the community because several similar facilities already existed there. The court ruled that the single-family home would not be distinguishable from any other home in the neighborhood and therefore allowed it to be established (*Town of Gates v. Commissioner of New York State Office of Mental Retardation and Developmental Disabilities and Finger Lakes Developmental Disabilities Services Office*, 1997).

Sigler and Lamb (1995) reported that successful community-based programs require the participation and support of the neighborhood in which they are placed.

They found that those who held some knowledge about community programs exhibited more positive attitudes toward such initiatives than those who knew nothing about them. They also found that court personnel expressed more positive views toward community-based corrections than did the general public. This may be related to their increased level of knowledge about such programs. It may also be attributable to an idea expressed by K. A. Carlson (1992). She stated that those most likely to hold positive attitudes toward prisons in communities are people who have business interests. Citizens are more likely to perceive them as more negative, or at least neutral, and those in the social services are more likely to examine the negative effects. Since the jobs of court personnel center around the issue of corrections, therefore creating a business interest, job holders may be more likely to view neighborhood-based corrections as positive.

Elrod and Brown (1996) conducted a study examining public support for community corrections. They focused solely on electronic house arrest for minor and serious offenders. Their findings suggest that more than half of the respondents felt that offenses such as stealing or damaging property valued at less than $1000, driving under the influence of alcohol, and technical probation violations were suitable for electronic house arrest. Respondents were also more likely to support the program for "minor offenses" if they thought that placing more offenders in jail would not decrease the amount of these crimes. Violations that respondents considered least appropriate for electronic house arrest were stealing or damaging property valued higher than $1000, crimes requiring medical care, selling illegal drugs, and criminal probation violations. Those participants who did favor using this program with serious offenders were more likely to be non-White and at least 50 years old. Therefore, public support for electronic house arrest depended on the nature of the crime that the offender committed. In a study conducted in 1995, Elrod and Brown (1996) found that the public was more likely to support this program if it was used in conjunction with incarcerating the offender for a period of time.

From these investigations one can tell that there is no straightforward answer for how to obtain support from local citizens for correctional programs. Various factors are involved in the process. P. Harris and Smith (1996) believe that gaining public support revolves around money. They stated that in order to convince the community to accept a program, information must be provided regarding the costs of incarceration and how rising costs are affecting other services. They also believe that in order to increase the chance of beginning a new program, there must be a close fit between the program and the community in which it is to be placed. In other words, do not try to implement a program that endorses practices and policies inconsistent with community beliefs. Cook (1997) also indicated increased sensitivity to neighborhood norms and concerns. He suggested that more education should be developed and that efforts to increase contact with neighbors may provide some positive experiences. Wenocur and Belcher (1990) cautioned developers of group homes to become familiar with a community's culture and sociopolitical composition and to be careful about which residents they inform and when they inform them. In the case of Susan and George, it is possible that George's beliefs and "culture" were incompatible with a community-based treatment approach for sex offenders. Thus, he may have relied upon any excuse to cause problems for Susan.

Forensic Psychology and Policy Implications

Because there are so many factors involved in garnering public support for community corrections, policy makers must begin to understand what these factors are. If they understand how citizens perceive community corrections, then they can develop educational campaigns to aid the public in overcoming their opposition to such programs. If policy makers do not learn about neighborhood attitudes, then programs that may actually benefit offenders and help decrease recidivism could be delayed or even destroyed (Elrod & Brown, 1996). Also, as previously discussed in the research by Sigler and Lamb (1995), people who are informed about community corrections hold more positive attitudes toward such initiatives. This indicates that policy makers need to educate society generally about community-based programs. If the community knows what these programs are about, then it may be more willing to accept them into its own "backyard." Wenocur and Belcher (1990) caution against notifying well-organized neighborhoods that have clearly identifiable leaders because they found such neighborhoods increase their opposition when informed in advance that a group home will be located there. If a community is well organized, their tactics to prevent the group home from being established are likely to be very effective.

   With the rising prison population it is inevitable that correctional agencies will increasingly turn to alternative sentencing options. If policy makers cannot provide the support required for these programs, then a great deal of time and money will be wasted in trying to implement new alternatives. As shown in the case illustration, a single member of the community can cause problems for a program if steps are not taken to ensure support.

Suggestions for Future Research

In order for policy makers to understand what factors are involved in obtaining public support, research must first be conducted. Steps have been taken toward gaining an understanding of why communities support certain programs, but much more needs to be learned. What factors will change public attitudes from negative to positive? How do public attitudes influence the way individuals in the justice system make decisions about what to do with offenders? Are community programs achieving their goals so that the neighborhood can be confident in supporting these programs? These are all areas that should be examined using a systematic method (Sigler & Lamb, 1995).

Another area that needs to be examined in order to learn what went wrong involves an assessment of prison programs unsuccessfully placed in communities. These situations can be compared to those initiatives that were successfully implemented. If we can learn why the public does not support a particular program versus why it does, then maybe the same mistakes can be avoided in the future. If Susan had learned why George disliked the group home so much, then she could have taken steps to address the problem instead of having to spend her time responding to each grievance.

MENTALLY DISABLED INMATES

Introduction

The prevalence of prisoners with mental retardation is relatively small, consisting of approximately 2% of inmates in state and federal prisons (Conley, Luckasson, & Bouthilet, 1992). However, this small population of inmates provides a great challenge to the correctional system given their need for specialized services. The dilemma that exists concerns the handling of prisoners with mental retardation. There is a concern for public safety due to their criminal behavior and there is a concern for providing appropriate services (Exum, Turnbull, Martin, & Finn, 1992). As a result, there is a constant struggle to maintain a balance between habilitation and punishment that does not occur with the typical offender.

> Richard, a 28-year-old with mental retardation, was sentenced to prison for $3\frac{1}{2}$ to 7 years for criminal mischief. This was his fifth arrest over a period of 3 years, and the judge did not know what else to do but place Richard in prison. Richard was living in a community home but had to be released because he resisted the services provided by staff, who also were at a loss as to what would be best for him. During a period of 6 months in prison, Richard committed four infractions. The disciplinary review board lost patience with him and decided to take away 6 months of good time for his last infraction of fighting with other inmates. The guards are aware that Richard is not like other prisoners, but they do not know how to help him stay out of trouble. Richard also does not know how to stay out of trouble and feels that he must continue fighting in order to keep harassment from other inmates to a minimum. He worries that he will not be safe if he lets his guard down. (Exum *et al.*, 1992)

Literature Review

With the rise in correctional populations all over the country, there also has been an increase in inmates like Richard who have mental disabilities and low IQs, falling in the mentally retarded range (J. N. Hall, 1992). Because of this, prisons have had to develop appropriate services and programs to assist these individuals. Before an inmate can be given these special services, he or she must first be diagnosed as mentally retarded. Screening and evaluating an inmate prior to placing the person in a housing unit is perhaps the most important aspect in developing appropriate services for a prisoner with mental retardation (Exum et al., 1992). This is the stage where mental disability characteristics can be determined for prisoners.

Bowker and Schweid (1992) reported a profile of the mentally retarded offender. Ninety-one percent were male, 57% were African American, 48% were between the ages of 20 and 24, 73% were single, 13% completed high school, 67% were repeat offenders, and the mean full-scale IQ was 68. A program in Florida reported that a majority of the mentally retarded inmates were male, African American, and under age 30. Due to the higher number of African-American mentally retarded inmates, Ho (1996) conducted a study which examined race as a factor in predicting those inmates who would be diagnosed as mentally retarded. The researcher found that the effect of race did not make any significant addition to the prediction. "Regardless of race, the offender who had a low IQ or a severe deficit in adaptive behavior was most likely to be diagnosed as having severe retardation" (Ho, 1996, p. 343). Ho reported that IQ was the strongest determinant for predicting mental retardation among offenders.

The type of instrument used to measure intelligence is an important factor to consider because the way in which inmates are screened can affect the prevalence of retardation. Often a group test is administered to incoming offenders because it saves time. Yet, Spruill and May (1988) found that group testing overestimates the prevalence of mental retardation. They found that if inmates were administered an individual intelligence test, such as the Wechsler Adult Intelligence Scale, then there was a lower prevalence of retardation. Upon questioning inmates who had been tested, they learned that many were very anxious upon entering prison, and the group testing did not allay their anxieties. The inmates also reported that they did not understand why they were being tested and, therefore, some did not try to do their best on the tests.

Despite this finding, prisons do still administer group screening tests because of the sheer volume of inmates that must be processed. Georgia State Prison has a mental retardation program which uses a group screening test to identify individuals who score less than 80 (J. N. Hall, 1992). The Texas Department of Corrections also screens all incoming inmates for mental retardation. If a prisoner scores less than 73 on a standard intelligence test, then he or she is sent to the mental retardation unit for a 30-day evaluation (Santamour, 1990).

Once an inmate has been identified with mental disabilities, what types of services are available? J. N. Hall (1992) describes two state approaches to treating this population. The South Carolina Department of Corrections has a Habilation Unit. This is a minimum-security unit reserved for those with developmental disabilities. Services such as special education, life-skills training, vocational preparation, recreation, counseling, and prerelease preparation are offered. These programs are run by a team of professionals which includes psychologists, special education teachers, and vocational specialists. The primary goal is to provide appropriate training which will improve the inmate's socialization skills. Therefore, the inmate will be prepared to live on the outside and hopefully not return.

The other program described by J. N. Hall (1992) is the Georgia State Prison Mental Retardation Unit. Unlike South Carolina's program, this is run through a maximum-security facility. The prisoners typically are repeat offenders who have committed violent crimes. Similar to South Carolina, this program teaches socialization and life-skills development. However, the goal is not to prepare the inmate for the outside world but to emphasize institutional adaptation. An effort is made to train the inmate on how to live inside the prison without committing further crimes.

Santamour (1990) describes a special program for prisoners with mental retardation that has been implemented in the Texas Department of Corrections. Once an inmate is identified as possibly disabled, the prisoner is sent to a special unit for evaluation. Multidisciplinary teams made up of doctors, social workers, educators, psychologists, vocational trainers, and security conduct the evaluations and work with inmates in the program. If the decision is made to admit the person into the program, then housing is available in one of five units designed to fit particular needs. One unit consists of dual-diagnosis inmates who have mental retardation and another psychological disorder. The prisoners housed in this unit also tend to act aggressively. A second unit houses inmates identified as being particularly vulnerable to abuse and therefore in need of extra protection. A third unit houses those inmates who are aggressive or disruptive and have histories of belligerent behavior. A fourth unit consists of those who have only mental retardation and no other identified problems. A fifth unit is reserved for model prisoners with mental retardation who are allowed the highest level of privileges. Once an inmate has been identified and housed, then an individualized habilitation and education plan is developed by the treatment team. This plan emphasizes four areas: (1) habilitation, which includes academic, vocational, and social skills; (2) social support, which includes counseling by psychologists and trained correctional officers who work as case managers; (3) institutional security; and (4) continuity of treatment, which prepares the inmate for the outside world when his or her release date approaches.

When an inmate is released from prison, he or she may still require special services. Therefore, an Ohio county has developed a Mentally Retarded Offender (MRO) Unit in their probation department (Bowker & Schweid, 1992). The criterion for being assigned to this unit is a score of 75 or lower on the Wechsler Adult Intelligence Scale, which must be administered by a licensed psychologist. This unit is run on a case management model where the probationer receives individualized services determined by the probation officer, the clinical director of the MRO unit, and others as deemed necessary. The supervision levels for these probationers range from "super-high," which means contact with the probation officer once a week, to "extended," which means only monthly contacts via mail with the probation officer. A probation officer working in this unit generally carries a caseload of approximately 55–65 individuals compared to the regular officers' caseloads of approximately 200. Due to the case management model, the MRO Unit officers take a much more active role in their probationers' postrelease services. If Richard, from the case illustration, had been assigned to such a unit, then more appropriate services may have been found for him, and he might have remained in the community instead of being sent to prison.

The programs that have been described all focus on aspects such as habilitation and vocational and social skills. Yet, are these skills important or even necessary for an inmate with mental retardation? A study conducted by Munson (1994) suggested that there are three important processes that take place once an offender is released to a community. These include beginning an appropriate occupation, selecting a home, and developing appropriate and positive leisure skills. He hypothesized that offenders who were provided career development training would score significantly higher than a control group on self-esteem and participation and commitment in the worker, homemaker, and leisure roles. His participants were youthful offenders who had mental retardation and/or learning disabilities as well as behavioral problems. He found that the offenders in the group who received career development training increased their self-esteem, while it decreased for those in the control group. Also, participation and commitment in the homemaker role increased more for the group receiving training than the control group. Although commitment to the worker and leisure roles did not show a significant difference between groups, the training did increase the offenders' commitment to finding and maintaining a home, and it did increase their self-esteem. These two benefits could provide enough incentive for released offenders to remain in the community and avoid criminal activities, which is the ultimate goal of most training programs.

Bowker and Schweid (1992) provide another reason for implementing specialized programs within prisons. Offenders with mental retardation, such as Richard in the case illustration, often become victims of physical attacks and psychological abuse. They also can be manipulated and blamed for incidents by more intelligent inmates. This type of behavior only becomes worse with overcrowding, and many prisons are overcrowded. If separate units are not created for those with mental retardation, then they must be housed with the mentally or physically ill, where they will not receive the types of services they need.

Placing inmates with mental retardation in the general population of a prison can create many conflicts. If the inmate breaks the rules, as Richard continuously did, then correctional officers may place him or her in disciplinary isolation because guards are not concerned with why the prisoner broke the rules, only that the person did. The stress of the punishment may only frustrate the mentally retarded inmate further, and he or she may verbally or physically act out this frustration because of a lack of understanding about what is happening. The aspects of prison life may actually place the mentally retarded prisoner at risk, despite attempts to help the person (J. N. Hall, 1992). This is why it is so important to develop separate units and programs for this population.

Forensic Psychology and Policy Implications

Although programs for mentally retarded inmates do exist, not all prisons have them, and not all of the programs are adequate. Policy makers need to develop programs which focus on the special needs of these inmates, especially their slower learning capabilities and limited ability to understand the rules of the prison. Policies should be developed that decrease mainstreaming them into the general population and increase the creation of special facilities (Spruill & May, 1988). Policies also need to be developed to create interagency communications which would smooth the way for a continuum of care from prison into the community (J. N. Hall, 1992). Psychologists, social workers, probation officers, and correctional staff should begin working together to assist prisoners in habilitating and transitioning back into the community so that they refrain from future criminal activities. Without this type of teamwork, offenders like Richard will keep cycling back through the system because they do not know how to live in their communities.

Suggestions for Future Research

Further research needs to be conducted on what types of programs are appropriate for inmates with mental retardation and those with additional problems or disabilities (J. N. Hall, 1992). Because of the difficulties inherent in group testing, more effective methods of screening for mental retardation should be studied further. The tests currently used for identifying mental retardation among inmates should be examined for validity with different ethnic groups (Ho, 1996). If these tests are culturally biased, then the reported higher prevalence of African-American inmates with mental retardation may not be accurate. Inmates who really are not retarded, but have been raised with different cultural values and ideals, may be receiving services that are not suitable for them. Research also should be conducted on community-based programs that have had success in housing and habilitating prior offenders so that more effective initiatives can be developed to help this population stay out of prison.

SOCIETY'S REACTION TO SEX OFFENDERS

Introduction

There are currently more than 200,000 convicted sex offenders in the United States (U.S. Department of Justice, 1996). These offenders are perhaps the most detested individuals in today's society. Since the late 1980s, there have been numerous movements calling for tougher penalties for sex offenders by law enforcement, legislatures, and communities. These movements support chemical castration, community notification, formalized registration, and civil commitment. At first glance, such actions may appear as proper precautions to ensure the safety of society against further victimization by convicted sex offenders. However, these actions also need to be examined in terms of whether they serve their intended function of curbing recidivism. Further, one needs to question whether the constitutional rights of the offender are violated. The case of Jose illustrates the repercussions that recent implementation of community notification laws have on both sex offenders and their families.

> José is a 19-year-old Latino male who has been participating in sex offender-specific treatment for the past 6 months. José attends high school and works 30 hours a week in order to pay for his treatment. One Monday night during a group therapy session, José disclosed the devastation that he and his family have encountered as a result of his sexual offense, and, specifically, the mandated registration and community notification laws. José revealed how he was recently confronted by five men whom he considered friends. They located José's name on the CD-ROM which contains information about all registered sex offenders. Accessible information included José's name, picture, zip code, and a description of his offense.
>
> José tearfully described how his friends did not stop after confronting just him. They also confronted José's sister, who, they learned, was his victim. They then took it upon themselves to notify José's girlfriend (who subsequently left him), José's place of employment (which subsequently fired him), and students at his school. Feeling extremely scared and alone, José disclosed his feelings of worthlessness and hopelessness. He stated, "I will never overcome my status as a sex offender, and no matter how much treatment I receive, I will continue to be hated by everyone. My family is being hurt because of me, and life is not worth it anymore." José then disclosed that he was intending to commit suicide.

Literature Review

The case of José is an example of a young man who has completed a jail sentence for his offense and is currently receiving outpatient sex-offender treatment while he is on probation. Despite these punishment and rehabilitation efforts, society imposes additional requirements for the protection of the community against individuals such as José. These additional requirements are explored in terms of their respective advantages and disadvantages within the literature. The three issues examined are the registration and community notification laws, the statute for Sexually Violent Predators, and chemical castration.

Sex-Offender Registration and Community Notification

The death of 7-year-old Megan Kanka sparked a nationwide movement to release information about the location and identity of sex offenders in the community. New Jersey was the first state to pass "Megan's Law" after the young girl was raped and murdered by a convicted child molester who had moved into her neighborhood. Currently, "Megan's Law" is upheld under federal legislation and is upheld in every state. The purpose of the law is to equip the community with information necessary for the protection of children against child molesters (Cody, 1997). According to this law, the identification of the victim is not to be released. However, as illustrated in the case of José, the victim's name does not need to be present in order for identification to occur. A description of the sexual offense is provided, which can, at times, be sufficient for victim identification. As in the case of José, victim identification occurred after it was stated that the sexual offense was committed against his sister. Regardless of the public's opinion on the rights (or lack thereof) of sex offenders, most would agree that the rights of victims, and particularly their identities, need to be protected.

In terms of the practical application of this law, it is important to examine whether it serves its intended purpose of protecting children from sexual abuse and reducing recidivism among sexual offenders. The law is too young for studies to have been conducted examining the rate of sexual offenses before and after its passage. However, the literature provides a great deal of information concerning sexual offenses and offenders which can help to address whether the law will meet its goals. Perhaps the most important issue is that most sexual offenses are not committed by strangers in the community; rather, most sexual offenses are perpetrated by members of the family. This illustrates one misperception by society that sexual offenders are crazed predators who are waiting to pounce on the first child they see. This misconception is easier for the public to understand than the fact that, by far, most offenses are incestuous in nature. As noted by Williams (1996), it is the stereotypic image of a sex offender that creates fear and misunderstanding within society. However, it is precisely such fear and misunderstanding that provide the basis for an emotional response by legislatures, as witnessed by the sex-offender registration and community notification laws.

Sexually Violent Predator Act

Another way in which society chooses to deal with sexual offenders is by following their incarceration with civil commitment. The definition of a Sexually Violent Predator varies slightly across states; however, the basic premise is the same. California has defined the statute in the following way:

> A person who has been convicted of one or more sexually violent offenses against two or more victims for which he or she received a determinate sentence and who has a diagnosed mental disorder that makes the person a danger to the health and safety of others in that it is likely that he or she will engage in sexually violent criminal behavior. (D. A. Cohen, 1997)

The purpose of the law is to identify, locate, apprehend, and prosecute habitual sexual offenders (D. A. Cohen, 1997). When examined more closely, there are numerous issues inherent in this statute that call into question its constitutionality. There has long been a debate as to whether sex offenders need treatment or imprisonment. The Sexually Violent Predator Act, which became effective in California on January 1, 1996, allows the state to subject the offender to both. In essence, this Act permits an indefinite civil commitment to be imposed on an offender after a full prison sentence has been served and prior to his release from prison. The *ex post facto* clause of the United States Constitution prohibits retroactive application of penal statutes. Given that the Sexually Violent Predator Act is a civil law, analysis of *United States v. Ward* (1980) extends the *ex post facto* clause to civil cases. In this case, it was found that civil laws violate the *ex post facto* law if the statute is "so punitive either in purpose or effect as to negate its intention." This applies to the Sexually Violent Predator Act in that the said intent was to provide mental health treatment to the offender; however, the underlying goal was to extend the confinement of the individual.

In a similar fashion, the Sexually Violent Predator Act is in conflict with prohibitions against double jeopardy. Double jeopardy is said to have occurred if one of three situations is present: (1) a second prosecution for the same offense after acquittal, (2) a second prosecution for the same offense after conviction, and (3) multiple punishments for the same offense. In terms of the Sexually Violent Predator Act, violations of the latter two occur. The major defense that has been used in court to claim this Act does *not* constitute double jeopardy is that a civil commitment is not punitive in character (*Department of Revenue of Montana v. Kurth Ranch*, 1994). One must determine whether the motivation for the commitment is truly for the offender to receive treatment or whether the purpose is to keep the offender confined in a secure facility apart from the rest of society. Further, if treatment is needed for the individual, such treatment needs to be provided immediately upon this determination rather than after a prison sentence has been completed.

Chemical Castration

Perhaps the most drastic measure that has been implemented as a means of protecting society against sex offenders is the chemical castration law. Again, this law varies slightly from state to state; however, the fundamentals of the law remain the same. In California, two-time sex offenders can be required to take Depo-Provera upon parole. Depo-Provera is a hormone-suppressing drug which lowers testosterone levels, thereby decreasing a man's sex drive. The court has also allowed for discretion in using this procedure for first-time sex offenders. In support of the chemical castration law, European studies have been cited in which offenders who underwent chemical castration had a recidivism rate under 15.0%. Review of the California Department of Corrections' statistics, however, reveals that sexual offenders who serve a prison sentence and do not receive treatment during incarceration have a recidivism rate of approximately 18.5%, whereas the recidivism rates for drug and violent offenders are approximately 25.0 and 30.0%, respectively (Lotke, 1996).

The American Civil Liberties Union of Florida has argued that the use of chemical castration is unconstitutional for several reasons (Spralding, 1997). First, chemical castration interferes with an individual's rights to procreate and to refuse treatment.

Second, Depo-Provera is not FDA-approved for chemical castration. Third, judges, not physicians, will be making the ultimate decision as to whether an offender should be given the drug and when the drug can be discontinued. Fourth, there are serious side effects from Depo-Provera which include diabetes, gallstones, hypertension, fatigue, weight gain, nightmares, and muscle weakness. For this reason, the chemical castration law can be viewed as judges practicing medicine without a license.

Perhaps one of the most important opposing arguments to the chemical castration law is that it will not curb recidivism in many offenders. The treatment strategy that has the best effect on curbing recidivism among sexual offenders is cognitive-behavioral therapy with a relapse prevention plan (Laws, 1989). Chemical castration does nothing to treat the psychological roots of sexually aberrant behavior. Numerous sexual offenders do not offend as a result of an overactive sex drive. Many offenders commit sexual offenses for reasons that have nothing to do with sex such as power, control, and anger. In fact, when comparing untreated sexual offenders to those who received sex-offender treatment, the recidivism rate drops from 18.5% to approximately 10.9% (Alexander, 1997). This clearly demonstrates that treatment can effectively reduce recidivism among sexual offenders.

Forensic Psychology and Policy Implications

There is a great need for forensic psychologists to provide information to the public and legislature regarding sexual offenders and their recidivism and treatment. It appears that several of the recent actions taken against sexual offenders will be ineffective in accomplishing the goal of protecting society. Cordoba and Chapel (1983) acknowledge that society is more willing to allow sex offenders back into the community if they have undergone antiandrogen therapy (chemical castration). It is important, however, to examine whether such measures are based simply on emotion and community misperceptions or whether thorough research was conducted to support their implementation. It appears that there is a direct conflict between society's outcry for severe punishment of sex offenders and mental health experts who maintain that there is effective treatment for such individuals. Given this conflict, the legislature has attempted to satisfy both sides through legally sanctioned penal and civil commitments.

Chemical castration, community notification, registration, and the Sexually Violent Predator Act are all aimed at protecting society from sex offenders who are likely to recidivate upon release from prison. In lobbying the chemical castration bill in California, proponents stated that recidivism would drop from almost 100 to 2% (E. Moses, 1996). In reviewing the literature on recidivism among sexual offenders, no study documents that recidivism occurs in almost 100% of the cases (Proulx et al., 1997). This illustrates the public's misperceptions about sexual offenders and specifically about their likelihood for reoffense. Furthermore, policy makers should be educated on the fact that public awareness needs to be focused primarily on the family, where most sexual offenses occur. Numerous studies have shown the effectiveness of treatment for sexual offenders in reducing recidivism. With this in mind, efforts need to be on funding prison and parole treatment programs which are designed specifically for this population.

Suggestions for Future Research

Sexually violent predator laws are all relatively new in the United States. Once they have been present for 5 to 10 years, analyses need to be conducted, examining recidivism rates before and after the laws. This will provide a more accurate measure of whether the laws are meeting their goal of curbing recidivism. In order to illustrate the discrepancy between society's perceptions of sex offenders, studies should be conducted which directly compare the statistical data gathered in the department of corrections with society's perceptions of recidivism among sex offenders and the effectiveness of treatment for this population. It is likely that the results will show that the legislature supports the misperceptions within society rather than the data available from corrections and mental health professionals.

WOMEN WORKING IN MALE PRISONS

Introduction

Today when you walk into a male prison it is not uncommon to see women there, not as inmates but as correctional officers (COs) guarding the male prisoners. Prior to the passage of Title VII of the Civil Rights Act of 1964, this would have been a rare sight. Women were delegated to work in all-female institutions and juvenile corrections (Etheridge, Hale, & Hambrick, 1984). Fortunately, Title VII prohibited sex discrimination by state and local governments, so female corrections officers began to move into the male prison system. Unfortunately, they have not had a warm welcome, especially by their male coworkers. The toughest task female COs have to face is not guarding the prisoners, but trying to find a way to coexist with the male COs in an atmosphere of hostility, harassment, and nonsupportiveness.

The following example illustrates the process that many female COs face when trying to fit into the male prison system.

> When Jane first began her career as a correctional officer, she chose to work in a female prison because there were more job openings and she felt more comfortable working with this population. After several years, she decided to move to an all-male prison because she had two kids to help support and needed the pay raise this job would bring. Although she was very familiar with the job requirements of a CO, she was aware that every prison had its own rules and had never worked in a male prison.

On her first day, she went in with a friendly, open attitude. She smiled and introduced herself to her new coworkers. She noticed that she was the only female CO in her unit. She got a couple of nods and one person even grunted hello. Nobody returned her friendly attitude, though. She knew the name of the CO who was to train her, but it took her half an hour to find him because he started his rounds without waiting for her. Upon finding him, he immediately ordered her to be quiet and watch everything he did. Several times that day she asked him questions about the job, and he often did not give her a sufficient answer or ignored her altogether. After one question, he accused her of being stupid and of not knowing anything about being a correctional officer.

During her lunch break, none of the male COs would sit with her. She overheard them talking and laughing about her, and one even cornered her and asked her to go out for a drink after work. After telling him she was married, he just laughed and said he was sure her husband expected such things since she worked with "real men." When Jane left work after that first day, she felt very discouraged and was afraid to return.

After thinking it over, she vowed to go back with a different attitude. She began to act more assertively and to not let her male coworkers demean her. She began to use more offensive language and joked around with the men so that she would fit in better. Gradually, the men began to accept her, but only after she showed she could be tough like them and not act feminine. She had to change her personality to fit their beliefs about how a CO should act. Her problem then became one of trying to leave her work personality at work. Her comments were that "it's a macho environment and I have to act aggressively to succeed. I work here all day, talk loud, act tough. I go home at night and find myself talking in a deep, loud voice to my kids" (Jurik, as cited in S. E. Martin & Jurik, 1996, p. 197). So, Jane found that she could fit into the male prison system, but at the cost of giving up her own identity to conform to her male counterparts.

Literature Review

Jane's situation is not an uncommon one among female correctional officers working in all-male prisons. Although Jane was able to fit in, she had to conform to the male officers' behaviors. When women do not conform, their experience can be very stressful because some male COs harass and discriminate against them.

The first signs of discrimination began after Title VII was passed. All-male prisons tried to prohibit women from even being hired by using the BFOQ clause, which states that sex discrimination can occur if it is a Bona Fide Occupational Qualification (Pollock-Byrne, 1990). *Dothard v. Rawlinson* (1977) is an example of this. The state of Alabama prohibited a woman from working in an all-male prison because it claimed the violence of the state prisons would be dangerous for women. The state used the BFOQ clause as their justification. The U.S. Supreme Court upheld the state's case, although it did overturn the use of height and weight restrictions in hiring unless it could be shown how it related to the job. Although this seems like a negative outcome for women, it was really a narrow ruling applying only to Alabama. Other states have had a difficult time proving that height, weight, or gender influence what is necessary to be a corrections officer (Pollock-Byrne, 1990).

Although prisons have not been able to prevent women from being hired, the male correctional officers have not welcomed them into their subculture. Fry and

Glaser (1987) conducted a study on female COs and found that they were not viewed positively by the male guards. In fact, they found that the male officers' resistance was the greatest problem the female COs faced in male prisons. S. E. Martin and Jurik (1996) found, more specifically, that it is in the area of actual security work in men's prisons where women are least likely to be included. Women consist of 43% of the total correctional work force, yet they only make up 13% of correctional officer security in men's prisons. Since their numbers are so low, it is not surprising that the biggest problem faced by female COs is being recognized and treated as equals (Szockyj, 1989). Jane's situation captures this problem.

This unequal position of female COs can often begin before they even start their job. Many do not receive any type of training before their first day of work (S. E. Martin & Jurik, 1996). They are supposed to receive on-the-job training, yet their trainers generally are male COs who do not want them there (Zimmer, 1987). Sometimes, they actively undermine the woman's ability to succeed by withholding information about how to deal with the inmates (Zimmer, 1987). In Jane's case, the training officer often refused to answer her questions about the job. S. E. Martin and Jurik (1996) also found that male coworkers excluded women COs from training exercises and even sabotaged them to the point of threatening the women's physical safety. They also reported that, due to this hostility by the coworkers, the inmates actually provided the needed information and training.

From their first day, women COs are confronted with the problem of fitting in with their coworkers. This problem does not always go away with time. Female COs face steady opposition and sexual harassment from the male guards (Zimmer, 1987). The opposition can take many different forms. Although male coworkers at times show overt hostility, they also engage in more subtle ways of undermining female COs. They can put pressure on women by constantly questioning or scrutinizing their performance (S. E. Martin & Jurik, 1996). They sometimes reverse decisions made by women, thereby undermining women's authority over prisoners (Zimmer, 1987). For women in supervisory positions, their male subordinates engage in subtle and blatant forms of resistance such as rolling their eyes, inattentiveness, and feigning an, inability to hear orders. They can also undermine a woman's authority by "going over her head," thus causing her to lose the respect of her superiors due to ineffective management (S. E. Martin & Jurik, 1996).

Sexual harassment is another technique male COs use to keep women in an unequal status. Women become victims of rumors and allegations of sexual misconduct. There are overt propositions by male COs and more subtle behaviors such as joking, teasing, and name calling (S. E. Martin & Jurik, 1996). In the case illustration, Jane was propositioned by her coworker and then ridiculed when she refused his advances. Women COs even report that male officers proposition them in front of male inmates (Pollock-Byrne, 1990). It seems as if this might encourage the inmates to behave in a similar manner, yet Horne (1985) reported that obscenities more often came from the male coworkers than from the inmates. In a study of San Quentin Prison, it was found that women COs were sexually harassed at work and by phone at home. The overtly sexist language and conduct was openly tolerated (Owen, as cited in S. E. Martin & Jurik, 1996). This sexual harassment makes relationships with male COs "difficult in that a balance always has to be struck between being friendly and being thought of as sexually available—being 'one of the boys' or designated as the fraternity whore" (Pollock-Byrne, 1990, p. 118). S. E. Martin and Jurik (1996) state that further problems arise when female COs refuse their counterparts' protection and sexual advances and attempt to show their competence. The male COs label them as "too mannish, 'man-haters', bitches, or lesbians" (S. E. Martin & Jurik, 1996, p. 174).

Women have had some success in trying to stop sexual harassment. For example, in *Bundy v. Jackson* (1981), a woman prison counselor was being harassed by her male supervisors. When she rejected their advances, they prevented her from advancing in her job. When she charged them with sexual harassment, the court ruled in her favor, saying that her employer had allowed a hostile and discriminating work environment that violated Title VII (S. E. Martin & Jurik, 1996). Despite cases like this, S. E. Martin and Jurik (1996) say that sexual harassment in all-male prisons has not decreased. The correctional field has been slow to prevent this type of behavior. Women fear that if they complain it may cause a negative evaluation of their job performance or even job loss.

Another aspect of opposition that female COs must face is that male COs evaluate women's job performances more negatively than they do their own (S. E. Martin & Jurik, 1996). A study by Fry and Glaser (1987), which gave questionnaires to staff, reported that the men found women COs less capable than themselves in duties that related to security and safety. Szockyj (1989) stated a similar finding in that male COs viewed themselves as more effective in handling situations that involved physical strength and preferred male back-up over female back-up. Male COs view women as too physically and emotionally weak to work in all-male prisons, and, therefore, they cannot do their jobs adequately in violent situations and will be injured (S. E. Martin & Jurik, 1996). There is also a fear that women will get too friendly with the inmates, so female officers' intentions with the prisoners are scrutinized, although male officers' intentions are rarely monitored (S. E. Martin & Jurik, 1996). Crouch (1985) found that the problem was not an inability by female COs to handle the job demands, but rather one of male guards' perceived standards of appropriate behavior for both genders. Therefore, it is often necessary for female COs to prove that they can perform their job well before being accepted, whereas this is not necessary for male COs. This negative view of women and their ability to do their job creates a disadvantage for promotions because they are often evaluated by male supervisors (Crouch, 1985). Thus, it is more difficult for women to get into positions of power where they could attempt to change the atmosphere of hostility female COs endure.

Because most of the resistance faced by female COs comes from male coworkers, some ideas have been offered that explain this occurrence. First, female COs are viewed as intruders in an all-male world (Horne, 1985). Female officers threaten an established subcultural code; they threaten a self-image held by male officers that guard work is dangerous and therefore only suitable for men. In other words, women are a status threat to men. One reason why men treat women in a sexually harassing way is to deny women acceptance on the job. Therefore, their status as men will not be diminished (Crouch, 1985). If women can perform the guard job as well as men, the job can no longer be used as a way of defining their masculinity (S. E. Martin & Jurik, 1996).

Another explanation is that women COs conduct their job in a different way than men. They are more likely to have a social worker's attitude about the job. They spend more time actually listening to the inmates' problems, having conversations about families, and assisting them in their plans for release. They do this as a way of creating alliances with the prisoners so that the inmates will voluntarily comply with orders and the women will not have to use force or intimidation (Zimmer, 1987). Male COs perceive this behavior as sympathy toward inmates and feel that female guards are incapable of handling the job properly.

Although there is no agreed-upon reason why male COs treat female officers with such opposition, what can be agreed upon is that women in "male" fields such as corrections face many hindrances, including expressed and subtle hostilities, exclusion from the male CO subculture, and sexual harassment (S. E. Martin & Jurik, 1996).

Forensic Psychology and Policy Implications

The hostility endured by female COs in all-male prisons is a significant social problem. The harassment women face "is a source of mistrust, resentment and job-related stress" (S. E. Martin & Jurik, 1996, p. 178). In fact, female COs experience more work-related stress than male COs. This reinforces the concept of women as outsiders and subordinates. In the absence of any support, they must adapt to the masculine culture (S. E. Martin & Jurik, 1996). This forces them to ignore and stifle their femininity, which is a part of who they are. Jane found that in order to fit in with her male coworkers she had to develop a macho persona. This behavior can lead to a negative self-image and low self-esteem, which can have adverse effects on health and family interactions. It could even influence a female guard's ability to do her job effectively, perpetuating the negative stereotypes placed on women by men and preventing job advancement. Thus, it is a self-fulfilling prophecy: female COs are treated as subordinates, causing them to do their job in a way they are uncomfortable with, thereby forcing them to be seen as incompetent, which leaves them in subordinate positions. Etheridge et al. (1984) emphasized that a major barrier to advancement by women is the expectancies held by the women themselves.

Because the numbers of female COs in all-male prisons are so small, they are often considered token employees. Therefore, their performance is highly visible, leading to further stress and pressure on the job (Crouch, 1985). They must represent the ability of all female COs, proving that they can do the job as well as their male counterparts. This can cause female COs to be wary of making mistakes, so they imitate the male officers, which may not be the most effective way to perform their job.

The fact that sexual harassment is still occurring in all-male prisons underscores an important political dynamic for women working as correctional officers. This type of behavior interferes with basic civil rights and therefore should be assessed by policy makers in an attempt to prevent women from having to endure such degrading experiences in their place of business. Sexual harassment further reinforces the notion that women are subordinate and not worthy of being treated as equals in the job environment. Policy analysts must address this false sentiment.

Suggestions for Future Research

Although work-related sexual harassment was dealt with to a certain extent during the first few decades after Title VII was passed, this trend has not continued. The effects of stricter, more defined sexual harassment laws in regard to women working in all-male prisons is a major area of needed research. Are women COs more willing to bring these situations out into the open now that sexual harassment is in the public eye? Do women now garner better results in getting this behavior to stop without having to sacrifice their jobs or level of respect by their coworkers?

Another area of inquiry should focus on the effects to family members. Developing a tougher, more aggressive personality could have a major impact on a female correctional officer's family. It could change the dynamics of the marital relationship or have an impact on the way she raises her children. In Jane's situation, she had a difficult time leaving her work personality at work. She spoke to her children the way she spoke to the inmates and guards. Consequently, does being a CO cause women to redefine their entire identity in order to succeed in the correctional setting? Research is needed in this area.

Finally, Zimmer (1987) proposes that maybe women should not be evaluated the same way that men are in these traditionally held male jobs. Specifically, an assessment could be undertaken, exploring the requirements for a correctional officer's job, followed by an evaluation as to whether the officer met them without looking at the manner in which they were met. A precedent needs to be set for acknowledging that women can perform their duties differently from men and be just as effective.

INMATE SEXUALITY

Introduction

For many people, it seems that the topic of sex and sexuality is one that causes discomfort and maybe even embarrassment. When viewing such an awkward topic in the context of inmates who are incarcerated in unisex prisons, people's discomfort levels seem to increase even further. This subject calls to mind the idea of gang rape, forced sexual interactions, and especially homosexuality. Despite the societal progress made in being able to openly discuss and understand homosexuality, it is still a subject that causes a great deal of concern and emotional reaction. Inmate homosexuality is not immune from this controversy. In fact, there are considerably more dilemmas found with same sex partnerships in prison. One controversy is the definition of homosexuality within a prison. This is an issue because many inmates who engage in homosexual behaviors while incarcerated are not homosexuals outside of prison (G. T. Long, 1993). This section discusses various aspects of inmate sexuality in order to provide a better understanding of this phenomenon.

> Sam was a 21-year-old first-time offender sentenced to a state prison where he knew no one. He was very lonely and depressed and was quickly befriended by Bud, who had been in the prison for several years and knew how the system worked. Bud took Sam under his wing and introduced him to prison life, including the inmate marriages between the "jockers" and the "punks." Bud stressed how normal an activity this was in prisons because he hoped to turn Sam into his punk. Once Bud had courted Sam for several weeks, he finalized the relationship by having Sam transferred to his cell where he could sodomize him away from the guards' view. (Huffman, as cited in G. T. Long, 1993)
>
> Charles was in his cell one morning when a large man entered asking to borrow something that belonged to his cellmate. The inmate asked Charles if he engaged in homosexual acts, and Charles emphatically stated no. The inmate threatened physical injury if Charles would not have sex with him. When Charles attempted to defend himself, three other inmates entered the cell and hit and kicked Charles until he fell down. They then ripped off his pants and each one sodomized Charles while the others restrained him. (Davis, as cited in G. T. Long, 1993)

Literature Review

The above case illustrations are very different, yet both situations exist in prisons as ways to engage in sexual behaviors and exert resistance to prison rules and regulations (Donaldson, 1990). In response to allegations of homosexuality, the perpetrators in these case illustrations would most likely deny that they are gay and might attack a fellow inmate who "accused" them of such. Donaldson states that the inmate subculture allows prisoners to be in the penetrating role without raising questions about their heterosexuality. Yet, one who submits to penetration is perceived as giving up his masculinity. Donaldson reports that the majority of prisoners engage in the former role and are called "jockers" or "men." The jockers engage in heterosexual behaviors both before and after their period of incarceration. A jocker's penetration of another prisoner only serves to validate his masculinity. It also serves to give the jocker some power by having control over other prisoners and thus diminishing the power the institution has over him.

Donaldson (1990) describes another class of inmates called "queens." These are men who exhibit homosexual patterns outside of the prison and thus exhibit similar behaviors while incarcerated. They are typically effeminate and are always in the role of a receiver. The queens are usually pressured by the jockers to maintain the feminine role. They typically consist of a small percentage of the inmate population. The queens often are separated from the other prisoners by guards in order to provide protection for them and attempt to diminish homosexual behaviors within the prison. The protection is necessary because homosexuals may be abused by the other inmates and correctional staff tend to believe that homosexuals are troublemakers (G. T. Long, 1993).

Donaldson (1990) reports that a third category of inmates is referred to as "punks." This category is typically larger than the queens, and the punks are considered to be the lowest class of inmates by other prisoners because they are forced into playing the receiver role. They are usually heterosexual, yet they are often "turned out" by other prisoners. This turning-out process typically involves rape, often gang rape. Charles is an example of a punk who was turned out by gang rape. These inmates are usually somewhat smaller and less experienced in the prison system. They usually have been charged with nonviolent offenses and may even have come from a middle-class upbringing. The punks will usually return to their heterosexual patterns once released from prison, but may experience distress in the form of rape trauma syndrome. However, G. T. Long (1993) reports that as a result of being turned out, those who were heterosexual may prefer homosexual behaviors once released from prison. In fact, all turnouts in one study reported to engage in exclusively homosexual behavior after being released from prison, although they were heterosexual before incarceration (Sagarin, as cited in G. T. Long, 1993).

As mentioned above, forcible rape exists in the prison subculture. It typically exists in a much higher percentage in maximum-security prisons because the inmates are usually incarcerated for more violent crimes and less worried about the risks involved with such prohibited behavior (Donaldson, 1990). Struckman-Johnson, Struckman-Johnson, Rucker, Bumby, and Donaldson (1996) found that in a state prison system, 22% of male inmates were pressured or forced to have sexual contact of some type. Those who were victims of forced sex stated that threat of harm and physical intimidation were the methods most often used by the perpetrators. Inmates' accounts of their turnouts reported that they were raped or "so completely terrified by physical threats that they were unable to resist" (Sagarin, as cited in G. T. Long, p. 155).

Those who engage in forcible rape do not need to worry about an inmate reporting them because there are serious consequences for informers in the prisoner subculture (Donaldson, 1990). The Struckman-Johnson *et al.* (1996) study found that of those males who had been pressured or forced into having sexual contact, only 29% reported the incident(s) to staff. In fact, often the sexual activities are engaged in as a group with prisoners watching out for guards and deterring other prisoners from the area being used (Donaldson, 1990). The Struckman-Johnson *et al.* (1996)

study reported that of the male inmates who were victims, 25% were forced to complete the entire act of intercourse by two or more inmates.

In addition to the after-effects of the rape trauma syndrome mentioned above, those who are forced into sexual behaviors may experience immediate distress. Struckman-Johnson et al. (1996) discovered that 75% of those who were forced to engage in sex experienced at least one negative consequence. Feelings of distrust, anxiety around others, and depression were the most common negative consequences. Sixteen percent of those forced into sexual behaviors received physical injuries. Sagarin (as cited in G. T. Long, 1993) stated that inmates reported feelings of shame, disgust, and humiliation after their first homosexual experience in prison. These feelings continued during their period of incarceration.

The above descriptions relate solely to sexual behaviors in all-male prisons, but female prisons share some of the same characteristics with respect to inmate sexuality. Donaldson (1990) reports that some women engage in lesbian relationships because they do not have access to members of the opposite sex. These women are labeled "penitentiary turnouts" and are similar to the jockers in male prisons. Those who engage in homosexual relationships outside of prison are labeled "lesbians" and are similar to the queens. The inmate who assumes the traditional female role in the relationship is called "femme" or "mommy," and the inmate who assumes the traditional male role is called "stud" or "daddy."

In contrast to the sexual behaviors committed by male prisoners, female homosexual relationships typically do not involve physical force or pressure. Struckman-Johnson et al. (1996) reported a low rate of 7% for forced or pressured sexual contact among women prisoners. Instead of basing the relationships upon fear and intimidation, they base them on consent between the inmates involved. Mahon (1996) found that female inmates reported widespread consensual sex which included mutual masturbation, sharing of sex toys, and oral and anal sex. The sexual behaviors occurred in places such as the showers, bathrooms, and cell areas. The relationships developed in prison take on a significant role for women because they provide a source for meaningful personal and social interconnections with other people. These relationships may develop due to what G. T. Long (1993) describes as "a need for intimacy and closeness with another person" (p. 158).

With the prevalence of sexual activity that occurs within prisons, it would seem that the administration and correctional staff would be aware of its existence. Although administrators may often deny that such sexual behavior occurs, Donaldson (1990) reports that they know that a prisoner who becomes difficult or is disliked by staff can be placed in a position where he will become a victim of forced sexual behaviors by other inmates. In fact, inmates may even be sexually victimized by prison staff. Struckman-Johnson et al. (1996) reported that 18% of their victimized sample were forced to engage in sexual behaviors with prison staff. Mahon's (1996) inmate participants informed her that nonconsensual and even consensual sexual activity occurred between prisoners and the male correctional staff. The reasons given were for protection, wanted items, privileges, and access to services.

There is a final category of inmates which is often overlooked and not taken seriously within the prison system. This category consists of both pre- and postoperative transsexuals. Transsexuals are those who identify themselves as the opposite gender from their biological genitalia and may attempt surgery to change their genitalia (R. Smith, 1995). Petersen, Stephens, Dickey, and Lewis (1996) indicate that these prisoners pose a significant difficulty to prison management, yet results from their survey reflect that only 20% of 64 corrections departments indicated the existence of any formal policy regarding housing or treating transsexuals. Their study indicated that nearly every department lacked specialized therapy for these inmates. For postoperative transsexuals, only 32% of the departments stated that they would definitely house the prisoners according to their new gender (i.e., male-to-female transsexuals would be sent to a female prison).

When viewing these inmates from a sexual behavior perspective, it would seem that they would be at greater risk for sexual assault and abuse. However, the Petersen *et al.* (1996) study found that 85% of the departments reported that this was not felt to be an important issue. In fact, less than 15% considered transsexual inmates to be at greater risk for sexual or physical assault. However, one particular Supreme Court case suggests that transsexuals are at risk for harm. *Farmer v. Brennan* (1994) involved a preoperative transsexual who exhibited feminine characteristics. He was transferred to a higher security penitentiary and claimed to have been beaten and raped by another inmate after being placed in the general population. The inmate brought suit against the prison officials who housed him in the general population upon being transferred. In his previous location he was segregated. The Supreme Court ruled that "prison officials may be held liable under Eighth Amendment for denying humane conditions of confinement only if they know that inmates face a substantial risk of serious harm and disregard that risk by failing to take reasonable measures to abate it" (p. 1270). Based on this ruling, prison officials may need to be more aware of how they handle transsexuals and take more seriously their risks for being harmed.

From this review, it appears that sexual behaviors do exist among inmates and that the sexual behaviors in prisons are not restricted solely to offenders. Mahon (1996) provides an appropriate summary in which she quotes a female jail inmate, "Male COs [correctional officers] are having sex with females. Female COs are having sex with female inmates, and the male inmates are having sex with male inmates. Male inmates are having sex with female inmates. There's all kinds, it's a smorgasbord up there" (p. 1212).

Forensic Psychology and Policy Implications

After examining the data on inmate sexual behaviors, one alarming concern is the extent of AIDS and the spread of HIV. Mahon (1996) reported that at the end of 1994, the rate of AIDS cases in state and federal prisons was seven times higher than that in the total United States' population. If prisoners are engaging in a prohibited activity, then it is highly unlikely that they are participating in it safely. Some type of policy must be developed to provide inmates the means to engage in safe sex. It would be next to impossible to ensure that inmates abandoned their sexual behaviors, so instead of pretending that it does not exist, policies need to be developed to ensure that it occurs safely.

Another consideration that should be examined is the provision of counseling for inmates raped and sexually assaulted. These prisoners most likely do not want to come forth and discuss their experiences, so measures should be taken to ensure confidentiality. The trauma that one experiences after being raped is considerable, and ignoring the consequences could lead to future acting-out behaviors by those victimized. The inmate code regarding informants is probably too strong for those who have been raped to ignore it. Policies need to be developed, allowing these inmates into protective housing without needing to inform the staff who sexually assaulted them.

Regarding transsexual inmates, formal policies must be enacted in each prison for handling these cases. R. Smith (1995) suggests that it is important to house the prisoner based on what the genitalia currently is. She suggests other considerations should include how long the inmate has been receiving hormone therapy, what type of surgical procedures have been conducted, what the psychosocial needs of the inmate are, and how long the person will be incarcerated.

Suggestions for Future Research

An area of research requiring attention includes effective methods for the prevention of HIV in the prisons and jails. Effective mental health intervention and treatment for inmates who have been victims of sexual assaults should also be examined (Struckman-Johnson et al., 1996). It is important to understand what types of treatments work for these offenders so that the impact of any trauma may be reduced. Another important area for future research concerns sexual relations between prison staff and inmates. Attempting to identify what types of staff characteristics are associated with such behavior could help in screening out these candidates at the beginning of the hiring process. Thus, future psychological harm to prisoners could be averted. Also, more in-depth studies of administrators' awareness of inmate sexual behaviors and their responses to it would provide a better understanding of exactly where officials stand on this issue and what needs to be done to educate them on the effects of sexual assaults.

CHAPTER 12

Family Forensics

OVERVIEW

Incarceration dramatically impacts families. Correctional psychologists examine where and how persons in and outside of the institution cope with the emotional pain that comes from separation, loss, shame, loneliness, and the like when a family member is criminally confined. Thus, similar to the preceding chapter on civil forensics and corrections, family forensics investigates many of the social, interpersonal, and intrapsychic variables that give rise to expert psychological practice in penal facilities.

This chapter reviews five issues at the center of the family forensic field. These topics are not exhaustive. They merely represent some of the more poignant concerns at the crossroads of corrections, psychology, and family studies. These issues include (1) "make-believe" families, (2) pregnant women in prison, (3) women inmates and mother–child separation, (4) family members of inmates, and (5) mothers in prison.

People have a fundamental need to express intimacy and affection. The same is true for persons in prison, especially women. One response to this need is to create "make believe" families. What emotional needs do surrogate or "play" families fill for women in prison? What specific roles do prisoners assume in these kinship systems? How do pseudofamilies operate in the correctional milieu? Some women in prison, prior to and once confined, get pregnant. What health and mental health-care services are provided to incarcerated pregnant women? What health and mental health-care services are availed to adolescent girls in youth facilities? What are the constitutional limits to receiving such medical treatment? What is the emotional impact to women receiving minimal prenatal and newborn infant care while incarcerated? Many female prisoners are mothers. What are the emotional and health-care consequences to both mothers and their children when the parent is incarcerated? How do children (and mothers) deal with the anxiety of separation? How can forensic psychologists help ease the pain of separation caused by criminal confinement? Other family members such as spouses are also traumatized by the incarceration of a loved one. Loneliness, depression, and anxiety are just a few of the symptoms experienced by many spouses. What services exist (i.e., support groups) to address these psychological problems? What advocacy work is being done to improve the standards for prison visitation by family members? Mothers in prisons represent a special group of offender. Who are they demographically? Is there a personality profile for this offender group? To what extent do mothers in prison feel shame, guilt, and grief as a result of their (criminal) life choices? How do they cope with the grief that comes from the loss of parental bonding and parenting?

At the intersection of corrections, psychology, and family studies are an array of issues and controversies affecting the lives of persons incarcerated and their loved ones. Forensic psychologists are uniquely trained to explore these dynamic issues and assist prison systems in meeting the challenges posed by such constituencies. As the sections of this chapter make evident, more and better research is essential if society is to adequately respond to the problems posed by the family forensic field. Indeed, while most would agree that criminal confinement for offenses committed is punishment in itself, questions remain about how best to address the debilitating and agonizing consequences of life in prison for those confined and for those family members who wait for the release of their spouse, their parent, or their loved one.

"MAKE-BELIEVE" FAMILIES

Introduction

When men and women who commit crimes are sent to prison, it is easy for many people to say that they are being punished and should not be entitled to those things to which ordinary citizens are entitled. However, some criminals spend many years confined in the prison environment, and they still experience the same emotions and feelings as when they were not imprisoned. It is unrealistic to assume that these inmates can shut themselves off from wanting intimacy and affection, especially in such a lonely environment where the need for affection is perhaps greater (Watterson, 1996). Male and female prisoners recreate their desires and needs inside of the correctional facility, yet they do so in different ways. In female prisons, women create caring relationships (MacKenzie, Robinson, & Campbell, 1989) which have been referred to as kinship systems (Giallombardo, 1966), "play" families (MacKenzie *et al.*, 1989), surrogate families (Church, 1990), and pseudofamilies (Pollock-Byrne, 1990).

> Kelly was 28 years old when she was convicted of selling drugs on the streets. She was sentenced to 5 years in a state correctional facility. Kelly had spent a few weeks in the local jail before, but she had never been to prison. She had heard all sorts of stories about prison and was not sure what to expect when she arrived. She was scared and felt very alone. She had no family to speak of, and her so-called friends were other drug dealers and addicts whom she could not rely on to be supportive during her time of need. On Kelly's first day in prison, she was placed in a cell with a 23-year-old inmate named Sabrina. Although Sabrina was 5 years younger than Kelly, she seemed much older and wiser. Sabrina instantly began sharing her feelings with Kelly in an attempt to have Kelly talk about her fears. Sabrina stated that it would make things easier if Kelly would talk about them. Kelly immediately felt a connection to Sabrina, which she had never experienced with anyone before. In a very short amount of time, Kelly began to view Sabrina as a mother figure and even began calling her "mom." She also was surprised to learn that Sabrina was married to another female inmate who was housed in a different unit. This inmate's name was Christina, but everyone called her Chris. Kelly soon began to call her "dad" because Chris behaved like a father and treated Kelly like her own daughter. The three of them were just like a regular family and Kelly was able to adjust to prison life with their help and support.

Literature Review

As exemplified in Kelly's case, women who are sentenced to serve time in prison find ways to cope with their environment. One way many of these women accomplish this is by modeling real families (Watterson, 1996). They use these "play" mothers, fathers, daughters, and lovers to make up for losing their real parents, children, and lovers (C. Burke, 1992). The inmates do not necessarily enter prison to consciously create these families, but when they are scared and lonely, they either retreat into their own misery or create new relationships which develop into substitute families (Watterson, 1996).

As one of the early researchers in this area, Giallombardo (1966) defined a prison family as "a group of related kin linked by ties of allegiance and alliance who sometimes occupy a common household and are characterized by varying degrees of solidarity" (p. 163). She expressed the notion that many of these women come together in homosexual relationships to create a marriage unit. Some of the prisoners take on the role of a man and adopt masculine traits such as wearing their hair short, wearing pants, and expressing typical societal male characteristics of strength and authority. Other inmates take on the feminine role of wife or mother and wear make-up and more feminine clothing (Giallombardo, 1966; Watterson, 1996).

Pollock-Byrne (1990) described the male and female roles as being stereotypical where the males are domineering and leading and the females are nurturing and pleasing. Because the inmates play these roles in such a stereotypical fashion, those playing the male role may seem so masculine that they are referred to as "he" and "him". These "men" also may become carried away with their roles and treat their wives as slaves, ordering them around. The women who go along with this behavior probably have been involved in similar relationships while outside of prison. Therefore, it is a habit for them to do anything in order to keep their man (Watterson, 1996).

Despite the sometimes negative consequences of developing prison marriages, these relationships actually serve to meet the inmates' needs for affection, and they provide closeness and a sense of belonging (Giallombardo, 1966). The women turn to each other for comfort and create these homosexual relationships and surrogate families (Church, 1990). The marriages may not even have anything to do with sex. In fact, some women may never consummate their marriage in a sexual manner (Watterson, 1996). Instead, possibly for the first time ever, the women base their relationships on kinship and intimacy as opposed to sex (Pollock-Byrne, 1990).

Relationships among female prisoners may not be restricted to homosexual unions. Entire families organize themselves by choice and give each other titles (MacKenzie et al., 1989). Women of varying ages assume roles of mothers, daughters, aunts, and fathers (Church, 1990; MacKenzie et al., 1989). As in Kelly and Sabrina's situation, age does not necessarily dictate what role the women play. These families are not bound by ethnic categories either. Many families will include members of several ethnicities (Church, 1990). Pollock-Byrne (1990) reported that the mother–daughter dyad is the most common familial relationship. A prison mother may have several daughters, and if she has a prison husband, then he may become their father, as Chris did for Kelly. Pollock-Byrne also indicated that when playing the role of mother in prison, the inmate may be a better parent to her role-playing daughter than she ever was to her real children on the outside. For the inmates playing the role of the child, their prison mother serves as a type of role model and may become like a real mother, who helps instead of neglects them (Watterson, 1996b). In Kelly's situation, Sabrina became a real mother for her.

Whether this is true in all situations, prison families, especially the roles of parent and child, are viewed as very special. The relationships consist of consideration and warmth (Giallombardo, 1966). The families are similar to regular friendships where the inmates support each other in order to decrease the stress of life in prison. Coming together as a family allows them to feel a sense of security, ease, and connection with others (Watterson, 1996). The family also serves as a form of protection for each member. If a member of the family is in physical danger from some other inmate, then the "father" or "brother" can protect that person (Giallombardo, 1966; Watterson, 1996).

Some researchers suggest that these prison families may not be as common as they used to be and may serve a purpose for only some women. MacKenzie *et al.* (1989) conducted a study and found that many women newly admitted to prison were involved in play families. However, those who had been in prison for a great deal of time did not partake in this phenomenon. The researchers suggested that these play families may assist inmates in adjusting to prison life, but then once acclimated, this need for safety and security disappears. Pollock-Byrne (1990) discussed something similar. She stated that when an inmate approaches her release date or when she maintains close ties to her real family, then the need for a pseudofamily is not as strong as for those inmates who are alone and have no outside connections. Kelly is an example of this latter type of inmate. Without those outside relationships, the prison families become real families. Pollock-Byrne also suggested that with increased efforts at family programming and community support, female inmates are able to preserve their outside connections, which therefore decreases the need for a prison family.

In a recent study conducted by Ansay (as cited in Silverman & Vega, 1996), it was found that the most common group in prison was more like a gang than a family. Approximately 6 to 12 inmates who were serving long sentences comprised these gang groups and had labels such as "associates" and "cousins," thus providing more support for the notion that prison families may not be as common as they once were.

Genders and Player (1990) questioned prison staff about these inmate families, and their responses appeared to concur with what inmates reported. They suggested that relationships were more about finding affection and emotional support than they were about engaging in sexual behaviors. The staff reported that many women engaged in lesbian behaviors at some time during their imprisonment. In fact, the staff indicated that this was an eventual phase for women serving long terms in prison; however, these women were not thought to be lesbians when not imprisoned. Prison administrators have indicated that they believe that fewer than 5% of female inmates have engaged in lesbian relationships outside of prison (Watterson, 1996).

Prison staff also reported that problems with these families can occur when a couple breaks up because jealous feelings and even suicidal thoughts can erupt (Genders & Player, 1990). Watterson (1996) indicated that problems occur when a female inmate "drops her belt" (p. 294). This is when the woman reverts back to her female role after playing a male role. It creates problems because there are not enough female inmates who want to play the male role. The woman is then seen as a phony and this is threatening to other inmates.

Despite the difficulties prison families can create, it appears as though they do offer something for which these women are searching. As one inmate stated, "... inside this place, when I do something with a girl, usually I feel like someone's comforting me and just making me feel good. It's not really a sex thing, even when it's sex, because in here you feel so damn little and alone ..." (Watterson, 1996, p. 285).

Forensic Psychology and Policy Implications

An important consideration in these make-believe families is to understand why the inmates find them necessary. As the literature has suggested, female inmates find that they are an important source of support and a necessity in adjusting to the prison environment. Psychologists and mental health workers should play a significant role in helping inmates and correctional staff identify this need. Policies should be implemented to assist these women in their initial adjustment to prison. Psychologists must make correctional staff aware of the types of issues these women confront upon entry into the prison system so that staff can assist them during the transition. This could prevent some acting-out behaviors that the women might otherwise exhibit out of fear and insecurity.

Policies also should be developed to prevent women from being labeled as lesbians and placed in separate housing units if these prisoners do not view themselves in such a manner. If female inmates assume a role in a homosexual relationship only while in prison, then when nearing release, they should be assisted in coming to terms with this. They also will need assistance in transitioning back into heterosexual relationships and into their real families.

Another dimension to consider when dealing with female inmates is their natural families on the outside. Policies should be developed to help women maintain connections with their friends and families so that the need to create make-believe ones will not be necessary. If a women enters prison and does not have any connections to anyone outside of prison, then correctional staff and psychologists should assist her in developing ties to the community in the form of education, vocation, and community service. In this way, the inmate may have something to look forward to upon release and not feel so alone upon having to leave her prison family.

Suggestions for Future Research

In recent years, not much research has been conducted on female inmates' make-believe families. Much of the research was conducted in the late 1960s and 1970s, with a few scattered studies in the early 1990s. If this is a phenomenon which is no longer as prevalent in prisons, then studies should be conducted to determine why this is so and what may have taken its place. If women no longer feel the need for these families, then what are they doing to adjust to prison life? More current investigations need to be implemented.

An area of research that has been neglected is learning how men adjust to and cope with prison life. If they do not create surrogate families in prison, then it is important to learn what they do instead? Are their mechanisms for coping effective, and, if not, then what can be done to assist them? If men are able to maintain ties with their real families, then it would be helpful to know how they manage to do so. In this way, maybe female prisons can implement the policies and programs that assist men in continuing their relationships with their families.

PREGNANT WOMEN IN PRISON

Introduction

The inmate population has been on the rise for several years, and the number of female inmates is increasing at the quickest rate (Flanagan, 1995; Safyer & Richmond, 1995). Incarcerated women pose significantly different problems for penal institutions than incarcerated men, especially in the area of health care. This is because of difficulties related to pregnancy and childbirth. Data reveal that approximately 6% of women arrested are pregnant, and more than 80% of incarcerated women fall in the age range for childbirth (Safyer & Richmond, 1995). Pregnant inmates create the need for appropriate health care and special services, which should be provided by all institutions housing women offenders. As is discussed later, many institutions have not implemented this type of programming for their pregnant prisoners.

> When Louwana was sent to a state prison she was pregnant. Her charges were not of a violent nature, and therefore she was not considered a maximum-security prisoner. However, she was confined around the clock and made to sleep on the floor of a cell which housed too many inmates. While confined with so many other prisoners, she came in contact with diseases such as tuberculosis and measles. Obstetric medical services were never provided to her during the entire course of her pregnancy. When her contractions started, signaling the beginning of labor, she was informed by the correctional staff that nobody from the medical unit was available at that time. Louwana was forced to wait outside the medical clinic, enduring labor pains for 3 hours. She finally gave birth where she was waiting. Once her baby was born, it was deprived of oxygen and survived for only a few months (Lays, as cited in Osborne, 1995).

Literature Review

Although Louwana's situation may seem extreme and unlikely to occur in modern prisons, it was not long ago that health care was not even a requirement for prisoners. It was the Supreme Court case of *Estelle v. Gamble* (1976) which declared that a disregard for health care was a violation of the cruel and unusual punishment clause of the Eighth Amendment. The Court ruled that this applied to the doctors treating the inmates and to the correctional staff whose job it was to transport the inmates to medical units and comply with medical directives. Although this case did not specifically discuss the issue of pregnancy, it did conclude that health care must be made available in all penal institutions, including women's prisons.

Despite the new law, it has been a long struggle for women, and especially pregnant women, to ensure that their health needs are met while in prison. Typically it is an institution-by-institution battle. For example, the inmates at Bedford Hills Correctional Facility in New York brought a class-action lawsuit against the institution for inadequate medical care. The Court found that the level of medical care was adequate, but the administrative and record-keeping procedures were not. Therefore, the inmates were denied medical attention for significant lengths of time. The Court ruled that the institution had to devise plans for better access to the medical care the facility provided (*Todaro v. Ward*, 1977).

Although these lawsuits reflect more general rulings regarding health care, the pregnant inmate benefits greatly because she usually has many more health concerns than the typical pregnant woman. Pregnant inmates are often exposed to more illnesses and diseases, including sexually transmitted diseases. These women tend to have backgrounds filled with abuse, poverty, poor nutrition, and drug use. These factors all contribute to increased risks for pregnancy complications (Safyer & Richmond, 1995). Incarcerated women also tend to smoke cigarettes and drink alcohol during pregnancy, they do not seek prenatal care until later in their pregnancies, they have fewer prenatal care visits, and this prenatal care is usually inadequate (S. L. Martin, Kim, Kupper, Meyer, & Hays, 1997). There are also the psychological adjustments these women must face, not only with the pregnancy, but with adapting to the prison environment, typically with a lack of familial or social support (Safyer & Richmond, 1995). The prison milieu is a stressful place with women being exposed to violence, aggression, and isolation. If support systems are created, they may be opposed to the prison authorities, decreasing the likelihood for pregnant inmates to seek prenatal care, especially if medical staff are viewed as part of the authority system (Hufft, 1992).

According to J. S. Wilson and Leasure (1991), the medical standards that have been developed in prisons focus only a small percentage on women's needs, and these standards typically are not very specific with regard to implementation. They suggest that if prenatal care is not provided on-site, then women often miss their prenatal appointments and classes because transportation for taking inmates to court appointments receives higher priority. They also note that pregnant inmates often do not have adequate knowledge about options available to them.

To determine what types of services are available for pregnant women within prisons, Wooldredge and Masters (1993) conducted a survey of facilities and found that only 48% of the institutions had actual policies in writing regarding health care for pregnant inmates. Programs for pregnant prisoners included prenatal counseling, lighter work loads, separate housing areas, assistance with infant placement, and postnatal counseling. These initiatives were improvements over what had been availed in the past, yet they were offered in only 21% of the facilities. The authors' survey also found that there were no programs which dealt specifically with the psychological aspects of being a pregnant inmate. Wardens from the prisons surveyed offered their opinions about the types of problems that existed for this population. These problems included poor resources for situations such as false labors, premature births or miscarriages, lack of maternity clothes, housing in inappropriate facilities, no facilities for mother and baby to stay together, no separate visiting areas for children, and overcrowded prisons.

If adult-female prisons have these inadequacies for pregnant inmates, then it is unlikely that youth facilities would provide better services. Although they are children themselves, teenage delinquents have babies of their own. A study conducted by Breuner and Farrow (1995) found that 68% of the youth facilities had approximately one to five pregnant adolescents. For those facilities with pregnant youths, "27% have no social work services available, 31% have no nursing or basic prenatal care, 38% have no obstetric prenatal services, 62% have no nutritionist available, 70% do not teach parenting, and 87% do not provide childbirth education classes" (p. 329). It seems that services for these young mothers-to-be would be even more crucial in youth facilities, yet they are not provided.

Despite the lack of services for pregnant inmates, studies have found that women incarcerated during portions of their pregnancies may actually benefit from their incarceration. Martin et al. (1997) reported that women who were incarcerated for longer periods of their pregnancies gave birth to babies who weighed more than did women who were incarcerated for shorter periods. Higher birth weight was considered to be a sign of good health. These women also did not have babies with significantly lower birth weights than women who had never been incarcerated. In another study comparing births for women incarcerated during part of their pregnancy and births while not incarcerated at all, S. L. Martin, Rieger, Kupper, Meyer, and Qaqish (1997) reported that although there were no significant differences in birth weights between the two, an increase in amount of time spent incarcerated was associated with an increase in birth weight. They hypothesized that because many of these pregnant women have such chaotic lives on the street, the prison provides a more stable environment with food, shelter, and safety, therefore improving the health of their future infants.

For institutions providing adequate prenatal assistance, what types of programs and standards do they include in their health care? Safyer and Richmond (1995) described the services in New York City where the Montefiore Medical Center provides health care to all inmates. For pregnant inmates, there are set standards which include comprehensive counseling, assistance, and medical care according to professional and legal requirements. If an inmate is identified as pregnant, she is automatically considered to be a high risk. The pregnant women are prescribed prenatal vitamins and iron supplements, and they are given routine prenatal care, seeing medical staff a minimum of once every 4 weeks. The doctor's visits become more frequent the closer the women are to delivery. Doctors are present in the institution around the clock. Prenatal counseling is provided to all pregnant women. This counseling incorporates information about HIV transmission as well as general pregnancy information. Women are also counseled about the negative effects of drug use on themselves and their unborn baby. If they are addicted to heroin upon incarceration, then they are placed on methadone maintenance for the rest of their pregnancy. The women are placed on a special diet, and, in their last 3 months of pregnancy, are housed together to develop a supportive environment for the soon-to-be mothers.

Flanagan (1995) described two different programs implemented in Maryland. The first program is called Healthy Start, and it provides health care to pregnant inmates, which can be continued upon release. The women are urged to decrease their high-risk behaviors, they are provided counseling and education about their pregnancy, and they are taught parenting techniques. The pregnant women are taught about appropriate diets and vitamins, and they are provided with information about the effects of drugs, alcohol, and cigarettes. Emphasis is also placed on keeping appointments with doctors. The second program is called Baby Talk and focuses more on educational topics than health care. Both pregnant inmates and prisoners who already have children participate in this program. Topics include:

> prenatal information; stages of fetal development; dealing with a second or third child; labor and delivery; postpartum information; postpartum blues; breast feeding; infant diet; food sensitivities and allergies; interacting with the infant; "high need" babies; colic; discipline; and nurturing, stimulating, and educating the baby. (p. 51)

Finally, Ryan and Grassano (1992) described a program in the Santa Rita County Jail in Alameda County, California, which developed following a lawsuit that pregnant inmates filed in 1986. A medical division was created to handle the needs of women, and pregnant inmates were moved to their own housing unit separate from the general population. Pregnant women are now provided with a special diet and counseling services. They even are able to have an abortion if they choose that option. The pregnant inmates also are provided with an exercise program and social services if necessary.

Forensic Psychology and Policy Implications

A significant problem that exists for pregnant inmates is the lack of standardized policies regarding their needs. Although the courts have continuously ruled that health care must be provided, specific state statutes still must be developed which define procedures for handling pregnant women who become incarcerated (Wooldredge & Masters, 1993). If standardized policies were implemented, then situations such as Louwana's might be avoided. Hufft (1992) suggested that maternity care should focus on assessment and intervention to help pregnant women adapt to the prison environment, especially regarding their limited physical and emotional surroundings and new social support systems. Policies also should focus on special medical skills for assessing the health of pregnant and postpartum inmates and on providing prenatal education and childbirth classes (J. S. Wilson & Leasure, 1991).

Wooldredge and Masters (1993) offered suggestions for several areas to be included in policies for pregnant inmates. They indicated that educational programs must be provided so that incarcerated and pregnant women can be aware of their options. Also, they should be taught parenting skills and child development. They stated that these women needed to be housed in separate living areas, eat special diets, wear maternity clothes, and have more contact with medical staff in case of complications. Counseling programs which focus on the psychological stress the pregnant inmates experience should also be included in prison policies. This appears to be the area with the least amount of services for this offender population.

Another problem for pregnant inmates involves their use of unhealthy and illegal substances. Detoxification programs designed specifically for pregnant women should be developed within prisons. These programs should focus on the withdrawal symptoms the mother and the unborn child experience (Ryan & Grassano, 1992). There are complications and concerns unique to pregnant substance abusers that should be dealt with in a separate program. These initiatives also could be developed outside the prison so that pregnant offenders continued to receive services once released. Women often do not spend their entire pregnancies incarcerated. One study reported that 52% of pregnant inmates were in prison for 8 weeks or less of their pregnancy (S. L. Martin *et al.*, 1997). Thus, in addition to substance abuse treatment, pre- and postnatal health care should be coordinated with the community so that women do not develop complications once they leave the prison or jail.

One major area neglected with regard to pregnant inmates is providing correctional staff with the appropriate knowledge and skills to help women have healthy pregnancies while in prison. Often the officers are unaware of what may be potentially harmful to an unborn fetus. Their primary concern is with the safety of the overall prison, and they must have the same rules for all inmates in order to accomplish this. However, these rules could be harmful to a pregnant woman, such as where the inmate sleeps, what type of food she eats, and what type of work and recreational activities in which she engages. If correctional staff are taught the key areas of concern for pregnant inmates and what their psychological state might be like because of them, then staff could be better prepared to handle physical and mental health situations as they arise instead of after the damage has already been done.

Suggestions for Future Research

Studies should be conducted on the effects of these short periods of incarceration in relation to the health of the pregnant inmate's newborn (Safyer & Richmond, 1995). It is important to learn if the prenatal care received is continued once the woman leaves prison, and, if not, what the consequences are for the baby. More in-depth evaluations also should be conducted of programs that have been implemented in institutions for pregnant women. Are adequate services being provided and are the women taking advantage of these services? Evaluations also could determine if the health care is meeting minimum standards defined by the courts. Although evaluations of existing programs come too late to help women like Louwana, it is important that they become model initiatives for all institutions housing female inmates so that adequate prenatal care, nutrition, and substance abuse treatment help improve the outcomes of these high-risk pregnancies (Safyer & Richmond, 1995).

Further research needs to be conducted on the psychological effects of incarceration for pregnant women. Once some of these effects are determined, then counseling services could be designed to meet the prisoner's needs. Even though adequate health care may be provided, if a woman experiences severe psychological stress, her unborn child could still be harmed. Learning how to help pregnant offenders cope and deal with their problems is an area that must be developed.

FEMALE PRISONERS AND MOTHER–CHILD SEPARATION

Introduction

Children of inmates are often-overlooked victims. Moreover, this group is not small. One estimate noted that there are 1.5 million children with an incarcerated parent or parents (Center for Children of Incarcerated Parents, as cited in Adalist-Estrin, 1994). Brownell (1997) reported that at least 75% of female inmates have children, with the average of two children per prisoner. Having a parent become incarcerated can be very traumatic and can lead to severe consequences for most children, including "anxiety, hyperarousal, depression, bedwetting, eating and sleeping disorders, behavior and conduct disorders, attention disorders, and prolonged developmental regression" (Center for Children of Incarcerated Parents, as cited in Adalist-Estrin, 1994, p. 165). As examined in this section, the mother–child separation can have negative consequences for the mother as well.

> When Annie was sent to prison for 1 to 3 years, she was 8-months pregnant. Upon giving birth in prison, her baby was taken away from her and sent to live with Annie's mother, who was interested in becoming a foster parent. Annie became depressed after being separated from her baby and upon realizing that she may lose custody. She is worried about the baby living with her mother because Annie reported being physically abused by this woman while growing up. Despite this, she feels there are no other alternatives: she cannot rely on the baby's father to help her because he beat and threatened her both before and during her pregnancy. Annie's depression has escalated to the point of her mentioning ways to commit suicide. (Brownell, 1997)
>
> Leslie is a first-time offender who is incarcerated. She has a 9-year-old son who was living with her prior to her incarceration. Her son now lives with his father from whom Leslie is separated. The father does not want their son to go to the jail but agreed to allow visitation. The son wants to visit his mother, yet he is afraid of the jail. Leslie is worried that her son will no longer respect her and that she may be causing psychological damage to him. Although she wants to see her son, she does not want him to see her in jail because she fears this will create more damage than has already been done (Hairston, 1991b).

Literature Review

As the case illustrations show, there are many issues involved when dealing with children of incarcerated parents. Indeed, children are not the only ones who can experience the negative consequences of being separated. In Leslie's instance, the incarcerated mother may feel embarrassed and guilty about being in jail and having to subject her children to such an environment. These mothers may not even want their children to visit them in jail or prison (Hairston, 1991b). Many incarcerated mothers report that the worst part of being incarcerated is having to be separated from their children (Church, 1990; Hairston, 1991b). Even if they want to see their children, other factors may prevent them from attending visiting days. Often women's prisons are in places far away from children's homes and in areas difficult to reach by public transportation, making it difficult for traveling (Church, 1990; Kiser, 1991).

Similar to Annie's case, sometimes the children are placed with foster families during the mother's incarceration, and the foster parents may not want the child to visit the mother because of their own desires to adopt the child (Osborne, 1995). Sometimes even the mother's own relatives do not want the children to visit her in prison (Kiser, 1991). A survey conducted by Hairston (1991b) found that 71% of incarcerated mothers had not had any visitation with their children during their period of confinement.

When children lose their mother to incarceration, there are many negative consequences. Kiser (1991) found that children felt they were to blame for their mother's offense and became very depressed. They continued to experience these negative emotions years after the mother's incarceration and some even attempted suicide. Falk (1995) noted that children feel powerless when they have to sit by and watch their mothers go to jail. Any attachments that are present must be put on hold until the mother returns. The author stated that these children experience grief emotions such as anger, denial, and depression. They may withdraw from others, or they may begin to act out and become aggressive. Feinman (1994) suggested that children experience emotions such as insecurity, lack of trust, confusion, and loneliness. These emotions can show themselves in mental and physical illnesses and a drop in school grades; M. C. Moses (1995) reported similar consequences for children. They "are more likely to experience anxiety, depression, post-traumatic stress symptoms, aggression, attention disorders, truancy and a decline in school performance. These children also are more likely to become pregnant in their teens" (M. C. Moses, 1995, p. 125).

If a child loses his or her mother to incarceration, then who takes care of the child? Hairston's (1991b) survey found that in 34% of the cases, the maternal grandmother became the caretaker. These children often live with relatives or friends of the mother. If these are not possibilities, then state-financed foster families care for them (Falk, 1995; Osborne, 1995). Occasionally, siblings have to be separated and live in different homes (Falk, 1995), thus increasing the loss they experience.

Feinman (1994) reported that some states have laws which allow the state to determine whether an incarcerated mother is unfit and to take away her children via a foster home or adoption. Once again, this creates additional loss for the child.

There are several solutions that could be implemented so that the child will not have to go through the trauma of enduring the incarceration of one's mother. Perhaps the most comprehensive is one that permits children to live with their mothers while in prison for a certain length of time (Feinman, 1994; Jaffe, Pons, & Wicky, 1997). Jaffe et al. (1997) report that the negative impact of this solution is that a child will have to experience the prison environment. The children may have to live in a small cell with their mother under very high levels of stress. Prison life is very regulated and limits the amount and type of information a child experiences, therefore placing a limit on the child's growth. The authors report that the mother is constantly watched and cannot freely care for her child. She also must rely on the prison to help meet the child's needs. Others opposed to this solution feel that prison is not a place for raising children and that these youths would learn to become criminals by associating with their offending mothers (Feinman, 1994). Jaffe et al. (1997) suggest the positive impact of this solution is that it emphasizes the mother–child bond and the important part it plays in a developing child. Being with one's mother is critical for a developing child and having her taken away during the early years could create some very negative consequences.

Some correctional institutions have implemented programs to allow children to remain with their incarcerated mothers. In the city of New York, the Legal Aid Society brought a lawsuit against the Department of Corrections based on the notion that separating a mother and newborn child is an action of cruel and unusual punishment under the Eighth Amendment. Apparently, there was a New York State law which allowed infants to remain in state prisons until the age of 1 year, so the Legal Aid Society wanted that law applied to the city jail. The court agreed with this argument, and, since 1985, incarcerated mothers have been allowed to have their newborn children remain with them in a special area of the jail designed for such a purpose (Feinman, 1994). The Bedford Hills Correctional Facility in New York has been a model prison for such programs as it was the first women's prison to implement a nursery for mothers and their infants (Brownell, 1997). Positive results have been reported in relation to these nursery programs. They decrease tensions and increase obedience and morale among female inmates. They also affect the staff in a positive way (Feinman, 1994).

A similar program in Nebraska was implemented in order to decrease the effects of separation between a mother and her child due to incarceration. Children younger than 18 months old can remain at the correctional facility with their mothers in a nursery equipped for six infants. The mothers must take prenatal courses, and other inmates can become involved by babysitting or providing support for the mothers (Hromadka, 1995).

California also offers incarcerated mothers a chance to remain with their children. The program is called Mother-Infant Care, and it is offered to minimum-security female prisoners. These women are allowed to live with their young children throughout the length of their sentence. However, they must participate in parental education courses and community service, and they are offered opportunities for job training and continuing education (Gifford, 1992).

Most programs which allow children to live with their mothers in prison have been developed for only very young children. There have been attempts to create other options for older children through visitation programs. Having children visit their mothers is viewed as an important ingredient to maintaining attachment bonds (Adalist-Estrin, 1994). Despite this, there are still few initiatives which provide visitation for children on a consistent basis (M. C. Moses, 1995). However, some alternatives that have been developed include expanded visitations, longer visitation hours, and overnight to week-long visits (Adalist-Estrin, 1994).

One of these types of programs is offered to children ages 5 to 12. Once a week, specified drivers take the children to have contact visits with their mothers in the correctional institution. One negative aspect of this program is that it may exclude one or more children in a family from visiting their mother (Falk, 1995). In Nebraska, the Mother-Offspring Life Development Program provides an opportunity for older children to have overnight visits with their mother within the correctional facility (Hromadka, 1995). Another unique project involves Girl Scout meetings within the correctional facility. This program was implemented in 1992, and daughters ages 5 to 13 meet with their mothers for two Saturdays every month and hold a Girl Scout meeting. This provides longer visiting hours and a chance for mothers to participate in their daughters' lives (M. C. Moses, 1995). These various initiatives represent what has been developed thus far in an attempt to decrease the negative effects of separation due to incarceration for both children and mothers.

Forensic Psychology and Policy Implications

Although efforts have been made to improve programs for children and their incarcerated mothers, there are still many issues that remain unresolved. For instance, as Falk (1995) pointed out, because of their restrictions, many of these projects exclude one or more children of the same family from visiting their mother. This could create a new set of problems for the family. It may be unreasonable for all of a woman's children to live with her in the prison, but programs should be developed where all the children in one family can visit their mother for extended periods of time.

Since incarcerated women have suggested that being separated from their children is the most difficult aspect of their confinement, support services designed specifically to assist them adjust to this separation should be developed further (Hairston, 1991b). Annie would have benefitted greatly from assistance on how to cope with being separated from her child. Psychologists can play an active role in this arena. Psychologists can also work with correctional staff and facilities on how best to implement and run programs where children live within the prison. Not all staff will be knowledgeable about how to provide a positive environment for children, so child development specialists should be involved in the programming. Also, the correctional facilities need to develop visitation areas which promote family bonding (Hairston, 1991b) and help children overcome their fears of going to the prison for visitation. As Leslie's case shows, children are afraid of jails and prisons and may not want to see their mothers for this reason.

Once programs and services have been developed within the correctional institution, then policies should be developed to assist these same women when released from prison. Currently, there is no set standard for continuing services outside of the prison (Adalist-Estrin, 1994). As in Annie's situation, these mothers may be struggling with someone who is seeking to terminate their parental rights, and they may need assistance with this process. Correctional facilities could have social workers on staff whose role it is to help these women transition back into their families.

One area that has been neglected is the development of more comprehensive programs for fathers who become incarcerated. In some situations, the father may have been the sole caretaker, and therefore his children would experience the same sense of grief over the loss of the parent. Even if the children have a mother at home, they still have a connection with their father and should be able to visit him in order to maintain that connection. Male correctional facilities could assist with this by also improving their visitation areas and allowing for extended visits by the children. If the father is the sole caretaker of a young child, then policies for developing live-in programs at male prisons also should be developed.

Suggestions for Future Research

An important area of research is to determine which situations are beneficial and which are detrimental for children who continue contact with their incarcerated parents (Hairston, 1991a). In some instances, seeking termination of parental rights may be in the best interest of the child, but a better understanding of what those instances are should be explored. Similarly, the effects on children of visiting or not visiting their incarcerated parent should be studied further (Hairston, 1991a).

Additional research should be conducted regarding the possible effects on children who live with their mothers in correctional institutions. More information is needed, particularly regarding whether this is beneficial or detrimental to youths. If benefits are assured, then examining whether they would extend to older children should be the next step.

Finally, research should examine what the effects are on children who have a father who becomes incarcerated, even if that father is not the sole provider. Do these children experience the same sense of loss as losing a mother? Are the bonds as strong with a father as they are with a mother? The father plays an important role in his children's lives, and more information needs to be learned about what kind of an effect his absence creates.

OTHER FAMILY MEMBERS OF INMATES

Introduction

The influx of incarcerated individuals in recent years has had an impact on millions of families. For every one person who is incarcerated, many others are affected, some of whom include spouses, parents, and children. Oftentimes family members of inmates suffer consequences ranging from financial hardship to emotional trauma. Spouses of inmates are often faced with loneliness, alteration of their role in the family, and financial crises to name a few. Similarly, children of prisoners frequently experience emotional and behavioral problems. Despite the large number of individuals affected by incarceration, there are limited resources available to assist family members of inmates. This is perhaps due to the fact that the needs of inmates' families are rarely considered by police officers, the courts, correctional institutions, and social service agencies (Hostetter & Jinnah, 1993). Furthermore, there is an inadequate amount of attention given to the families of prisoners by researchers (B. E. Carlson & Cervera, 1992; Kiser, 1991). While there remains a dearth of resources for family members, recently pioneering efforts have been initiated aimed at addressing this need. Current programs have been established which focus on familial support groups as well as on enhancing the visitation experience for family members of inmates.

> Nancy and Mike have been married for 9 years and have four children under the age of 6. Four months ago Mike was incarcerated as the result of a conviction for drug-related charges. Because of Mike's drug addiction, the family has had difficulty paying the bills for the past 3 years. However, despite his addiction, Mike was able to maintain steady employment in construction.
>
> After Mike's incarceration, the family began to deteriorate. Nancy never finished high school and married Mike when she was 17 years old. Thus, she did not have the necessary skills to secure employment. Nancy and Mike's children had never spent any significant amount of time away from home since Nancy had always stayed there to care for them. When the home utilities were turned off, Nancy started working at two local fast food restaurants to ensure that the bills were paid. Nancy's new role in the family meant that the four children spent every day and some nights away from home. Two of the children started to display aggressive behavior and one child started to withdraw from everyone.
>
> After 9 months of incarceration, Mike has only seen his children once. Nancy works 18 hours a day in order to pay the bills and simply does not have time to visit her husband, much less take the children to the prison. Nancy has sought assistance from social services, but has been told that there is nothing they can do to help her and that she seems to be managing fine.

Literature Review

Among those most affected by an individual's incarceration are the inmate's spouse and children, as depicted in the case illustration of Nancy and Mike. At any given time, over 1.5 million children have a parent who is incarcerated (Hostetter & Jinnah, 1993). It is widely recognized that children who have an incarcerated parent experience a host of behavioral and emotional difficulties. One reason for such difficulties is the absence of contact that children have with the incarcerated parent. For various reasons, research has shown that children of incarcerated fathers rarely visit their fathers while they are in jail or prison. Hairston (1989) reports that nearly one-third of the incarcerated fathers in her sample had not received a visit from their children since the time of their incarceration. Among the reasons given for the absence of contact between father and child are lack of transportation to the prison, opposition by the mother of the child, and objection by the incarcerated father. Many fathers in prison have reportedly made the decision themselves to forego visitation with their children due to the potential negative effects that such visitation could have on their offspring (Johnston & Gabel, 1995). In the study conducted by Hairston (1989), approximately one-fifth of the fathers in the sample reported that their children could not visit them because the mother of the child objected.

Regardless of the reason for the absence of contact between the incarcerated parents and their children, the lives of such children are dramatically affected by this separation. Norman (1995) notes that many children of incarcerated parents are affected by the separation for the rest of their lives. According to Norman (1995), such children may experience difficulty with close relationships in the future and a heightened sensitivity to separation and rejection by others. Moreover, particularly for infants and toddlers who experience separation from their incarcerated parent, separation anxiety often results (Johnston, 1995a). This is largely due to the fact that young children develop their sense of security from the presence of their primary caretaker (Johnston, 1995a). Therefore, when incarceration takes one parent from the child, the young child often experiences the trauma of parental abandonment.

While it is apparent that children of incarcerated parents have needs to which psychological and social service agencies should attend, there is a scarcity of such assistance available in the United States (Johnston, 1995b). The Center for Children of Incarcerated Parents is one service that pioneers therapeutic intervention programs for children of inmates (Gabel & Johnston, 1995). This Center recommends that treatment be targeted toward children who display signs of aggression, withdrawal, anxiety, or excessive delinquent behavior such as lying and stealing (Johnston, 1995b). The Center further advocates comprehensive assessments of the children which include behavioral, developmental, familial, and medical needs. While the Center for Children of Incarcerated Parents established such a program in 1991 (i.e., the Early Therapeutic Intervention Project), it was terminated in 1993.

In addition to the deleterious effects incarceration creates for children of inmates, spouses of prisoners are also affected in many ways. Similar to the children of incarcerated parents, spouses suffer from the separation resulting from the confinement. However, the effects of the separation give rise to different issues for the adult spouse than for the young child. For example, extreme financial burdens are often placed on the spouse of an inmate. As noted by Hostetter and Jinnah (1993), many wives of inmates are often forced into the job market with limited skills on which to rely and consequently are forced to place their children in daycare for the first time. Moreover, collect calls are frequently the means by which spouses remain in contact with their incarcerated partner, thereby placing the financial burden once again on the nonincarcerated party.

Coupled with the practical concerns of financial hardship, spouses of inmates endure a great deal of emotional strain. Among the concerns experienced by spouses are fear and anxiety about the well-being of their partner in prison, feelings of loneliness and isolation, and sexual frustration (B. E. Carlson & Cervera, 1992). Moreover, spouses are often faced with the stereotyping that accompanies incarceration. Many wives report moving from their place of residence as a result of the stigma placed on them and in an attempt to be closer to the husband's place of confinement (Fishman, 1990). Further, as a result of the shame and stigma associated with prison, wives of inmates often receive pressure from family and friends to divorce their husband while he is incarcerated (B. E. Carlson & Cervera, 1992).

Perhaps one of the most beneficial means of assisting prisoner spouses is through the establishment of support groups. B. E. Carlson and Cervera (1992) report that there are currently a few isolated programs which offer such opportunities. These authors note that such support groups offer an invaluable time during which spouses receive validation for their emotional experiences and have an opportunity to share information and feelings in a safe and supportive environment. Additionally, counseling is provided within a few prisons to inmates and their families. This type of service is based on the premise that prisoners with familial support will be more equipped to change their maladaptive behavior patterns upon release from prison (B. E. Carlson & Cervera, 1992). Despite the existence of several programs aimed at providing support and counseling to spouses of inmates, greater availability of such services is needed to assist spouses in dealing with the loss of a loved one to incarceration and the resulting effects (Hostetter & Jinnah, 1993).

Forensic Psychology and Policy Implications

The number of individuals incarcerated in the United States continues to increase and, as a result, the number of families disrupted continues to rise at an alarming rate. Public policy has historically focused on offenders themselves while virtually ignoring the families of inmates (Bloom, 1995). Given this restrictive approach, it is not surprising that the needs of spouses and children are wholly neglected.

Incarceration does not simply affect the one who is imprisoned; rather, the impact of incarceration extends beyond the individual and includes the family system. Despite the large number of families affected in a deleterious manner by incarceration, the resources available to the nonoffending loved ones are extremely sparse. Thus, the psychological well-being of over 1 million children is severely compromised. (Hostetter & Jinnah, 1993). Similarly, thousands of spouses do not receive the financial or emotional support needed to sustain them through the time during which their partners are incarcerated. Without services available to families, it is likely that children will continue to be removed from their homes and placed in foster care, spouses and children will continue to suffer the psychological repercussions resulting from the physical and emotional loss of a loved one, and communities in general will continue to see an increasingly larger percentage of the population experiencing behavioral, financial, and emotional difficulties.

Suggestions for Future Research

A dearth of scholarship exists which addresses families of inmates. Current research follows public policy trends and focuses on offenders, both individually and collectively. There is a dire need for future research to address the needs of family members of incarcerated individuals. Perhaps the lack of literature in this area reflects the limited amount of available resources for families of prisoners on which to base such studies. Initially, future research would do well to identify the reasons for the paucity of services available to families. Such inquiries would entail investigating the legislative, mental health, and criminal justice system factors, preventing the availability of such services. Additionally, program evaluations need to be conducted on those programs which currently exist in order to identify their strengths and weaknesses. Future research would do well to conduct both qualitative and quantitative studies to determine the differences in overall functioning between those families of inmates who do receive services and those who do not.

FEMALE INMATES: MOTHERS IN PRISON

Introduction

While it has been widely recognized that the United States has the highest incarceration rate in the world, women prisoners have not received as much attention from the media, the legislature, and the fields of psychology and criminology as have their male counterparts. Yet the recent trend toward retributive justice dramatically effects the incarceration rates of women. This is primarily because most women in prison are incarcerated as a result of nonviolent offenses (Watterson, 1996). The vast majority of female offenders commit drug-related crimes. While the increase in prison populations may create a sense of security in the community, there are numerous detrimental effects which result from incarcerating less serious offenders. Among the most important issues regarding incarcerated women is their status as mothers. Therefore, confinement serves to emotionally and physically separate mothers from children, which in turn creates a host of debilitating effects on both the women and their children. Additionally, the majority of women prisoners have a substance abuse problem for which they do not receive treatment while imprisoned (Boudin, 1998). The lack of services provided to women prisoners contributes greatly to their perpetual criminal behavior, and this is connected to their drug addiction. The following case depicts a scenario which is quite typical of women prisoners.

> Nancy is a 28-year-old Latino woman who is currently being incarcerated for the eighth time in her life. She was 15 years old when she was arrested for the first time. All of her charges have been drug related. Nancy has a long history of substance abuse that began when she was 11 years old, at which time her father gave her some of his cocaine. Nancy has three children under the age of 10 for whom she is the sole provider.
>
> Nancy's most recent arrest was 5 months ago for possession of narcotics. As a result of her incarceration, all of her children are now in separate foster homes. The first few times that Nancy was incarcerated, her mother took care of her children. However, Child Protective Services has now insured that the Court has custody of the children and is initiating a movement to have Nancy's parental rights terminated.
>
> While Nancy does have a lengthy history of incarceration and substance abuse, she has never received any treatment for her substance abuse problem. The correctional officers know Nancy very well and refer to her as one of the inmates caught in the "revolving door." Without proper substance abuse treatment for her drug and alcohol addictions, it is likely that Nancy will continue to engage in the same behaviors upon release from prison and thus continue her pattern of incarceration.
>
> While Nancy is serving her punishment, her children are separated from one another as well as from their mother. They live over 100 miles from Nancy's place of incarceration and approximately 45 miles from one another, thereby making visitation next to impossible. The family has lost all physical contact with one another. As a result, Nancy and all of her children are exhibiting signs of severe emotional distress including depression, suicidal ideation, guilt, and a variety of acting-out behaviors.

Literature Review

Women comprise one of the fastest growing prison populations in the United States (Reed & Reed, 1998). In the 9-year period between 1986 and 1995, the number of incarcerated women in the United States increased by more than 250% (A. J. Beck & Gilliard, 1995). The criminal justice system is much more likely to sentence a woman to prison now than ever before (Watterson, 1996b). Further, women are receiving much longer prison sentences at both the state and the federal levels (Watterson, 1996). However, this is not to suggest that women are becoming more violent or committing more crimes than they were previously; rather, the criminal justice system has broadened the scope of criminal behavior for which it deems incarceration a necessary remedy. Due largely to the "War on Drugs," California prisons actually showed a decrease in their percentage of violent offenders from 1985 to 1991, while their percentage of substance abuse offenders doubled (California Department of Corrections, 1991). As depicted in the case of Nancy, the majority of women prisoners are incarcerated as a result of drug-related crimes. Thus, it is clear why this population has been particularly affected by the new laws which require stiffer sentences for drug offenses.

Given the recent influx of women prisoners nationwide, it is important to look at the overall impact that such a movement has on society. First, there are numerous psychological considerations that pertain to incarcerated women that do not pertain to incarcerated men. Boudin (1998) identifies three central issues that women prisoners encounter during their period of confinement. Since the vast majority of women inmates are mothers, the issue of parenting permeates throughout all three of these core concerns. First, Boudin claims that a woman's personal traumatic experiences that occurred prior to incarceration have dramatic effects on her life choices before, during, and after confinement. The U.S. Department of Justice (1994) reports that over 40% of incarcerated women report a history of physical or sexual abuse. Fletcher, Rolison, and Moon (1993) report that the typical female prisoner was sexually abused in childhood by a male member of her immediate family. While Boudin (1998) agrees that there is a high prevalence of physical, sexual, and emotional abuse in the lives of women prisoners, she reports that there are very few opportunities for women to receive help in resolving such matters during the time they are incarcerated.

Second, Boudin (1998) states that women experience a great deal of shame and guilt as a result of their life choices and experiences. For example, Boudin reports that many women in prison have lives filled with years of substance abuse and addiction. As a result of their addictions, the women do not care for their children in an appropriate manner, expressed through abuse or neglect. According to Boudin, this results in shame and guilt among women prisoners as they reflect on their lives during their period of incarceration. Similar to those women who have been traumatized by physical or sexual abuse, those women who are addicted to drugs or alcohol rarely receive treatment during their period of confinement.

Third, most women prisoners who are mothers experience grief as a result of being separated from their children. Watterson (1996) reports that 80% of women in prison are mothers. The case of Nancy depicts a common scenario in that 85% of women prisoners had custody of their children prior to their incarceration (Watterson, 1996). An additional 6–9% of incarcerated women are pregnant upon entering prison (U.S. Department of Justice, 1994). As a result, hundreds of thousands of children have lost their mothers to penal confinement (Reed & Reed, 1998). The experience of delivering a child during a period of incarceration is particularly traumatic. Since prisons are not equipped to handle childbirth, pregnant prisoners are sent to a local hospital to give birth and are then immediately separated from their babies and returned to prison (Watterson, 1996). The lack of time permitted for proper bonding to occur between mother and child has extreme consequences for the psychological well-being of the child and the mother.

According to a fact sheet provided by the Chicago Legal Aid to Incarcerated Mothers (1997), nearly 90% of male prisoners report that while they are incarcerated their children are being cared for by the children's mothers, whereas only 25% of similarly confined women report that their children are being cared for by their fathers. The result is that thousands of children end up in "the system." At times, relatives will care for the children of incarcerated mothers; however, all too often the children are placed in foster homes, separated from their siblings, and denied visitation with their mothers. Fifty-four percent of the mothers in a study conducted by Bloom and Steinhart (1993) reported that their children had never visited them while they were in prison. Participants in this study attributed the distance between their place of residence and their mother's place of incarceration as a primary reason for the lack of visitations. Thus it becomes obvious how the incarceration of mothers has a great impact on society overall, not solely on the lives of the women in prison.

Perhaps being separated from their children is the most difficult issue faced by women prisoners. Watterson (1996b) reports that 75% of the jails in 1994 did not allow contact visits between prisoners and their children. When such visits are allowed, it is often a traumatic experience for everyone involved. Children have a difficult time with the intimidating environment of a prison. They often do not understand why they have limited or no contact with their mothers, and they have difficulty saying goodbye to their mothers once the visit is over. For the mother, once a contact visit is granted, she knows that in order to be with her child she may be subject to the humiliation of a strip-search immediately after the visit.

> [T]he reality is that she knows before she begins that after seeing her children and family and perhaps feeling very good about herself, she will have to take off all her clothing and stand naked in front of the guards, who will check under her arms and breasts for contraband. She'll have to open her mouth and let them look under her tongue and in her cheeks. Then she has to squat, pull apart her buttocks and cough, so the guard in charge can check her vagina and anus for any hidden objects. (Watterson, 1996, p. 214).

For this reason, contact visits can simultaneously be a rewarding and positive experience as well as a humiliating and punishing one. Acknowledging the importance of interaction between mothers and children, programs were developed in the 1980s to support such contact. However, in the 1990s such programs were largely discontinued due to a loss of state and federal funding (Watterson, 1996).

Forensic Psychology and Policy Implications

The number of women incarcerated in the United States is increasing with every new law that requires stiffer sentences for minor offenses. Although the vast majority of women prisoners are incarcerated as a result of drug-related crimes, few programs exist inside the prisons to provide the treatment that such women need to assist them in recovering from their addictions. Research has repeatedly shown that incarceration alone does not alter the subsequent criminal behavior of drug-abusing offenders (Moon, Thompson, & Bennett, 1993; National Institute of Corrections, 1991). Policy reforms are drastically needed given that most women prisoners are substance abusers, most prisons do not offer substance abuse treatment, and incarceration without a treatment component does not curb recidivism for offenders who abuse drugs or alcohol.

Forensic psychologists can also be instrumental in developing programs which support contact between imprisoned mothers and their children. Given that such programs did exist for a short period of time, it can be assumed that the legislature once saw promise in such initiatives, yet no longer deems them to be beneficial or cost effective. With the expertise of both criminological and psychological approaches to the issues at hand, forensic psychologists have valuable services to offer in this area.

Suggestions for Future Research

Compared to the literature on male prisoners, the research on women confined is relatively scarce. Female prisoners have only recently received concentrated attention as a separate cohort from their male counterparts. While the existing research strongly supports contact between women prisoners and their children, studies are needed that compare those women who do receive such visits with those who do not in terms of their psychological well-being, their behavioral conduct within the prison, and their future criminal behavior. One of the primary goals of the criminal justice system is the reduction of future criminal behavior. Therefore, recidivism studies need to be conducted that compare women who receive substance abuse treatment while incarcerated with those who do not. Finally, for many reasons, alternative sentencing programs need to be examined for women who have committed nonviolent offenses. If such programs are found to be equally effective at reducing recidivism among women offenders as are correctional placements, then their implementation would be sensible economically, psychologically, and criminologically.

REFERENCES

Abadinsky, H., & Winfree, L. (1992). *Crime and justice: An introduction* (2nd ed.). Chicago: Nelson-Hall.

Abram, K. M., & Teplin, L. A. (1991). Co-occurring disorders among mentally ill jail detainees: Implications for public policy. *American Psychologist, 46*(10), 1036–1045.

Adalist-Estrin, A. (1994). Family support and criminal justice. In S. L. Kagan & B. Weissbourd (Eds.), *Putting families first America's family support movement and the challenge of change* (pp. 161–185). San Francisco: Jossey-Bass.

Albers, E., & Evans, W. (1994). Suicide ideation among a stratified sample of rural and urban adolescents. *Child and Adolescent Social Work Journal, 11*(5), 379–389.

Alessi, N. E., McManus, M., Brickman, A., & Grapentine, L. (1984). Suicidal behavior among serious juvenile offenders. *American Journal of Psychiatry, 141,* 286–287.

Alexander, M. A. (1997). *Sex offender treatment probed anew.* Unpublished manuscript.

Allen, H., & Simonsen, C. E. (1989). *Corrections in America.* New York: Macmillan.

American Bar Association. (1980). *Juvenile justice standards on dispostions.* Cambridge, MA: Ballinger Press.

American Psychiatric Association Insanity Defense Work Group. (1983). American Psychiatric Association Statement on insanity defense. *Am. J. Psychiatry, 140,* 681–688.

American Psychiatric Association. (1987). Diagnostic and Statistical Manual of Mental Disorders (3rd ed. revised). Washington, DC: Author.

American Psychiatric Association (APA). (1994). *Diagnostic and statistical manual of mental disorders* (4th ed.). Washington, DC: American Psychiatric Association.

American Psychological Association. (1992). Ethical principles of psychologists and code of conduct. *American Psychologist, 47*(12), 1597–1611.

Anastasi, A., & Urbina, S. (1997). *Psychological testing* (7th ed.). Upper Saddle River, NJ: Prentice Hall.

Anonymous. (1984, April). Forensic guidelines: Collection and preservation of arson evidence. *The Police Chief,* pp. 56–58.

Anonymous. (1997). Hell on Block 1G. *Westchester County Weekly* [On-line]. Available: http://www.westchesterweekly.com/articles/suicied2.html

Arcaya, J. M. (1989). The police and the emotionally disturbed: A psychoanalytic theory of intervention. *International Journal of Offender Therapy and Comparative Criminology, 33*(1), 37–48.

Arens, D. A. (1993). What do the neighbors think now? Community residences on Long Island, New York. *Community Mental Health Journal, 29,* 235–245.

Arrigo, B. (1993). Paternalism, civil commitment, and illness polictics: Assessing the current debate and outlining a future direction. *Journal of Law and Health, 7*(3/4), 131–168.

Arrigo, B. (1996). *The contours of psychiatric justice: A postmodern critique of mental illness, criminal insanity, and the law.* New York: Garland.

Arrigo, B. (1999). A review of graduate training models in forensic psychology: Implications for practice. *J. Forensic Psychol. Practice, 1*(1), 1–20.

Arrigo, B., & Garsky, K. (1997). Police suicide: A glimpse behind the badge. In R. Dunham & G. Alpert (Eds.), *Critical issues in policing* (pp. 609–626). Prospect Heights, IL: Waveland Press.

Arrigo, B., & Tasca, J. (1999). Right to refuse treatment, competency to be executed, and therapeutic jurisprudence: Toward a systemic analysis. *Law and Psychology Review, 23*(1), 1–47.

Baca, S. V. (1987, August). Domestic violence: One police department's solution. *The Police Chief,* pp. 40–41.

Bachrach, L. (1980). Is the least restrictive environment always the best? Sociological and semantic implications. *Hospital and Community Psychiatry, 31,* 97–103.

Bagley, C., & Young, L. (1987). Juvenile prostitution and child sexual abuse: A controlled study. *Canadian Journal of Community Mental Health, 6,* 55–126.

Baker, T. E., & Baker, J. P. (1996, October). Preventing police suicide. *FBI Law Enforcement Bulletin,* pp. 25–27.

Baker, W. D. (1995, September). Prevention: A new approach to domestic violence. *FBI Law Enforcement Bulletin*, pp. 18–20.

Banach, M. (1998). The best interests of the child: Decision-making factors. *Families in Society, 79*, 331–340.

Barr, W. P. (1992). Violent youths should be punished as adults. In M. D. Biskup & C. P. Cozic (Eds.), *Youth violence*. San Diego, CA: Greenhaven Press.

Barrett, S. E. (1997). Children of lesbian parents: The what, when, and how of talking about donor identity. *Children's Rights, Therapists' Responsibilities, 20*, 43–55.

Batterman-Faunce, J. M., & Goodman, G. S. (1993). Effects of context on the accuracy and reliability of child witnesses. In G. S. Goodman & B. L. Bottoms (Eds.), *Child victims, child witnesses: Understanding and improving testimony* (pp. 301–330). New York: Guilford Press.

Battle, A. O., Battle, M. V., & Tolley, E. A. (1993). Potential for suicide and aggression in delinquents at juvenile court in a southern city. *Suicide and Life Threatening Behavior, 23*(3), 230–244.

Battle staff burnout with critical incident stress debriefing. (1997, November 7). *Corrections Professional*, p. 3.

Bayley, D. H., & Garafalo, J. (1989). The management of violence by police patrol officers. *Criminology, 27*, 1–25.

Beck, A. J., & Gilliard, D. K. (1995). *Prisoners in 1994*. Washington, DC: Bureau of Justice Statistics Bulletin.

Beck, J. (1990). Home confinement and the use of electronic monitoring with federal parolees. *Federal Probation, 54*, 22–31.

Belcher, J. R. (1988). Are jails replacing the mental health system for the homeless mentally ill? *Community Mental Health Journal, 24*(3), 185–195.

Bell, D. J., & Bell, S. L. (1991). The victim offender relationship as a determinate factor in police dispositions of family violence incidence: A replication study. *Policing and Society, 1*, 225–237.

Bennett, W., & Hess, K. (1996). *Management and supervision in law enforcement* (2nd ed.). St. Paul, MN: West Publishing.

Benson, C., & Matthews, R. (1995). Street prostitution: Ten facts in search of a policy. *International Journal of the Sociology of Law, 23*, 395–415.

Bergmann, L. H., & Queen, T. R. (1987). The aftermath: Treating traumatic stress is crucial. *Corrections Today, 49*, 100–104.

Berube, M. S. (Ed.). (1982). *The American Heritage dictionary* (2nd ed.). Boston: Houghton Mifflin.

Beutler, L. E., Nussbaum, P. D., & Meredith, K. E. (1988). Chaging personality patterns of police officers. *Professional Psychology: Research and Practice, 19*(5), 503–507.

Beutler, L. E., Storm, A., Kirkish, P., Scogin, F., & Gaines, J. A. (1985). Parameters in the prediction of police officer performance. *Professional Psychology: Research and Practice, 16*, 324–335.

Binder, A., & Scharf, P. (1980). The violent police-citizen encounter. *Annals of the American Academy of Political and Social Science, 452*, 111–121.

Bindman, S. (1991, October 14). Top court revisits abuse defense. Murder conviction appeal to focus on instructions to jury about "battered-woman syndrome." *The Ottawa Citizen*, p. A1.

Blak, R. (1995). *Use of deadly force. The psychological impact of officerinvolved shootings*. Available at the Institute for Psychology, Law, and Public Policy, Fresno, CA.

Blak, R., & Sanders, S. (1997). *Post traumatic stress (PTSD) in law enforcement*. Available at the Institute for Psychology, Law, and Public Policy, Fresno, CA.

Blanchette, K. (1996). *Sex offender assessment, treatment and recidivism: A literature review*. Unpublished manuscript.

Bloom, B. (1995). Public policy and the children of incarcerated parents. In K. Gabel & D. Johnston (Eds.), *Children of incarcerated parents* (pp. 271–284). New York: Lexington Books.

Bloom, B., & Steinhart, D. (1993). *Why punish the children? A reappraisal of the children of incarcerated mothers in America*. San Francisco: National Council on Crime and Delinquency.

Blumberg, M. (1989). The AIDS epidemic and the police. In R. Dunhamand & G. Alpert (Eds.), *Critical issues in policing: Contemporary readings* (pp. 208–219). Prospect Heights, IL: Waveland Press.

Borum, R., & Grisso, T. (1995). Psychological test use in criminal forensic evaluations. *Professional Psychology: Research and Practice, 26*(5), 465–473.

Bottoms, B. L. (1993). Individual differences in perceptions of child sexual assault victims. In G. S. Goodman & B. L. Bottoms (Eds.), *Child victims, child witnesses: Understanding and improving testimony* (pp. 229–261). New York: Guilford Press.

Boudin, K. (1998). Lessons from a mother's program in prison: A psychosocial approach supports women and their children. *Women & Therapy, 21*(1), 103–125.

Bourque, B. B., Cronin, R. C., Felker, D. B., Pearson, F. R., Han, M., & Hill, S. M. (1996). Boot camps for juvenile offenders: An implementation evaluation of three demonstration programs [On-line]. Available: askncjrs@aspensys.com Message: NCJ 157316

Bowker, A. L., & Schweid, R. E. (1992). Habilation of the retarded offender in Cuyahoga County. *Federal Probation, 56*, 48–52.

Bracco, K. (1997). Patriarchy and the law of adoption: Beneath the best interests of the child. *The Alberta Law Review, 35*, 1035–1055.

Brantley, A. C., & DiRosa, A. (1994). Gangs: A national perspective. *FBI Law Enforcement Bulletin, 63*(5), 1–6.

Breci, M. G., & Simons, R. (1987). An examination of organizational and individual factors that influence police response to domestic disturbances. *Journal of Police Science and Administration, 15*(2), 93–104.

Breuner, C. C., & Farrow, J. A. (1995). Pregnant teens in prison: Prevalence, management, and consequences. *Western Journal of Medicine, 162*, 328–330.

Briscoe, J. (1997). Breaking the cycle of violence: A rational approach to at-risk youth. *Federal Report, 61*, 3–13.

Brooks, L. (1997). Police discretionary behavior: A study of style. In R. Dunham & G. Alpert (Eds.), *Critical issues in policing* (3rd ed.). Prospect Heights, IL: Waveland Press.

Brown, G. L., Linnoila, M. I., & Goodwin, F. K. (1992). *Impulsivity, aggression, and associated affects: Relationship to self-destructive behavior and suicide.* New York: Guilford Press.

Brown, J. G. (1994). The use of mediation to resolve criminal cases: A procedural critique. *Emory Law Journal, 43*, 1–45.

Brown, V. B., Ridgely, M. S., Pepper, B., Levine, I. S., & Ryglewicz, H. (1989). The dual crisis: Mental illness and substance abuse. *American Psychologist, 44*, 565–569.

Browne, A., & Finkelhor, D. (1986). Impact of child sexual abuse: A review of the research. *Psychological Bulletin, 99*(1), 66–77.

Browne, K., & Herbert, M. (1997). *Preventing family violence.* New York: Wiley.

Brownell, P. (1997). Female offenders in the criminal justice system: Policy and program development. In A. R. Roberts (Ed.), *Social work in juvenile and criminal justice settings* (2nd ed., pp. 325–349). Springfield, IL: Charles C. Thomas.

Buerger, M. E. (1994). A tale of two targets: Limitations of community anticrime action. *Crime & Delinquency, 40*(3), 411–436.

Buhrke, R. A. (1996). *A matter of justice: Lesbians and gay men in law enforcement.* New York: Routledge.

Burke, C. (1992). *Vision narratives of women in prison.* Knoxville: University of Tennessee Press.

Burke, M. (1993). *Coming out of the blue: British police officers talk about their lives in "the job" as lesbians, gays, and bisexuals.* New York: Cassell.

Burke, M. (1994). Homosexuality as deviance: The case of, the gay police officer. *British Journal of Criminology, 34*(2), 192–203.

Bussey, K., Lee, K., & Grimbeck, E. J. (1993). Lies and secrets: Implications for children's reporting of sexual abuse. In G. S. Goodman & B. L. Bottoms (Eds.), *Child victims, child witnesses: Understanding and improving testimony* (pp. 147–168). New York: Guilford Press.

Bussey, M. (1996). Impact of kids first seminar for divorcing parents: A three-year follow-up. *Journal of Divorce and Remarriage, 26*, 129–149.

Butcher, J. N. (1990). *MMPI-2 in psychological treatment.* New York: Oxford University Press.

Buzawa, E. S., & Buzawa, C. G. (1997). Traditional responses to domestic violence. In R. G. Dunham & G. P. Alpert (Eds.), *Critical issues in policing: Contemporary readings* (3rd ed., pp. 243–264). Prospect Heights, IL: Waveland Press.

California Department of Corrections. (1991). *California prisoners and parolees 1990.* Sacramento: State of California.

Canada, G. (1993, August). Developing stress-resistant police families. *The Police Chief*, pp. 92–95.

Carlson, B. E., & Cervera, N. (1992). *Inmates and their wives: Incarceration and family life.* Westport, CT: Greenwood Press.

Carlson, K. A. (1992). Doing good and looking bad: A case study of prison/community relations. *Crime and Delinquency, 38,* 56–69.

Carpenter, M. (1978). Residential placement for the chronic psychiatric patient: A review and evaluation of the literature. *Schizophrenia Bulletin, 4,* 384–398.

Ceci, S. J., & Bruck, M. (1993). Suggestibility of the child witness: A historical review and synthesis. *Psychological Bulletin, 113,* 403–439.

Ceci, S. J., & Bruck, M. (1995). *Jeopardy in the courtroom: A scientific analysis of children's testimony.* Washington, DC: American Psychological Association.

Chamelin, N. (1975). *Introduction to criminal justice.* Englewood Cliffs, NJ: Prentice Hall.

Chan, R. W., Raboy, B., & Patterson, C. J. (1998). Psychosocial adjustment among children conceived via donor insemination by lesbian and heterosexual mothers. *Journal of Child Development, 69,* 443–457.

Chance, P. (1988). *Learning and behavior* (2nd ed.). Belmont, CA: Wadsworth.

Chandler, R., & Plano, J. (1988). *The public administration dictionary.* Santa Barbara, CA: ABC-Clio.

Chesney-Lind, M. (1988). Girls in jail. *Crime and Delinquency, 34,* 150–168.

Chesney-Lind, M., & Shelden, R. G. (1992). *Girls, delinquency, and juvenile justice.* New York: Brooks/Cole.

Chicago Legal Aid to Incarcerated Mothers. (1997). *Women in prison: Fact sheet* [On-line]. Available: http://www.c-l-a-i-m.org/factsheet.htm

Church, G. J. (1990). The view from behind bars. *Time, 135,* 20–22.

Cody, B. (1997). San Mateo county sheriff's office: Megan's law in the state of California [On-line]. Available: http://www.5mcsheriff.com/n-f/is-m.htm#top

Cohen, D. A. (1997). Sexual psychopaths [On-line]. Available: http://members.tripod.com/~dazc/sexopat.htm#watiz

Cohen, H. S., & Feldberg, M. (1991). *Power and restraint: The moral dimension of police work.* New York: Praeger.

Conley, R. W., Luckasson, R., & Bouthilet, G. N. (Eds.). (1992). *The criminal justice system and mental retardation.* Baltimore, MD: Paul H. Brookes.

Cook, J. R. (1997). Neighbors' perceptions of group homes. *Community Mental Health Journal, 33,* 287–299.

Cooper, C. (1997). Patrol police officer conflict resolution processes. *Journal of Criminal Justice, 25*(2), 87–101.

Cooprider, K. W. (1992). Pretrial bond supervision: An empirical analysis with policy implications. *Federal Probation, 56,* 41–49.

Corbett, C., & Simon, F. (1991). Police and public perceptions of the seriousness of traffic offences. *British Journal of Criminology, 31*(2), 153–164.

Cordner, G. W. (1997). Community policing: Elements and effects. In R. G. Dunham & G. P. Alpert (Eds.), *Critical issues in policing: Contemporary readings* (pp. 451–468). Prospect Heights, IL: Waveland Press.

Cordoba, O. A., & Chapel, J. L. (1983). Medroxyprogesterone acetate antiandrogen treatment of hypersexuality in a pedophiliac sex offender. *American Journal of Psychiatry, 140,* 1036–1039.

Correia, M. E. (1997). Boot camps, exercise, and delinquency. An analytical critique of the use of physical exercise to facilitate decreases in delinquent behavior. *13,* 94–113.

Cortina, J. M., Doherty, M. L., Schmitt, N., Kaufman, G., & Smith, R. G. (1992). The "Big Five" personality factors in the IPI and MMPI: Predictors of police performance. *Personnel Psychology, 45,* 119–140.

Cowley, G., Springen, K., Miller, S., Lewis, S., & Titunik, V. (1993, August 16). Who's looking after the interests of the children? *Newsweek,* pp. 54–55.

Crank, J. P. (1992). Police style and legally serious crime: A contextual analysis of municipal police departments. *Journal of Criminal Justice, 20,* 401–412.

Crank, J. P., Payn, B., & Jackson, S. (1993). The relationship between police belief systems and attitudes toward police practices. *Criminal Justice and Behavior, 20*(2), 199–221.

Crockenberg, S., & Forgays, D. (1996). The role of emotion in children's understanding and emotional reactions to marital conflict. *Merrill-Palmer Quarterly, 42,* 22–47.

Crosby-Currie, C. (1996). Children's involvement in contested custody cases: Practices and experiences of legal and mental health professionals. *Law and Human Behavior, 20,* 289–310.

Crouch, B. M. (1985). Pandora's box: Women guards in men's prisons. *Journal of Criminal Justice, 13,* 535–548.

Davis, M. (1995). Critical incident stress debriefing: The case for corrections. *The Keeper's Voice* [Online], *16.* Available: http://www.acsp.uic.edu/iaco/kv160145.htm

Dawson, J. M., & Langan, P. A. (1994). *Murder in families.* Washington, DC: Bureau of Justice Statistics.

Defina, M., & Wetherbee, L. (1997, October). Advocacy and law enforcement: Partners against domestic violence. *FBI Law Enforcement Bulletin,* pp. 22–26.

D'Emilio, J. (1983). *Sexual politics, sexual communities: The making of a homosexual minority in the United States 1940–1970.* Chicago: University of Chicago Press.

De Wilde, E. J., Kienhorst, I. C., Diekstra, R. F., & Wolters, W. H. (1992). The relationship between adolescent suicidal behavior and life events in childhood and adolescence. *American Journal of Psychiatry, 149*(1), 45–51.

Dexter, H., Cutler, B., & Moran, G. (1992). A test of voir dire as a remedy for the prejudicial effects of pretrial publicity. *Journal of Applied Social Psychology, 22*(10), 819–832.

Diamond, S. (1990). Scientific jury selection: What social scientists know and do not know. *Judicature, 73,* 178–183.

Dietrich, J. (1989, November). Helping subordinates face stress. *The Police Chief,* pp. 44–47.

DiIulio, J. (1987). *Governing prisons.* New York: Free Press.

DiPietro, A. L. (1993, July). Lies, promises, or threats: The voluntariness of confessions. *FBI Law Enforcement Bulletin,* pp. 27–31.

Dodge, K. S. (1993). "Bashing back": Gay and lesbian street patrols and the criminal justice system. *Law & Equality: A Journal of Theory and Practice, 11,* 295–368.

Dolgin, J. L. (1996). Why has the best interest standard survived? The historic and social context. *Children's Legal Rights Journal, 16,* 2–10.

Dolon, R., Hendricks, J., & Meagher, M. (1986). Police practices and attitudes toward domestic violence. *Journal of Police Science and Administration, 14*(3), 187–192.

Donaldson, S. (1990). Prisons, jails, and reformatories. In W. R. Dynes (Ed.), *Encyclopedia of homosexuality.* New York: Garland.

Douglas, J. E., & Burgess, A. E. (1986, December). Criminal profiling: A viable investigative tool against violent crime. *FBI Law Enforcement Bulletin,* pp. 9–13.

Doyle, J. (1996). Homosexuals in law enforcement: A contemporary study. *Journal of California Law Enforcement, 30*(4), 77–81.

Dripps, D. A. (1988). Supreme court review. Foreword: Against police interrogation—and the privilege against self incrimination. *Journal of Criminal Law and Criminology, 78*(4), 699–734.

Dunphy, F. R., & Garner, G. (1992, April). A guide to effective interaction with the news media. *The Police Chief,* pp. 45–48.

Eck, J. E. (1982). *Solving crimes: The investigation of burglary and robbery.* Washington, DC: Police Executive Research Forum.

Elias, R. (1986). *The politics of victimization*. New York: Oxford University Press.

Elrod, P., & Brown, M. P. (1996). Predicting public support for electronic house arrest Results from a New York county survey. *American Behavioral Scientist, 39*, 461–473.

Ericson, R. V. (1991). Mass media, crime, law, and justice: An institutional approach. *British Journal of Criminology, 31*(3), 219–249.

Etheridge, R., Hale, C., & Hambrick, M. (1984). Female employees in all-male correctional facilities. *Federal Probation, 48*, 54–65.

Evans, W., Albers, E., Macari, D., & Mason, A. (1996). Suicide ideation, attempts and abuse among incarcerated gang and nongang delinquents. *Child and Adolescent Social Work Journal, 13*, 115–126.

Evers, T. (1998). A healing approach to crime: Victim-offender mediation. *The Progressive Inc., 9*(62), 30–36.

Ewing, C. P. (1997). *Fatal families: The dynamics of intrafamilial homicide*. Thousand Oaks, CA: Sage.

Exum, J. G., Turnbull, H. R., Martin, R., & Finn, J. W. (1992). Points of view: Perspectives on the judicial, mental retardation services, law enforcement, and corrections systems. In R. W. Conley, R. Luckasson, & G. N. Bouthilet (Eds.), *The criminal justice system and mental retardation* (pp. 1–16). Baltimore: Paul H. Brookes.

Falk, J. A. (1995). Project exodus: The corrections correction. In L. Combrinck-Graham (Ed.), *Children in families at risk: Maintaining the connections* (pp. 375–392). New York: Guilford Press.

Federal Bureau of Investigation (FBI). (1985a, August). The men who murdered. *FBI Law Enforcement Bulletin*, pp. 2–11.

Federal Bureau of Investigation (FBI). (1985b, August). Crime scene and profile characteristics of organized and disorganized murderers. *FBI Law Enforcement Bulletin*, pp. 18–25.

Federal Bureau of Investigation (FBI). (1994). *Uniform Crime Report 1993*. Washington, DC: U.S. Government Printing Office.

Federal Bureau of Investigation (FBI). (1997). Facts about deterrence and the death penalty [On-line]. Available: http://www.essential.org/dpic/dete...f

Feinman, C. (1994). *Women in the criminal justice system* (3rd ed). Westport, CT: Praeger.

Finn, M. A., & Stalans, L. J. (1997). The influence of gender and mental state on police decisions in domestic assault cases. *Criminal Justice and Behavior, 24*(2), 157–176.

Firush, R., & Shukat, J. R. (1995). Content, consistency, and coherence of early autobiographical recall. In M. S. Zaragoza, J. R. Graham, G. C. N. Hall, R. Hirschman, & Y. S. Ben-Porath (Eds.), *Memory and testimony in the child witness* (pp. 5–23). Thousand Oaks, CA: Sage.

Fishbein, P., Davis, J. M., & Hamparin, D. (1984). *Restitution programming for juvenile offenders*. Columbus: Ohio Serious Juvenile Offender Program, Department of Corrections.

Fishman, L. T. (1990). *Women at the wall: A study of prisoners' wives doing time on the outside*. Albany: State University of New York Press.

Flaherty, M. G. (1983). The national incidence of juvenile suicide in adult jails and juvenile detention centers. *Suicide and Life Threatening Behavior, 13*, 85–93.

Flaks, D. K., Ficher, I., Masterpasqua, F., & Joseph, G. (1995). Lesbians choosing motherhood: A comparative study of lesbian and heterosexual parents and their children. *Developmental Psychology, 31*, 105–114.

Flanagan, L. W. (1995). Meeting the special needs of females in custody: Maryland's unique approach. *Federal Probation, 59*, 49–53.

Fletcher, B. R., Rolison, G. L., & Moon, D. G. (1993). The woman prisoner. In B. R. Fletcher, L. D. Shaver, & D. G. Moon (Eds.), *Women prisoners: A forgotten population* (pp. 15–26). Westport, CT: Praeger.

Flowers, R. B. (1995). *Female crime, criminals and cellmates: An exploration of female criminality and delinquency*. Jefferson, NC: McFarland.

Flowers, R. B. (1998). *The prostitution of women and girls*. Jefferson, NC: McFarland.

Freeman-Longo, R. E., & Knopp, H. F. (1992). State-of-the-art sex offender treatment: Outcome and issues. *Annals of Sex Research, 5*(3), 141–160.

Fritsch, E., & Hemmens, J. D. (1995). Juvenile waiver in the United States 1979–1995: A comparison and analysis of state waiver statutes. *Juvenile and Family Court Journal, 46*(3), 17–35.

Fry, L. J., & Glaser, D. (1987). Gender differences in work adjustment of prison employees. *Journal of Offender Counseling, Services, and Rehabilitation, 12,* 39–52.

Furby, L., Weinrott, M. R., & Blackshaw, L. (1989). Sex offender recidivism: A review. *Psychological Bulletin, 105,* 3–30.

Fyfe, J. J. (1985). The split-second syndrom and other determinants of police violence. In A. Campbell & J. Gibbs (Eds.), *Violent transactions: The limits of personality* (pp. 207–223). New York: Basil Blackwell.

Fyfe, J. J. (1996). Methodology, substance, and demeanor in police observational research: A response to Lundman and others. *Journal of Research in Crime and Delinquency, 33*(3), 337–348.

Fyfe, J. J., Klinger, D. A., & Flavin, J. M. (1997). Differential police treatment of male-on-female spousal violence. *Criminology, 35*(3), 455–473.

Gabel, K., & Johnston, D. (1995). *Children of incarcerated parents.* New York: Lexington Books.

Garner, B. A. (Ed.). (1996). *Black's law dictionary.* St. Paul, MN: West Publishing.

Gavin, T. (1997, March). Truancy: Not just kids' stuff anymore. *FBI Law Enforcement Bulletin.*

Geller, W. A. (1994, January). Research forum: Videotaping interrogations and confessions. *FBI Law Enforcement Bulletin,* pp. 24–27.

Genders, E., & Player, E. (1990). Women lifers: Assessing the experience. *The Prison Journal, 80,* 46–57.

Genova, J. (1989, April). Automating crime labs and evidence control. *The Police Chief,* pp. 34–40.

Giallombardo, R. (1966). *Society of women: A study of a women's prison.* New York: Wiley.

Gifford, E. A. (1992). California's mother-infant care program: An alternative model for prison mothers. *UCLA Women's Law Journal, 2,* 279–281.

Glick, B. (1992). In New York: Governor's task force tackles growing juvenile gang problem. *Corrections Today, 54,* 92–97.

Godschalx, S. M. (1984). Effect of a mental health educational program upon police officers. *Research in Nursing and Health, 7,* 111–117.

Goldstein, J., Solnit, A. J., Goldstein, S., & Freud, A. (1996). *The best interests of the child: The least detrimental alternative.* New York: Free Press.

Goodman, G. S., Tobey, A. E., Batterman-Faunce, J. M., Orcutt, H., Thomas, S., Shapiro, C., & Sachsenmaier, T. (1998). Face-to-face confrontation: Effects of closed circuit technology on children's eyewitness testimony and jurors' decisions. *Law and Human Behavior, 22,* 165–203.

Gottesman, I. I., & Bertelsen, A. (1989). Confirming unexpressed genotypes of schizophrenia. Risk in the offspring of Fischer's Danish identical and fraternal discordant twins. *Archives of General Psychiatry, 46,* 867–872.

Gottman, J. S. (1990). Children of gay and lesbian parents. In F. W. Bozett & M. B. Sussman (Eds.), *Homosexuality and family relations* (pp. 177–196). New York: Harrington Park Press.

Graham, J. R. (1993). *MMPI-2 assessing personality and psychopathology.* New York: Oxford University Press.

Graves, W. (1996). Police cynicism: Causes and cures. *FBI Law Enforcement Bulletin, 65,* 16–20.

Gray, L., & Harding, A. (1988). Confidentiality limits with clients who have the AIDS virus. *Journal of Counseling and Development, 66,* 219–223.

Greene, A. F., Coles, C. J., & Johnson, E. H. (1994). Psychopathology and anger in interpersonal violence offenders. *Journal of Clinical Psychology, 50,* 906–912.

Greer, D. (1994). A transatlantic perspective on the compensation of crime victims in the United States. *Journal of Criminal Law and Criminology, 85*(2), 333.

Griffin, J. L. (1993, August 25). Primary label for gay police officers is cop. *Chicago Tribune,* p. 5.

Grisso, T. (1996a). Pretrial clinical evaluations in criminal cases: Past trends and future directions. *Criminal Justice and Behavior, 23*(1), 90–106.

Grisso, T. (1996b). Society's retributive response to juvenile violence: A developmental perspective. *Law and Human Behavior, 20*(3), 229–247.

Grossi, E. L., & Berg, B. L. (1991). Stress and job dissatisfaction among correctional officers: An unexpected finding. *International Journal of Offender Therapy and Comparative Criminology, 35,* 73–81.

Groves, B., Zuckerman, B., Marans, S., & Cohen, D. (1993). Silent victims: Children who witness violence. *JAMA, Journal of the American Medical Association, 269,* 262–264.

Hagan, J. (1982). Victims before the law: A study of victim involvement in the criminal justice process. *Journal of Criminal Justice, 73,* 317–330.

Hairston, C. F. (1989). Men in prison: Family characteristics and family views. *Journal of Offender Counseling, Services, and Rehabilitation, 14*(1), 23–30.

Hairston, C. F. (1991a). Family ties during imprisonment. Important to whom and for what? *Journal of Sociology and Social Welfare, 18,* 87–104.

Hairston, C. F. (1991b). Mothers in jail: Parent-child separation and jail visitation. *Affilia, 6,* 9–27.

Hall, A. S., Pulver, C. A., & Cooley, M. J. (1996). Psychology of best interest standard: Fifty state statutes and their theoretical antecedents. *American Journal of Family Therapy, 24,* 171–180.

Hall, G. C. N. (1990). Prediction of sexual aggression. *Clinical Psychology Review, 10,* 229–245.

Hall, J. N. (1992). Correctional services for inmates with mental retardation: Challenge or catastrophe? In R. W. Conley, R. Luckasson, & G. N. Bouthilet (Eds.), *The criminal justice system and mental retardation* (pp. 167–190). Baltimore, MD: Paul H. Brookes.

Hansen, M. (1994a, March). Troopers' wrongdoing taints cases. *American Bar Association Journal,* p. 22.

Hansen, M. (1994b, November). Fears of the heart. *American Bar Association Journal,* pp. 58–63.

Hansen, M. (1997). Repairing the damage: Citizen boards tailor sentences to fit the crimes in Vermont. *American Bar Association Journal, 83*(20), 1–2.

Hanson, R. K., & Bussiere, M. T. (1996). Sex offender risk predictors: A summary of research results [On-line]. Available: http://www.csc-scc.gc.ca/crd/forum/e082/e082c.htm

Hanson, R. K., Steffy, R. A., & Gauthier, R. (1993). Long-term recidivism of child molesters. *Journal of Consulting and Clinical Psychology, 61*(4), 646–652.

Harlan, S., Rodgers, L. L., & Slattery, B. (1981). *Male and female adolescent prostitution: Huckleberry Sexual Minority Youth Services Project.* Washington, DC: U. S. Department of Health and Human Services.

Harris, G., Rice, M., & Quinsey, V. (1993). Violent recidivism of mentally disordered offenders: The development of a statistical prediction instrument. *Criminal Justice and Behavior, 20,* 315–335.

Harris, P., & Smith, S. (1996). Developing community corrections: An implementation perspective. In A. T. Harland (Ed.), *Choosing correctional options that work: Defining the demand and evaluating the supply* (pp. 183–222). Thousand Oaks, CA: Sage.

Hastings, J. E., & Hamberger, L. K. (1988). Personality characteristics of spouse abusers: A controlled comparison. *Violence and Victims, 3,* 31–48.

Hazelwood, R. R. (1983, September). The behavior-oriented interview of rape victims: The key to profiling. *FBI Law Enforcement Bulletin,* pp. 8–15.

Hecker, S. (1997). Race and pretextual traffic stops: An expanded role for civilian review board. *Columbian Human Rights Law Review, 28,* 1–37.

Heide, K. M. (1992). *Why kids kill parents: Child abuse and adolescent homicide.* Columbus: Ohio State Press.

Heilbrun, K. (1992). The role of psychological testing in forensic assessment. *Law and Human Behavior, 16*(3), 257–272.

Heilbrun, K., Radelet, M. L., & Dvoskin, J. (1992). The debate on treating individuals incompetent for execution. *American Journal of Psychiatry, 149*(5), 596–605.

Helfer, R. E., & Kempe, C. H. (Eds.). (1986). *Child abuse and neglect: The family and the community.* Cambridge, MA: Ballinger.

Hess, J. E., & Gladis, S. D. (1987, July). Benevolent interrogation. *FBI Law Enforcement Bulletin,* pp. 20–23.

Higgins, S. E. (1993). Interjurisdictional coordination of major gang interventions. *The Police Chief, 60*(6), 46–47.

Ho, T. (1996). Assessment of retardation among mentally retarded criminal offenders: An examination of racial disparity. *Journal of Criminal Justice, 24,* 337–350.

Hoffman, P., & Faust, L. (1977). Least restrictive treatment of the mentally ill: A doctrine in search of its senses. *San Diego Law Review, 14,* 1100–1154.

Hoffman, P., & Silverstein, M. (1995). Safe streets don't require lifting rights. In M. W. Klein, C. L. Maxon, & J. Miller (Eds.), *The modern gang reader.* Los Angeles: Roxbury.

Holub, R. J. (1992). *Forensic psychological testing: A survey of practices and beliefs.* Unpublished manuscript, Minnesota School of Professional Psychology, Bloomington.

Hopkins, N., Hewstone, M., & Hantzi, A. (1992). Police-schools liaison and young people's image of the police: An intervention evaluation. *British Journal of Psychology, 83,* 203–220.

Horne, P. (1985). Female correction officers: A status report. *Federal Probation, 49,* 46–54.

Hostetter, E. C., & Jinnah, D. T. (1993). Families of adult prisoners [On-line]. Available: http://www.ifs.univie.ac.at/uncjin/mosaic/famcorr/fmcorrpt.html

Hromadka, P. (1995). Innovative York program allows babies to stay with inmate moms. *Nebraska Nurse, 28,* 14.

Hufft, A. G. (1992). Psychosocial adaptation to pregnancy in prison. *Journal of Psychosocial Nursing, 30,* 19–23.

Hunt, G., Riegel, S., Morales, T., & Waldorf, D. (1993). Changes in prison culture: Prison gangs and the case of the Pepsi generation. *Social Problems, 40*(3), 398–409.

Icove, D. J. (1994). Police use of discretion: A comparison of community, system, and officer expectations [On-line]. Available: http://www.totse.com/files/FA019/res_rev.htm

Inciardi, J. A. (1993). *Criminal justice.* Orlando, FL: Harcourt Brace Jovanovich.

Ingrassia, M., & Springen, K. (1993, May 3). Standing up for fathers. *Newsweek,* pp. 52–53.

Ingrassia, M., & Springen, K. (1994, March 21). She's not baby Jessica anymore. *Newsweek,* pp. 60–65.

Inwald, R. (1988). Five-year follow-up study of departmental terminations as predicted by 16 preemployment psycholgical indicators. *Journal of Applied Psychology, 73,* 703–710.

Inwald, R., Knatz, H., & Shusman, E. (1983). *Inwald Personality Inventory manual.* New York: Hilson Research.

Ivanoff, A., Jang, S. J., & Smyth, N. (1996). Clinical risk factors associated with parasuicide in prison. *International Journal of Offender Therapy and Comparative Criminology, 400,* 135–146.

Jackson, P. I. (1989). *Minority group threat, crime, and policing: Social context and social control.* New York: Praeger.

Jacobs, C. (1998). California to execute man with schizophrenia [On-line]. Available: http://w1.480.telia.com/~u48003561/kellyhorace.htm

Jacobs, P. (1966). *Prelude to riot.* New York: Vintage Press.

Jaffe, P. D., Pons, F., & Wicky, H. R. (1997). Children imprisoned with their mothers: Psychological implications. In S. Redmonds, V. Garrido, J. Perez, & R. Barberet (Eds.), *Advances in psychology and law: International contributions* (pp. 399–407). Berlin: de Gruyter.

Jaskiewicz-Obydzinska, T., & Czerederecka, A. (1995). Psychological evaluation of changes in testimony given by sexually abused juveniles. In G. Davies & S. Lloyd-Bostock (Eds.), *Psychology, law, and criminal justice: International developments in research and practice* (pp. 160–169). Berlin: de Gruyter.

Jefferson, T., & Walker, M. (1993). Attitudes to the police of ethnic minorities in a provincial city. *British Journal of Criminology, 33,* 251–266.

Jesson, J. (1993). Understanding adolescent female prostitution: A literature review. *British Journal of Social Work, 23,* 517–530.

Johnson, J. (1992). *Teen prostitution.* Danbury, CT: Franklin Watts.

Johnston, D. (1995a). Effects of parental incarceration. In K. Gabel & D. Johnston (Eds.), *Children of incarcerated parents* (pp. 59–88). New York: Lexington Books.

Johnston, D. (1995b). Intervention. In K. Gabel & D. Johnston (Eds.), *Children of incarcerated parents* (pp. 199–236). New York: Lexington Books.

Johnston, D., & Gabel, K. (1995). Incarcerated parents. In K. Gabel & D. Johnston (Eds.), *Children of incarcerated parents* (pp. 3–20). New York: Lexington Books.

Joseph, K. L. (1996). Victim-offender mediation: What social and political factors will affect its development? *Ohio State Journal of Dispute Resolution, 11*(207), 1–14.

Joseph, T. M. (1994, September). Walking the minefields of community-oriented policing. *FBI Law Enforcement Bulletin*, pp. 8–12.

Kagle, J., & Kopels, S. (1994). Confidentiality after Tarasoff. *Health and Social Work, 19*(3), 217–222.

Kain, C. (1988). To breach or not to breach: Is that the question? A response to Gray and Harding. *Journal of Counseling and Development, 66*, 224–225.

Kamerman, J. (1995). Correctional officer suicide. *The Keeper's Voice* [On-line], *16*. Available: http://www.acsp.uic.edu/iaco/kv160307.htm

Kandel, R. F. (1994). Just ask the kid! Towards a rule of children's choice in custody determinations. *University of Miami Law Review, 49*, 299–376.

Kannady, B. (1993, August). Developing stress-resistant police families. *The Police Chief*, pp. 92–95.

Katz, L. F., & Gottman, J. M. (1997). Buffering children from marital conflict and dissolution. *Journal of Clinical Child Psychology, 26*, 157–171.

Keilitz, S. (1994). Legal report: Civil protection orders: A viable justice system tool for deterring domestic violence. *Violence and Victims, 9*, 79–84.

Kelley, J. B. (1997). The best interests of the child: A concept in search of meaning. *Family and Conciliation Courts Review, 35*, 377–387.

Kennedy, D. M., & Moore, M. H. (1997). Underwriting the risky investment in community policing: What social science should be doing to evaluate community policing. In R. G. Dunham & G. P. Alpert (Eds.), *Critical issues in policing: Contemporary readings* (pp. 469–488). Prospect Heights, IL: Waveland Press.

Keyes, D., Edwards, W., & Perske, R. (1998). Mental retardations and the death penalty [On-line]. Available: http://www.essential.org/dpic/dpicmr.html

Kiely, J., & Hodgson, G. (1990). Stress in the prison service: The benefits of exercise programs. *Human Relations, 43*, 551–572.

Kinder, K., Veneziano, C., Fichter, M., & Azuma, H. (1995). A comparison of the dispositions of juvenile offenders certified as adults with juvenile offenders not certified. *Juvenile and Family Court Journal, 46*(3), 37–42.

Kiser, G. C. (1991). Female inmates and their families. *Federal Probation, 55*, 55–63.

Klein, M. W. (1995). Attempting gang control by suppression: The misuse of deterrence principles. In M. W. Klein, C. L. Maxon, & J. Miller (Eds.), *The modern gang reader*. Los Angeles: Roxbury.

Klinger, D. A. (1994). Demeanor or crime? Why "hostile" citizens are more likely to be arrested. *Criminology, 32*(3), 475–493.

Klinger, D. A. (1996). Bringing crime back in: Toward a better understanding of police arrest decisions. *Journal of Research in Crime and Delinquency, 33*(3), 333–336.

Klockars, C. B. (1984). Blue lies and police placebos. *American Behavioral Scientist, 27*(4), 529–544.

Knox, G., & Tromanhauser, E. (1991). Gangs and their control in adult correctional institutions. *The Prison Journal, 71*(2), 15–21.

Koehler, S. P., & Willis, F. N. (1994). Traffic citations in relation to gender. *Journal of Applied Social Psychology, 24*(21), 1919–1926.

Kornfeld, A. D. (1995). Police officer cadidate MMPI-2 performance: Gender, ethnic, and normative factors. *Journal of Clinical Psychology, 51*(4), 536–540.

Krisberg, B., & DeComo, R. (1993). *Juveniles taken into custody: Fiscal year 1991 report*. Washington, DC: United States Department of Justice, Office of Juvenile Justice and Delinquency Prevention.

Kroes, W. H. (1976). *Society's victim: The policeman*. Springfield, IL: Charles C. Thomas.

Kurtz, L. (1997). Comment: Protecting New York's children: An argument for the creation of a rebuttable presumption against awarding a spouse abuser custody of a child. *Albany Law Review, 60*, 1345–1376.

Labecki, L. A. (1994). Monitoring hostility: Avoiding prison disturbances through environmental screening. *Corrections Today*, *56*(5), 104–111.

Lamb, D., Clark, C., Drumheller, P., Frizzell, K., & Surrey, L. (1989). Applying Tarasoff to AIDS-related psychotherapy issues. *Professional Psychology: Research and Practice*, *20*, 37–43.

Lanyon, R. I. (1986). Psychological assessment procedures in court-related settings. *Professional Psychology: Research and Practice*, *17*(3), 260–268.

Laws, R. D. (Ed.). (1989). *Relapse prevention with sex offenders*. New York: Guilford Press.

Lee, M. (1997). Post-divorce interparental conflict, children's contact with both parents, children's emotional processes, and children's behavioral adjustment. *Journal of Divorce and Remarriage*, *27*, 61–82.

Leiber, M., Nalla, M., & Farnworth, M. (1998). Explaining juvenile's attitudes toward the police. *Justice Quarterly*, *15*(1), 151–173.

Leinen, S. (1993). *Gay cops*. New Brunswick, NJ: Rutgers University.

Leo, R. A. (1996). Criminal law: Inside the interrogation room. *Journal of Criminal Law and Criminology*, *86*(2), 266–303.

Levinson, A., & Fonagy, P. (1999). *Adult attainment patterns in forensic nonpsychiatric patients*. Manuscript submitted for publication.

Levinson, D. (1988). Family violence in cross-cultural perspective. In V. Van Hasselt, R. L. Morrison, A. S. Bellack, & M. Herson (Eds.), *Handbook of family violence* (pp. 435–456). New York: Plenum.

Levy, R., & Rubenstein, L. (1996). *The rights of people with mental disabilities*. Carbondale: Southern Illinois University Press.

Lewis, D. O., Pincus, J. H., Bard, B., Richardson, E., Prichep, L. S., Feldman, M., & Yeager, C. (1988). Neuropsychiatric, psychoeducational, and family characteristics of 14 juveniles condemned to death in the United States. *American Journal of Psychiatry*, *145*, 584–589.

Liebling, A. (1993). Suicides in young prisoners: A summary. *Death Studies*, *17*(5), 381–409.

Lilly, R. J. (1992). The Pride Inc. program: An evaluation of 5 years of electronic monitoring. *Federal Probation*, *54*, 42–47.

Lillyquist, M. J. (1985). *Understanding the changing criminal behavior*. Englewood Cliffs, NJ: Prentice Hall.

Linney, J. A. (1982). Alternative facilities for youth in trouble: Descriptive analysis of a strategically selected sample. In J. F. Handler & J. Zatz (Eds.), *Neither angels nor thieves: Studies in deinstitutionalization of status offenders*. Washington, DC: National Academy Press.

Lipsey, M. (1992). Juvenile delinquency treatment: A meta-analytic inquirey into the variability of effects in meta-analysis for explanation: A casebook (T. Cook *et al.*, eds.). New York: Russell Sage Foundation.

Long, E., Long, J., Leon, W., & Weston, P. B. (1975). *American minorities*. Englewood Cliffs, NJ: Prentice Hall.

Long, G. T. (1993). Homosexual relationships in a unique setting: The male prison. In L. Diamant (Ed.), *Homosexual issues in the workplace*. Washington, DC: Taylor & Francis.

Lorr, M, & Strack, S. (1994). Personality profiles of police candidates. *Journal of Clinical Psychology*, *50*(2), 200–207.

Los Angeles City Attorney Gang Prosecution Section. (1995). Civil gang abatement: A community based policing tool of the office of the Los Angeles City Attorney. In M. W. Klein, C. L. Maxon, & J. Miller (Eds.), *The modern gang reader*. Los Angeles: Roxbury.

Lotke, E. (1996). Sex offenders: Does treatment work? *Corrections Compendium*, *21*(5), 1–8.

Love, B. (1994). Program curbs prison violence through conflict resolution. *Corrections Today*, *56*(5), 144–156.

Lundman, R. (1993). *Prevention and control of juvenile delinquency* (2nd ed.). New York: Oxford University Press.

Lundman, R. J. (1996a). Demeanor and arrest: Additional evidence from previously unpublished data. *Journal of Research in Crime and Delinquency*, *33*(3), 306–323.

Lundman, R. J. (1996b). Extralegal variables and arrest. *Journal of Research in Crime and Delinquency*, *33*(3), 349–353.

MacKenzie, D. L., Robinson, J. W., & Campbell, C. S. (1989). Long-term incarceration of female offenders: Prison adjustment and coping. *Criminal Justice and Behavior, 16*, 223–228.

MacKenzie, D. L., & Souryal, R. (1994). Results of a multisite study of boot camp prisons. *Federal Probation, 58*, 60–66.

Maghan, J. (1997). Prison violence. *Crime and Justice International, 13*(9), 18–21.

Mahon, N. (1996). New York inmates' HIV risk behaviors: The implications for prevention policy and programs. *American Journal of Public Health, 86*, 1211–1215.

Mann, C. (1984). *Female crime and delinquency*. Birmingham: University of Alabama Press.

Marion, N. (1995). The federal response to crime victims. *Journal of Interpersonal Violence, 10*(4), 419–436.

Marquart, J. W., Cuvelier, S. J., Burton, V. S., Adams, K., Gerber, J., Longmire, D., Flanagan, T. J., Bennett, K, & Fritsch, E. (1994). A livited capacity to treat: Examining the effects of prison population control strategies on prison education programs. *Crime and Delinquency, 40*(4), 516–531.

Marshall, W. L. (1996). The sexual offender: Monster, victim, or everyman? *Sexual Abuse: A Journal of Research and Treatment, 8*, 317–336.

Marshall, W. L., & Barbaree, H. E. (1990). An integrated theory of the etiology of sexual offending. In W. L. Marshall, D. R. Laws, & H. E. Barbaree (Eds.), *Handbook of sexual assault: Issues, theories, and treatment of the offender* (pp. 257–275). New York: Plenum Press.

Martin, D. (1989). Human immunodeficiency virus infection and the gay community: Counseling and clinical issues. *Journal of Counseling and Development, 68*, 67–71.

Martin, S. E., & Jurik, N. C. (1996). *Doing justice, doing gender: Women in law and criminal justice occupations*. Thousand Oaks, CA: Sage.

Martin, S. L., Kim, H., Kupper, L. L., Meyer, R. E., & Hays, M. (1997). Is incarceration during pregnancy associated with infant birth weight? *American Journal of Public Health, 87*, 1526–1531.

Martin, S. L., Rieger, R. H., Kupper, L. L., Meyer, R. E., & Qaqish, B. F. (1997). The effect of incarceration during pregnancy on birth outcomes. *Public Health Reports, 112*, 340–346.

Martinez, A. R. (1997). Corrections officer: The other prisoner. *The Keeper's Voice* [On-line], *18*. Available: http://www.acsp.uic.edu/iaco/kv1801/180108.shtml

Mastrofski, S. D., Ritti, R. R., & Snipes, J. B. (1994). Expectancy theory and police productivity in DUI enforcement. *Law and Society Review, 28*(1), 113–146.

Maung, N. (1995). *Young people, victimization and the police: British crime survey findings on experiences and attitudes of 12 to 15 year olds*. London: H. M. Stationery Office.

McCord, J. (1991). The cycle of crime and socialization process. *Journal of Criminal Law and Criminology, 82*, 211–228.

McCorkle, R. C., Miethe, T. D., & Drass, K. A. (1995). The roots of prison violence: A test of the deprivation, management, and "not-so-total" institution models. *Crime and Delinquency, 41*(3), 317–331.

McCormack, R. (1991). Compensating victims of violent crime. *Justice Quarterly, 8*(3), 329–343.

McCormack, R. (1994). United States crime victim assistance: History, organization and evaluation. *International Journal of Comparative and Applied Criminal Justice, 18*(2), 209–220.

McGrath, R. (1991). Sex-offender risk assessment and disposition planning: A review of empirical and clinical findings. *International Journal of Offender Therapy and Comparative Criminology, 35*(4), 328–350.

McIntyre, N. (1996). Project SODA FY95 progress report [On-line]. Available: http://www.dccn.org/communit/projsoda/soda.htm

McMurray, H. L. (1990). Attitudes of assaulted police officers and their policy implications. *Journal of Police Science and Administration, 17*(1), 44–48.

McWhirter, E. H., & Linzer, M. (1994). The provision of critical incident stress debriefing services by EAPs: A case study. *Journal of Mental Health Counseling, 16*, 403–414.

Melancon, R. (1998). Arizona's insane response to insanity. *Arizona Law Review, 40*, 287.

Melton, G., Petrila, J., Poythress, N., & Slobogin, C. (1987). *Psychological evaluations for the courts: A handbook for mental health professionals and lawyers*. New York: Guilford Press.

Melton, G., Petrila, J., Poythress, N., & Slobogin, C. (1997). *Psychological evaluations for the courts: A handbook for mental health professionals and lawyers* (2nd ed.). New York: Guilford Press.

Mignon, S., & Holmes, W. (1995). Police response to mandatory arrest laws. *Crime and Delinquency, 41*(4), 430–442.

Miller, G. (1993). The psychological best interests of the child. *Journal of Divorce and Remarriage, 19,* 21–36.

Miller, K. S., & Radelet, M. L. (1993). *Executing the mentally ill: The criminal justice system and the case of Alvin Ford.* Newbury Park, CA: Sage.

Miller, M., & Morris, N. (1988). Predictions of dangerousness: An argument for limited use. *Violence and Victims, 3*(4), 263–283.

Miller, R. (1990). Involuntary civil commitment. In R. Simon (Ed.), *Annual review of psychiatry and the law.* Washington, DC: American Psychiatric Press.

Miller, R. (1992). An update on involuntary civil commitment to outpatient treatment. *Hospital and Community Psychiatry, 43*(1), 79–81.

Mills, L. (1996). Empowering battered women transnationally: The case for postmodern interventions. *Social Work, 41,* 261–267.

Milner, J. S., & Campbell, J. C. (1995). Prediction issues for practitioners. In J. C. Campbell (Ed.), *Assessing dangerousness: Violence by sexual offenders, batterers, and child abusers.* Thousand Oaks, CA: Sage.

Monahan, J. (1981). *The clinical prediction of violent behavior.* Beverly Hills, CA: Sage.

Monahan, J. (1996). Violence prediction: The past twenty and the next twenty years. *Criminal Justice and Behavior, 23*(1), 107–120.

Moon, D. G., Thompson, R. J., & Bennett, R. (1993). Patterns of substance use among women in prison. In B. R. Fletcher, L. D. Shaver, & D. G. Moon (Eds.), *Women prisoners: A forgotten population* (pp. 45–54). Westport, CT: Praeger.

Moran, R. (1981). Knowing right from wrong. *Corrections Today, 57,* 124–126, 142.

Morash, M., & Rucker, L. (1990). A critical look at the idea of boot camp as a correctional reform. *Crime and Delinquency, 36,* 204–222.

Moses, E. (1996). Ogles proposes castration law [On-line]. Available: http://www.bhip.com/news/9ogles.htm

Moses, M. C. (1995). A synergistic solution for children of incarcerated parents.

Munetz, M., & Geller, J. (1993). The least restrictive alternative in the postinstitutional era. *Hospital and Community Psychiatry, 44*(10), 967–973.

Munson, W. M. (1994). Description and field test of a career development course for male youth offenders with disabilities. *Journal of Career Development, 20,* 205–218.

Murphy, C. M., Meyer, S. L., & O'Leary, K. D. (1993). Family of origin violence and MCMI-II psychopathology among partner assaultive men. *Violence and Victims, 8,* 165–175.

Murphy, J. J. (1972). Current practices in the use of the psychological testing by police agencies. *Journal of Criminal Law, Criminology, and Police Science, 63,* 570–576.

Myers, J. E. (1983–1984). Involuntary civil commitment of the mentally ill: A system in need of change. *Villanova Law Review, 29,* 367–433.

Myers, J. E. B. (1993a). A call for forensically relevant research. *Child Abuse and Neglect, 17,* 573–579.

Myers, J. E. B. (1993b). The competency of young children to testify in legal proceedings. *Behavioral Sciences and the Law, 11,* 121–133.

National Broadcasting Corporation (NBC) Research. (1998). [On-line]. Available: http://www.msnbc.com/news/wld/iframes/schoolshootings.asp

National Center for Health Statistics. (1996). A generation at risk [On-line]. Available: http://www.rainbows.org/Rain5a.htm

National Center for Health Statistics. (1997). Teen suicide rate [On-line]. Available: http://home.ptd.net/~buzz/fam-cide.htm

National Center on Child Abuse and Neglect. (1994). *Child maltreatment 1992: Reports from the states to the National Center on Child Abuse and Neglect.* Washington, DC: U.S. Department of Health and Human Services.

National Institute of Corrections. (1991). *Intervening with substance-abusing offenders: A framework of action* (Report No. 296-934/40539). Washington, DC: U.S. Government Printing Office.

Newman, G. R. (1990). Popular culture and criminal justice: A preliminary analysis. *Journal of Criminal Justice, 18*(3), 261–272.

New York State Investigation Commission. (1981). *Corruption and abuses in the correctional system: The Green Haven correctional facility.* New York: New York State Investigation Commission.

Nicholson, R., & Kugler, K. (1991). Competent and incompetent criminal defendants: A quantitative review of comparative research. *Psychological Bulletin, 109*(3), 355–370.

Niederhoffer, A. (1967). *Behind the shield.* New York: Doubleday.

Norman, J. A. (1995). Children of prisoners in foster care. In K. Gabel & D. Johnston (Eds.), *Children of incarcerated parents.* New York: Lexington.

Nunnally, J. C. (1961). *Popular conceptions of mental health.* New York: Holt, Rinehart, & Winston.

Oppenheim, E., & Bussiere, A. (1996). Adoption: Where do relatives stand? *Child Welfare League of America, 5*(47), 1–488.

Oppenheimer, K., & Swanson, G. (1990). Duty to warn: When should confidentiality be breached? *Journal of Family Practice, 30*(2), 179–184.

Osborne, O. H. (1995). Jailed mothers: Further explorations in public sector nursing. *Journal of Psychosocial Nursing, 33,* 23–28.

Osler, M. W. (1991). Shock incarceration: Hard realities and real possibilities. *Federal Probation, 55,* 34–42.

Owens, R. P., & Wells, D. K. (1993). One city's response to gangs. *The Police Chief, 60*(2), 25–27.

Parrish, P. (1993, September). Police and the media. *FBI Law Enforcement Bulletin,* pp. 24–25.

Patch, P., & Arrigo, B. A. (1999). Police officer attitudes and use of discretion in situations involving the mentally ill: The need to narrow the focus. *International Journal of Law and Psychiatry, 22*(1), 23–25.

Pate, A. M., Wycoff, M. A., Skogan, W. G., & Sherman, L. W. (1986). *Reducing fear of crime in Houston and Newark: A summary report.* Washington, DC: Police Foundation.

Patterson, C. (1994). Children of the lesbian baby boom: Behavioral adjustment, self-concepts, and sex-role identity. In B. Greene & G. Herek (Eds.), *Contemporary perspectives on gay and lesbian psychology: Theory, research, and applications* (pp. 156–175). Beverly Hills, CA: Sage.

Patterson, C. J., & Redding, R. E. (1996). Lesbian and gay families with children: Implications of social science research for policy. *Journal of Social Issues, 52,* 29–50.

Patterson, J. (1995, November). Community policing: Learning the lessons of history. *FBI Law Enforcement Bulletin,* pp. 5–10.

Penner, N., & Oss, M. E. (1996, November). Barred on the inside: Mental illness in prisons. *Open Minds.*

Perlin, M., Gould, K., & Dorfman, D. (1995). Therapeutic jurisprudence and the civil rights of institutionalized mentally disabled persons: Hopeless oxymoron or path to redemption. *Psychology, Public Policy, and the Law, 1*(1), 80–119.

Peters, J. M., & Murphy, W. D. (1992). Profiling child sexual abusers: Legal considerations. *Criminal Justice and Behavior, 19*(1), 38–53.

Petersen, M., Stephens, J., Dickey, R., & Lewis, W. (1996). Transsexuals within the prison system: An international survey of correctional services policies. *Behavioral Sciences and the Law, 14,* 219–229.

Peterson, E. (1996). Juvenile boot camps: Lessons learned [On-line]. Available: http://www.ncjrs.org/txtfiles/fs-9636.txt

Peterson-Badali, M., & Abramovitch, R. (1993). Grade related changes in young people's reasoning about plea decisions. *Law and Human Behavior, 17,* 537–552.

Pipe, M. E., & Goodman, G. S. (1991). Elements of secrecy: Implications for children's testimony. *Behavioral Sciences and the Law, 9,* 33–41.

Pitt, S., & Bale, E. (1995). Neonaticide, infanticide, and filicide: A review of the literature. *Bulletin of the American Academy of Psychiatry and Law, 23,* 375–386.

Podboy, J. W., & Kastl, A. J. (1993). The intentional misuse of standardized psychological tests in complex trials. *American Journal of Forensic Psychology, 11*, 47–54.

Pollock-Byrne, J. M. (1990). *Women, prison, & crime.* Belmont, CA: Wadsworth.

Prentky, R., & Burgess, A. (1990). Rehabilitation of child molesters: A cost benefit analysis. *American Journal of Orthopsychiatry, 60*, 108–117.

Prentky, R. A., Knight, R. A., & Lee, A. F. (1997). Child sexual molestation: Research issues [On-line]. Available: http://www.ncjrs.org/txtfiles/163390.txt

President's Commission on Mental Health. (1978). *Report to the President.* Washington, DC: U.S. Government Printing Office.

Pritchett, G. L. (1993, July). Interpersonal communication: Improving law enforcement's image. *FBI Law Enforcement Bulletin*, pp. 22–26.

Proulx, J., Pellerin, B., Paradis, Y., McKibben, A, Aubut, J., & Ouimet, M. (1997). Static and dynamic predictors of recidivism in sexual aggressors. *Sexual Abuse: A Journal of Research and Treatment, 9*(1), 7–27.

Pursley, R. D. (1994). *Introduction to criminal justice.* New York: Macmillan.

Pyle, A. (1995). County takes first step to prohibiting gangs from parks. In M. W. Klein, C. L. Maxon, & J. Miller (Eds.), *The modern gang reader.* Los Angeles: Roxbury.

Quinsey, V. L. (1998). Comment on Marshall's "A Monster, victim, or everyman." *Sexual Abuse: A Journal of Research and Treatment, 10*, 65–69.

Quinsey, V. L., Lalumiere, M. L., Rice, M. E., & Harris, G. T. (1995). Predicting sexual offenses. In J. C. Campbell (Ed.), *Assessing dangerousness: Violence by sexual offenders, batterers, and child abusers* (pp. 114–137). Thousand Oaks, CA: Sage.

Radelet, M. L., & Akers, R. L. (1995). Deterrence and the death penalty: The views of the experts [On-line]. Available: http://sun.soci.niu.edu/~critcrim/dppapers/mike.deterrence

Radelet, M. L., & Miller, K. S. (1992). The aftermath of Ford v. Wainwright. *Behavioral Sciences and the Law, 10*, 339–351.

Reed, D. F., & Reed, E. L. (1998). Children of incarcerated parents. *Social Justice, 24*(3), 152–169.

Reid-MacNevin, S. A. (1997). Boot camps for young offenders. *Journal of Contemporary Criminal Justice, 13*, 155–171.

Reisner, R., & Slobogin, C. (1990). *Law and the mental health system: Civil and criminal aspects.* St. Paul, MN: West Publishing.

Reming, G. C. (1988). Personality characteristics of supercops and habitual criminals. *Journal of Police Science and Administration, 16*(3), 136–167.

Renzema, M., & Skelton, D. T. (1990). *The use of electronic monitors by criminal justice agencies.* Kutztown, PA: Kutztown University Foundation.

Reppucci, N. D., & Crosby, C. A. (1993). Law, psychology, and children: Overarching issues. *Law and Human Behavior, 17*, 1–10.

Reske, H. J. (1995). Victim-offender mediation catching on: Advocates say programs, typically for nonviolent offenses, benefit both parties. *American Bar Association Journal, 81*(14), 1–4.

Rigby, K., & Black, D. (1993). Attitudes toward institutional authorities among aboriginal school children in Australia. *Journal of Social Psychology, 133*(6), 845–852.

Robinson, D. (1992). Commitment, attitudes, career aspirations and work stress: The experiences of correctional staff. *Focus on Staff* [On-line], *4*. Available: http//198.103.98.138/crd/forum/e04/e04li.htm

Rosenbaum, D. P. (1988). Community crime prevention: A review and synthesis of the literature. *Justice Quarterly, 5*, 328–395.

Rosenbaum, D. P., & Lurigio, A. J. (1994). An inside look at community policing reform: Definitions, organizational changes, and evaluation findings. *Crime and Delinquency, 40*(3), 299–314.

Ross, D. L., & Jones, M. (1996). Frequency of training in less-than lethal force tactics and weapons: Results of a two-state survey. *Journal of Contemporary Criminal Justice, 12*(3), 250–263.

Rouzan, J. T., & Knowles, L. (1985, January). A streamlined truancy sweep program that really works. *The Police Chief*, pp. 44–45.

Roy, S. (1993). Two types of juvenile restitution programs in two midwestern counties: A comparative study. *Federal Probation*, 57, 48–53.

Russell, H. E., & Beigel, A. (1982). *Understanding human behavior for effective police work*. New York: Basic Books.

Ryan, T. A., & Grassano, J. B. (1992). Taking a progressive approach to treating pregnant offenders. *Corrections Today*, 57, 184–186.

Saathoff, G. B., & Buckman, J. B. (1990). Diagnostic results of psychiatric evaluations of state police officers. *Hospital and Community Psychiatry*, 41(4), 429–432.

Safyer, S. M., & Richmond, L. (1995). Pregnancy behind bars. *Seminars in Perinatology*, 19, 314–322.

Santamour, M. B. (1990). Mentally retarded offenders: Texas program targets basic needs. *Corrections Today*, 52, 52, 92, 106.

Saywitz, K. J. (1995). Improving children's testimony: The question, the answer, and the environment. In M. S. Zaragoza, J. R. Graham, G. C. N. Hall, R. Hirschman, & Y. S. Ben-Porath (Eds.), *Memory and testimony in the child witness* (pp. 113–140). Thousand Oaks, CA: Sage.

Schaffer, B., & DeBlassie, R. R. (1984). Adolescent prostitution. *Adolescence*, 19(75), 689–696.

Schifferle, C. J. (1997). After Whren v. United States: Applying the equal protection clause to racially discriminatory enforcement of the law. *Michigan Law and Policy Review*, 2, 1–25.

Schmallenger, F. (1997). *Criminal Justice: A Brief Introductions* (2nd ed.). Upper Saddle River, NJ: Prentice Hall.

Schmidt, A., & Curtis, C. (1987). Electronic monitors. In B. R. McCarthy (Ed.), *Intermediate punishments* (pp. 137–152). Monsey, NY: Willow Tree Press.

Schwartz, I. M. (1992). Juvenile crime-fighting policies: What the public really wants. In I. M. Schwartz (Ed.), *Juvenile justice and public policy: Toward a national agenda*. Lanham, MD: Lexington Books.

Scrivner, E. M. (1994). Controlling police use of excessive force. *Series: National Institute of Justice Research in Brief* [On-line]. Available: http://www.ncjrs.org/txtfiles/ppsyc.txt

Sereny, G. (1984). *The invisible children*. London: Pan Books.

Severson, M. M., & Bankston, T. V. (1995). Social work and the pursuit of justice through mediation. *Social Work*, 40, 683–690.

Shader, R. I., Jackson, A. H., Harmatz, J. S., & Applebaum, P. S. (1977). Patterns of violent behavior among schizophrenic patients. *Diseases of the Nervous System*, 38(1), 13–16.

Shalala, D. E. (1994). Domestic terrorism. *Vital Speeches of the Day*, 15, 450–453.

Shapiro, J. (1993, August 9). Bonds that blood and birth cannot assure. *US News and World Report*, p. 13.

Shearer, R. W. (1993, August). Police officer stress: New approaches for handling tension. *The Police Chief*, pp. 96–99.

Sherer, R. A. (1998). Allegations of poor psychiatric care in county jails prompt increased funding [On-line]. Available: webmaster@mhsource.com

Shilts, R. (1982). *The mayor of Castro Street: The life and times of Harvey Milk*. New York: St. Martin's.

Short, J. L. (1998). Evaluation of a substance abuse prevention and mental health promotion program for children of divorce. *Journal of Divorce and Remarriage*, 28, 139–155.

Siegal, N. (1997). Ganging up on civil liberties: Anti-gang policing and civil rights. *The Progressive*, 61(10), 28–31.

Siegel, L. J., & Senna, J. J. (1994). *Juvenile delinquency, theory, practice, and law* (5th ed.). St. Paul, MN: West Publishing.

Sigler, R. T., & Lamb, D. (1995). Community-based alternatives to prison: How the public and court personnel view them. *Federal Probation*, 59, 3–9.

Silverman, I. J., & Vega, M. (1996). *Corrections: A comprehensive view*. St. Paul, MN: West Publishing.

Skogan, W. G. (1994). *The challenge of community policing: Testing the promises*. Thousand Oaks, CA: Sage.

Skolnick, A. (1998). Solomon's children: The new biologism, psychological parenthood, attachment theory, and the best interests standard. In M. A. Mason & A. Skolnick (Eds.), *All our families: New policies for a new century* (pp. 236–255). New York: Oxford University Press.

Slobogin, C. (1994). Involuntary community treatment of people who are violent and mentally ill: A legal analysis. *Hospital and Community Psychiatry, 45*(7), 685–689.

Smith, B., Sloan, J., & Ward, R. (1990). Public support for the victim's rights movement: Results of a statewide survey. *Crime and Delinquency, 36*(4), 488–502.

Smith, D., & Klein, J. (1984). Police control of interspersonal disputes. *Social Problems, 31*(4), 468–481.

Smith, R. (1995). Transgendered . . . and taken to jail. *Journal of Psychosocial Nursing, 33*, 44–46.

Snow, C. R. (1997). *Family violence: Tough solutions to stop the violence*. New York: Plenum Press.

Soler, M. (1988). Litigation on behalf of children in adult jails. *Crime and Delinquency, 34*, 190–208.

Solomon, P. (1983). Analyzing opposition to community residential facilities for troubled adolescents. *Child Welfare, 62*, 361–366.

Solomon, R., & Horn, J. (1986). Post-shooting traumatic reactions: A pilot study. In J. Reese & H. Goldstein (Eds.), *Psychological services for law enforcement*. Washington, DC: U.S. Government Printing Office.

Soto, G., & Miller, M. (1992, August). Keeping kids in school. *Police Practices*.

Southworth, R. (1990, November). Taking the job home. *FBI Law Enforcement Bulletin*, pp. 8–11.

Spralding, L. H. (1997). Chemical castration: A return to the dark ages. *American Civil Liberties Union* [On-line]. Available: http://www.shadow.net/aclu/t-chem.htm

Spruill, J., & May, J. (1988). The mentally retarded offender: Prevalence rates based on individual versus group intelligence tests. *Criminal Justice and Behavior, 15*, 484–491.

Stalans, L. J. (1996). Family harmony or individual protection? *American Behavioral Scientist, 4*, 433–448.

Stalans, L. J., & Lurigio, A. (1995a). Responding to domestic violence against women. *Crime and Delinquency, 41*(4), 387–398.

Stalans, L. J., & Lurigio, A. J. (1995b). Public preferences for the court's handling of domestic violence situations. *Crime and Delinquency, 41*, 399–413.

Stanard, R., & Hazler, R. (1995). Legal and ethical implications of HIV and duty to warn for counselors: Does Tarasoff apply? *Journal of Counseling and Development, 73*, 397–400.

Steadman, H., McGreevy, M., Morrissey, J., Callahan, L., Robbins, P., & Cirincione, C. (1993). *Before and after Hinckley: Evaluating insanity defense reform*. New York: Guilford Press.

Steadman, H., Monahan, J., Hartstone, E., Davis, S., & Robbins, P. (1982). Mentally disordered offenders: A national survey of patients and facilities. *Law and Human Behavior, 6*, 31–38.

Steadman, H. J., McCarty, D. W., & Morrissey, J. P. (1989). *The mentally ill in jail: Planning for essential services*. New York: Guilford Press.

Steinhart, D. (1988). California legislature ends the jailing of children: The story of a police reversal. *Crime and Delinquency, 34*, 169–189.

Stone, A. (1975). *Mental health and law: A system in transition*. Rockville, MD: National Institute of Mental Health.

Straus, M. B. (1994). *Violence in the lives of adolescents*. New York: W. W. Norton.

Streib, V. (1987). *The death penalty for juveniles*. Bloomington: Indiana University Press.

Streib, V. (1996). Current death row inmates under juvenile death sentences [On-line]. Available: http://www.essential.org/dpic/juvchar.html

Streib, V. (1998). Juveniles and the death penalty: Brief facts and figures [On-line]. Available: http://www.prince.essential.org/dpic/juvchar.html

Struckman-Johnson, C., Struckman-Johnson, D., Rucker, L., Bumby, K., & Donaldson, S. (1996). Sexual coercion reported by men and women in prison. *Journal of Sex Research, 33*, 67–76.

Swerling, J. B. (1978). *A study of police officers' values and their attitudes toward homosexual officers*. Dissertation, California School of Professional Psychology, Los Angeles.

Sykes, G. M. (1967). *Crime and society*. New York: Random House.

Szockyj, E. (1989). Working in a man's world: Women correctional officers in an institution for men. *Canadian Journal of Criminology, 31*, 319–328.

Tasker, F., & Golombok, S. (1995). Adults raised as children in lesbian families. *American Journal of Orthopsychiatry*, *65*, 203–215.

Territo, L. (1989). *Crime and justice in America*. St. Paul, MN: West Publishing.

Texeira, M. T. (1995). Policing the internally colonized: Slavery, Rodney King, Mark Fuhrman and beyond. *Western Journal of Black Studies*, *19*, 235–243.

Thurman, Q. C., Giacomazzi, A., & Bogen, P. (1993). Research note: Cops and community policing: An assessment of a community policing demonstration project. *Crime and Delinquency*, *39*(4), 554–564.

Tobey, A. E., Goodman, G. S., Batterman-Faunce, J. M., Orcutt, H. K., & Sachsenmaier, T. (1995). In M. S. Zaragoza, J. R. Graham, G. C. N. Hall, R. Hirschman, & Y. S. Ben-Porath (Eds.), *Memory and testimony in the child witness* (pp. 214–239). Thousand Oaks, CA: Sage.

Toch, H. (1985). The catalytic situation in the violence equation. *Journal of Applied Social Psychology*, *15*(2), 468–481.

Toch, H. (1992). *Violent men: An inquiry into the psychology of violence*. Washington, DC: American Psychological Association.

Toller, W., & Tsagaris, B. (1996). Managing institutional gangs. *Corrections Today*, *58*(6), 110–112.

Tomasevski, K. (1986). *Children in adult prisons: An international perspective*. London: Printer.

Torok, W. C., & Trump, K. S. (1994). Gang intervention: Police and school collaboration. *FBI Law Enforcement Bulletin*, *63*(5), 13–17.

Turco, R. N. (1990, September). Psychological profiling. *International Journal of Offender Therapy and Comparative Criminology*, pp. 147–154.

Umbreit, M. S. (1993). Crime victims and offenders in mediation: An emerging area of social work practice. *Social Work*, *38*, 69–73.

Umbreit, M. S. (1994). Victim meets offender: The impact of restorative justice and mediation. Monsey, NY: Criminal Justice Press.

Umbreit, M. S. (1995). Holding juvenile offenders accountable: A restorative justice perspective. *Juvenile and Family Court Journal*, *46*(2), 31–42.

Umbreit, M. S., & Bradshaw, W. (1997). Victim experience of meeting adult vs. juvenile offenders: A cross-national study. *Federal Probation*, *61*, 33–39.

U.S. Department of Justice. (1994). *Special report: Women in prison* (Report No. NCJ-145321). Washington, DC: Bureau of Justice Statistics.

U.S. Department of Justice, Bureau of Justice Statistics. (1997). Criminal offender statistics [On-line]. Available: http://www.ojp.usdoj.gov/bjs/crimoff

U.S. Department of Justice, Federal Bureau of Investigation. (1996). *Crime in the United States: Uniform Crime Reports 1995*. Washington, DC: U.S. Government Printing Office.

Useem, B., & Kimball, P. A. (1989). *States of siege: U.S. prison riots 1971–1986*. New York: Oxford University Press.

Violanti, J. (1995). The mystery within: Understanding police suicide. *FBI Law Enforcement Bulletin*, *64*, 19–23.

Violanti, J. M., & Aron, F. (1993). Sources of police stressors, job attitudes, and psychological distress. *Psychological Reports*, *72*, 899–904.

Violanti, J. M., & Aron, F. (1995). Police stressors: Variations in perception among police personnel. *Journal of Criminal Justice*, *23*(3), 287–294.

Violanti, J. M., Marshall, J. R., & Howe, B. (1985). Stress, coping, and alcohol use: The police connection. *Journal of Police Science and Administration*, *13*(2), 106–110.

Waddington, P., & Braddock, Q. (1991). Guardians or bullies? Perceptions of the police amongst adolescent black, white and Asian boys. *Policing and Society*, *2*(1), 31–45.

Wadman, R. C., & Ziman, S. M. (1993, February). Courtesy and police authority. *FBI Law Enforcement Bulletin*, pp. 23–26.

Wahl, O. F. (1993). Community impact of group homes for mentally ill adults. *Community Mental Health Journal*, *29*, 247–259.

Wakefield, H., & Underwager, R. (1993). Misuse of psychological tests in forensic settings: Some horrible examples. *American Journal of Forensic Psychology*, *11*, 55–75.

Walker, A. G. (1993). Questioning young children in court: A linguistic case study. *Law and Human Behavior, 17*, 59–81.

Walker, M., Schmidt, L., & Lunghofer, L. (1993). Youth gangs. In M. I. Singer, L. T. Singer, & T. M. Anglin (Eds.), *Handbook for screening adolescents at psychosocial risk* (pp. 504–552). New York: Lexington Books.

Wall, J. C., & Amadio, C. (1994). An integrated approach to child custody evaluation: Utilizing the Best Interest of the child and family systems frameworks. *Journal of Divorce and Remarriage, 21*, 39–57.

Walters, P. M. (1993). Community-oriented policing: A blend of strategies. *FBI Law Enforcement Bulletin, 62*, 20–23.

Warshak, R. A. (1996). Gender bias in child custody decisions. *Family and Conciliation Courts Review, 34*, 396–409.

Watterson, K. (1996). *Women in prison: Inside the concrete womb* (Rev. ed.). Boston: Northeastern University Press.

Weaver, R. S. (1992). Violent youth need rehabilitation, not harsh punishment. In M. D. Biskup & C. P. Cozic (Eds.), *Youth violence*. San Diego, CA: Greenhaven Press.

Weinberg, M. S., & Williams, C. J. (1974). *Male homosexuals: Their problems and adaptations*. New York: Penguin.

Weisberg, D. K. (1985). *Children of the night: A study of adolescent prostitution*. Lexington, MA: Lexington Books.

Weiss, M. (1997). A legal evaluation of criminal competency standards. *Journal of Contemporary Criminal Justice, 1*(3), 213–223.

Welch, M. (1997). A critical interpretation of correctional bootcamps as normalizing institutions: Discipline, punishment and the military model. *Journal of Contemporary Criminal Justice, 13*(2), 184–205.

Wenocur, S., & Belcher, J. R. (1990). Strategies for overcoming barriers to community-based housing for the chronically mentally ill. *Community Mental Health Journal, 26*, 319–333.

Wertlieb, D. (1997). Children whose parents divorce: Life trajectories and turning points. In I. H. Gotlib & B. Wheaton (Eds.), *Stress and adversity over the life course* (pp. 179–195). New York: Cambridge University Press.

West, D. J. (1988). Psychological contributions to criminology. *British Journal of Criminology, 28*(2), 77–89.

Weyer, M., & Sandler, I. (1998). Stress and coping as predictors of children's divorce-related ruminations. *Journal of Clinical Psychology, 27*, 78–86.

White, E. K., & Honig, A. L. (1995). Law enforcement families. In M. Kurke & E. Scrivener (Eds.), *Police psychology into the 21st century* (pp. 189–205). Hillside, NJ: Erlbaum.

Widom, C. S. (1992). The cycle of violence. *Journal of Marriage and the Family, 43*, 331–337.

Widom, C., and Kuhns, J. (1996). Childhood victimization and subsequent risks for promiscuity, prostitution, and teenage pregnancy: A prospective study. *Am. J. Public Health 86*(11), 1607–1612.

Williams, S. M. (1996). A national strategy for managing sex offenders. *Forum on Corrections Research, 8*(2), 33–35.

Wilson, C., & Gross, P. (1994). Police-public interactions: The impact of conflict resolution tactics. *Journal of Applied Social Psychology, 24*(2), 159–175.

Wilson, J. S., & Leasure, R. (1991). Cruel and unusual punishment: The health care of women in prison. *Nurse Practitioner, 16*, 32–39.

Winick, B. (1995). Ambiguities in the meaning of mental illness. *Psychology, Law, and Public Policy, 1*(3), 534–611.

Winick, B. J. (1992). Competency to be executed: A therapeutic jurisprudence perspective. *Behavioral Sciences and the Law, 10*, 317–337.

Wintersmith, R. F. (1974). *Police and the black community*. Lexington, MA: Lexington Books.

Woodhull, A. (1993). *Police communication in traffic stops*. Rochester, NY: Schenkman Books.

Wool, R. J., & Dooley, E. (1987). A study of attempted suicides in prisons. *Medicine Science Law, 27*(4), 297–301.

Woolard, J. L., Reppucci, N. D., & Redding, R. E. (1996). Theoretical and methodological issues in studying children's capacities in legal contexts. *Law and Human Behavior, 20*, 219–228.

Wooldredge, J. D., & Masters, K. (1993). Confronting problems faced by pregnant inmates in state prisons. *Crime and Delinquency, 39*, 195–203.

Worden, R. (1989). Situational and attitudinal explanations of police behavior: A theoretical reappraisal and empirical assessment. *Law and Society Review, 23*(4), 667–711.

Worden, R. E., Shepard, R. L., & Mastrofski, S. D. (1996). On the meaning and measurement of suspects' demeanor toward the police: A comment on "demeanor and arrest." *Journal of Research in Crime and Delinquency, 33*(3), 324–332.

Wrightsman, L., Nietzel, M., & Fortune, W. (1994). *Psychology and the legal system* (3rd ed.). Pacific Grove, CA: Brooks/Cole.

Wrightsman, L. S. (Ed.). (1991). *Psychology and the legal system* (2nd ed.). Belmont, CA: Wadsworth.

Wynne, E. E. (1997). Children's rights and the biological bias in biological parent versus third-party custody disputes. *Child Psychiatry and Human Development, 27*, 179–191.

Zatz, J. (1982). Problems and issues in deinstitutionalization: Historical overview and current attitudes. In J. F. Handler & J. Zatz (Eds.), *Neither angels nor thieves: Studies in deinstitutionalization of status offenders*. Washington, DC: National Academy Press.

Zimmer, L. (1987). How women reshape the prison guard role. *Gender and Society, 1*, 415–431.

CASES

Alaska Statute Title 11, Chapter 56, Article 4, Section 610-As 11.56.610 (1997).

Barefoot v. Estelle, 103 S. Ct. 3383, 463 U.S. 880 (1983)

Bartley v. Kremens, 402 F. Supp. 1039 (1975)

Baston v. Kentucky, 476 U.S. 79 (1986)

Baumgartner v. City of Long Beach, Civil No. C-54782 (L.A. Super. 1987)

Bundy v. Jackson, 641 F. 2d 934 (D.C. Cir. 1981)

Chambers v. Mississippi, 410 U.S. 284 (1973)

Coleman v. Wilson, 912 F. Supp. 1282 (1995)

Coy v. Iowa, 108 S. Ct. 2798 (1988).

Daubert v. Merrell, 509 U.S. 579, 591 (1993)

Davis v. United States, 512 U.S. 452-464 (1994)

Department of Revenue of Montana v. Kurth Ranch, 511 U.S. 128 L.Ed. 2d 767, 777 (1994)

Dodd v. Hughes, 81 Nev. 43, 398 P.2d 540 (1965)

Dothard v. Rawlinson, 433 U.S. 321 (1977)

Durham v. United States, 214 F.2d 862 (D.C. Cir. 1954)

Dusky v. United States, 362 U.S. 402 (1960)

Eddings v. Oklahoma, 455 U.S. 104 (1982)

Estelle v. Gamble, 429 U.S. 97 (1976)

Farmer v. Brennan, 114 S. Ct. 1970 (1994)

Fasanaro v. County of Rockland, 166 Misc. 2d 152, 632 N.Y.S. 2d 453 (NY 1995)

Finlay v. Finlay, 240 N.Y. 429, 148 N.E. 624 (1925)

Ford v. Wainwright, 477 U.S. 399 (1986)

Foucha v. Louisiana, 504 U.S. 71 (1992)

Frye v. United States, 293 F. 1013 (D. C. Cir 1923)

Garrett v. Collins, 951 F. 2d 57, 58 (5th Cir. 1992)

Gregg v. Georgia, 428 U.S. 1301 (1976)

Guardianship of Richard Roe III, 421 N.E. 2d 40 (1981)

In re Gault, 387 U.S. 1 (1967)

In re Winship, 397 U.S. 358 (1970)

Jackson v. Indiana, 406 U.S. 715 (1972)

Jennings v. New York State Office of Mental Health, 90 N.Y.2d 227 (1997)

Juvenile Justice and Delinquency Prevention Act, 42 U.S.C. 5603(23) (1974)

Katz v. United States, 389 U.S. 347 (1967)

Kent v. United States, 383 U.S. 541 (1966)

Knecht v. Gillman, 488 F. 2d 1136 (1973)

Lake v. Cameron, 364 F. 2d 657 DC Cir (1966)

Maryland v. Craig, 110 S. Ct. 3157 (1990)

McKeiver v. Pennsylvania, 403 U.S. 528 (1971)

North Carolina v. Alford, 400 U.S. 25 (1970)

Olmstead v. United States, 277 U.S. 438, 48 S. Ct. 564 (1928)

Parham v. J. R., 442 U.S. 584 (1978)

Penry v. Lynaugh, 109 S. Ct. 2934 (1989)

People v. Aris, N.E. 005418 Cal. App. Lexis 1187 (1989)

People v. Presley, 47 Ill. 2, 50 (1974)

Perry v. Louisiana, 111 S. Ct. 449 (1990)

Rex v. Brasier (1770)

Roach v. Aiken, Warden *et al.*, 474 U.S. 1039 (1986)

Robbins v. Glenn County, No. CIVS-85-0675 RAR (U.S.D.C., E.D. Ca. 1986)

Rock v. Arkansas, 107 S. Ct. 2704 (1987)

Santobello v. New York, 404 U.S. 257 (1971)

Schall v. Martin, 104 S. Ct. 2403 (1984).

Singleton v. State, 90-CP-36-66 (Newberry County) (1991)

Stanford v. Kentucky, 492 U.S. 361 (1989)

Swain v. Alabama, 380 U.S. 202 (1965)

Tarasoff v. Regents of the University of California, 551 P.2d 334 (1976)

Tennessee v. Garner, 471 U.S. 1 (1985)

Terry v. Ohio, 392 U.S. 1 (1968)

Thompson v. Oklahoma, 487 U.S. 815 (1988)

Todaro v. Ward, 431 F. Supp. 1129 (1977)

Town of Gates v. Commissioner of New York State Office of Mental Retardation and Developmental Disabilities and Finger Lakes Developmental Disabilities Services Office, 667 N.Y.S. 2d 568 (1997)

United States of America v. Michael A. Whren, 324 U.S. App. D.C. 197 (1997)

United States v. Salerno, 481 U.S. 739 (1987).

United States v. Sanusi, 813 F. Supp. 149 (1992)

United States v. Ward, 448 U.S. 242, 248 (1980)

Washington v. Harper, 494 U.S. 210, 110 S. Ct. 1028 (1990)

Wertz v. Workmen's Compensation Appeal Board, 683 A.2d 1287 (Pen. 1996)

Wheeler v. United States, 159 U.S. 523 (1895)

Wilkins v. Missouri, see Stanford v. Kentucky, 492 U.S. 361 (1989)

Yellen v. Ada County, Civil No. 83-1026 (U.S.D.C. Idaho 1985)

Index